DIASPORAS
NEW PARTNERS IN GLOBAL DEVELOPMENT POLICY

Kathleen Newland, Editor
Migration Policy Institute

Foreword by Karen D. Turner, Career Minister
Director, Office of Development Partners,
US Agency for International Development

November 2010

FROM THE AMERICAN PEOPLE

MIGRATION POLICY INSTITUTE

This edited volume was made possible in part by the generous support of the American people through the US Agency for International Development under The QED Group, LLC for the Knowledge-Driven Microenterprise Development project. The Migration Policy Institute's work on diasporas, including this project, is made possible through the support of the John D. and Catherine T. MacArthur Foundation. The contents are the responsibility of MPI and do not necessarily reflect the views of USAID, the United States government, or the MacArthur Foundation.

Migration Policy Institute
Washington, DC

© 2010, Migration Policy Institute.

Library of Congress Cataloging-in-Publication Data

Diasporas : new partners in global development / Kathleen Newland, editor.
    p. cm.
ISBN 978-0-9742819-7-1 (pbk)
1. Economic development--Developing countries. 2. Globalization--Economic aspects. I. Newland, Kathleen. II. Title.

HD82.D494 2010
338.90089'0091724--dc22

                                        2010038866

Cover Photo: airliners.nl
Cover Design and Typesetting: April Siruno, MPI

Suggested citation: Newland, Kathleen, ed. 2010. *Diasporas: New Partners in Global Development Policy.* Washington, DC: Migration Policy Institute.

Printed in the United States of America.

CONTENTS

FOREWORD

By Career Minister Karen D. Turner

Diaspora groups and individuals are being recognized as both major stakeholders and potentially powerful actors that are using their influence and financial resources to contribute to the development of their home countries. Today, the transnational flow of persons, information, knowledge, and ideas across political, economic, security, and sociocultural domains is greater than ever.

As the US government's lead development agency with field presence around the world, the US Agency for International Development (USAID) is well positioned to leverage its ability to connect US-based diasporas with USAID-supported programs and activities and vice versa in order to enhance development outcomes and contribute to the body of experience and learning regarding the role of diasporas in development and development effectiveness.

This volume, produced by the Migration Policy Institute (MPI) in a partnership with USAID, explores six channels of diaspora engagement: philanthropy, volunteerism, heritage tourism and nostalgia trade, entrepreneurship, investment in capital markets, and advocacy. Kathleen Newland and her MPI colleagues carefully document the wide array of activities that diasporas undertake in their homelands. With their research supplemented by discussions with public officials, private investors, scholars, and nonprofit actors from the United States and countries of origin, the authors have produced thoughtful in-depth analyses and a menu of key policy options.

Today, cooperation with development stakeholders is more important than ever. President Obama has identified global engagement and partnership as hallmarks of his foreign policy — a vision that places diaspora engagement at the heart of US foreign assistance strategies. The challenges facing the developing world can, at times, appear daunting. No agency alone can expect to provide comprehensive and sustainable solutions. Addressing these issues requires innovation, collaboration, and commitment. As the examples in this book illustrate, diasporas bring critical resources — human as well as financial — to this common endeavor.

We hope the analysis and information in this volume will add to the global awareness of the critical role of diaspora groups and individuals in development and stimulate increased attention to leveraging the resources and know-how of diaspora networks.

Karen D. Turner, Career Minister
Director, Office of Development Partners
United States Agency for International Development

CHAPTER 1

SIX STUDIES AND A ROAD MAP:
Diasporas as Partners in Development

Kathleen Newland, Migration Policy Institute

Introduction

Diaspora populations are a legacy of past migrations and a defining feature of the current age of heightened mobility. Their impact on development in their countries of origin is hard to measure but impossible to miss, and its manifestations are wildly diverse. Intrepid diaspora investors in Afghanistan have defied the risk environment there to open a $25 million Coca-Cola bottling plant and the nation's first shopping mall. An Indian investment group based in Silicon Valley, The Indus Entrepreneurs, raised $500,000 in the immediate aftermath of the 2001 Gujarat earthquake to help the victims. Moroccan emigrants in France and their families in Morocco are pioneering rural tourism by restoring traditional dwellings and opening them as inns and restaurants. The promotion of human rights in Vietnam became a campaign issue in a 2010 congressional election in California. A Somali-American was appointed prime minister of Somalia in 2010. Quite apart from the huge volume of money they send home as family remittances, migrants and their descendants are deeply engaged in the affairs of their countries of origin or ancestry.

Beginning in fall 2009, analysts at the Migration Policy Institute (MPI) undertook the study of several forms of diaspora engagement in countries of origin or ancestry within the framework of the United States Agency for International Development's (USAID's) Diaspora Networks Alliance. The forms of engagement studied were as follows:

- Direct investment by diaspora entrepreneurs
- Investment in country-of-origin capital markets
- Diaspora tourism and trade in "nostalgia goods"
- Diaspora philanthropy
- Diaspora volunteerism
- Diaspora advocacy and diplomacy

Examination of each of these areas has yielded a rich set of observations on how emigrants and their descendants perceive and interact with opportunities and constraints in their countries of origin or ancestry. This introductory chapter synthesizes these observations and draws from them some implications for the development agenda. Appended to the overview is a "road map" for governments of both countries of diaspora origin and countries of settlement as they seek to involve migrants and their descendants in the development of diasporas' ancestral homelands.

The MPI studies were conducted at a time when diasporas were assuming a central role in the global discussion of the links between migration and development. Diasporas are assumed to be "resource multipliers" for their countries of origin, but all too often, only the short-term gains from remittances and investments are considered. This is unfortunate, as the longer-term benefits of diaspora engagement — such as greater integration of the country of origin into the global economy and newfound access to concentrations of talent that the home market cannot sustain — may be even more important to development.

Two senior officials from the French government's development agency, the *Agence Française pour le Développement*, have written that foreign assistance is going through a "triple revolution" of new goals, new actors, and new tools.[1] Although not mentioned by these authors, diasporas are among the new actors in development, and forms of engagement such as philanthropy and capital market investment are new tools that go beyond official development assistance and may leverage additional bilateral flows. Diaspora individuals and organizations can deploy their resources faster and more flexibly than official-aid agencies, which are inhibited by bureaucratic requirements.[2]

---

1 Jean Michel Severino and Olivier Ray, "The End of ODA: Death and Rebirth of a Global Public Policy," Working Paper 167, Center for Global Development, March, 2009.
2 See Andrew Natsios, "The Clash of the Counter-Bureaucracy and Development," essay, Center for Global Development, July 2010.

Government agencies often find it challenging to engage with diaspora groups and individuals. Favoritism (or its appearance), hidden agendas, and factionalism are common challenges. It can be hard to discern whether an organization is truly representative of the population for which it claims to speak. And while some diaspora groups are well funded and highly skilled in pursuing their agendas, many have great enthusiasm but a limited capacity to play a role in development. The governments of countries where diasporas have settled must keep in mind that some diaspora groups have political objectives along with developmental, humanitarian, or economic goals, and that associating with such groups can bring accusations of meddling in the domestic affairs of these diasporas' origin countries. And yet in many, if not most, settings, there is ample common ground among diasporas, homeland authorities, and settlement-country actors.

Box I. A Note on Terminology

To many people, "Diaspora" has a tragic connotation, associated with forcible dispersal, a strong sense of loss, and a longing to return to the ancestral homeland. The historical archetypes in this sense are the persecution of the Jews and the African slave trade. The contemporary use of the term in the social sciences is much more positive, as in the definition offered by Gabriel Scheffer: "Modern Diasporas are ethnic minority groups of migrant origins residing and acting in host countries but maintaining strong sentimental and material links with their countries of origin — their homelands."[3] At a minimum, it implies the retention of a distinct identity relating to a community of origin.

"Diaspora" is now commonly used to refer to migrant communities even if they do not share the classic diaspora attributes of forced dispersal, residence in many countries over several generations, and a longing to return. Although "diaspora" implies a settled community, it is increasingly common to use the term to include migrants who have left their countries only temporarily (though perhaps long-term). What both recent arrivals and long-settled communities have in common is that they identify with and remain engaged with their country of origin or ancestry even while absent from it.

The US government has long worked with diaspora populations, particularly in the aftermath of natural disasters. But like governments in many other developed and developing countries, it is therefore seeking

---

3 Gabriel Sheffer, "A New Field of Study: Modern Diasporas in International Politics," in Gabriel Sheffer, ed., *Modern Diasporas in International Politics* (London: Croom Helm, 1986), 3. Quoted in Khalid Koser, "New African Diasporas: An Introduction," in Khalid Koser, ed., *New African Diasporas* (London: Routledge, 2003), 5.

to engage strategically with them in its pursuit of foreign policy goals. Diasporas are seen to be potential partners in diplomatic work, security efforts, and development programs. But such engagement is, thus far, ad hoc. Various US government agencies are pursuing diaspora-related activities that may be either synergistic or contradictory, but no mechanism exists for gathering that information systematically and sharing it widely. The recent upsurge of interest in diasporas at the White House and the State Department may, however, be about to change that.

While USAID is far from integrating diaspora issues throughout its programs, it has devised a framework, known as the Diaspora Networks Alliance (DNA), that aims to "intensify the flow of knowledge and resources of Diaspora to their home countries to promote economic and social growth."[4] The alliance is, appropriately, located in the agency's Office of Development Partnerships. The six scoping studies conducted by MPI in partnership with USAID lay the groundwork for a more intensive implementation of the DNA framework.

I. Observations from the Scoping Studies

A. Diaspora Entrepreneurship

Diaspora entrepreneurs are uniquely positioned to recognize opportunities in their countries of origin and to exploit such opportunities as "first movers." Not all forms of entrepreneurship contribute equally to economic development. Necessity entrepreneurs, or those who are self-employed because they cannot find other work, have little effect on economic development. At best, they help to reduce overt unemployment by supporting themselves. Opportunity entrepreneurs, on the other hand, are much more likely to have a positive impact on economic development as they take advantage of market openings in growing sectors of the economy. Research shows that countries with a high ratio of opportunity entrepreneurship to necessity entrepreneurship tend to have higher levels of income, higher exports as a share of gross domestic product (GDP), and higher licensing receipts — and spend more on research and development (R&D) and education — than those with a low ratio.

---

4   United States Agency for International Development (USAID), "Global Diaspora Networks Alliance Framework," draft briefing paper, unpublished, 2009.

According to the MPI study, donors should aim to assist governments in designing and implementing policies that respond to the major challenges that diaspora entrepreneurs face in establishing or running businesses in their countries of origin. In some cases, this may be a question of opening existing programs for domestic entrepreneurs to members of the diaspora; in others, special programs designed for diaspora members may be needed. Specific policy measures include the following:

- Encourage access to capital, especially for small-scale diaspora entrepreneurs. This might include offering easier (but still well-regulated) access to loans, competitive grant-based support for promising projects, and risk-sharing mechanisms and instruments for investors.

- Provide high-quality education and vocational training in business, science, technology, engineering, and mathematics to individuals in the diaspora interested in pursuing opportunities in knowledge-based industries. This is likely to require increased government spending on R&D and on world-class research facilities and universities.

- Lower tariffs on imported raw materials and equipment into the country of origin to help diaspora entrepreneurs begin transnational businesses.

- Establish mechanisms that encourage regular consultations with diaspora professionals to help governments identify strategic economic areas and attract diaspora resources to them.

- Make it very clear that diaspora entrepreneurs are welcome in their countries of origin.

- Adopt policies that make it easy for diaspora business owners and investors to travel between their country of origin and their country of settlement. Offering multiple reentry permits, long-term visas, or dual citizenship to transnational entrepreneurs would encourage them to actively supervise their investments.

B. Diaspora Investment in Capital Markets

Financial flows from migrants and their descendants are at the heart of the relationship between migration and development. Accordingly, most policy attention to date has focused on migrants' remittances. But while there is little doubt that remittances are a large and extremely important financial flow, they represent only one of the potential private financial flows originating from diasporas, and a limited one at best. Remittances merely redistribute migrants' incomes; the greater challenge is to mobilize diaspora wealth. Capital markets perform precisely this function — mobilizing savings and channeling them into productive investments.

This chapter describes five vehicles that have been used to mobilize diaspora wealth via capital markets: deposit accounts, securitization of remittance flows, transnational loans, diaspora bonds, and diaspora mutual funds. It also explores the potential of four additional options that could be considered in the future: subnational debt issues, diaspora private equity funds, institutional investment, and corporate debt and equity. There is ample evidence that diasporas hold substantial assets that could be mobilized for portfolio investment in their countries of origin, but they face many of the same barriers to investing in developing and emerging countries as other international investors do — such as access to credit and appropriate training. Several existing USAID and other US government programs could help reduce these barriers. For instance, USAID's Development Credit Authority and the Overseas Private Investment Corporation have the potential to mitigate the risks of diaspora investment. USAID's Volunteers for Economic Growth Alliance and the US Treasury Department's Government Debt Issuance and Management Program could provide technical assistance to diaspora members hoping to create new investment vehicles in their countries of origin. Finally, USAID's Global Development Alliance could provide credibility to diaspora investment initiatives, and its country missions' needs assessments could help identify promising investment opportunities.

C. Diaspora Tourism and "Nostalgia" Trade

Diaspora populations can play an important role in opening markets for new tourism destinations as well as markets for goods produced in and associated with the culture of their countries of origin. Tourists from the diaspora are more likely than other international travelers to have or make connections with the local economy by staying in small, locally owned accommodations (or with relatives), eating in local restaurants, shopping in locally owned shops, and so forth — rather than staying in foreign-owned tourist enclaves with little connection to their surroundings. The many forms of diaspora tourism include medical tourism, business-related tourism, heritage (or "roots") tourism, exposure or "birthright" tourism, educational tourism, VIP tourism, and "peak experience" tourism. Not all forms are aimed exclusively at the diaspora, but many are encouraged by country-of-origin governments as part of their efforts to bind the diaspora more closely to the homeland.

Trade in "nostalgia" goods earns significant revenue for countries of diaspora origin. As Manuel Orozco's research has shown, migrant households are regular and heavy consumers of home-country goods, particularly foodstuffs. Nostalgia goods tend to be labor intensive to produce and, often, artisanal, so earnings are likely to be enjoyed at the local and household level. In addition, the diaspora market for nostalgia goods can offer a measure of protection to small or artisan producers who may be threatened by the standardization of large-scale production for the global market. In some cases, the availability of nostalgia goods in the migrant niche market leads to broader popularization of the goods in the mass market and can significantly boost export earnings of the homeland — as long as production is not diverted to destination-country manufacturers.

The producers of nostalgia goods often find it difficult to distribute their products and to take advantage of economies of scale, however. Access to credit guarantee schemes and assistance in forming producer cooperatives could help them build more robust enterprises. Technical assistance in business planning, accounting, marketing, food safety standards, and export requirements might be useful as well.

As for tourism, donor agencies can support country-of-origin tourism departments in reaching out to diaspora populations through marketing campaigns and specialized tourist offerings for the heritage traveler. The preservation and development of historic sites should also be a funding priority, as such sites appeal both to diaspora tourists and to international tourists more generally. Public-private partnerships are well suited to the sensitive conversion of traditional structures to hotels or restaurants.

D. Diaspora Philanthropy

Private philanthropy plays an increasingly important role in development efforts. According to economist Homi Kharas of the Brookings Institution, private philanthropy already accounts for a larger share of total economic engagement with developing countries than does official development assistance (ODA).[5] While they may lack the expertise and public resources of official development agencies and the long-term

---

5 Homi Kharas, *The New Reality of Aid* (Washington, DC: Wolfensohn Center for Development, Brookings Institution, 2007).

development potential of private business, private philanthropies serve as important catalysts and innovators, and in some cases provide significant resources. They also involve migrants and diasporas more than ever before. While philanthropic undertakings in the past were typically associated with wealthy industrialists, many middle-income and even relatively poor individuals now make meaningful donations to charitable causes. The MPI study describes a wide range of diaspora philanthropists, ranging from wealthy individuals such as magnates, celebrities, and international sports stars to associations, foundations, and Web sites that pool the donations of hundreds or even thousands of smaller-income donors

The study suggests that diaspora philanthropists have been particularly adept at mobilizing resources for humanitarian relief and during national crises, but their role as social innovators and agents of change is less understood. The more ambitious diaspora philanthropists are, the greater the challenges they are likely to face. Moving beyond palliative charitable contributions to actions that address the sources of deprivation, for example, are likely to draw philanthropists into contentious political debates. Collective action also presents challenges. For example, when migrant organizations pool the donations of many individuals, it is often difficult to identify priorities. It can also be difficult for philanthropists to find partners in the home country, as many diaspora members mistrust the established social-service institutions in their countries of origin

There is a clear consensus that public policy must tread lightly in promoting specific private causes, but rather should establish conditions that encourage philanthropy in general. The United States, for example has been very successful in promoting philanthropy using tax regulations — perhaps the most effective policy tool available. (Charitable contributions have been tax deductible in the United States since 1917.) Tax policy is beyond the mandate of development agencies, and calls for cross-departmental cooperation between them and finance ministries and/or legislatures. In the wake of recent natural disasters, for example, the US Congress approved legislation that gave special tax treatment for charitable contributions to relief and recovery efforts in Haiti (e.g., extending the deadline for contributions that could be claimed as tax deductions in the current year). Donor agencies might consider sponsoring workshops with diaspora organizations to acquaint them with the requirements and the process of acquiring tax-exempt status. Donors could also play a role in vetting social-service organizations in developing countries as potential partners for diaspora philanthropists, and help to educate diasporas about strategic donations.

E. Diaspora Volunteering

Extensive, if scattered, evidence documents the ways in which diasporas devote time to community development projects and provide pro bono professional advice and training to institutions in their countries of origin. They may provide medical care in underserved areas, teach a university course, train people in a particular skill, or provide much-needed advice to budding entrepreneurs. In some cases, they take extended leaves of absence or devote their vacation time to volunteer service. Many diaspora members volunteer for causes or raise funds for philanthropic activities in or related to their countries of origin. Some who volunteer do so through a wide range of nonprofit and community-based organizations. Still others, by virtue of their homeland ties, have the contacts and capacity to undertake volunteer work outside of formal programs.

The research conducted by MPI identifies six "clusters" of programs that aim to recruit volunteers. These are centered on the following areas: business growth and technical advice, public health capacity building, postconflict relief and recovery, higher education capacity building, public policy advisory services, and youth programs. In addition, some volunteer programs target multiple categories of volunteers. Still other programs have a specific purpose and no particular diaspora focus, but nonetheless attract significant numbers of diaspora volunteers. On balance, volunteer programs are incredibly diverse and illustrate the wide range of opportunities open to diaspora volunteers — as well as the pitfalls of different approaches.

Over the past half century, the United States has promoted a multitude of international volunteer programs as a means to advance foreign policy goals. USAID initiatives often rely (intentionally or inadvertently) on diaspora volunteers. On balance, the MPI research suggests two complementary approaches to promoting diaspora volunteerism:

- Encourage greater diaspora participation in existing international volunteer programs.

- Partner with diaspora groups (such as community-based organizations, professional associations, and faith-based groups, among others) to promote new volunteer opportunities for their members.

F. Diaspora Advocacy

Of all the roles that diasporas play in development, advocacy, and diplomacy are among the least studied. The MPI scoping study surveys a number of examples of diaspora activism to identify the forms of diaspora advocacy and diplomacy, the primary concerns targeted, and the means by which the chosen causes are advanced. Diaspora organizations are enormously diverse. They include associations of migrants originating from the same locality, ethnic affinity groups, religious organizations, professional associations, charitable organizations, developmental nongovernmental organizations (NGOs), investment groups, affiliates of political parties, humanitarian relief organizations, virtual networks, federations of associations, and others. Members of any of these organizations, as well as individuals, may engage in "outward" advocacy (directed at authorities in their countries of origin or ancestry) or "inward" advocacy (directed at actors in the countries where they or their ancestors settled). Thus, diaspora investors have lobbied their country-of-origin governments to take specific steps to improve their business climate while at the same time lobbying their destination-country governments to adopt free-trade agreements with their countries of origin.

Diasporas use a variety of means to influence governments, international organizations, mass media, and potential allies. Their strategies include direct lobbying, media campaigns, electronic communication, and electoral participation. Whether these efforts are successful is determined by the strength of the advocates' personal contacts and transnational social networks, and by the resonance that their goals have for the broader diaspora community and among key interest groups in their homeland or settlement countries. In this vein, the MPI study pays special attention to ways in which diasporas have leveraged funds, contacts, and expertise to gain voting rights in their countries of origin and dual citizenship in their countries of origin and settlement.

Diaspora populations are major contributors to relief efforts when their homelands are affected by storms, earthquakes, and other natural disasters. At such times, the humanitarian response often trumps political differences within and among diaspora groups and their homeland governments, with diaspora members and groups not merely contributing to relief efforts but working to secure more funding and make existing programs more effective. Diaspora members also have an increasingly prominent voice in development efforts, advocating for projects, fundraising, identifying and prioritizing needs, and contributing expertise. Such work brings diaspora advocates into the same realm as many bilateral and international aid organizations. Finding ways to communicate with diaspora groups — which tend to be smaller and less well organized and financed than their more established counterparts — is an important step that country-of-destination governments can make to include more views in development and foreign policymaking. Governments in destination countries such as the United States, the Netherlands, and the United Kingdom have made strides in encouraging diaspora members to organize themselves so that they can speak more effectively on behalf of development-related policy measures.

II. Overarching Needs and Potential Donor Responses

USAID and other donors have several means of expanding diasporas' opportunities to contribute to development efforts in their countries of origin. These actions fall into four categories:

- Actions to strengthen the capacity of diaspora groups

- Actions to help country-of-origin governments engage more effectively with their diasporas

- Actions to strengthen donors' capacity to create partnerships with diasporas

- Actions to build and share knowledge among diasporas

All of the following recommendations should be vetted with diaspora members themselves before being considered for implementation.

A. Strengthening the Capacity of Diaspora Groups

Many diaspora groups are small and underfunded, with entirely volunteer staff, donated office space (if any), and a minimal operating budget. Because most members of these groups hold regular jobs, they may have difficulty finding the time to participate in training or information sessions or to organize the affairs of the group. To address this problem, donors may want to consider forming or supporting some kind of consolidated service center for diaspora organizations that meet certain criteria, to bring economies of scale to central functions such as accounting tasks, legal issues, funds management, travel services, and the like. Community foundations often perform these functions for philanthropic family foundations. More broadly, the San Francisco–based Tides Foundation provides services for many small nonprofit organizations. Centralized services might include establishing trust funds for diaspora-donated funds to safeguard them and ensure that they are used as intended and matched as promised.

Donors could also support technical assistance and training for diaspora groups in financial management, fundraising, project management, reporting requirements, and other areas. Rather than doing this directly or through a contractor, the government of Canada, for example, twins diaspora organizations with established Canadian NGOs in a mentorship arrangement that allows diaspora members to acquire practical organizational skills. Diaspora organizations with a proven track record may qualify for direct support as contractors or grantees of donor agencies. In a similar vein, donors could issue a contract to create a business incubator for small-to-medium-scale diaspora investors. IntEnt, in the Netherlands, is one such business incubator for diasporas, supported in part by the Netherlands Foreign Ministry. Scholarships to philanthropy workshops could be provided to new diaspora philanthropists.

B. Help Countries of Origin Engage Diasporas More Effectively

Foreign assistance strategies for diaspora engagement tend to focus on the diaspora rather than the country of origin. But as the MPI roundtables associated with the scoping studies revealed, many country-of-origin governments need help in establishing effective knowledge bases, structures, and methods of interacting with diaspora populations. Providing such assistance is, in many ways, an easier and more accepted way for donor agencies to promote diaspora engagement than direct support for diaspora groups, and should be part of the donors' repertory for strengthening diasporas' roles in their homelands. One of the themes that emerged throughout the MPI roundtables was the difficulty that governments in countries of origin have in understanding the locations, capabilities, and interests of their diaspora populations. These governments need diaspora skill inventories, descriptions of diaspora organizations and their capabilities, and surveys of diaspora needs and interests. Donor agencies could help provide such information by connecting these governments with national census organizations and with analysts who can carry out surveys and analyze census and survey data.

Countries of origin also need reliable and regular ways of communicating with diaspora populations. Donors could therefore provide funds for technical assistance in communications — especially in social media, ethnic media in the countries of destination, and new narrowcast media. Researching and analyzing diaspora bonds and their impact in countries of origin is another area where donor agencies can help. The Ministry of Overseas Indian Affairs, for example, has established ties with Jawaharlal Nehru University to tap into its expertise on migration issues. Donors may support such institutions in poorer countries of origin and promote interaction with country-of-destination universities and think tanks that specialize in diaspora issues.

Finally, the many ministries, subministries, and government departments that countries of origin have established to promote ties with diasporas are often woefully underfunded. Budget support to such ministries, along with technical assistance and training, would boost countries' ability to gather information from, provide services to, and work in cooperation with their diasporas.

C. Developing Donor Capacity

Donor governments' efforts to promote diaspora engagement are, as noted earlier, mostly ad hoc and uncoordinated. Commonly, one agency does not know what the others are doing. An important first step to ensure that various government efforts add up to more than the sum of their parts is to promote information sharing across government offices, departments, and agencies. In the United States, information sharing is particularly important between USAID and the Department of State. It would be useful to designate officials as focal points for diaspora information and engagement in USAID and State Department country or regional desks, with each given the responsibility to keep both State and USAID offices, as well as US embassies, informed of diaspora-related activities.

Another useful step would be to create an informal platform for communication with diaspora organizations in the country of destination. Participation should be fluid in order to avoid creating an entrenched group (which might also be perceived as being privileged or co-opted by the country-of-destination government). Diaspora members could regularly be invited to participate in consultations or to serve on advisory committees or task forces relating to their countries or regions of origin.

D. Knowledge Management

A solid evidence base is a prerequisite for the formulation of diaspora engagement strategies and for sound policymaking. Donors should routinely make use of the knowledge of diaspora members and experts in both areas. Another important knowledge management task is to disseminate successful models of diaspora activities, such as the Indicorps model discussed in the chapter on diaspora volunteerism. Sharing experiences among diaspora groups and with policymakers is a simple but effective way to learn. To promote understanding of good practices, donor agencies could hold sector-specific workshops and commission written or video case studies to develop wider understanding of good practices.

In assessing the progress and benefits of engaging diasporas in development activities, it is important to set realistic expectations and time frames. Metrics are important, but they should not simply borrow from conventional ODA frameworks. The process of building capacity among diasporas — and building trust between diaspora groups and governments (see the "road map" for diaspora engagement below) — is a long-term proposition that requires flexibility in its implementation.

III. Conclusion

There is much more to learn about diaspora engagement. Part of its promise lies in its extraordinary diversity — there is a diaspora partner for every dimension of development and for every corner of the earth. But for diaspora engagement policy to be most effective, it needs to move beyond the familiar language of using, tapping, or even exploiting diaspora ties into the language — and practice — of mutuality and reciprocity. Diasporas do not see their role as merely utilitarian. They want to be seen as stakeholders in the development of their countries of origin, and they need to know that both their practical contributions and their vital ideas are being taken into account. Diaspora engagement is a two-way street. If diasporas are to respond to the priorities of governments, they expect governments to respond to their priorities. If they are expected to listen, they also expect to be heard. In working with diaspora partners, a number of donor governments have found that the most successful projects and programs are those that build on existing diaspora initiatives rather than those that start with a call for partnership in a top-down initiative.

Appendix.
A Road Map for Diaspora Engagement

The road map for diaspora engagement presented below shows the major elements of a strategy for governments of origin or destination countries that want to engage diaspora populations more fully. It was developed by MPI for the third Global Forum on Migration and Development (GFMD) in 2009. The road map is not meant to be a one-size-fits-all model but rather an aid to integrating the many elements of a diaspora policy into a coherent strategy that can be adapted to the circumstances of different countries and diaspora populations. The road map will be permanently "under construction" as it is applied to specific cases.

Strategic Policies and Practices for Diaspora Partnerships

A government's strategy for diaspora engagement needs to include the following elements: identifying goals, mapping diaspora geography and skills, creating a relationship of trust between diasporas and governments of both origin and destination countries, and, ultimately, mobilizing diasporas to contribute to sustainable development. The "destination" is arrived at when the diaspora is established as a true partner in the development of its country of origin. Throughout its implementation, a diaspora engagement strategy must devote attention to strengthening the capacity of both government institutions and diaspora communities to work with one another and with other stakeholders. The central boxes in the diagram represent the major elements of the strategy. Although they are presented as a series of stages, in fact these elements will proceed concurrently, loop back upon each other, and leap-frog over any orderly progression from one stage to the next. Above all, there must be constant feedback among the processes in each stage.

The arrows show the processes necessary to get from one stage to the next (remembering that no stage is ever complete but must always remain in a state of dynamic interaction with the others). The balloons to the side are representative of the kind of actions associated with each stage of the strategy; they are neither exhaustive nor compulsory. Not all actions will be relevant for all governments, as some are specific to countries of origin and others to countries of destination. The different steps of the road map and the actions associated with each step are illustrated, below, by examples of best practices and lessons learned.

Figure 1. A Road Map for Diaspora Engagement

A Road Map for Diaspora Engagement

Match goals to diaspora resources (human and financial)

Identify goals and capacities (e.g., investment, knowledge, remittances).

Strengthen existing diaspora institutions and programs

Consultations / Research

National / Regional / Local

Identify opinion shapers within the diaspora

Analyze census data

'Listening exercises'

Know your diaspora.

Map diaspora organizations

Inventory skills

Coordination within gov't / Capacity building

Sponsor cultural events, language promotion

Grant Dual citizenship

Explain and get feedback on gov't diaspora policy

Build trust.

Provide services to the diaspora (documents, classes, social services)

Intervene with host governments

Grant privileges to nonresident expatriates and descendants

Flexible project implementation

Pilot projects

Time

Activate consular networks

Capacity building

Create or adapt government institutions (consular networks, ministries, councils)

Twinning

High-profile events

Diaspora spokespersons

Mobilize stakeholders (government, diaspora, civil society).

Facilitate investment (one-stop centers)

Sponsor travel for opinion leaders, youth

Integrate diasporas into development planning and policy implementation

Adaptation / Evaluation

Volunteer corps

Promote partnerships

Effectively engage diaspora in development.

©Migration Policy Institute 2010.

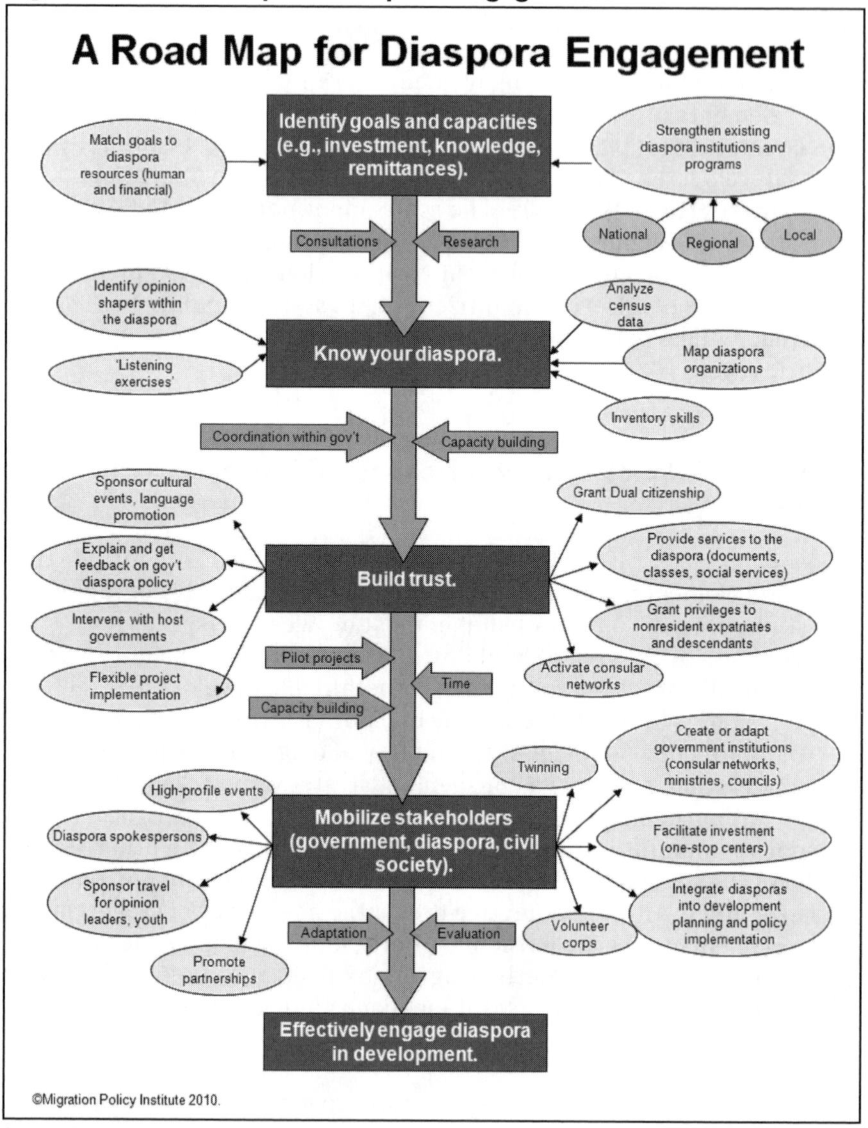

Source: Author's rendering.

1. Identification of Goals and Capacities

Any government devising a strategy for stronger diaspora involvement in development should first identify its own goals in undertaking this pursuit and define the internal tools and mechanisms (administrative, financial, and so on) it requires. For countries of destination, this approach will differ according to the specific circumstances and origin of potential diaspora partners. Governments can then ascertain how well their own capacities — as well as those of the diaspora — match their goals, and what they must seek to create or find in other actors.

If, for example, the country of origin seeks to reduce poverty or support the national balance of payments, its policy will likely focus on remittances, business investments, and, perhaps, capital markets. If, however, its goal is to improve national competitiveness, its policy is more likely to emphasize the knowledge and skills that diasporas can channel, whether through their own efforts or by connecting home-country institutions of learning and enterprise to institutions in the country of destination.

The government of the Philippines, for example, pursues a strategy of large-scale contract labor deployment overseas to reduce unemploy-ment and maintain a stream of remittance income. India and China, by contrast, have in recent years given priority to encouraging diaspora entrepreneurs and highly skilled professionals to develop activities in their countries of origin. If the goal of a destination country is to provide technical support for development, its diaspora engagement strategy is likely to focus on highly skilled members of a diaspora. If, however, its priority is poverty reduction, it is likely to emphasize measures such as lowering the cost of remittances.

Beyond these domestic policy considerations, goals may also be identi-fied as a result of dialogue between the governments of countries of origin and destination. For a country of origin, partnership with the country of destination could facilitate the involvement of diasporas via cooperation in spreading information in diaspora communities, enabling mobility, or providing financial support for projects involving the diaspora. For a country of destination that has decided to work with a specific diaspora, it is important to ascertain that the country of origin is willing to involve its diaspora in development activities, and that the goals defined by the destination country are consistent with the development priorities of the country of origin.

2. Know Your Diaspora

Once its goals are reasonably well articulated, the second, crucial step for a government is to know its diaspora. This involves collecting data (through a migrant/diaspora census) and mapping the diaspora popu-lation's skills and experience; creating inventories of relevant information; and conducting extensive listening exercises to understand what the diaspora has to offer, what it is willing to offer, and what it expects from the government in turn. It is crucial to acknowledge the diversity of diaspora agendas, interests, and strategies. Through the establishment of a continuous dialogue with diasporas, governments should try to reconcile — or at least understand — differing and often diverging views. Successful government interventions are the result of years of continuous, open engagement.

The Indian government, for example, tasked the High Level Committee on the Indian Diaspora to analyze the location, situation, and potential development role of the estimated 20 million nonresident Indians (NRIs) and persons of Indian origin (PIOs). The information resulting from this two-year exercise led to a new direction for India's diaspora policy, including the creation of a Ministry for Overseas Indian Affairs in 2004.

For countries of destination, a "know-your-diaspora" exercise would involve the collection of data in national censuses and surveys to reveal the birthplaces and ancestries of residents in the aggregate, while protecting the identity of subgroups and individuals. Using this aggregate information, countries of destination can judge where best to invest their efforts. More detailed information about diaspora populations can be gathered by both origin and destination countries through cooperation with diaspora organizations such as professional associations, "hometown" clubs, and alumni associations. Embassies and consular offices can also play an important role in gathering information about diaspora capacities and interests. The government of Ghana, for example, is directing resources to the management of migration data — and to diaspora profiles in particular.

The numbers, distribution, skills, prosperity, and level of integration of diaspora groups, along with their history, will define the universe of possibilities for diaspora partnerships. Realistic policy options, for example, will be different for a large and concentrated diaspora residing chiefly in one or a few countries (Mexico) than for a small and highly dispersed diaspora (Ghana). Similarly, the country of destination's policy will differ depending on its historical relationship with its diasporas' countries of origin, and on how successfully its diaspora communities are integrated in the destination country.

3. Building Trust

The long-term project of building partnerships between governments and diasporas is much more likely to succeed if it has a strong foundation of good communication and mutual trust. Partnership is a two-way street. Too often, diasporas have felt that country-of-origin governments see them simply as cash cows, while some country-of-destination governments see diaspora groups demanding support even though they are not capable of delivering on mutual objectives. Both parties must feel that they are deriving value from the relationship. Building trust is therefore a necessary third element of diaspora engagement strategy.

For the governments of countries of origin, building trust with diaspora populations may also involve creating a welcoming environment for diaspora engagement in development activities. This would include steps to improve the business climate, such as greater transparency in regulations and licensing requirements and more consistent application of property law. Other elements of good governance and rule of law are also important in attracting diaspora engagement. Countries of destination, collectively or individually, can support these efforts. The European Commission, for example, has funded projects in a number of migrant-origin countries, intended to help their governments develop sound legal, regulatory, and/or institutional frameworks that will encourage increased diaspora investment.

Few governments have taken the task of gaining the trust of a diaspora as seriously as the government of Mexico. From the late 1990s, the government has invested in communication with and service to the diaspora.[6] The creation of the Institute for Mexicans Abroad (IME) in the Ministry of Foreign Affairs in 2002 brought coherence to these efforts and set up a dense network of over 56 consular offices in North America. IME works with organized diaspora groups on the well-known 3x1 Program, through which three levels of government match the contributions of migrant organizations to infrastructure projects in their communities of origin. Thousands of projects have been financed — 1,613 in 2007 alone, in 443 municipalities.[7] A key trust-building element of Mexico's diaspora engagement strategy is the Consultative

---

6 See Carlos Gonzalez Gutierrez, "The Institute of Mexicans Abroad: An Effort to Empower the Diaspora," *Closing the Distance: How Governments Strengthen Ties with Their Diasporas*, ed. Dovelyn Rannveig Agunias (Washington, DC: Migration Policy Institute, September, 2009).

7 The 3x1 Program is best understood as a solidarity program rather than a development program. The choice of projects follows a logic of collaboration and interconnection between diaspora and "hometown" communities rather than an economic logic. Some critics charge that it diverts government development resources to communities that are not the neediest, since they are already in receipt of remittances and charitable contributions from migrant "Hometown Associations."

Council of IME, composed primarily of elected leaders from diaspora communities. The council makes recommendations to the government about its diaspora policies and helps set IME's agenda. The council freely criticizes and disagrees with government positions when it feels called upon to do so, which — paradoxically perhaps — consolidates the confidence of both parties that disagreement does not mean alienation.

As Mexico's example shows, the establishment of joint diaspora-government decisionmaking is extremely important in building trust. At the institutional level, Israel and its diaspora have taken this process a step further through the development of an increasingly autonomous, quasi-governmental Jewish Agency for Israel. Its institutions and programs are governed jointly by government and diaspora representatives. At a more local level, Partnership 2000 is a prime example of building trust through twinning Israeli municipalities and diaspora communities. Programs have organizational structures that feature representation from both sides, whether on governing boards or professional committees consulting on program development and implementation. This allows for the voice and influence of both sides in key areas such as the identifying of needs, priority setting, and resource allocation.

Partnerships of trust can be built around many different kinds of programs. In addition to the kinds of services provided by IME, many governments offer privileges to nonresident citizens (and, in some cases, their descendants) such as duty-free imports, tax-free repatriation of foreign-currency income, or the ability to buy assets or hold jobs normally reserved for resident citizens. Successful examples of diaspora activities identified by the EC-UN Joint Migration and Development Initiative (JMDI) reinforce the notion that there is a positive link between diaspora privileges (such as the existence of a special fiscal regime or streamlined processes to set up businesses) and the impact of diaspora initiatives.[8]

Many governments sponsor cultural events in countries that have a diaspora presence; some, including China, also promote learning of the "mother tongue" by subsidizing lessons and providing teachers. Politi-

---

8   This global and multiannual initiative is funded by the European Commission (EC) and implemented by the United Nations Development Programme (UNDP) in partnership with the International Organization for Migration (IOM), International Labour Organization (ILO), United Nations Population Fund (UNFPA), and United Nations High Commissioner for Refugees (UNHCR). It is engaged in the provision of direct financial support to concrete projects in the field of migration and development, and the identification and analysis of good practices with a view to drawing lessons learned to ultimately feed into policymaking at national and international levels.

cal rights are often a high priority of diasporas; governments can both demonstrate and earn trust by facilitating overseas voting and other forms of political participation by expatriates. Ghana, for example, passed a law permitting dual citizenship in 2000 and granting voting rights to Ghanaians abroad in 2006. Such activities are designed to instill a sense of belonging to the country of origin, and thus to foster deeper engagement.

For the governments of destination countries, building trust with engaged diaspora populations involves acknowledging that their dual sense of belonging and their commitment to their homelands is compatible with thorough integration in the adopted country. Dual citizenship is one signal that a government can send that it trusts people who have multiple commitments to meet all the obligations of full citizenship.

Destination-country governments can take the message of trust to a deeper level — and one more specific to development — by accepting that diaspora expertise is an important input in development policies relating to their countries of origin. The UK country offices of the Department for International Development (DFID) are encouraged to consult diaspora groups in formulating DFID country assistance plans, for example. Furthermore, the United Kingdom supports a Senior Executive Service drawn from diaspora members to fill senior positions in governments of postconflict countries.

4. Mobilization

Once trust has been established between governments and diasporas, the characteristics of diasporas well understood, and the objectives of diaspora engagement clearly articulated, partnerships for development involving diasporas can be more successfully mobilized. This may require the creation of new government institutions or the evitalization of existing ones.[9] Senegal was one of the first countries to pioneer this kind of arrangement, in 1993, with a landmark initiative that overhauled the Ministry of Foreign Affairs to include oversight for Senegalese abroad. An ever-increasing number of migrant-origin countries are creating ministries dedicated to diaspora issues, such as India's Ministry for Overseas Indian Affairs, Mali's Ministry of Malians Abroad and African Integration, Armenia's Ministry of the Diaspora, and Haiti's Ministry of Haitians Living Abroad. Still more have offices

---

9   See Dovelyn Rannveig Agunias, "Institutionalizing Diaspora Engagement within Migrant-Origin Governments," in Dovelyn Rannveig Agunias, ed., *Closing the Distance: How Governments Strengthen Ties with Their Diasporas* (Washington, DC: Migration Policy Institute, 2009).

at the subministerial level or special institutions elsewhere in government. Delegates at the 2007 GFMD's diaspora roundtable repeatedly made the point that countries of origin need an institutional framework at the national level to communicate with diasporas, coordinate policies, and provide support and follow-up.

Yet even if it succeeds in building trust, a governmental institution is not necessarily the most suitable channel for the mobilization of diaspora investment. Israel's experience has demonstrated the advantages of an independent and accountable mechanism for the transfer of philanthropic funds from the diaspora to the homeland — in Israel's case, the American Jewish Joint Distribution Committee is governed solely by diaspora members. Diaspora Jews and overseas Israelis raise well over $1 billion in philanthropic contributions annually, which indicates that formal institutions for diaspora engagement can be augmented by initiatives from civil society. It is also worth noting that in a framework of origin-destination country cooperation, a nongovernmental mechanism for the transfer of funds might enjoy tax benefits or incentives in some host countries.

Strategies for diaspora mobilization may include high-profile events, such as India's annual Pravasi Bharatiya Divas, the first of which, in 2003, brought together more than 2,000 high-profile diaspora Indians for a conference attended by most of India's senior politicians as well as by Nobel Prize winners of Indian nationality or descent. Jamaica, too, holds an annual celebratory gathering of expatriates and descendants of emigrants.

Governments of origin countries may appoint well-known diaspora members as spokespersons on diaspora issues, sponsor travel to the country of origin for opinion leaders and youth, or establish diaspora volunteer programs. For example the "Birthright" program initiated by Israel in 2001 provides free educational trips to Israel for young diaspora adults aged 18 to 26. Since its inception, over 200,000 diaspora youth from 52 countries have participated in the program. Origin-country governments may also establish centers or programs to facilitate financial flows from the diaspora, such as India's "one-stop shop" for diaspora investors.

Country-of-destination governments, acting alone or in regional organizations, may partner with country-of-origin governments in development initiatives, particularly those that would benefit from technical assistance or financial support. The European Commission from 2003 to 2005 supported a "Return of Qualified Afghans" program for Afghan nationals living in European Union Member States. In cooperation with the government of Afghanistan, and employing the International Organization for Migration (IOM) as an implementing partner, the program identified Afghans with relevant qualifications and experience and assisted their return to Afghanistan for assignments of six to 12 months in both the public and the private sector. The program was small and relatively high cost, but an evaluation found that the participating Afghans provided needed skills that were appropriately used.[10] The Netherlands is currently implementing a similar program (Temporary Return of Qualified Nationals) in Afghanistan, Georgia, Ethiopia, Bosnia-Herzegovina, Sudan, and Sierra Leone. It also cooperates with the IOM/ Migration for Development in Africa (MIDA) program in Ghana to support the temporary return of medical doctors in the diaspora to Ghana.

Canada's International Development Agency (CIDA) uses a number of techniques to mobilize diaspora groups for development in their countries of origin. It directly funds development projects executed by diaspora groups with experience in implementing development projects, such as the Association of Haitian-Canadian Engineers and Scientists. Since many diaspora groups do not have relevant experience, however, CIDA has created tripartite partnerships among diaspora organizations, Canadian development NGOs, and NGOs in the countries of origin. (The practice has the added advantage of avoiding the impression that diaspora policy is supporting an organized political opposition in exile.) Linking diaspora organizations to Canadian NGOs with solid country experience has enabled diaspora organizations to gain the knowledge and expertise needed to seek donor funds and work independently. CIDA experience shows that many Haitian diaspora organizations, after working with Canadian civil society organizations for several years, now approach CIDA for separate funding to execute development projects in Haiti on their own.

Several donor governments have found it useful to create and/or support platforms to facilitate diaspora involvement in development, such as Diasporas for Development in the Netherlands, the *Regroupement des Organismes Canado-Haïtiens pour le Développement* in Canada, and Connections for Development in the United Kingdom. These encourage the systematic sharing of ideas and information while also serving as vehicles for capacity building. In some cases, they may also evolve into operational partners for national development agencies.

---

10 Altai Consulting, *An Evaluation of the EU-RQA Program for the International Organization for Migration and the European Commission* (Kabul: IOM, 2006).

A number of donor governments or consortia, after experiments in working with diaspora partners, have found that the most successful projects and programs are those that build on existing diaspora initiatives. The EC-UN JMDI observes that "policies too strongly driven by governments can act as a deterrent for diaspora engagement."[11] ↲

11 EC-UN Joint Migration and Development Initiative (JMDI) contribution to Global Forum on Migration and Development (GFMD), "Mainstreaming Migration in Development Planning — Key Actors, Key Strategies, Key Actions," GFMD Background Paper 1.2, undated.

CHAPTER 2

MOBILIZING DIASPORA ENTREPRENEURSHIP FOR DEVELOPMENT

Kathleen Newland and Hiroyuki Tanaka, Migration Policy Institute

Introduction

Development practitioners and policymakers are beginning to examine the role of diaspora entrepreneurs in gearing investments toward their home countries, thereby creating jobs, spurring innovation, and fostering networks. Compared with remittances or diaspora bonds, entrepreneurial investments give diaspora members more direct control over the use of their funds.[1] Given their ties to their countries of origin, diaspora members are often more willing than non-diaspora investors to risk starting or engaging in business activities in high-risk or emerging markets.[2] Moreover, their knowledge of the local political, economic, and cultural environment, as well as their personal connections and linguistic abilities, may give members of diasporas a "first mover" advantage over others when investing in or starting businesses in their countries of origin.[3]

---

1 The inability to control and oversee the development projects that they help finance can be a source of frustration for those who would like to play a more active role and engage themselves directly in the development of their countries of origin. However, as some experts note, many diaspora members do not actively or consciously seek to contribute to the development of their home countries. Instead, their everyday actions such as remitting money to family members only happen to contribute to economic development.

2 Kate Gillespie, Liesl Riddle, Edward Sayre, and David Sturges, "Diaspora Interest in Homeland Investment," *Journal of International Business Studies* 30, no. 3 (1999): 623–35; Ravi Ramamurti, "Developing Countries and MNEs: Extending and Enriching the Research Agenda," *Journal of International Business Studies* 35, no. 4 (2004): 277–85.

3 David Leblang, "Another Link in the Chain: Migrant Networks and International Investment," Presentation at the World Bank Conference on Diaspora and Development in Washington, DC, July 14, 2009, http://siteresources.worldbank.org/INTPROSPECTS/

Despite the advantages of attracting diaspora direct investors and entrepreneurs to their countries, many developing countries have experienced only limited success in actually doing so. Countries at war or those experiencing internal conflict and social upheaval remain unattractive to all but the most intrepid diaspora private investors and business people.[4] But even when societies are at peace, governments may still require aspiring entrepreneurs to follow complex procedures and clear many administrative hurdles to register and operate businesses. Complicated tax laws, limited access to local financing, and corruption are all conditions that can deter individuals from pursuing economic activities in a given country and persuade them to look for opportunities elsewhere.

This chapter seeks to identify the nature of diaspora entrepreneurship and suggest ways that the United States Agency for International Development (USAID) and other donors can constructively promote its developmental impact. The chapter draws from the academic and policy literature — including, importantly, research presented at the World Bank Conference on Diaspora and Development held in Washington, DC, on July 14, 2009 — as well as interviews with experts in the field. The study first outlines why entrepreneurship, in particular among diasporas, is important for development and how governments can support it. It then identifies the major patterns of diaspora entrepreneurship, offering examples of initiatives that have encouraged and supported migrants to engage in entrepreneurial activities.[5] Next, the chapter outlines some policy approaches that are likely to enhance diaspora entrepreneurship, suggesting how countries can construct environments that are conducive to investment and sustainable business growth. Finally, it notes the constraints on engaging diaspora entrepreneurs or those who seek to become entrepreneurs, including the potential for perverse or unintended consequences.

Resources/334934-1110315015165/Leblang.pdf; Yevgeny Kuznetsov and Charles Sabel, "International Migration of Talent, Diaspora Networks, and Development: Overview of Main Issues," in *Diaspora Networks and the International Migration of Skills: How Countries Can Draw on Their Talent Abroad*, ed. Yevgeny Kuznetsov (Washington, DC: World Bank, 2006).

4   Stephen C. Lubkemann, "Remittance Relief and Not-Just-for-Profit Entrepreneurship: The Case of Liberia," in *Diasporas and Development: Exploring the Potential*, ed. Jennifer M. Brinkerhoff (Boulder, CO: Lynne Rienner Publishers, Inc., 2008).

5   Many of the activities in these areas are not initiated by governments. Rather, they spring from the private or voluntary sectors, which offer a useful record of experience for those seeking ways to promote diaspora engagement through government programs or public-private partnerships.

I. Why Focus on Diaspora Entrepreneurship?

Since at least the 1970s, researchers have studied entrepreneurship among immigrants in their countries of destination. Studies have emphasized immigrants' contributions to local economies through the small and medium enterprises (SMEs) that they establish and run, their role in creating and expanding niche markets in immigrant communities, and their ability to offer jobs to natives and other immigrants.[6]

Recent research shows that entrepreneurship among immigrants living in the world's advanced economies is on the rise, and that the bulk of immigrant entrepreneurs in more than ten advanced economies of the world work in the retail, wholesale, restaurant, and catering businesses.[7] Numerous studies have tried to assess the economic impact of both high- and low-skilled immigrants in their countries of destination. One study of Chinese and Indian entrepreneurs in Silicon Valley, for example, shows that companies founded by immigrants employed 45,000 workers and generated $52 billion in revenue in 2006.[8]

Even though very little research has been completed on how diaspora entrepreneurs contribute to the economic development of their countries of origin, through what is sometimes called diaspora direct investment (DDI),[9] there is reason to believe that diaspora entrepreneurship has the potential to contribute to development in four ways:

---

6   See, for example: Roger Waldinger, Howard Aldrich, and Robin Ward, *Ethnic Entrepreneurs: Immigrant Business in Industrial Societies* (New York, NY: Sage Publications, 1990); Roger Waldinger, *Through the Eye of the Needle: Immigrants and Enterprise in New York's Garment Trades* (New York, NY: New York Univ. Press, 1986); Robert Kloosterman and Jan Rath, eds., *Immigrant Entrepreneurs: Venturing Abroad in the Age of Globalization* (Oxford, United Kingdom and New York, NY: Berg, 2003); Robert Watson, Kevin Keasey, and Mae Baker, "Small Firm Financial Contracting and Immigrant Entrepreneurship," in *Immigrant Businesses: The Economic, Political and Social Environment*, ed. Jan Rath (Basingstoke, United Kingdom and New York, NY: Macmillan and St. Martin's, 2000).

7   These findings apply to the United States, Canada, Australia, South Africa, the United Kingdom, the Netherlands, Italy, France, Belgium, Austria, and Germany. See Kloosterman and Rath, *Immigrant Entrepreneurs*.

8   Vivek Wadhwa, AnnaLee Saxenian, Richard Freeman, Gary Gereffi, and Alex Salkever, *America's Loss is the World's Gain: America's New Immigrant Entrepreneurs, Part IV* (Kansas City, MO: Kauffman Foundation, March 2009).

9   United States Agency for International Development (USAID), *Global Diaspora Networks Alliance Framework* (Washington, DC: USAID, 2008); USAID, *Diaspora Networks Alliance: Leveraging Migrant Resources for Effective Development* (Washington, DC: USAID, 2008).

1. *Diaspora entrepreneurship fosters business development, job creation, and innovation.* Substantial investment by members of the diaspora, if successful, creates jobs both directly and indirectly and spurs competition; both effects may lead to further innovation, businesses, and jobs.

2. *DDI creates economic, social, and political capital through global networks.* One of the characteristics of poor countries is their relative isolation from global flows of trade, capital, and knowledge. Diaspora members have a comparative advantage in their ability to connect with a wide range of potential partners and supporters in both their countries of origin and their countries of destination. These connections may create opportunities for investment, trade, and outsourcing; foster strategic partnerships; and tap into sources of political and financial capital that can facilitate the transfer of knowledge and technology from developed to developing countries.[10] Diaspora entrepreneurs may also leverage their access to relatively cheap labor and, in some cases, large talent pools in their countries of origin into a comparative advantage in manufacturing or knowledge-process outsourcing (such as information systems integration and insurance underwriting).[11] All of these actions can help developing economies grow.

3. *Diaspora entrepreneurship taps into social capital through cultural and linguistic understanding.* Many diaspora members have advantages over other entrepreneurs investing in countries of diaspora origin, such as their understanding of cultural and social norms, distinct business cultures, and local languages. Such familiarity can help develop trust and thereby open up opportunities closed or unknown to other investors or entrepreneurs.[12]

4. *Entrepreneurship and economic development are positively linked.* According to research comparing entrepreneurship in more than 40 countries, higher levels of entrepreneurship are positively correlated with higher levels of economic development.[13] While it is difficult to pinpoint the causality in this virtuous cycle — do high levels of entrepreneurship spur economic growth, or do high levels of economic growth encourage entrepreneurship? — the association is strong.

---

10 Given the important role that diaspora and immigrant networks play in fostering entrepreneurship and helping people find employment, this comparative advantage is arguably the most important point on which policymakers should focus to help foster diaspora entrepreneurship.

11 Abhishek Pandey, Alok Aggarwal, Richard Devane, and Yevgeny Kuznetsov, *India's Transformation to Knowledge-based Economy — Evolving Role of the Indian Diaspora* (Gurgaon, India: Evalueserve, 2004), http://info.worldbank.org/etools/docs/library/152386/abhishek.pdf.

12 Gillespie et al., "Diaspora Interest in Homeland Investment."

13 Zoltán J. Ács, "How is Entrepreneurship Good for Economic Growth?" *Innovations* (Winter 2006): 96–107, www.mitpressjournals.org/doi/pdf/10.1162/itgg.2006.1.1.97?cookieSet=1.

Not all forms of entrepreneurship contribute equally to economic development. Recent research shows the importance of distinguishing between "necessity entrepreneurs" and "opportunity entrepreneurs," as the two groups have very different effects on development. (Joseph Schumpeter, among others, has defined necessity entrepreneurs as those who are simply self-employed and opportunity entrepreneurs as those who "reform or revolutionize the pattern of production.")[14]

A greater number of necessity entrepreneurs may not correlate with higher levels of economic growth. In fact, an abundance of necessity entrepreneurs may suggest the exact opposite — that individuals are setting up their own businesses or working for themselves because they cannot find opportunities in the labor market.

Unskilled immigrants or returnees who establish their own businesses, mainly out of necessity, have different networking opportunities and approaches to starting businesses than high-skilled immigrants with business experience abroad — in Silicon Valley or the City of London, for example.[15] Those running businesses that require little education and low start-up costs usually work in sectors that are oversaturated with competitors and have razor-thin profit margins, thus making social capital extremely important for survival. While self-employment can create value for entrepreneurs and any employees they might have, research shows that necessity entrepreneurship has no effect on economic development.[16] At best, it reduces overt unemployment and enables people to support themselves.

Opportunity entrepreneurs are much more likely to have a positive impact on economic development.[17] Skilled individuals who specialize in high-demand and rapidly growing sectors of the knowledge-based economy can create huge economic opportunities and profits for businesses and their countries. Even those with little education but strong business acumen may perceive and take advantage of market openings. The roles of diasporas in developing knowledge-based sectors in China,

---

14 Joseph Alois Schumpeter, *Capitalism, Socialism and Democracy*, 4th edition (London, United Kingdom: Unwin, 1974), 132.

15 Kloosterman and Rath, *Immigrant Entrepreneurs*.

16 Zoltán J. Ács and Attila Varga, "Agglomeration, Entrepreneurship and Technological Change," *Small Business Economics* 24, no. 3 (2005): 323–34; Leora Klapper and Juan Manuel Quesada Delgado, *Understanding Entrepreneurship: Influences and Consequences of Business Creation* (Washington, DC: World Bank, 2007); Zoltán J. Ács and Laszlo Szerb, "Entrepreneurship, Economic Growth, and Public Policy," *Small Business and Economics* 28, nos. 2–3 (2007): 109–22; Zoltán J. Ács, David B. Audretsch, and Robert J. Strom, eds., *Entrepreneurship, Growth, and Public Policy* (Cambridge, United Kingdom: Cambridge Univ. Press, 2009).

17 Ibid.

India, Ireland, and Israel are now well known.[18] They have provided venture capital and connections to trade networks, facilitated technology and knowledge transfers, and pioneered development of robust special economic zones in their countries of origin.

The Global Entrepreneurship Monitor (GEM) is an academic research consortium that tracks, evaluates, and compares the level of entrepreneurial activity in 54 developed and developing countries and analyzes how it relates to national economic growth. It finds that countries with a high opportunity-to-necessity entrepreneurship ratio tend to have higher levels of income, exports as a share of GDP, licensing receipts, R&D expenditures, and spending on education compared to those with a low ratio.[19] Moreover, GEM finds that necessity entrepreneurship plays a relatively small role in innovation-driven economies. Nonetheless, most governments in developing countries continue to promote necessity entrepreneurship rather than opportunity entrepreneurship.

Given these research findings, this chapter focuses on how organizations and individuals can promote high-value-added opportunity entrepreneurship among diasporas (while not forgetting that some necessity entrepreneurs may transition into this category if they can overcome the constraints on their businesses). While job creation and employment are important economic indicators, they offer limited value if they are concentrated in already oversaturated markets in largely informal sectors of the "bazaar" economy.[20] One of the major downsides of informal firms is that many of the owners or entrepreneurs of these firms operate on a small scale, do not pay taxes, and cannot obtain formal bank credit, as they lack a formally registered property to use as collateral. Such obstacles then lead them to seek credit elsewhere, such as from friends or family — or from money lenders who charge extremely high interest rates.[21]

---

18 AnnaLee Saxenian, *The New Argonauts: Regional Advantage in a Global Economy* (Cambridge, MA: Harvard Univ. Press, 2006).

19 GEM uses harmonized definitions and standards to compare entrepreneurship levels across developed and developing countries. Researchers have emphasized the difficulty in comparing entrepreneurship across countries. International comparisons are difficult because different countries adopt different definitions of entrepreneurship (some define entrepreneurs as all self-employed individuals while others define them as those who register businesses). Moreover, national data on employment vary from country to country, making comparisons difficult, and some countries collect data on immigrants, while others do not (Global Entrepreneurship Monitor, home page, www.gemconsortium.org).

20 Mohammad A. Qadeer, *Urban Development in the Third World: Internal Dynamics of Lahore, Pakistan* (New York, NY: Praeger, 1983).

21 William J. Baumol, Robert E. Litan, and Carl J. Schramm, *Good Capitalism, Bad Capitalism and the Economics of Growth and Prosperity* (New Haven, CT: Yale Univ. Press, 2007).

While encouraging diaspora members to reproduce familiar businesses such as taxi companies, beauty salons, or corner shops may create jobs in the short run, it is not the best strategy for long-term economic growth. Policymakers would be better advised to shift their focus from encouraging job creation in these low-value-added sectors to helping entrepreneurs identify and exploit opportunities that will boost economic development. Once public and private leaders identify such opportunities, they should facilitate investment by diaspora members and help fill the gaps in education, mentoring, training, and funding that constrain entrepreneurs' ability to invest in these strategic sectors. The government, however, should limit its role to defining and implementing policies and regulations that are likely to spur investment, entrepreneurship, and new businesses in accordance with its national development strategy; it should not extend its reach into telling private businesses what to do and what not to do.

For Mauritius, the end of the Multi-Fiber Agreement (MFA) — a preferential trade agreement with the United States and the European Union on textiles and clothing — in 2005 led to increased exposure to global competition in the textile industry, which had been a bedrock of the Mauritian economy. Growing unemployment and a weakening global economy pushed the government to rethink how it could put Mauritius back on a sustainable growth path. In 2005, the government created a ten-year Economic Reform Programme; in 2007, it passed the Business Facilitation Act that laid out steps for development of an environment conducive to the creation of SMEs. In addition, it restructured several of its government agencies, including the Small Enterprises and Handicrafts Development Agency (SEHDA), the Board of Investment (BOI), and Enterprise Mauritius (EM). As a result of such restructuring, the government has attracted more foreign direct investment, increasing its volume from 2.8 billion rupees in 2005 to 11.4 billion rupees in 2008, and the number of registered SMEs from 75,000 in 2002 to 92,000 in 2007.[22] In addition to economic restructuring, since the 1990s Mauritius has made building competitive and knowledge-driven information technology (IT), financial services, and medical industries a national objective. Relying on its diaspora members and their networks has become one of the major strategies in this endeavor.[23]

---

22 Joyker Nayeck, "Circular Migration — The Case for Mauritius," Presentation at the International Conference on Diaspora for Development, World Bank, Washington, DC, July 14, 2009, http://siteresources.worldbank.org/INTPROSPECTS/Resources/334934-1110315015165/Nayeck.pdf.

23 United Nations Conference on Trade and Development (UNCTAD), *Investment Policy Review: Mauritius* (New York and Geneva: UNCTAD, 2001), www.gov.mu/portal/sites/ncb/mac/nlibrary/efiles/dig4.pdf.

The Indian diaspora has contributed significantly to India's economic development, most notably that of its IT industry. In the late 1980s, many Indian engineers working in the United States reached top management positions in US IT companies. Some of these business leaders mentored Indian programmers and invited them to enhance the quality and performance standards of their companies' outsourced operations in India — a move that, in turn, helped upgrade these programmers' skills.[24] As more Indian diaspora members in the United States became entrepreneurs, venture capitalists, and top executives in US companies, they began playing a much more active role in promoting and supporting the growth of India's IT industry. In 1992, a group of successful Indians, many of them engineers living in the San Francisco Bay Area, founded The Indus Entrepreneurs (TiE) with the intent to support and mentor promising Indian entrepreneurs in Silicon Valley. The organization now offers these and other networking opportunities to 11,000 members and 2,500 charter members in 53 chapters in 12 countries.[25] In addition, it has lobbied the Indian government to reform regulations to promote the venture capital industry.[26] Finally, as the United States faced the "Y2K" scare in the late 1990s, Indian-origin executives at major US corporations influenced their companies to outsource work to India.[27] Partly as a result, some Indians in the United States returned to India to supervise outsourced projects and investments and to train Indian professionals in meeting US standards. In sum, the positive contributions of the Indian diaspora have helped build India's reputation as a go-to place for US and European companies seeking to outsource high-quality work at all skill levels; as a source of exported goods and services, including R&D; and as a promising destination for investment.[28]

While experts debate the extent to which the Indian diaspora was central to the growth of the IT industry in India, people of Indian origin, particularly in the United States, have undoubtedly played a key role in its development. As the case of the Indian diaspora illustrates, policies that encourage diaspora entrepreneurship can be a useful component of a country's national development strategy. As people around the world become increasingly mobile and interconnected due

24 Devesh Kapur, "Diasporas and Technology Transfer," *Journal of Human Development* 2, no. 2 (2001): 265–86, www2.ssc.upenn.edu/about/Diasporas and Technology Transfer.pdf.
25 The Indus Entrepreneurs (TiE), "Overview," www.tie.org/chapterHome/about_tie/ OverView200706189912181967/viewInnerPagePT.
26 Devesh Kapur, "The Causes and Consequences of India's IT Boom," *India Review* 1, no. 2 (2002): 91–110.
27 Steve Hamm, *Bangalore Tiger: How Indian Tech Upstart Wipro is Rewriting the Rules of Global Competition* (New York, NY: McGraw-Hill, 2007).
28 Kapur, "Diasporas and Technology Transfer"; Hamm, *Bangalore Tiger*.

to declining travel costs and the widespread use of new information and communication technologies, the nexus of globalization, migration, transnationalism, and entrepreneurship promises to be a potent driver of economic development.[29]

II. What Spurs Entrepreneurship? The Opportunity Structure

If governments want to encourage entrepreneurship among diaspora populations, they first need to know what spurs entrepreneurship in general so that they can support members of the diaspora to pursue and realize their entrepreneurial ambitions. Research shows that in addition to personal goals and traits, a combination of economic, political, financial, and sociocultural factors also influences an individual's decision to become an entrepreneur. The personal attributes of an entrepreneur — such as risk-taking and optimism — may be inherent, but the opportunity structure is susceptible to policy intervention. Several factors that foster entrepreneurism are discussed below.

A strong economy. First, individuals are more likely to start a business in a country with robust economic growth, a high level of formal sector participation, a high-quality and business-friendly legal and regulatory environment, and relatively easy access to finance.[30] Economic growth, in turn, is positively correlated with new business registrations and entry rates.[31] According to the World Bank's World Development Indicators, the time required to start a business has a strong negative correlation with a nation's overall income level — a trend that has been observed since 2003.[32] For example, in 2008 it took 13 days on average to start a business in high-income member countries of the Organization for Economic Cooperation and Development (OECD), 20 days in other high-income countries, 43 days in middle-income countries, and

---

29 Linda G. Basch, Nina Glick-Schiller, and Cristina Szanton Blanc, *Nations Unbound: Transnational Projects, Postcolonial Predicaments, and De-territorialized Nation-States* (Amsterdam, The Netherlands: Gordon and Breach, 1994); Peggy Levitt, "Transnational Migration: Taking Stock and Future Directions," *Global Networks* 1, no. 3 (2001): 195–261; Peggy Levitt, *The Transnational Villagers* (Berkeley, CA: Univ. of California Press, 2001).

30 Leora Klapper, Raphael Amit, Mauro F. Guillén, and Juan Manuel Quesada, *Entrepreneurship and Firm Formation across Countries* (Washington, DC: World Bank, August 2007), http://knowledge.wharton.upenn.edu/papers/1345.pdf.

31 Ibid.

32 2003 is the first year for which data from the World Development Indicators are available for the number of days required to start a business.

47 days in low-income countries.[33] This suggests that low- and middle-income countries should try to reform regulatory frameworks in ways that would make it easier and quicker for diaspora members to register businesses, acquire business licenses, and protect property rights.[34]

However, government failures can also open opportunities for entrepreneurs, such as the water sellers who bring in tank trucks to poor neighborhoods not supplied by public water services and the cell-phone sellers who profit from Somalia's ruined communications infrastructure. (Similarly, Somalia's *hawala* system, organized by diaspora entrepreneurs, substitutes for conventional banking and money-transfer systems.)

Diaspora engagement policies. Governments can and should tap into the wealth, knowledge, and skills of their diaspora members to foster the establishment and growth of businesses, training centers, and educational institutions. Relevant policies might include offering tax breaks to diaspora entrepreneurs and investors along with special legal status, lowering import barriers, and providing information about business regulations and laws. For example, when Dominica tried to set up a tertiary educational institution, the Dominica State College, it turned to members of its diaspora who had served in management positions in US universities to help develop the curriculum, structure the college, and launch the institution. Those diaspora members who were involved in establishing the college offered their services free of charge.[35] In another example, the Ethiopian Investment Agency wooed Ethiopians living abroad, mostly in the United States, to invest in Ethiopia by giving them special privileges; however, when economic conditions pushed the government to discontinue this practice, diaspora investment in the homeland declined.[36] These experiences indicate that diaspora engagement policies can have positive effects but are not likely to be sustained unless underlying conditions are right.

---

33 World Bank Group, "Quick Query Selected from World Development Indicators," *World Development Indicators* (Washington, DC: World Bank, 2009), http://ddp-ext.worldbank.org/ext/DDPQQ/report.do?method=showReport.

34 William J. Baumol, Robert E. Litan, and Carl J. Schramm, *Good Capitalism, Bad Capitalism and The Economics of Growth and Prosperity* (New Haven, CT: Yale Univ. Press, 2007).

35 Thomson Fontaine, "Tracing the Diaspora's Involvement in the Development of a Nation: The Case of Dominica," Paper prepared for the George Washington University's Research Workshop and Edited Book Project on The Role of Diasporas in Developing the Homeland, 2006, www.thedominican.net/articles/diasporaPaper.pdf.

36 Elizabeth Chaco and Marie Price, *The Role of the Diaspora in Development: The Case of Ethiopia and Bolivian Immigrants in the USA* (Washington, DC: George Washington Univ., 2009), http://iussp2009.princeton.edu/download.aspx?submissionId=92786.

Special privileges for diaspora investors and entrepreneurs must be carefully designed not to distort the market for capital by directing it toward less-productive uses. By the same token, domestically based entrepreneurs should not be put at a disadvantage. That said, special incentives to attract diaspora direct investment are appropriate to level the playing field, since investing from abroad often carries extraordinary financial and administrative costs. Thus India established a "one-stop shop" for diaspora investment in India shortly after a report commissioned by the government showed that overwhelming red tape and obscure regulations were major obstacles faced by potential diaspora investors.[37]

Good governance. Investors favor countries, regardless of their level of economic development, with better governance; that is, countries with relatively little corruption and with well-functioning public institutions. There is evidence that good governance is positively correlated with high rates of business entry: countries with good governance have higher business registrations and entries than those with poor governance.[38] The United Nations Development Programme (UNDP) has implemented several programs, including the UNDP Qualified Somali Technical Support Program (QUEST) and the Transfer of Knowledge Through Expatriate Nationals (TOKTEN) program, that seek to improve governance and the functioning of public institutions (among other goals) by sponsoring temporary returns of qualified diaspora members. In general, there are positive correlations among good governance, entrepreneurship, and economic growth. Diaspora entrepreneurs are likely to respond to the same conditions as other potential investors.

Access to financial capital. Access to financial capital is particularly important for individuals seeking to pursue entrepreneurial activities, whether large or small, skill-based or unskilled. The micro-credit and micro-savings revolution has opened a path to entrepreneurs who operate on a very small scale, at least initially. The clients for these tiny loans are necessity entrepreneurs who typically contribute little to the growth of their countries, but some may be able to expand their businesses as loans enable them to take advantage of new opportunities.

37 Kathleen Newland with Erin Patrick, "Beyond Remittances: The Role of Diasporas in Poverty Reduction in their countries of Origin," Scoping Study for the Department for International Development, United Kingdom, July 2004, www.migrationpolicy.org/pubs/Beyond_ Remittances_0704.pdf.
38 See the Doing Business Project, www.doingbusiness.org, for government indices. Strong positive correlation between business entry rates and good governance (voice and accountability; political stability; government effectiveness, regulatory quality, rule of law and control of corruption) even after controlling for GDP per capita.

Even if on a small scale, they do contribute to poverty reduction. A number of micro-finance schemes are funded by diaspora organizations.[39]

At the other end of the spectrum, diaspora investors may underwrite the creation of new industries and the growth of established sectors. As noted above, the role of the Indian diaspora in providing venture capital to Indian entrepreneurs in the United States and start-ups in India has been important in expanding IT and business-process outsourcing industries. It has also created positive spillover effects such as helping the Indian venture capital industry grow.

Favorable sociocultural perceptions of entrepreneurship. Cultural perceptions of entrepreneurs and entrepreneurship can affect the decision to become an entrepreneur.[40] Some societies, such as that of the United States, attach high value to individual initiative and reward successful entrepreneurs with social status as well as wealth. These cultural predilections are conducive to entrepreneurship. Other cultures favor group action and attach guilt or shame to individuals whose ventures fail, a viewpoint that is common among many countries in East Asia. As a result, aspiring entrepreneurs may be discouraged from pursuing risky business ventures; indeed, research shows that despite the high value placed on innovation in East Asia, relatively few people actually pursue entrepreneurial activities.[41] The very success of the Japanese and Korean models of industrial growth, resting on close cooperation between the central government and large industrial conglomerates, has been blamed for choking off entrepreneurship. Diaspora members, on the other hand, often lead lives that transcend a single culture, and as such may develop different perceptions of entrepreneurship than those dominant in the country of their origin or ancestry. Bridging differences and introducing new business ideas and attitudes are some of the valuable contributions diaspora members are well positioned to make. Several countries, from India to Nigeria, have started to hold high-profile events that celebrate the accomplishments and contributions of diaspora entrepreneurs. China has made attracting diaspora entrepreneurs a pillar of its "One Thousand Talents" Initiative, an element of its high-profile National Medium- and Long-Term

---

39 Development Marketplace for African Diaspora in Europe, "The Development Marketplace for African Diaspora in Europe: Promoting Diaspora Investment Projects and Innovative Entrepreneurial Activities in Africa," 2009, www.dmade.org/admindb/docs/D-MADE_Competition-Guidelinesweb.pdf.
40 Thomas M. Begley and Wee-Liang Tan, "The Socio-Cultural Environment for Entrepreneurship: Comparison between East Asian and Anglo-Saxon Countries," *Journal of International Business Studies* 32, no. 3 (2001): 537–53.
41 Ibid.

Talent Development Plan. According to Dr. Wang Huiyao, the plan "aims to import top brains and groom local talent to produce a new generation of political leaders, scientists, engineers, technology professionals, entrepreneurs, educators, agricultural experts and social workers," bringing China's talent pool up from 114 million skilled people in 2010 to 180 million by 2020.[42]

A critical mass of human and social capital. Individuals with high levels of human capital tend to be more entrepreneurial than those without. However, knowledge and education alone do not spur entrepreneurship. Individuals working in economic clusters or areas saturated with like-minded and experienced professionals in specific sectors have access to valuable social capital, including networks and knowledge transfers, which facilitates joint ventures and partnerships among current and former colleagues.[43] Encouraging "hot spots" of technological and educational institutions is one way that governments can create conditions conducive to entrepreneurship, and several — such as those of China, Taiwan, South Korea, Mauritius, Chile, and India — have taken this step and encouraged diaspora members to take part in them.[44] Research suggests that highly skilled individuals make their decisions on where to migrate based on a variety of factors, including:

- The presence of other talented professionals — and the subsequent opportunities to create synergistic work environments and virtuous circles of innovation and success

- Capital infrastructure (such as advanced science and engineering colleges and state-of-the-art research labs) that promote professional growth and offer a dynamic and transformative environment

- The promise of good returns on one's own human-capital investments.[45]

---

42 Tracy Quek, "China's Not-so-little talent blueprint," *Straits Times,* Sept. 26, 2010, http://wanderingchina.wordpress.com/2010/09/26/chinas-not-so-little-talent-blueprint-straits-times/. Dr. Wang is one of the authors of the plan, and is director of the Centre for China and Globalization in Beijing, as well as vice chairman of the Western Returned Scholars Association in China.

43 Henning Madsen, Helle Neergaard, and John P. Ulhøi, "Factors Influencing the Establishment of Knowledge Intensive Ventures," *International Journal of Entrepreneurial Behavior & Research* 14, no. 2 (2008): 70–84.

44 AnnaLee Saxenian, "International Mobility of Engineers and the Rise of Entrepreneurship in the Periphery," Research Paper No. 142, United Nations Univ., Tokyo, Japan, 2006, www.wider.unu.edu/publications/working-papers/research-papers/2006/en_GB/rp2006-142/_files/78091822234994961/default/rp2006-142.pdf; Wadhwa et al., "America's Loss Is the World's Gain."

45 Demetrios G. Papademetriou, Will Somerville, and Hiroyuki Tanaka, "Talent in the 21st Century," in *Talent, Competitiveness and Migration,* eds. Bertelsmann Stiftung and Migration Policy

Lifestyle plays a part in migration decisions as well, especially for diaspora entrepreneurs who return to their countries of origin, many with their families, after having become accustomed to the amenities of life in the West. Thus, the government of Taiwan constructed Western-style housing and upgraded neighborhood schools in the vicinity of the Hinschu Industrial Park in order to attract returning migrants and diaspora members.[46] Amenities such as good transportation infrastructure and recreational facilities may make a difference, as does the enforcement of environmental protection regulations.

III. Five Levels of Commitment to Diaspora Entrepreneurship

Over the past decade, a number of governments and other organizations have established programs to encourage emigrants and their descendants to invest in their home countries. Initiatives range from those that are privately run and funded to those that are government-led or lodged in multilateral organizations, but most involve some sort of public-private partnership. These organizations play multiple roles and offer a variety of services to encourage and support entrepreneurship among members of diaspora groups. While some initiatives are nationality based, others are open to all individuals with an interest in contributing to the development of a particular country.

Below, we briefly profile 16 organizations and initiatives that promote diaspora entrepreneurship to further economic development in countries of origin. While each has unique programs, ways of working, and sources of funding, each also offers one or more of the following kinds of support to entrepreneurs in the country of origin:

- Networking
- Mentoring
- Training[47]
- Investment
- Venture capital and partnerships

Institute (Guetersloh: Bertelsmann Stiftung, 2009).
46 Newland with Patrick, "Beyond Remittances."
47 Training may be offered in such areas as market research, financial literacy, and access to financial capital.

Organizations that focus on networking tend to be more passive in their support for diaspora entrepreneurship, while involvement becomes progressively more intense through mentoring, investment, venture capital, and strategic partnerships. Many of the organizations profiled below are hybrids and promote activities in several of the above categories. For example, some organizations run competitions for aspiring diaspora entrepreneurs, combining mentoring, training, investment (through cash prizes for the winners), and partnership functions. All of these variables play an important role in supporting diaspora entrepreneurship. This study categorizes the organizations according to their main function; where an organization combines two or more in roughly equal proportions, we include the organization in the most active category.

A. Networking Organizations

Networking organizations are those that promote diaspora entrepreneurship by offering opportunities for diaspora and local business leaders and professionals to meet one another and discuss potential business and investment opportunities in the homeland. Some networking organizations, such as the Mexican Talent Network and The African Network (TAN) offer forums for networking in person. Others, such as the Business in Development (BiD) Network, offer virtual networking opportunities between entrepreneurs and financiers via the Internet. Some networking organizations are involved in public-private partnerships to facilitate meetings between locals and members of the diaspora, while others promote networking among diaspora business leaders to foster business partnerships and opportunities in countries of diaspora origin.

I. Mexican Talent Network

The government of Mexico is trying to leverage the resources of its highly qualified diaspora members to develop a knowledge-driven economy. In 2005, the Secretariat of Foreign Relations founded the Mexican Talent Network, in partnership with the Institute of Mexicans Abroad and the National Council on Science and Technology (CONACYT) and with the financial support of the United States-Mexico Foundation for Science.[48] The Mexican Talent Network aims to promote ties between Mexico and its highly qualified professionals living abroad, to support high-value-added projects in the

---

48 The name in Spanish is *la Red de Talentos Mexicanos*.

areas of business development and education for global innovation, and to promote Mexico's image as a favorable business destination for global investors. Among its many projects, the Mexican Talent Network is working to establish internship programs for undergraduate students, professors, and researchers in companies suggested by network members; to create a program that enables network members to provide expertise in the use of plastics in automotive and aerospace industries; and to develop a strategy for raising the visibility of Mexican companies that could provide outsourcing services.

2. The African Network

The African Network (TAN) is a US-based nonprofit organization, founded in Silicon Valley in 2004 and modeled on TiE. Its mission is to alleviate poverty through entrepreneurship and job creation — by empowering people of African descent to sustain themselves through entrepreneurship. The organization has two main programs in addition to its monthly networking dinners: TAN Conference (TANCon) and TAN Empowerment (TEP). TANCon is a biannual forum held in Africa and the United States where current and aspiring entrepreneurs, venture capitalists, investors, business leaders, community leaders, and policymakers can network to discuss business opportunities. TEP has a special focus on mobilizing diaspora resources to support and develop low-income, needy, and underserved communities in Africa.[49]

3. The Business in Development (BiD) Network

The BiD Network offers migrant and nonmigrant entrepreneurs assistance in developing business plans and raising funds for entrepreneurial ventures in 12 developing countries (Argentina, Bolivia, Colombia, Ecuador, Mexico, Peru, Jordan, Kenya, Uganda, Rwanda, Tanzania, and the Philippines). The BiD Network allows entrepreneurs seeking start-up money to post their business plan on the network's Web site, where thousands of investors and experts will have the opportunity to view their plans and contact those with promising projects.[50] Approximately 70 percent of the business plans submitted to the BiD Network are for start-up companies, and 27 percent were submitted by female entrepreneurs.[51]

---

49 The African Network, "What is The Africa Network?" www.theafricannetwork.org.
50 For examples of businesses that have successfully been matched with investors via the BiD Network, see BiD Network, "SMEs Matched via BiD Network," www.bidnetwork.org/page/121645.
51 BiD Network, "BiD Network Results," www.bidnetwork.org/page/92869/en.

But it is a fairly passive mechanism, and the matches that come to fruition are a small proportion of the applications. As of August 2009, the BiD Network had 27,144 members and had received 9,520 applications, 1,651 business plans, and 149 BiD-grade plans; it had brought about 51 matches between entrepreneurs and financiers.

4. South African Diaspora Network

The South African Diaspora Network, created as a pilot project by the University of Cape Town's Centre for Innovation & Entrepreneurship (with the support of the World Bank Development Marketplace) in 2001, attempted to help South Africans in South Africa and those living overseas connect with one another for business-related purposes. The network targeted South African businesspeople living in South Africa who sought assistance, guidance, and support in expanding their businesses to overseas markets. Those offering advice and guidance from overseas included approximately 40 well-established business leaders living in the greater London area who were connected with the South African Business Club in London and the University of Cape Town Graduate School of Business Alumni Association. The network suspended operation in 2003 due to lack of funding and support staff.

5. The Korean IT Network (KIN)[52]

Korean engineers and businessmen in Silicon Valley noted that diaspora networks formed by Indian and Chinese contemporaries helped their members get ahead, and formed KIN in 2001. The organization has had strong backing from the Korean government: 100 percent financing for the first three years and 50 percent for the next three. It organizes annual conferences, with sponsorship from large Korean companies, Korean-owned companies in Silicon Valley, and the government. Despite this support, KIN has not established the kind of internal dynamism that led other diaspora networks to become indispensable to entrepreneurs in the home country and abroad. It has been criticized for focusing on "show-up" events that satisfy government sponsors but do little to advance the interests of members. Unlike its newer rival organization, the K Group, it has been unable to help its members find jobs and start companies in a systematic way.

---

52 The material for this profile was drawn from Jeong Hyop Lee and AnnaLee Saxenian, "Do We Need a Double-Edged Sword?; Triggering Networking of Silicon Valley Korean Diaspora and Their Contribution to Home Country Institution Transformation," Paper presented at the International Conference on Diaspora for Development, World Bank, Washington, DC, July 13–14, 2009.

B. Mentoring Organizations

Mentoring organizations are more actively involved in supporting entrepreneurship among diaspora members than pure networking organizations, in that they try to match aspiring entrepreneurs or business owners seeking to expand their operations abroad with seasoned diaspora experts and business leaders. Some mentors offer one-off services such as assistance in conducting market research or a feasibility study, while others provide internships or even job opportunities in their corporations. While mentorship definitely helps diaspora entrepreneurs gain business knowledge, it often falls short of providing hands-on training or funds to actually launch a business in the country of origin.

1. GlobalScot

GlobalScot is Scotland's diaspora-based framework for promoting economic development. In 2001, Scottish Enterprise (Scotland's main economic, enterprise, innovation, and investment agency, largely funded by the Scottish government) launched GlobalScot as an international network of Scottish business leaders and those interested in supporting the development of the Scottish economy.[53] GlobalScot's mission is to market Scotland as an attractive place for investors through its members. Since its creation, GlobalScot has helped generate more than GBP £30 million in gross value added to Scotland.[54] GlobalScot encourages its 850 members (or "GlobalScots"), all of whom hold senior positions within their respective organizations, to serve on one another's boards and to encourage and educate students about the various business opportunities in Scottish and global firms.[55] GlobalScots have helped entrepreneurs identify business opportunities abroad, and offered advice on how to enter markets, negotiate business deals, make strategic business plans, and expand business networks. In their role as mentors to Scottish students, GlobalScots have served as mentors and invited speakers in schools and universities, offered guidance on developing skills that are in demand, and provided internship placements and employment opportunities.

---

53 GlobalScot, *GlobalScot: Building International Business Networks for Scotland* (Glasgow, Scotland: Scottish Enterprise, 2009), www.globalscot.com/web/FILES/GlobalScot_Brochure_2009.pdf; Scottish Enterprise, "What We Do," www.scottish-enterprise.com/about-us/se-whatwedo.aspx; Mairi MacRae with Martin Wight, "A Model Diaspora Network: The Origin and Evolution of Globalscot," in *Diaspora Networks and the International Migration of Skills: How Countries Can Draw on Their Talent Abroad*, ed. Yevgeny Kutznetsov (Washington, DC: World Bank, 2006).
54 Scottish Enterprise, "GlobalScot," Press Release, October 15, 2009.
55 Ibid.

2. Armenia 2020

Armenia 2020 is an organization that engages the Armenian diaspora to identify a variety of development scenarios for the Republic of Armenia until 2020. Through its discussions and forums, it seeks to feed advice into the policymaking process for Armenia's development process. A number of the organization's board members sit on the National Competitiveness Council of Armenia (NCCA), which assists the prime minister in setting policies to attract vital investments to Armenia. In partnership with the Harvard Alumni Club of Armenia among others, Armenia 2020 organized the first Armenian National Business Contest that sought applications from Armenian entrepreneurs to present their business plans to international business leaders. The winners of the contest were given the opportunity to present their business plans at the annual International Business Plan Competition held by the Entrepreneurs Club of Harvard Business School.[56]

3. The Indus Entrepreneurs (TiE)

TiE is a nonprofit organization formed in 1992 by a group of Silicon Valley entrepreneurs with roots in the Indian subcontinent. TiE does not present itself as a diaspora organization and its membership is open to anyone, although its board, staff, and chapter presidents are all of South Asian origin. Of its 54 chapters in 13 countries, 25 are in the United States and 22 in India. TiE's membership has been growing, on average, at the rate of 20 percent per year (although general membership dipped slightly during the recession), making it perhaps the largest entrepreneurial organization in the world. TiE does acknowledge a particular interest in promoting entrepreneurship in the Indus region (comprising India and Pakistan), although its broader goal is to "democratize entrepreneurship" globally. The organization's singular focus on entrepreneurship incorporates special programs focused on women entrepreneurs, young entrepreneurs, start-up ventures, specific industry groups, and more. In partnership with Microsoft Corporation, TiE is implementing a program that provides young start-up companies with free access to Microsoft software and technical support along with TiE's networking, mentoring, and educational services. TiE's roots are in the information and communications technology industry, but it is branching out into clean energy, agricultural technology, and life sciences using a characteristic model: a group of its senior members from each industry are being asked to mentor at least five entrepreneurial ventures in that industry.

---

56 Armenia 2020, "News," Press Releases, October 23 and July 31, 2007.

C. Training Organizations

Training organizations help aspiring diaspora entrepreneurs acquire the knowledge and skills to set up and run a successful business. These training programs (sometimes combined with provision of start-up business services such as help in developing a business plan, incorporating, and registering a business) range from transferring knowledge from diaspora experts to country-of-origin entrepreneurs to offering lessons on business management to providing guidance on how to find financing to start a business. Some organizations, such as pS-Eau, *Programme Solidarité Eau*, offer training tailored to the entrepreneur's country of origin. These groups operate on the principle that training and educating future entrepreneurs promotes the success and sustainability of their ventures.

I. Ethiopia Commodity Exchange[57]

The Ethiopia Commodity Exchange (ECX) is a cooperative initiative between the Ethiopian government and the Ethiopian diaspora, which has received $1 million in support from USAID. It allows farmers to access real-time information about national and international agricultural products and sell their products on a commodity exchange. Eleni Gabre-Mahdin, an American-educated Ethiopian economist, created the exchange to address Ethiopia's malnutrition and other food-related problems, including the inefficient and obscure nature of Ethiopian agricultural trade, which has traditionally been based on trust between known buyers and sellers. The exchange gives buyers and sellers an improved framework for transactions, offering warehousing, a reliable payment system, real-time market information, and quality control. In addition, Gabre-Mahdin, now chief executive of the exchange, is working with Yohannes Assefa, an Ethiopian American trade lawyer, to transmit the business and technology know-how of Ethiopians living abroad to local employees of the exchange. Ethiopian Americans who possess the appropriate skills are offered three-year job contracts at the exchange to transfer their skills to at least one local resident. Since its inception in April 2008, the ECX has granted 461 coffee suppliers membership on the exchange.[58]

---

57 Phillip Kurata, "Ethiopia Launches Commodity Exchange to Develop Agriculture," America.gov, October 31, 2008, www.america.gov/st/econ-english/2008/October/20081031174240cpata ruk0.134823.html; Phillip Kurata, "African Migrants Invest in Their Home Countries," America. gov, November 9, 2009, www.america.gov/st/develop-english/2009/November/2009110617 3018cpataruk0.2806055.html.

58 ECX (Ethiopia Commodity Exchange), "About Us," www.ecx.com.et/CompanyProfile.aspx#AU.

2. IntEnt

IntEnt, based in the Netherlands, was created in the 1996 by Social-Economical Entrepreneurship in the Netherlands (SEON),[59] FACET BV,[60] and Triodos Bank[61] at the request of the former Dutch minister of international development, J. P. Pronk. Its purpose is to stimulate entrepreneurship among immigrants. The organization offers fee-based support to entrepreneurs seeking assistance in developing their business plans to promote development in Morocco, Turkey, Surinam, Ghana, Ethiopia, Afghanistan, and the Antilles.[62] Its services include providing information about entrepreneurship; orientation sessions and training courses; counseling; advisory services; market information; referral and mediation; assistance during and after starting a business in the program countries; networking; management training; online services; and supplementary financing. These services help entrepreneurs to overcome credit limitations and high interest rates at local banks; time-consuming and complicated bureaucracy; unfamiliarity with local procedures and markets; lack of updated statistics on markets; unstable political, economic, and security environments; and cultural differences. Between 1998 and the end of 2007, IntEnt helped launch 236 businesses, finished 194 business plans, trained 1,176 participants, and admitted 1,693 clients. Together, these businesses created sustainable investment worth more than 14.5 million euros and almost 990 jobs. The average IntEnt entrepreneur invested 62,000 euros.

3. Economic Initiatives and Migration Program

The Economic Initiatives and Migration Program (PMIE)[63] was created by the nonprofit organization *Programme Solidarité Eau* (pS-EAU) in 2001 to help African immigrants in France implement economic projects in France and their countries of origin. The program receives financial support from the French ministries of Foreign Affairs and Labor, Employment and Social Cohesion, as well as from the European Commission and the Catholic Committee against Hunger and for Development.[64] In 1996, pS-Eau began coordinating the Micro Enterprise

---

59 SEON offers advice to small and middle-size companies, group training, and personal advice for entrepreneurs who wish to start their own company in the Netherlands.
60 FACET BV is an organization that gives advice on developing micro and small businesses in developing and transitional economies in Central and Eastern Europe.
61 Triodos Bank is an independent Dutch bank that has branches in 30 developing countries and helps IntEnt manage the IntEnt Guarantee Fund.
62 IntEnt is currently exploring the possibility of extending its programs to some of the countries in the Great Lakes region in East Africa.
63 The acronym is derived from its French name, *Programme Migrations et Initiatives Economiques* (PMIE).
64 *Programme Migration et Initiatives Economiques*, "The Economic Initiatives and Migration Programme," www.pseau.org/outils/ouvrages/pmie_presentation_ve.pdf.

Support Group (GAME),[65] a network of development organizations, migrant associations, and public authorities that supports business projects initiated by immigrants residing in France. GAME offers immigrants guidance on how to implement a business project in their countries of origin, how to invest in or otherwise support a project initiated by a business partner living in Africa, and how to begin a project in France. Today, the network consists of 27 support organizations in four French regions and ten countries in Africa and the Indian Ocean that annually offer support to approximately 1,000 African entrepreneurs. To date, immigrants have initiated projects in a wide range of sectors[66] in 16 African countries.

D. Investment Organizations

Investment organizations provide initial start-up funds or subsequent capital infusions, usually in the form of pooled private and public funds or matching grants, to diaspora entrepreneurs with creative business ideas that will likely spur development in their countries of origin. Some investment organizations take a hands-off approach to the money they offer entrepreneurs, while others are more involved in overseeing how their money is spent at various stages of project implementation. While these organizations may not always provide business training, they do provide the critical resources that enable aspiring diaspora entrepreneurs to realize their business plans.

I. African Diaspora Marketplace

The African Diaspora Marketplace (ADM) was a competition held in 2009, sponsored by USAID and Western Union, in which US-based members of the African diaspora — either US citizens or legal permanent residents — presented business plans for SMEs that would contribute to economic development in Sub-Saharan Africa.[67]

---

65 The French name is *Groupe d'Appui à la Micro Entreprise* (GAME).
66 These sectors include market garden production, poultry farming and fishing, construction, arts and crafts, agrofood processing, commerce (retail, wholesale, import/export), IT (cyber cafés, maintenance and sale of hardware), tourism, driving schools, printing, and other services.
67 The ADM defines *diaspora member* according to the African Union's definition of *diaspora:* "people of African origin living outside the continent, irrespective of their citizenship and nationality and who are willing to contribute to the development of the continent and the building of the African Union." The competition adopts the International Finance Corporation's definition of small and medium enterprises, namely that a company must satisfy at least two of the following three criteria: (1) have between ten and 300 employees; (2) possess assets ranging from $100,000 to $15 million; and (3) have a total annual sales figure ranging from

Applicants were required to have a partner organization in Africa to help them execute their projects, and to own at least 25 percent of the proposed company. The goal of the ADM was to spur job creation, generate income, and produce goods and services, preferably in designated sectors,[68] by offering matching grants to African-diaspora member living in the United States. Judges were drawn from business; nongovernmental organizations; and diaspora, development, and academic groups. They evaluated applications based on the quality of the business idea, its proposed management plan, its sustainability, its results orientation, and its ability to capitalize on diaspora resources. In mid-January 2010, ADM announced the 14 winners, who were awarded matching grants of up to US$100,000 to help fund businesses in seven countries.[69] (Winners were required to match these grants through financial or in-kind contributions.) The initiatives included a business that would increase production of school, hospital, and agricultural supplies in Ethiopia and a franchise business that would offer health care to populations living in rural areas in Ghana. Upon receipt of the grant, winners were allowed 18 months to fully execute their business plans.

2. 1x1 Program, Mexico

In January 2009, the federal government of Mexico initiated an investment program called 1x1, which matches individual migrants' investment funds for business projects with government money. A migrant fills out a simple application for a matching loan of up to 300,000 Mexican pesos (approximately US$25,000). The applicant must attach a copy of his or her consular identification card (*matricula consular*) to confirm his or her identity as a migrant (the card cannot be obtained in Mexico). The loan is repayable within three years and carries no interest. The unique feature of the 1x1 program is that repayment is not made in cash to the government but rather in the form of a contribution to a social investment through the remittance-based Tres por Uno (3x1)

$100,000 to $15 million. Business projects must occur in one of the following 19 Sub-Saharan countries: Angola, Burundi, Ethiopia, Ghana, Kenya, Liberia, Malawi, Mali, Mozambique, Namibia, Nigeria, Rwanda, Senegal, Sierra Leone, South Africa, Sudan, Tanzania, Uganda, and Zambia — countries in which USAID has a local presence and can provide technical assistance to entrepreneurs.

68 Designated sectors included agribusiness, handicrafts, textiles, tourism, environmental services (such as waste management), construction and infrastructure, logistics and transportation, manufacturing and assembly, fisheries, livestock, and information and communication technologies (ICTs). But applications in other sectors were also accepted.

69 ADM (African Diaspora Marketplace), "U.S.-Based African Diaspora Entrepreneurs to Spur Job Growth in Their Native Countries with Innovative Business Plans," press release, January 13, 2010, www.diasporamarketplace.org/sites/default/files/African_Diaspora_Marketplace_Winners_Release_1–13-10_0.pdf.

program, in which contributions from Mexican hometown associations (HTAs) abroad are matched by federal, state, and local governments in Mexico. The migrant invests the amount of the loan in a social project approved by his or her HTA (such as rebuilding a school or equipping it with computers), and the amount of the repayment is matched by federal, state, and municipal governments.[70] Thus, the 1x1 program supports both individual business investment by small entrepreneurs and collective community investment.

E. Venture Capital and Partnership Organizations

Venture capital and partnership organizations provide more than just the funds to launch a business. They usually are heavily involved in business projects that they believe will be profitable, often taking part in management in the early stages of an investment. Often they form strategic alliances with other venture capitalists, business leaders, engineers, and other professionals. For these organizations, the number of strategic partnerships or projects supported by venture capital usually matters less than the quality of the proposed investment, the high potential for return on investment, and the impact that such partnerships and investments are likely to have on economic growth in strategic sectors. For others, such as the Migration for Development in Africa (MIDA) projects in Italy, strategic partnerships are also about fostering trust and long-term relationships among key public and private institutions in countries of origin and destination.

I. Fundación Chile

Fundación Chile is a small public-private foundation that seeks to leverage the Chilean diaspora to bring Chile into the knowledge-based economy. The foundation helps entrepreneurs launch technically innovative agribusinesses in Chile by including them in professional networks and offering financial support from its venture capital fund. It has helped create 76 companies with more than 50 domestic and international partners (the partners include private corporations, universities, and institutes of technology), and currently has a share in 23 of them.[71] One of Fundación Chile's flagship programs is ChileGlobal, an organization that designs and finances business projects through

---

70 Efrain Jimenez, projects coordinator, Zacatecan Federation of Clubs in Southern California, posted January 26, 2010 to the m4d listserve (m4d@groups.dev-nets.org) hosted by the EC-UN Joint Migration and Development Initiative.
71 Fundación Chile, "I'm an Investor: Invest in Your Dreams," http://ww2.fundacionchile.cl/portal/web/guest/inversionista.

its network of about 80 influential Chileans living in the United States, Canada, Europe, and Chile. Its mission is to promote and facilitate the development of key economic clusters in Chile by reinforcing their links with Chileans (and some non-Chileans) residing abroad who are working to introduce innovative technologies to Chile. ChileGlobal introduces innovations in both the production and services sectors, boosts human capital to augment productivity,[72] attracts innovative businesses to Chile, and promotes technology and knowledge transfers to and from Chile.[73]

2. Migration for Development in Africa (MIDA)

The International Organization for Migration's (IOM) MIDA program, launched in 2001, seeks to build capacity in African countries by working with the African diaspora to transfer technical skills and resources to their countries of origin. MIDA uses four major channels to connect diaspora professionals with their countries of origin: (1) virtual or communications-based IT systems; (2) sequenced or repeat visits; (3) investment; and (4) permanent return.[74] Working with the diaspora in Italy and with funding from the Italian government, MIDA Italy has made entrepreneurship a major focus of its program, with the aim of creating jobs and bringing positive social and economic change to countries of origin.[75] MIDA Italy selected five SME projects in Ghana (out of a total of 26 applications) and seven SME projects in Senegal (out of a total of 56 applications) to support in 2006 and 2007. All of the projects were designed to set up SMEs and promote partnerships among Italian, Ghanaian, and Senegalese communities in a way that would benefit Ghana and Senegal. The selected SMEs focused on agriculture (cultivation and processing), woodwork, reforestation, and tourism. Forty entrepreneurs received training from specialized institutions in Ghana and Senegal on business creation and management, as well as access to credit.[76]

---

72 ChileGlobal, "¿Quiénes Somos?" (Who Are We?), www.chileglobal.org/quienes-somos/.

73 Yevgeny Kuznetsov, "Por que ChileGlobal? Red de Talentos en el Exterior para Desarrollo Tecnologico de Chile," Presentation at the first meeting of ChileGlobal in San Francisco, June 10, 2005, http://info.worldbank.org/etools/docs/library/201209/ChileDiaspora.pdf.

74 IOM (International Organization for Migration), "Migration for Development in Africa (MIDA)," www.iom.int/jahia/Jahia/mida-africa/.

75 MIDA (Migration for Development in Africa), "The MIDA Italy Experience," presentation given at the Conference on International Migration and Development: Continuing the Dialogue Legal and Policy Perspectives, New York, January 2008, www.un.int/iom/MIDA%20Rome.pdf; Ndioro Ndiaye, "The MIDA Experience and Beyond," presentation given at the World Bank Conference on Diaspora and Development, Washington, DC, July 13, 2009, http://siteresources.worldbank.org/INTPROSPECTS/Resources/334934-1110315015165/Ndiaye.pdf.

76 MIDA can make a maximum contribution of up to 30 percent of the total proposed budget.

3. The African Foundation for Development (AFFORD)

The African Foundation for Development (AFFORD), which was founded in 1994 by Africans living in the United Kingdom, helps the African diaspora in the United Kingdom create wealth and jobs in Africa. Its main program, Supporting Entrepreneurs and Enterprise Development in Africa (SEEDA), uses the skills, knowledge, and wealth of the African diaspora to support SMEs in Africa. Its efforts thus far have focused on entrepreneurship in the Democratic Republic of the Congo, Ghana, Nigeria, Sierra Leone, and Uganda. With the support of the UK Voluntary Services Overseas (VSO) Diaspora Volunteering Initiative, SEEDA has organized five missions to Africa. As of July 2009, 70 diaspora members had contributed time and money worth GBP £200,000, offering 800 businesses in Sierra Leone and Ghana services ranging from business planning and marketing to help with bookkeeping and opening bank accounts. SEEDA has also contributed to the creation of two new business development centers in Sierra Leone that provide business advice and advocate for a better business environment in the country.

IV. Major Observations

Organizations that support diaspora entrepreneurship take on multiple roles, sometimes creating networking opportunities among business leaders and at other times forming strategic institutional partnerships to foster long-term economic growth in knowledge-intensive sectors.

The five types of involvement listed above — networking, mentoring, training, investment, and venture capital and partnerships — describe ascending levels of commitment to the entrepreneurial project (see Figure 1). While a combination of all five levels of engagement is likely to foster entrepreneurship, for a variety of reasons — including availability of resources and time, and the different actors involved at each level — the more passive forms of support (toward the base of the pyramid) are likely to proliferate and dissipate more quickly than the more active forms of support near the peak.

Figure 1. Levels of Commitment to Diaspora Entrepreneurship

Venture Capital and Partnerships

Investment

Training

Mentoring

Networking

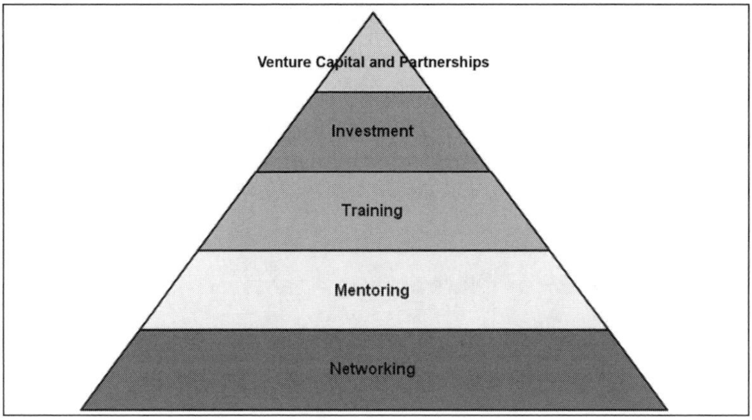

Source: Authors' rendering

Differences among Organizations

The 16 organizations profiled above provide a wide range of services to aspiring diaspora entrepreneurs. While all of them share the goal of promoting diaspora entrepreneurship to further economic development in countries of diaspora origin, they differ on many fronts, including, but not limited to, the following:

- *Different targets.* Some organizations focus on developing the national economy, while others focus on developing the entrepreneurial skills of individual diaspora members.

- *Different levels of selectivity for membership.* Some organizations restrict their membership to professionals or to members of a specific diaspora, while others are open to individuals of all nationalities and skill levels. GlobalScot and ChileGlobal, for example, have cultivated an aura of exclusivity, making membership a desirable status indicator, while other institutions welcome all aspiring entrepreneurs.

- *Focus on different economic sectors.* Some organizations focus on building knowledge-intensive and high-value economic sectors, such as biotechnology, that are driven by new technologies and innovation, while others maintain a more neutral approach toward the economic sectors in which diaspora members wish to start their businesses. Likewise, some organizations emphasize the growth of trade between countries of origin and destination through SMEs in areas such as textiles, handicrafts, or agriculture, while others support specific subsets of potential business creators, such as micro entrepreneurs or women entrepreneurs.

- *Different types of services offered.* Some organizations offer financial or business services, while others provide networking or mentoring opportunities for diaspora members. Some offer their services free of charge, while others impose fees.

- *Different geographic focus.* Some organizations foster diaspora entrepreneurship primarily for the benefit of one country or even a single town, municipality, or province, while others offer services to entrepreneurs from an entire region or continent.

Box 1. Another View of Diasporas as Agents of Entrepreneurship

Yevgeny Kuznetsov of the World Bank Institute outlines six models of how professional diaspora networks serve as catalysts for entrepreneurship:

1. **Top executives model:** Members of the diaspora who are top executives of firms abroad use their managerial experience and technical know-how to persuade their respective companies to invest in or outsource knowledge-intensive operations to their countries of origin

2. **Mentoring/venture capital model:** Diaspora members who are managers or owners of firms whose parent companies are in their countries of destination work with start-ups in their countries of origin to help them develop and finance commercially viable projects.

3. **Diaspora members as investors model:** Diaspora members use their knowledge of their home countries to mitigate risks in making investments back home. Personal and professional networks between diaspora members and business partners in their countries of origin help reduce transaction costs to start up new businesses.

4. **Setting new strategic direction/identifying new opportunities model:** Diaspora members are able to identify niche markets back home based on their professional experiences abroad in business consulting and other sectors and capitalize on business opportunities by turning them into actual business projects.

5. **Return of talent model:** Governments implement policies that encourage members of the diaspora to return to their countries of origin to contribute to economic development.

6. **Basic outsourcing model:** Successful diaspora members who own companies abroad create opportunities to outsource activities such as R&D or programming in their countries of origin.

Kuznetsov's concept of a network goes far beyond the relatively passive concept described in this paper's model of levels of engagement. In fact, it incorporates most kinds of systematic interactions of diaspora members, from networking to investment and partnerships.

V. Policy Options and Conclusions

The *New Oxford English Dictionary* defines an entrepreneur as "a person who organizes and operates a business, taking on greater than normal risks in order to do so." The word derives from a French verb *entreprendre*, meaning "to undertake." An entrepreneur undertakes new ventures, and if successful he or she creates wealth and jobs. It is little wonder that development practitioners are interested in trying to harness this tremendous force for economic growth and dynamism. Diaspora entrepreneurs are uniquely well equipped to recognize opportunities in their countries of origin. They have an advantage over other entrepreneurs in exploiting such opportunities as "first movers." In many cases, they are especially motivated to contribute to job creation and economic growth in their native lands. They have a foot in each of two worlds.

Diaspora entrepreneurs have caught the attention of policymakers who recognize that most poor countries suffer from a deficit of entre-preneurship, and that this is both a cause and a consequence of their poverty. The dilemma for governments is that their role in promoting entrepreneurship is circumscribed. Their most important tasks — establishing the rule of law, ensuring access to quality education and other public services, creating and maintaining infrastructure, regulat-ing excesses, providing a safety net when the market fails, and so forth — promote entrepreneurship indirectly, and they can take additional steps to ease the way for the entrepreneurially inclined. The following policy options are directed at this work of facilitation.

Don't neglect small and medium-size enterprises. Programs that aim to support the efforts of diaspora entrepreneurs to create wealth and jobs in their homelands often focus on the ends of the business spectrum: micro enterprises and high-value-added, knowledge-intensive industries. But small and medium-size companies should not be neglected, as they are often the most prolific job creators and are closely attached to local demand. In addition, they are least able to overcome bureaucratic impediments to business creation, corruption, and gaps in market information.

Foster the transformation of "necessity entrepreneurs" into "oppor-tunity entrepreneurs." As we have seen, necessity entrepreneurs nor-mally contribute little to economic growth, although they do contribute to poverty reduction. In many cases, however, the constraints on necessity entrepreneurs are not intrinsic to them or their businesses; rather, they result from an economic environment unfriendly to small businesses and a dearth of external resources to help owners of such businesses improve their skills, raise adequate capital, and connect them with the larger market. Programs that aim to promote diaspora entrepreneurship should be alert to small-scale businesses with potential to grow. For example, one immigrant who returned to Mexico from the United States[77] built a small fruit-processing factory and found that his products were in demand. He managed to get his products accepted by the local Walmart — a breakthrough for a small entrepreneur. However, Walmart's just-in-time stocking procedure meant that he was responsible for replacing his products as they sold, almost jar by jar. Since the Walmart was two hours' drive from his factory, the transportation costs were uneconomical and he could not maintain the retail link. This is the kind of problem that a cooperative effort among small producers might have been able to resolve, with support and advice from other companies, government programs, or public-private partnerships. The diaspora entrepreneur in question here was fortunately able to seize another opportunity: bottling water from a spring on his property for the local hotel trade, whose clients preferred to drink a natural, local product. In trying to build his customer base for one set of products, he discovered a market for another.

Create and/or support diaspora business forums. This was among the recommendations of a 2008 seminar, "Engaging African Diaspora in Europe as Strategic Agents for Development in Africa," convened by the African Diaspora Policy Centre in the Netherlands.[78] Some activities of this nature have already been implemented at the national level. For example, the Ministry of Foreign Affairs of the Democratic Republic of Congo convened the first "Congolese Diaspora Investment Forum" in August 2009, in collaboration with the Centre for Migrants and Congolese Abroad and other partners. Its purpose was threefold: to assess the support of the diaspora for development efforts in the Democratic Republic of Congo (DRC), to analyze the difficulties that diaspora members have when they do try to invest in the DRC, and to develop proposals to overcome the difficulties and promote investment. The forum gave members of the diaspora an opportunity to share their experiences of obstacles to entrepreneurship and their ideas for solutions to them.[79] Such opportunities for communication among stakeholders — in this case, other diaspora members and government

---

77 Salvatore Chaves, interview with Kathleen Newland facilitated by Rolando Garcia Zamora, Zacatecas, March 2009.

78 African Diaspora Policy Centre, "Engaging African Diaspora in Europe as Strategic Agents for Development in Africa," Seminar Report, Brussels, June 25–26, 2008, www.diaspora-centre. org/Migration_Development/Expert_Meetings/Enhancing_Dialogue_between_A/Engaging_African_Diaspora_in.

79 Posting by the Centre for Migrants and Congolese Abroad on m4d listserve, July 14, 2009.

officials — may open the door to greater cooperation. Donors may consider supporting diaspora meetings, helping to ensure that they are designed to reach the right set of participants and have practical follow-up mechanisms.

Consider innovative programs, such as matching grants, to help capitalize new ventures or expand existing ones. Access to capital is one of the persistent problems for entrepreneurs, especially those who operate on a small scale. Many financial institutions are not accustomed to dealing with small loans that lack conventional collateral. A recent survey on return migration and small enterprise development in Algeria, Morocco, and Tunisia found that access to finance ranked first among the problems faced by returning migrant investors.[80] A number of programs, such as Mexico's 1x1 program and the ADM, profiled above, offer matching grants to small-scale entrepreneurs. In addition, the government of Norway in 2008 initiated a matching grant program for Pakistani residents of Norway who wished to invest in Pakistan, and Western Union has provided small grants to diaspora investors in Mexico.

Preserve the role of competition in allocating capital. One concern about a grant-based model of support for small-scale entrepreneurship is that no market mechanism is necessarily built in to direct capital to its most productive use. Some grant programs, such as USAID's ADM, use a contest in lieu of the market mechanism, an effective way (assuming expert judges) to reinject competition into the allocation of resources. Competitions also help to overcome another obstacle for SMEs: the difficulty of making their ventures known to partners who might be able to help them grow.

Establish risk-sharing mechanisms. Programs to support entrepreneurs should consider establishing risk-sharing mechanisms, mimicking the operations of commercial venture-capital firms. If an investment proves profitable, the program's share of the rewards could be invested in a fund that would make additional investments possible. Unlike loan programs (which may also be valuable), the investment fund model does not create a liability for the entrepreneur, which may allow more latitude for risk-taking. Loan insurance programs and credit guarantees are additional means of reducing the risk of investing in a new business.

---

80 Flore Gubert and Christophe J. Nordman, 2009, "Return Migration and Small Enterprise Development in the Maghreb," Presentation at the World Bank Conference on Diaspora for Development, Washington, DC, July 14, 2009, http://siteresources.worldbank.org/ INTPROSPECTS/Resources/334934-1110315015165/Gubert_Nordman.pdf.

Insist on rigorous evaluation of programs to encourage diaspora entrepreneurship. Programs funded by nonprofit organizations or governments need to make the same effort to rigorously evaluate their own progress that private investors make when their own money is at stake. Real-time evaluations of ongoing programs are essential to making course corrections, and retrospective evaluations are key to designing effective future programs for the future, and avoiding the repetition of mistakes made in the past. The scarcity of capital makes it important to spend money productively and to avoid creating "moral hazard" on the part of entrepreneurs who do not have a business plan robust enough to survive without subsidy. (It also points to the importance of making information, mentoring, and training available to small-scale entrepreneurs so they can use their limited financial capital effectively to become self-sufficient or, better yet, profitable.)

Incorporate diaspora entrepreneurs in the planning of high-tech nodes of industrial development. Many of the hot spots of global innovation are areas where universities, research laboratories, and high-tech industries are gathered together to create a critical mass of talent, skills, and investors. Government-backed R&D and world-class research facilities and universities will attract diaspora entrepreneurs to invest in their home countries.[81] But diaspora entrepreneurs can also contribute to planning and populating these technology parks or special industrial zones, advising governments on the skill sets needed to attract venture capital and setting up businesses tied to global markets and networks. They may also play a direct role by locating businesses in the zones of innovation, mentoring local entrepreneurs, and training knowledge workers.[82] Millennium Science Initiatives (MSI) in Chile and Latvia offer models for engaging diaspora members in efforts to channel incremental government R&D resources into centers of excellence.[83] Perhaps even more important, diaspora entrepreneurs

---

81 Baumol, Litan, and Schramm, *Good Capitalism, Bad Capitalism.*
82 Mendoza Emprende 2008 in Argentina is a good example of how diaspora members offer to develop entrepreneurial skills among youth. See Agustina S. Paglayan and Mariano Lafuente, "Reversing the Brain Drain: The Role of the Argentine Diaspora in Building the Entrepreneurial Skills of Argentine Youth," presentation at the World Bank Conference on Diaspora and Development, Washington, DC, July 14, 2009, http://siteresources.worldbank.org/INTPROSPECTS/Resources/334934-1110315015165/Paglayan_Lafuente.pdf; Agustina S. Paglayan and Mariano Lafuente, *Mendoza Emprende: Enhancing Youth Entrepreneurship in Argentina by Leveraging Its Diaspora* (Washington, DC: World Bank, 2008), http://siteresources.worldbank.org/INTARGENTINA/Resources/MendozaEmprendeDisseminationReport.pdf.
83 The World Bank provided a $5 million loan and the Chilean government provided an addition $10 million to support Chile's MSI project. The MSI will fund three institutes (at $1 million per year for five years) and ten centers of excellence (at $300,000 per year for three years). See Alfred Watkins and Natalia Agapitova, "Creating a 21st-Century National Innovation System for a 21st-Century Latvian Economy," Policy Research Working Paper 3457, World Bank,

can help foster a culture of entrepreneurship in countries where it is not a traditional approach to business. Traditions of rote learning, exam-driven, or seniority-based systems of advancement, extreme deference to superiors, nepotism as a normal practice, avoidance of risk-taking, and other such cultural traits stifle entrepreneurism. The presence, example, and visible success of diaspora entrepreneurs may encourage local business people and professionals to shed these practices. High-tech industrial parks in emerging economies often strive to attract high-achieving diaspora members with the intention of creating a "culture within a culture" that is more conducive to entrepreneurship.[84]

Regular consultations with diaspora professionals can help governments to identify strategic economic areas and attract diaspora resources to them. India, for instance, has identified heath-care-related export services and medical tourism as important business opportunities, attracting customers looking for alternatives to the high prices charged in such countries as the United Kingdom, Canada, and the United States. India seeks to leverage its medical workforce to meet the global demand for health-care-related services and sees the diaspora as an important ally in this effort.

Use special incentives for diaspora entrepreneurship with caution. Governments commonly offer financial, social, and political incentives for diaspora members to create or invest in businesses in the country of origin. These include tax breaks or tax credits for businesses in strategic economic areas; ready access to policymakers; and reduction of bureaucratic and administrative red tape associated with establishing and operating a business. Removing obstacles to diaspora investment is highly desirable, but some special privileges invite misuse. Ethiopia used to permit diaspora members to bring in a car for personal use tax-free, which led to a thriving import and resale business, open exclusively to expatriates, that evaded high customs and excise taxes on automobiles. China's favorable tax treatment of diaspora direct investment for a time led to the "round-tripping" of capital as Chinese investors sent their money to Hong Kong or Macau so that it could be brought back to China under the favorable provisions supposedly reserved for expatriates.

Roll out the welcome mat for diaspora entrepreneurs. A simple and

---

Washington, DC, 2004, www-wds.worldbank.org/servlet/WDSContentServer/WDSP/IB/2004/12/07/000012009_20041207121312/Rendered/PDF/WPS3457.pdf.
84 The authors are indebted to Dr. Hiuyao Wang, director-general of the Centre for China and Globalization, for stimulating this line of thought.

perhaps obvious (but not necessarily easy) step that governments can take is to establish beyond a doubt that diaspora entrepreneurs are welcome in their countries of origin. Entrenched business interests may not welcome outsiders, even of a common origin, especially if they threaten to shake up established practices — such as the cozy relationships between government ministries and industrial conglomerates in East Asia or the oligarchies that dominate many other developing economies. A number of governments are not only reaching out to diaspora entrepreneurs but publicly celebrating their accomplishments and welcoming them as important economic actors.

Facilitate circular migration for diaspora entrepreneurs. An important step in promoting diaspora entrepreneurship is to make it easy for diaspora business owners or investors to travel between their country of origin and their country of settlement. Multiple reentry permits, long-term visas, and dual citizenship are all tools that enable transnational entrepreneurs to actively supervise their investments. Other market opening measures, such as reducing tariffs on imported raw materials and equipment into the country of origin, may also be essential to a transnational business.

Conclusion

Encouraging members of the diaspora to pursue entrepreneurial ventures seems a matter of common sense as an element of development policy. But it is, in some settings, controversial — especially in countries where state intervention in business is strong. State-run enterprises may see diaspora entrepreneurs as threats, and local businesses may resent incentives given to the diaspora if the same measures are not available to nondiaspora ventures. A more fundamental concern is over-reliance on diaspora entrepreneurship as a panacea for sluggish job creation and economic growth, especially in the context of return migration. Not all members of the diaspora or returning emigrants have the capabilities to become successful entrepreneurs. Many small businesses fail, wiping out savings and hope in the process.

Interventions to promote entrepreneurship must walk a fine line between opening opportunity and distorting markets. Development will not benefit from the creation of firms too weak to survive in a competitive environment; if enough businesses are created that survive only with external support, they may become a strong enough lobby to demand subsidies and exclude more competitive businesses.

As might be expected, research confirms that potential diaspora entrepreneurs are discouraged from investing or starting businesses if their home countries are wracked by violence (political or criminal); lack transparent local information on investment risks; exhibit a historically poor business environment; and lack infrastructure and amenities such as reliable water and electricity supplies, decent schools, and transportation links.[85] Peace, stability, and the construction of basic infrastructure are prerequisites for substantial diaspora investment, as they are for so many other development processes.

Diaspora entrepreneurs, like all entrepreneurs, succeed by identifying opportunities and moving to take advantage of them. Members of a diaspora have both advantages and disadvantages in pursuing opportunities in their countries of origin. They are more likely than people without ties to the country to understand the opportunity structure and to have connections and "cultural capital" that facilitate their undertakings. They also bring knowledge and understanding acquired outside the country that may help them to see possibilities that are not apparent to people who have never lived elsewhere. On the other hand, diaspora entrepreneurs often encounter entrenched attitudes, resentment from nonmigrants, and administrative barriers in bringing money, materials, and equipment from abroad. However, the most abundant resources of the entrepreneur are ingenuity and persistence. Governments, multilateral institutions, diaspora organizations, and other civil society groups can help diaspora entrepreneurs to tap the resources they need and clear obstacles to realizing their ventures — or at the very least, they can get out of the way. ↵

---

85 Hassan Sheikh and Sally Healy, *Somalia's Missing Million: The Somali Diaspora and Its Role in Development* (New York, NY: United Nations Development Programme, 2009), www.so.undp.org/index.php/View-document-details/70-Forging-Partnerships-with-the-Somali-Diaspora.html

CHAPTER 3

DIASPORA INVESTMENT IN DEVELOPING AND EMERGING COUNTRY CAPITAL MARKETS:

Patterns and Prospects

Aaron Terrazas, Migration Policy Institute

Introduction

Recent years have witnessed a renewed interest in the complex relationship between migration and development. The role of diasporas — defined throughout this volume to include migrants and their descendants who maintain ties with their countries of origin — has often been overlooked or is discussed only in general terms. Yet a growing body of evidence, including earlier chapters of this book, suggests that diasporas play a critical role in supporting sustainable development by transferring resources, knowledge, and ideas back home, and in integrating their countries of origin into the global economy.[1]

Financial flows from migrants and their descendants are at the heart of the relationship between migration and development. Most policy attention to date has focused on migrants' remittances. There is little doubt that these remittances are large: to developing countries alone, they were estimated at nearly $316 billion in 2009 — lower than the $335 billion recorded in 2008 but still more than three times the $76

---

1 For an early discussion of the role of diasporas in development, see Kathleen Newland and Erin Patrick, *Beyond Remittances: The Role of Diaspora in Poverty Reduction in Their Countries of Origin* (Washington, DC and London: MPI and the UK Department for International Development [DFID], 2004).

billion recorded a decade earlier, in 1999.[2] Despite a downturn due to the global economic crisis, remittances have proven much more stable and far less volatile than other private financial flows to developing and emerging economies.[3]

Still, it is widely acknowledged that remittances represent only a fraction of the potential private financial flows originating from diasporas. As Dilip Ratha of the World Bank highlights, *remittances tap the incomes of migrants, but the greater challenge is to mobilize the wealth of diasporas.*[4] This chapter explores a less understood way that diasporas contribute to development in their countries of origin — through participation in capital markets — and identifies opportunities where development policy might enhance this contribution.[5] Capital markets include any institution that matches savings and investments via markets where private- and public-sector entities are able to borrow mid- to long-term funds from multiple lenders, for instance, through stock or bond sales, or through managed funds. International investment in capital markets is known as portfolio investment, and is different from direct investment in enterprises. (The two topics are closely related, however, and direct investment in enterprises is addressed in Chapter 2.[6])

I.   Capital Markets and Development

When they function properly, financial markets efficiently mobilize savings for investment, and there is a general consensus that financial market development and economic growth influence each other positively. Effective capital markets set the stage for innovation and private-sector expansion, which in turn further the growth

---

2   This growth reflects both an increase in the number of migrants sending remittances, as well as improved data coverage and the transfer of substantial remittance flows from informal to formal corridors. See World Bank Development Prospects Group, Remittances Data, April 2010, http://go.worldbank.org/SSW3DDNLQ0.

3   These data include only remittances sent through formal banking challenges. Estimates taking into account informal flows may differ substantially. Dilip Ratha, Sanket Mohapatra, and Ani Silwal, *Outlook for Remittance Flows 2010–11* (Washington, DC: World Bank, April 2010). For an alternative view, see Ceyhun Bora Durdu and Serdar Sayan, "Emerging Market Business Cycles Discussion Paper No. 946, Board of Governors of the Federal Reserve System, September 2008.

4   In line with convention, *income* is the flow of money that individuals receive from labor, government transfers, intrahousehold transfers, or investments. *Wealth*, or net worth, refers to the accumulated stock of savings, real estate, retirement funds, stocks, bonds, and trust funds.

5   The terms *financial market* and *capital market* are used interchangeably throughout this chapter. They include markets for loans, bonds, equity, asset-backed securities, and derivatives.

6   See Chapter 2 "Mobilizing Diaspora Entrepreneurs for Development," in this volume.

of these markets.[7] Importantly, the economists Thorsten Beck, Asli Demirgüç-Kunt, and Ross Levine writing for the National Bureau of Economic Research (NBER) find that financial market development is "pro-poor" in that it disproportionately boosts the incomes of the poor.[8]

Global capital markets are composed of creditors (investors), debtors (debt issuers), and intermediaries who coordinate the exchanges of savers, investors, and consumers:

- **Creditors** include both private- and public-sector investors. Private investors are individuals, corporations, and institutions (e.g., pension and other funds that pool and collectively manage individual investments) that save funds in order to purchase a claim on future earnings. Public-sector investment can originate from traditional national account surpluses (i.e., when a government's expenditures are lower than its revenues) as well as from profitable publicly owned corporations and accrued revenues to sovereign wealth funds (typically funded from commodity export earnings).

- **Debtors** include both sovereign (i.e., government) and corporate borrowers who seek funds from domestic or foreign sources. Among corporate borrowers, an important distinction is between *debt* and *equity*. Debt instruments such as bonds require regular repayment of borrowed funds regardless of the borrower's economic circumstances. Historically, both governments and corporations in developing and emerging markets have been far more likely to seek debt financing from banks than from capital markets.[9] Equity relies more on risk sharing between the lender and the debtor and offers potentially large payouts during good economic times and little to no returns during bad economic times.[10] Many stocks perform poorly even during good economic times, and some do well during bad ones. Equity contracts involve substantially more risk on the part of the lender than debt contracts, are more costly for debtors to issue, and require corporations to cede partial control to shareholders.

7   Ralph Chami, Connel Fullenkamp, and Sunil Sharma, "A Framework for Financial Market Development," IMF Working Paper WP/09/156, International Monetary Fund, Washington, DC, July 2009.

8   Thorsten Beck, Asli Demirgüç-Kunt, and Ross Levine, "Finance, Inequality, and Poverty: Cross-Country Evidence," Cambridge, Massachusetts. National Bureau of Economic Research Working Paper 10979, December 2004.

9   Gerd Häusler, Donald J. Mathieson, and Jorge Roldos, "Trends in Developing-Country Capital Markets Around the World," in *The Future of Domestic Capital Markets in Developing Countries*, ed. Robert E. Litan, Michael Pomerleano, and V. Sundararajan (Washington, DC: The Brookings Institution, 2003), 21–44.

10 This point is taken from Peter Blair Henry and Peter Lombard Lorentzen, "Domestic Capital Market Reform and Access to Global Finance: Making Markets Work," in Litan, Pomerleano, and Sundararajan, *The Future of Domestic Capital Markets in Developing Countries*, 179–214.

- **Financial intermediaries** link savers with investors within and across countries.[11] The spectrum of intermediaries ranges in sophistication and scale from rotating credit associations to micro-finance operators to traditional banks to brokers, hedge funds, and other financial markets, among others. Financial intermediaries offer a range of investment vehicles, from rotating funds to micro- and traditional loans to equity and debt. In some instances, these intermediaries perform additional functions, such as assessing and managing the risks associated with investment (for instance, the risk that a borrower will not be able to pay back the borrowed funds or, in the case of international lending, the risk that exchange rates will change rapidly, altering the profitability of an investment) or fostering good corporate and public financial governance by actively monitoring the sustainability of borrowers' debts.[12]

The rapid growth desired (and, in some cases, experienced) by many developing and emerging economies requires high, sustained rates of investment. This investment is typically financed through a combination of domestic and foreign savings. Some developing countries are able to sustain high household savings to finance corporate and state investment domestically (e.g., China), whereas others rely on earnings largely from commodity exports (e.g., Angola) and still others rely more directly on foreign lending (e.g., Mexico and Brazil during the 1960s and 1970s and Eastern Europe during the 2000s).

Financial market development takes a unique path in each country, and different economies face distinct challenges. But in recent years a standard narrative has evolved to broadly outline the common challenges faced by financial markets in developing and emerging economies:[13]

- **Underdeveloped financial systems hinder savings and investment.** Informal saving is widespread due to limited access to (and, often, mistrust of) formal banking institutions; this and the predominance of cash transactions limit opportunities for households and small businesses to establish credit histories. Macroeconomic or political instability can prompt the already limited pool of formal savers to hold their savings abroad or in a foreign currency. As a result, the domestic pool of savers and the domestic market for investment are typically limited. Yet, critical mass is necessary for financial market development. Economists Robert McCauley and

---

11 The academic literature typically distinguishes between traditional banks, which are considered intermediaries, and financial markets, which directly link savers and investors. This report considers both traditional banks and financial markets along a spectrum of intermediaries.

12 See the Commission on Growth and Development, *The Growth Report: Strategies for Sustained Growth and Inclusive Development* (Washington, DC: World Bank, 2008).

13 This section draws on Beck, Demirgüç-Kunt, and Levine, "Finance, Inequality, and Poverty."

Eli Remolona of the Bank for International Settlements (BIS) estimate that between $100 billion and $200 billion of capitalization is
necessary to ensure sufficient liquidity in sovereign debt markets.[14]
Todd Moss, Vijaya Ramachandran, and Scott Standley of the Center
for Global Development estimate that foreign institutional investors
are hesitant to enter private equity markets smaller than $50 bil-
lion in size or $10 billion worth of shares traded annually, and that
for the emerging market asset class, the most pressing challenge
faced by African capital markets was "mostly one of size."[15]

- **Large, safe borrowers dominate formal borrowing, and smaller,
  riskier borrowers must resort to informal financial markets.** As
  a result of the limited pool of domestic savings, traditional
  financial intermediaries in many developing economies are highly
  conservative in their lending practices, and formal borrowing tends
  to be dominated by governments and large, safe companies. Smaller
  and less established firms, as well as households, must often resort
  to informal (and often, although not always, less efficient) lenders
  such as rotating community funds.[16] In recent years, micro-finance
  lenders have played a growing role in providing finance to small
  and medium-sized borrowers and households perceived as too
  risky by traditional lenders.

- **Substantial foreign financing is necessary to fund investment
  due to the small pool of domestic savings.** Another result of a
  limited pool of domestic savings is that it is typically necessary
  to attract substantial foreign capital to fund domestic investment
  (there are, of course, important exceptions to this generalization).
  The appropriate balance of foreign and domestic financing has
  been much considered in recent years — particularly in light of
  the global economic crisis.[17] External finance (i.e., foreign savings)
  can be highly volatile and susceptible to sudden changes in direction.[18] It often lacks long-term perspective — as illustrated by the

---

14 Robert McCauley and Eli Remolona, "Size and Liquidity of Government Bond Markets," *Bank for International Settlements Quarterly Review*, November 2000.

15 Todd Moss, Vijaya Ramachandran, and Scott Standley, "Why Doesn't Africa Get More Equity Investment? Frontier Stock Markets, Firm Size, and Asset Allocation of Global Emerging Mar-ket Funds," Center for Global Development Working Paper No. 112, February 2007, www.cgdev.org/content/publications/detail/12773.

16 Jack Glen and Ajit Singh, "Capital Structure, Rates of Return and Financing Corporate Growth: Comparing Developed and Emerging Markets, 1994–00," ESRC Centre for Business Research, Univ. of Cambridge, Working Paper No. 265, June 2003, www.cbr.cam.ac.uk/pdf/wp265.pdf.

17 See Commission on Growth and Development, *Post-Crisis Growth in Developing Countries: A Special Report of the Commission on Growth and Development on the Implications of the 2008 Financial Crisis* (Washington, DC: World Bank, 2010). For a retrospective on the lessons from earlier financial crises in emerging market economies, see John Williamson, *Curbing the Boom-Bust Cycle: Stabilizing Capital Flows to Emerging Markets* (Washington, DC: Peterson Institute for International Economics, 2005).

18 See Carmen Reinhart and Guillermo Calvo, "When Capital Inflows Come to a Sudden Stop: Consequences and Policy Options," in *Reforming the International Monetary and Financial System*, ed. Peter Kenen and Alexandre Swoboda (Washington, DC: IMF, 2000): 175–201.

financial crises in emerging countries over the past two decades. Overall, experts agree that financial liberalization and integration with the global economy are indispensable for economic growth and improved living standards. But, as noted by the Commission on Growth and Development, there is "no case of a sustained high investment path not backed up by high domestic savings" — i.e., domestic savings are necessary but not sufficient.[19]

- **High potential growth should attract foreign investment, but international investors have proven reluctant to invest in developing economies.** In theory, the higher potential growth rates of developing and emerging economies should attract foreign capital flows. (More recently, low interest rates in most developed economies have also spurred international investors to seek higher returns in emerging market economies.[20]) In reality, substantial barriers to cross-border capital flows exist, and private financiers are often reluctant to invest in developing countries (especially in the poorest, resource-poor economies) for a wide variety of reasons, including perceptions of risk, lack of information, and doubts about enterprise profitability.

II. What Is the Role of Diasporas?

Broadly framed, developing and emerging economy capital markets face two interrelated sets of challenges: (1) mobilizing *sufficient* resources to finance development through both domestic and external pools of savings, and (2) ensuring that international investment is *sufficiently stable* to promote long-term growth. The first challenge relates to savings and assets, the second to investment.

Is there a role for migrants and diasporas in helping countries overcome these challenges? Of the substantial research on diasporas investing in their countries of origin, most focuses on direct investment. Portfolio investment has been less studied, along with the savings and assets of diasporas. Only recently have researchers begun to focus on the role of remittances in promoting savings, and some banks and micro-finance lenders have begun to leverage remittances to expand lending in developing countries.

From the point of view of diasporas, there may be advantages to investment via capital markets. Portfolio investments are more liquid (if less visible and less personal) than enterprises or real estate — two

---

19 Commission on Growth and Development, *The Growth Report*, 54.
20 Swati R. Ghosh, "Dealing with the Challenges of Capital Inflows in the Context of Macrofinancial Links," World Bank, Economic Premise No. 19, June 2010.

common investments made by diasporas in their countries of origin. While property may provide psychological benefits, the flexibility and returns are often less than those of other investment vehicles, such as bonds or corporate equity. Capital market investment provides diasporas the option to invest in their country of origin through a more liquid mechanism with greater spillover benefits to the local economy.

But important questions remain — particularly in regard to implementation. Although global markets have become increasingly integrated in recent decades, substantial legal and technical barriers exist to the cross-border movement of capital and assets. Do diasporas face the same cross-border barriers to capital mobility as other investors? Are diaspora investors in a distinct class or does their behavior align with either domestic or international portfolio investors?

A. Mobilizing Assets: Diasporas as Savers

A robust body of literature examines the *impact of remittances on household savings* and the use of formal banking institutions.[21] Banks, money transfer operators, credit unions, micro-finance institutions, and other private-sector actors have paid increasing attention to designing savings accounts and other banking products tailored to the needs and preferences of transnational families. Banks, governments, and community organizations have also been increasing their focus on financial education for low income households.[22] The research agenda

---

21 Douglas S. Massey and Emilio Parrado, "Migradollars: The Remittances and Savings of Mexican Migrants to the USA," *Population Research and Policy Review* 13, no. 1 (March 1994): 3–30; Reena Aggarwal, Asli Demirgüç-Kunt, and Maria Soledad Martinez Peria, *Do Workers' Remittances Promote Financial Development?* (Washington, DC: World Bank, 2005); Una Okonkwo Osili, "Remittances and Savings from International Migration: Theory and Evidence Using a Matched Sample," *Journal of Development Economics* 83, no. 2 (2007): 446–65; Sanjeev Gupta, Catherine Patillo, and Smita Wagh, "Impact of Remittances on Poverty and Financial Development in Sub-Saharan Africa," IMF Working Paper WP/07/38, International Monetary Fund, February 2007; Fernando Rios Avila and Eva Schlarb, "Bank Accounts and Savings — The Impact of Remittances and Migration: A Case Study of Moldova," Kiel Institute for the World Economy, Working Paper No. 448, May 2008. A distinct view argues that in countries with underdeveloped financial systems, remittances serve as a substitute for financial system development although this view is far less widespread. See Paola Guiliano and Marta Ruiz-Arranz, "Remittances, Financial Development and Growth," IZA Discussion Paper No. 2160, June 2006.

22 See, for example, the work of the Inter-American Dialogue and the Global Financial Education Program. Nancy Castillo, Landen Romei, and Manuel Orozco, *Toward Financial Independence: Financial Literacy for Remittance Senders and Recipients* (Washington, DC: Inter-American Dialogue, June 2010), www.thedialogue.org/page.cfm?pageID=32&pubID=2400 and Microfinance Opportunities and Freedom from Hunger, Global Financial Education Program, www.globalfinancialed.org/.

appears to have shifted away from knowledge and toward operations and experience: it is no longer a question of *whether* remittances contribute to savings and to the use of formal banking services, but rather *how* to profitably provide financial education and banking services to low-income households (or at least how to do so without incurring a loss).

On balance, there is little doubt that remittances represent a substantial resource for development and can provide an incentive for formal banking institutions to compete for low- and middle-income clients in developing countries. Accordingly, the focus on remittance sending and receiving as an entry point for broader financial engagement is well founded. However, diasporas also hold substantial assets outside their countries of origin.

Although the question has not been studied in depth, labor migration flows likely include a society's more prolific savers. The age range when savings rapidly increase overlaps with the demographic profile of the immigrant population in the United States (69 percent of immigrants in the United States were of working age in 2008).[23] Evidence from developed countries suggests that individual savings increase rapidly during the prime working-age years, peaking around age 40 to 50, and decline gradually thereafter; there are, of course, differences by generation and across the business cycle.[24] A more limited research base supports this notion in emerging and developing economies.[25]

Migrants in the United States admittedly face many barriers to accumulating wealth. Some are trapped in low-wage jobs due to their low level of education, limited English proficiency, or lack of legal immigration status. Although they are widely recognized as voluntary intrahousehold transfers, remittances inevitably generate extra demands on the income of the sender. Data from the first wave of the US Census Bureau's 2008 Survey of Income and Program Participation

---

23 Aaron Terrazas and Jeanne Batalova, "Frequently Requested Statistics on Immigrants and Immigration in the United States," *Migration Information Source*, October 2009, http://www.migrationinformation.org/USFocus/display.cfm?ID=747.

24 See Axel Börsch-Supan, ed., *Life-Cycle Savings and Public Policy: A Cross-National Study in Six Countries* (Amsterdam and Boston: Academic Books, 2003); Frederic Lambert and Matteo Pignatti, "Saving Behavior over the Life-Cycle Does Not Differ across Countries. Portfolio Choices Do," Working Paper, Banque de France, August 2008; Steffan G. Ball, *Stock Market Participation, Portfolio Choice and Pensions over the Life-Cycle* (Washington, DC: Federal Reserve Board, Finance and Economics Discussion Series, Divisions of Research and Statistics and Monetary Affairs, November 2008).

25 See, for instance, Jehad Yasin, *Demographic Structure and Private Savings: Some Evidence from Emerging Markets*, Working Paper, Department of Economics, Population Studies Center, Fort Valley State Univ., 2007.

(SIPP) suggest that working-age adult immigrants are less likely to hold a wide range of formal financial assets than the native born (see Table 1). It is not clear from the data where the assets are held, which may result in underreporting of checking and savings accounts and rental property among immigrants.

Table 1. Share of Employed Adult Immigrants in the United States Who Own Various Financial Assets, 2008

	Native Born (%)	Foreign Born (%)
US government savings bond	11	3
IRA or Keogh account	25	13
401k or thrift plan	44	28
Interest-earning checking account	39	25
Savings account	58	43
Money market deposit account	15	9
Certificate of deposit	10	7
Mutual funds	13	6
Stocks	17	9
Municipal or corporate bonds	1	<1
Rental property	5	4

Note: Includes employed adults aged 18 to 65.
Source: Migration Policy Institute (MPI) analysis of US Census Bureau, 2008 Survey of Income and Program Participation, Wave 1.

But many migrants are also able to accumulate substantial assets. Based on data from specially designed surveys, Manuel Orozco and his colleagues at the Inter-American Dialogue estimate that even among relatively marginalized immigrant communities — for instance, those from Mexico, El Salvador, Guatemala, and Haiti — upward of 80 percent save or invest their earnings, although many do so outside formal banking institutions.[26] Still, given the large number of immigrants in the United States, many hold formal financial assets: SIPP data indicate that over 9 million employed, working-age adult immigrants hold savings accounts; around 6 million hold individual retirement accounts (IRAs) or 401k tax-deferred retirement savings accounts; nearly 2 million hold stocks or money market deposit accounts; about 1.5 million hold certificates of deposit or stocks; and less than 1 million own US government savings bonds, municipal or corporate bonds, or

26 Manuel Orozco, "Financial Access among Remittance Senders," Presentation at the Inter-American Dialogue, Washington, DC, June 14, 2010.

US government securities.[27]

The data do not distinguish among the countries of origin of these immigrants, but if the annual income of prime working-age males (18 to 55 years old) is considered as a benchmark of a household's savings and investment capacity, then migrants from several developing and emerging countries appear to hold substantial potential for diaspora-targeted savings and investment vehicles. Among prime working-age males, immigrants from 18 developing and emerging countries (including India, South Africa, Sri Lanka, Lebanon, Malaysia, Croatia, Romania, Turkey, Egypt, Pakistan, Bulgaria, the Philippines, Syria, and Nigeria[28]) have a median annual income equal to or above that of native-born prime working-age males ($40,000)

B. Diasporas as Investors

A distinct body of research focuses on the role of *diasporas* as *investors* — both directly in enterprises or indirectly as portfolio investors. Two common assumptions regarding diaspora investors merit critical consideration: (1) that diaspora investors benefit from special information regarding investment opportunities in their countries of origin, and (2) that diaspora investors accept below-market rates of return on investment due to patriotic sentiments.

First, it is often argued that diasporas have superior knowledge about investment opportunities and business practices in their countries of origin, and that these information asymmetries make diasporas open to investments that other international investors perceive as too risky — particularly in postconflict or natural-resource-poor countries (e.g., Ethiopia, Iraq, Liberia). Extensive evidence documents the role of diasporas as direct investors in small businesses in their countries of origin.[29] When diasporas invest in businesses owned and operated by others, the investment decision is often based on family or community ties rather than pure profit seeking. While a number of these businesses prove highly successful, as with domestic entrepreneurial undertakings many are ill-conceived and poorly executed. (Of course, a high business failure rate is typical of any dynamic economy: for instance,

---

27 These data are based on MPI analysis of Wave 1 of the US Census Bureau's 2008 Survey of Income and Program Participation, conducted during the first four months of 2008. It includes employed working-age adults aged 18 to 65 to control for low asset holdings among youth and asset draw down by the unemployed and retirees.

28 Data include only countries for which a sufficient sample is included in the American Community Survey.

29 Chapter 2, "Mobilizing Diaspora Entrepreneurs for Development."

in the United States only one-third of new businesses established in 1992 were still operating a decade later.[30]) On balance, a healthy dose of skepticism is merited toward the assumption that diaspora investment is any more informed than other foreign investment — particularly since more traditional foreign investors often benefit from expert advice while diaspora investors are often (although not always) novice entrepreneurs.

While specialized knowledge is particularly important for direct investment, it plays a less important role in portfolio investment — in particular since portfolio investment is typically channeled through professional managers.[31] As a result, informational asymmetries among portfolio managers rather than among investors may be the relevant lens through which to examine diaspora investment in capital markets. To our knowledge, no existing study on the allocation of international portfolio investment examines the national origins or cultural affinities of portfolio managers.

Second, it is often argued that it may be less costly for the country-of-origin governments to borrow from diasporas since diasporas might perceive investment risk in their countries of origin differently than other investors. This difference in risk perception can lead to a "patriotic discount" on expected returns. Evidence suggests that patriotic discounts are particularly meaningful among first-generation immigrants and when the country of origin faces an external threat. This discount, however, appears to deteriorate over succeeding generations. Evidence also suggests that diasporas are less forgiving when their countries of origin face financial challenges due to domestic mismanagement. While it is occasionally argued that encouraging diasporas to invest in their countries of origin for patriotic motives violates canon investment principles such as profit maximization, many other investors accept less-than-optimal returns for a variety of other

---

30 Scott Shane, *The Illusions of Entrepreneurship: The Costly Myths that Entrepreneurs, Investors, and Policy Makers Live By* (New Haven, CT: Yale Univ. Press, 2008), 99.
31 Assaf Razin, Efraim Sadka, and Chi-Wa Yuen, "Excessive FDI Flows under Assymetric Information," Federal Reserve Bank of San Francisco Working Paper No. 27-99, August 1999, www.frbsf.org/economics/conferences/990923/papers/razin_sadka_yuen.pdf; Juan Carlos Hatchondo, "Asymmetric Information and the Lack of International Portfolio Diversification," Federal Reserve Bank of Richmond Working Paper No. 05-07, September 2007, www.richmondfed.org/publications/research/working_papers/2005/pdf/wp05-7.pdf; Wioletta Dziunda and Jordi Mondria, "Assymetric Information, Portfolio Managers and Home Bias," AFA 2010 Atlanta Meetings Paper, February 2009, http://papers.ssrn.com/sol3/papers.cfm?abstract_id= 1359280&rec=1&srcabs=1344880; and Sandro C. Andrade and Vidhi Chhaochharia, "Information Immobility and Foreign Portfolio Investment," *The Review of Financial Studies* 23, no. 6 (2010): 2429–63.

investments such as socially responsible or progressive funds.[32]

From a policy perspective, the question of *how* diasporas invest in their countries of origin may be more relevant than *why* they invest.

Similar to other domestic investors in developing countries, diasporas tend to rely on accumulated savings (often held informally) rather than credit to finance investment. To a lesser extent, some diasporas may obtain bank credit in their country of residence to finance investment in their country of origin. Indeed, access to bank credit is often easier in the country of residence since the latter typically has more developed financial markets, and migrants often have developed credit histories while abroad. But transnational investments financed through borrowing in the country of residence require diasporas to assume currency risk (i.e., the probability that currency exchange rates will change rapidly, altering the profitability of an investment). If lending is secured in the country of origin, of course, this risk does not exist. Diaspora investment in targeted portfolio investment vehicles such as debt and equity is exceedingly rare — at least in part because of the limited number of opportunities.

Evidence on the stability of diasporas' portfolio investment is less conclusive. Such investment appears to behave similar to other sources of foreign portfolio investment, for instance, in the ways it responds to exchange-rate fluctuations and is prone to investor activism. Similar to global venture capitalists and private equity funds, diaspora investors may take a proactive approach to ensuring good corporate governance and sovereign fiscal responsibility rather than simply withdrawing from investments when challenges or strategic differences arise.

But in other respects, capital inflows from diasporas are more similar to pools of domestic capital, characterized by long-return horizons rather than a constant rush for profit expatriation. Moreover, diasporas are more likely than other investors (although perhaps less likely than direct investors) to have liabilities denominated in the developing country's domestic currency. This reduces foreign exchange risk — the risk that an investment's value will change due to changes in currency exchange rates — since diasporas will often accept repayment or returns in the domestic currency or can be easily convinced to make the initial investment in the domestic currency.

---

32 See, for example, Alexander Kempf and Peer C. Osthoff, "The Effect of Socially Responsible Investing on Portfolio Performance," *European Financial Management* 13, no. 5 (November 2007): 908–22; Meir Statman, "Socially Responsible Mutual Funds," *Financial Analysts Journal* 56, no. 3 (May/June 2000): 30–39.

Overall there is little conclusive evidence that capital inflows from diasporas are any more or less stable or farsighted than other forms of foreign investment. The nature of such inflows depends on the structure of the investment vehicle: direct investment is typically less volatile than long-term bonds, which in turn are less volatile than short-term bonds and deposit accounts.

III. Options and Investment Vehicles

Some indirect evidence suggests that diasporas may participate in mainstream capital markets in their countries of origin. For instance, political economist David Leblang estimates that a 1 percent increase in the migrant stock from source country A in destination country B increases portfolio investment from country B to country A by 0.2 percent — or an average of $450 in portfolio investment per migrant.[33] (Obviously, the focus on the mean obscures a polarized distribution with a large majority investing little or nothing and a small minority investing substantial amounts.) Economists Mark Grinblatt and Matti Keloharju observe that private investors in Finland prefer to hold and trade equities in firms whose chief executive officer is of similar origin, although this bias is weaker among "financially savvy institutions" than among amateur investors.[34] According to Suhas Ketkar, pricing trends in Lebanese sovereign debt suggest that the diaspora plays an important role although the country's financial institutions have not specifically targeted investment vehicles to diaspora investors.[35] But diasporas also face important barriers to direct participation in mainstream capital markets: a domestic bank account is often a prerequisite, and few investors have the capacity or expertise to individually manage a transnational portfolio.

For the most part, it is extremely difficult if not impossible, given available data, to identify mainstream capital market participation by diasporas. While it is presumably often present, it is indistinguishable from other foreign investments. Further research is clearly necessary, possibly using specially designed surveys among diaspora communities. Although diaspora-targeted investment vehicles may or may not

---

33 David Leblang, "Diaspora Bonds and Cross Border Capital," Working Paper, Department of Politics, Univ. of Virginia, March 2009.
34 Mark Grinblatt and Matti Keloharju, "How Distance, Language, and Culture Influence Stockholdings and Trades," *The Journal of Finance* 56, no. 3 (June 2001): 1053–73.
35 Suhas Ketkar, comments at USAID-MPI Roundtable on Diaspora Investment in Country of Origin Capital Markets, June 1, 2010.

be widespread — it is impossible to be certain — their experience is certainly more "knowable." The following section reviews several targeted investment vehicles that have been used in the recent past to mobilize diaspora wealth for investment in the country of origin including via deposit accounts, securitization of remittance flows, sovereign debt bonds, and mutual funds. Many of the experiences described draw on the pioneering work of financial economists Suhas Ketkar and Dilip Ratha in this field.

A. Deposit Accounts

Among the most basic ways that diasporas contribute to capital market development in their countries of origin is through the maintenance of deposit accounts. Deposit accounts increase domestic bank assets, allowing banks to expand lending and onward investment. Diasporas maintain deposit accounts in their countries of origin when they have ongoing financial obligations in these countries (known as current liabilities) or expect to have them in the future (known as contingent liabilities). Current liabilities could include remittance obligations or property maintenance, while contingent liabilities could include future retirement plans. For instance, using data from the German Socio-Economic Panel, economists Christian Dustmann and Josep Mestres estimate that about 48 percent of immigrant households in Germany hold savings in their country of origin.[36] In many cases, diasporas also receive favorable terms and interest rates for maintaining these accounts.

Although not strictly capital market investments, deposit accounts expand bank capitalization and are often a prerequisite to direct participation in country-of-origin capital markets:

- **Expanding bank capitalization.** For most countries, reserve requirements for deposit-taking institutions (i.e., the deposits and other assets that a bank must hold per increment of lending) are set according to a complex formula outlined in the Bank for International Settlement's Basel II accords.[37] As a result, the limited pool of bank deposits — the Consultative Group to Assist the Poor (CGAP) estimates that developing-country banks hold 0.52 deposits per adult compared to 1.77 deposits per adult in

---

36 For years 1992 to 1994 only. Christian Dustmann and Josep Mestres, "Savings, Asset Holdings, and Temporary Migration," Centre for Research and Analysis of Migration, Discussion Paper No. 05/10, 2010, www.econ.ucl.ac.uk/cream/pages/CDP/CDP_05_10.pdf.
37 See www.bis.org/publ/bcbs128.htm.

developed countries — limits lending.[38]

■ *Facilitating direct participation in capital markets.* The
costs associated with directly marketing investment vehicles
to foreign nationals (including diasporas) can be significant
given regulatory requirements. The alternative of domiciling the
investment vehicle in the country of origin inevitably limits the
investor pool, but it also allows the borrowing entity to avoid
registering the investment vehicle with securities and exchange
authorities in the destination country, often a complicated and
costly process.

One critical distinction is between accounts denominated in *foreign*
versus *local* currency. In the former case, the bank assumes the foreign-
exchange risk whereas, in the latter, the account holder assumes the
risk. Foreign-currency deposit (FCD) accounts have typically been
discussed in the context of macroeconomic instability when domestic
savers use these accounts to maintain the real value of their savings
(for instance, in Latin America during the 1980s when many countries
confronted high inflation).[39] But diasporas may also use FCD accounts
to hold assets in their country of origin without assuming currency
risk.

Another critical distinction is between *current* and *fixed-term* deposit
accounts. Current deposit accounts allow the holder to withdraw funds
at any time, although there is often a minimum balance. Fixed-term
deposit accounts have stricter limitations on when the principal can
be withdrawn from the account but, in exchange, the holder typically
receives a higher interest rate. For obvious reasons, fixed-term deposits are less volatile than current deposits.

In recent years a number of developing and emerging economies
— including Albania, Ethiopia, India, Kenya, Nigeria, Sri Lanka, and
Turkey — have liberalized their banking regulations and aimed to
attract diaspora savers to FCD accounts. For instance, the Central Bank
of Turkey offers foreign-currency-denominated fixed-term deposit
accounts and "Super FX" accounts (similar to certificates of deposit in
the United States) for Turkish passport holders residing abroad.[40] These
accounts can be denominated in euros, US dollars, British pounds, or
Swiss francs (Super FX accounts are only available in euros and US

---

38 CGAP (Consultative Group to Assist the Poor), *Financial Access* 2009 (Washington, DC: CGAP,
   2009).
39 See Koji Kubo, "Do Foreign Currency Deposits Promote or Deter Financial Development in
   Low-Income Countries? An Empirical Analysis of Cross-Country Data," Institute of Developing
   Economies Discussion Paper No. 87, January 2007.
40 Central Bank of the Republic of Turkey, "FX Deposit Accounts," www.tcmb.gov.tr/iscidvz/
   iscidozengyeni.htm.

dollars). By the end of 2009, nonresident Turks held about $5.5 million in FCDs.[41] Similarly, in 2004 the National Bank of Ethiopia authorized the establishment of FCD accounts — in US dollars, euros, or British pounds — for members of the Ethiopian diaspora, including Ethiopian nationals residing abroad and foreign nationals of Ethiopian origin.[42]

There are fewer examples of countries that have managed to convince diasporas to hold their savings in domestic-currency-denominated accounts. (In any case, it is difficult to distinguish domestic-currency-denominated deposit accounts held by the diaspora from other deposit accounts.) India, however, provides nonresident Indians (NRIs) the option of holding their savings in foreign currency or in rupee-denominated accounts.[43] (FCD accounts available to NRIs are distinct from FCD accounts available more generally to foreigners.[44]) By March 2010, NRIs held an estimated $14.3 million in foreign-currency-denominated accounts and $33.6 million in rupee-denominated accounts.[45] Evidence from the recent global crisis suggests that nonresident Turks and Indians drew on their country-of-origin accounts as they faced financial challenges; in both cases, balances stagnated over the course of the recession after years of growth.

Finally, some emerging and developing country banks have attempted to establish a presence in countries that host their diasporas and market banking services directly to the diasporas where they reside. For instance, India's ICICI Bank reportedly maintains small retail operations in Britain and Canada.[46] According to *The Economist*, Banco do Brasil has plans to open 15 new branches in the United States to target the nearly 400,000 Brazilians estimated to reside in the country. In 2007 Minsheng Bank — a Chinese bank — reportedly bought a 10 percent stake in the San Francisco–based UCBH Holdings, which held

---

41 Data current as of December 31, 2009. Central Bank of the Republic of Turkey, *Balance of Payment Statistics and International Investment Position* (Ankara: Central Bank of Turkey, March 2010), www.tcmb.gov.tr/yeni/eng/.

42 National Bank of Ethiopia, "Directive No. FXD/25/2004, Amendment to Directive No. FXD/24/2004, Establishment and Operation of Foreign Currency Account for Non-Resident Ethiopians and Non-Resident Ethiopian Origin," July 12, 2004, www.mfa.gov.et/Ethiopians_Origin_Abroad/Services.php?Page=Home.htm.

43 See Muzaffar A. Chishti, *The Phenomenal Rise in Remittances to India: A Closer Look* (Washington, DC: MPI, May 2007), www.migrationpolicy.org/pubs/MigDevPB_052907.pdf.

44 Reserve Bank of India, "Features of Various Deposit Schemes Available to Non-Resident Indians," www.rbi.org.in/scripts/FAQView.aspx?Id=69.

45 Provisional data. Reserve Bank of India, "NRI Deposits — Outstandings and Inflows(+)/Outflows(-)," *RBI Bulletin*, May 12, 2010, www.rbi.org.in/scripts/BS_ViewBulletin.aspx.

46 The information in this paragraph draws on *The Economist, A Special Report of Banking in Emerging Market Economies*, May 15, 2009.

a strong position in serving Chinese-American communities.[47] But UCBH failed in 2009, and Minsheng Bank wrote off the $130 million investment.[48] More recently, BBVA Bancomer, originally a Spanish bank that has established a deep presence throughout Latin America, has purchased several small, regional banks in areas of the United States that have attracted recent immigration flows from Mexico.

B. Securitization of Remittance Flows

Another mechanism through which diasporas can contribute — albeit inadvertently — to broadening the assets held by domestic banks in their countries of origin is through the securitization of remittance flows. Future-flow securitization is a fairly recent financial innovation that essentially allows issuers of debt to provide intangible, illiquid, or expected assets as collateral for debt and thereby gain access to more favorable lending terms.[49] (The term "future-flow securitization" refers specifically to the use of expected or future assets to secure debt.) This section summarizes the work of Suhas Ketkar and Dilip Ratha in this field.

Securitization is the process of taking an illiquid asset, or group of assets, and converting it into stocks, bonds, or rights to ownership (derivatives) that can be assigned value and risk, and can ultimately be traded.[50] Issuers of debt securitized by future flows can include public entities, private corporations, and banks that have some sort of periodic receivables with a proven record of stability. A wide variety of flows have been used in future-flow securitizations including residential mortgage loans, credit card vouchers, telecommunications receipts, natural resource revenues, tax liens, mutual fund fees, and workers' remittances. Ketkar and Ratha estimate that between 1992 and 2006, assets worth nearly $84 billion were securitized through 387 future-flow transactions. Mexican debt issuers accounted for nearly one-third of total future-flow securitizations between 1992 and 2006, followed by Turkey and Brazil, which together accounted for approximately one-third of all transactions. Remittances were used in a fairly small share of these transactions (2.1 percent), and $1.8 billion worth of assets were securitized.[51] Securitized transactions peaked in 2006 but have

---

47 Reuters, "China's Minsheng Bank to Buy into UCBH," October 8, 2007, www.reuters.com/article/idUSSHA20222420071008.

48 Dow Jones, "China Minsheng Bank 2009 Net Profit Soars 53%," April 19, 2010.

49 Akerman Senterfitt, *A Primer on Securitization* (New York: World Services Group, October 2006), www.hg.org/articles/article_1723.html.

50 Scotia Capital, *A Securitization Primer* (Toronto: Scotia Capital, June 2000).

51 Suhas Ketkar and Dilip Ratha, "Future-Flow Securitization for Development Finance," in

largely been at a standstill since the collapse of the US investment bank Lehman Brothers in September 2008 and the outbreak of the global financial crisis; the recovery of the market is expected to be delayed due to recent reforms to financial regulations in the United States and pending reforms in the European Union.[52]

The biggest benefits of future-flow securitization are likely to accrue when a debt transaction from a country whose investments are graded "speculative" by a ratings agency such as Standard & Poor's (S&P) subsequently receives an investment grade rating. In at least five cases, remittance-backed securities have received better ratings from debt ratings agencies than the sovereign debt rating of the originating country: Banco Cuscatlan's (El Salvador) issue of $50 million in 1998, Banco do Brasil's (Brazil) issue of $250 million in 2002, Banco Salvadoreno's (El Salvador) issue of $25 million in 2004, Banco de Credito del Peru's (Peru) $50 million issue in 2005, and Banco Brades-co's (Brazil) $400 million issue in 2007. Ketkar and Ratha estimated an untapped potential of about $12 billion for remittance-based, future-flow securitization from countries such as Indonesia, Philippines, Vietnam, Albania, Georgia, Serbia, Montenegro, Tajikistan, Turkey, Ukraine, Brazil, Colombia, Costa Rica, El Salvador, Guatemala, Peru, Egypt, Jordan, Morocco, Yemen, Bangladesh, India, Pakistan, Sri Lanka, Nigeria, and Senegal. (The estimates were performed before the recent economic crisis.) Although the benefits of future-flow securitization of remittances to Mexico, the world's third-largest recipient of remittances, were limited in recent years due to the country's investment grade sovereign debt rating (BBB); the downgrade of Mexico's sovereign debt rating by one notch (BBB-) by Fitch Ratings in November 2009 likely enhanced the attractiveness of future-flow securitization of remittances to the country, although the rating still classified Mexico's debt as investment grade. (Other ratings agencies such as S&P's did not downgrade Mexico's credit rating.)

C. Transnational Loans

Transnational loans are generally small loans provided by banks or micro-finance lenders that allow immigrants to apply for and service a loan in their countries of origin while residing abroad.[53] Financial

---

Innovative Financing for Development, ed. Suhas Ketkar and Dilip Ratha (Washington, DC: World Bank, 2009), 25–57.

52 See "Earthbound," *The Economist*, March 27, 2010.

53 The section is based on Joan Hall, *Diez años de innovación en remesas: Lecciones aprendidas y modelos para el futuro* (Washington, DC: Multilateral Investment Fund, Inter-American

intermediaries have experimented with transnational loans for business expansion, home improvement, home purchase, and education
expenses; mortgage lending has been the most successful. Transnational loans enable migrants to provide credit to their family members back
home while leveraging their credit history (established in their country
of residence) and retaining ultimate control over the loan. Migrants
are typically not able to use assets accumulated in their country of
residence (e.g., housing) as collateral for transnational loans due to the
divergence of bankruptcy laws and enforcement across countries.

A number of public and private entities have begun offering transnational loans. For instance, the Philippine government's Pag-ibig
Overseas Program is a voluntary savings fund that allows overseas
Filipinos to access home loans after two years of contributing to
the fund. Similarly, Mexico's Sociedad Hipotecara Federal (SHF) is a
government-based financial institution with a mandate to foster the
development of primary and secondary mortgage markets. Through
partnerships with financial intermediaries (the largest of which was
Hipotecaria Su Casita, S.A.), SHF offers transnational loans to migrants
in the United States denominated in pesos and either/or US dollars.
Critically, migrants are not required to return to Mexico to finalize the
transaction but can do so remotely through a power of attorney. Finally,
since 2006, Microfinance International Corporation (MFIC), a US-based
financial services corporation, has partnered with micro-finance
lenders and remittance transaction operators in El Salvador,
Guatemala, and Bolivia to provide transnational mortgage loans to
immigrants in the United States and Spain.

Between 2004 and 2008, SHF and its affiliates issued about 3,500
migrant loans. But the economic crisis in the United States — and its
severe impacts on both the housing and real estate sectors and on
the Mexican and US economies in general — severely weakened SHF's
portfolio, forcing Su Casita to default. Still, observers note that the
default of Su Casita was primarily due to weakness in the company's
domestic portfolio; the performance of its international portfolio did
not suffer the same degree of loss.[54] MFIC's transnational loan portfolio
for El Salvador — which benefits from a partial default guarantee from
the United States Agency for International Development's (USAID's)
Development Credit Authority (DCA) for loans below $40,000 — is

Development Bank, January 2010); MPI interviews with Ana Luisa Pinto, Office of Development Credit, USAID, and Diego Rios, international credit analyst, Microfinance International
Corporation; and Dovelyn Agunias and Aaron Terrazas, "Leveraging Diaspora Investment for
Development: Lessons from the Housing Sector," Unpublished draft, MPI, September 2008.
54 Alberto Barranco, "Sigue Su Casita," *El Universal*, June 17, 2010.

much smaller, but the default rate has not increased notably despite much tighter credit and labor markets.

D. Diaspora Bonds

Diaspora bonds are long-dated sovereign debt agreements that are marketed to diasporas.[55] Issuers of diaspora bonds gain access to fixed-term funding, often (although not always) at discounted interest rates. In this respect, diaspora bonds are similar to fixed-term domestic-currency deposit accounts, although they also have some unique features, described in greater detail below.

Diaspora bonds offer several potential advantages to debt issuers. Discussions of the benefits of diaspora bonds typically focus on the "patriotic discount" — that is, the difference between the market interest rate for government debt and the interest rate that diasporas are willing to accept. But as the experiences of Israel, India, and other countries illustrate, this "discount" is often small and does not always materialize. Rather, as Ketkar and Ratha point out, diaspora bonds allow governments to leverage a relatively small amount of charity from the diaspora into substantial resources for development.

Beyond the psychological benefits of "doing good," holders of diaspora bonds may believe that holding such bonds allows them some degree of policy influence back home. More importantly, the default risk normally associated with international sovereign-debt holdings may be reduced for diasporas. According to Ketkar and Ratha, "the worst-case default risk associated with diaspora bonds is that the issuing country would be unable to make debt service payments in hard currency. But the issuing country's ability to pay interest and principal in local currency terms is perceived to be much stronger, and therein lies the attractiveness of such bonds to diaspora investors."[56] Several countries have experimented with diaspora bonds in recent years — and many more are reportedly interested in the concept:[57]

---

55 This section draws on the groundbreaking work of Suhas Ketkar and Dilip Ratha, "Development Finance via Diaspora Bonds," in Ketkar and Ratha, *Innovative Financing for Development.*
56 Ketkar and Ratha 2009, 72.
57 For instance, see Paul Wong, *Leveraging the Jamaican Diaspora for Development* (Washington, DC: USAID Office of Development Credit, November 2003), www.tcgillc.com/tcgidocs/Jamaica031124.pdf; George Grant, "Can a Diaspora Bond Help Grenada?" Caribbean Net News, October 4, 2009, www.caribbeannetnews.com/article.php?news_id=22475.

- Israel has issued bonds to the Jewish diaspora annually since 1951 through the Development Corporation to raise long-term infrastructure investment capital.

- Egypt reportedly issued bonds to Egyptian workers throughout the Middle East in the late 1970s.[58]

- India issued diaspora bonds in 1991, 1998, and in 2000 to avoid balance-of-payments crises and to shore up international confidence in India's financial system at times of financial sanctions or special needs.

- In 2007, the government of Ghana issued a $50 million "Golden Jubilee" savings bond targeted at Ghanaians both in Ghana and in the diaspora.[59]

- Ethiopia issued the Millennium Corporate Bond in 2008 to raise capital for the state-owned Ethiopian Electric Power Corporation (EEPCO).

As Table 2 illustrates, countries' use of diaspora bonds varies widely. Israel has regularly issued diaspora bonds to finance long-term infrastructure development needs, whereas India has issued them on three occasions to fund current account imbalances at times when other international investors had lost confidence in Indian sovereign debt. Ethiopia's one experience issuing diaspora bonds is more recent and aimed to raise funds for the country's state-owned electricity corporation to expand its distribution grid. In India's case, there was little to no patriotic discount, while in Israel's case the initial, substantial discount diminished over time. Ethiopia's bond implies a substantial patriotic discount, although it is not clear the extent to which the diaspora has been willing to subscribe to these terms.[60] Initial subscriptions to Ethiopia's Millennium Bond do not appear to have met expectations. As of June 2009, EEPCO had raised about $200,000 through the bond issue, reportedly far less than projected.[61] Israel's diaspora bonds are not strictly limited to members of the diaspora, whereas India's and

---

58 J. S. Birks and C. A. Sinclair, "Human Capital on the Nile: Development and Migration in the Arab Republic of Egypt and the Democratic Republic of the Sudan," International Labor Organization, World Employment Program, Working Paper 2-26/WP 27, May 1978.

59 Ghana Ministry of Finance and Economic Planning, "Golden Jubilee Savings Bond," www.mofep.gov.gh/gj_bond.htm.

60 Minga Negash, "Ethiopian Diaspora Investment Potential and EEPCO's Millennium Bond," Working Paper, Univ. of Witwatersrand, March 2009, http://papers.ssrn.com/sol3/papers.cfm?abstract_id=1370515.

61 Muluken Yewondwossen, "Ethiopia — EEPCo and Diaspora to Bond with Agents," Nazret.com, August 3, 2009, http://nazret.com/blog/index.php?title=ethiopia_eepco_and_diaspora_to_bond_with&more=1&c=1&tb=1&pb=1.

Ethiopia's bonds are limited to individuals with Indian or Ethiopian ancestry.

Table 2. Comparison of Diaspora Bonds Issued by Israel, India, and Ethiopia

Israel	India	Ethiopia
• Annual issuance since 1951	• Opportunistic issuance in 1991, 1998, and 2000	• Single issue in 2008
• Development oriented borrowing	• Balance-of-payments support	• State-owned corporate financing
• Large though declining patriotic discount	• Small patriotic discount, if any	• Large patriotic discount
• Fixed- and floating-rate bonds and notes	• Fixed-rate bonds	• Fixed-rate bonds
• Maturities from 1 to 20 years with bullet repayment	• Five year with bullet maturity	• Five-, seven-, and ten-year maturities
• Direct distribution by the Development Corporation for Israel (DCI)	• Distributed by the State Bank of India (SBI) in conjunction with international banks	• Distribution through the Commercial Bank of Ethiopia
• Targeted toward but not limited to diaspora	• Limited to members of the diaspora (must be identified as persons of Indian origin)	• Limited to members of the Ethiopian diaspora (Ethiopian passport holders and persons able to trace origins to Ethiopia)
• Registered with US Securities and Exchange Commission	• No SEC registration	• No SEC registration
• Nonnegotiable	• Nonnegotiable	• Nonnegotiable
		• Minimum $500 (or equivalent)

Source: Israel and India: Suhas Ketkar and Dilip Ratha, "Development Finance via Diaspora Bonds," in *Innovative Financing for Development,* edited by Suhas Ketkar and Dilip Ratha (Washington, DC: World Bank, 2009); Ethiopia: Commercial Bank of Ethiopia.

As Figure 1 illustrates, there were about 11.2 million immigrants in the United States from countries with a sovereign credit rating below investment grade (BB+ or lower). Over half (57 percent) were from countries with a speculative credit rating (BB+ to BB-), and about one-third (39 percent) were from countries with a "highly speculative" (B+ to B-) rating; the remaining 4 percent of immigrants were from countries that lacked a credit rating from S&P.[62] The median annual income in 2008 of employed adult immigrants from countries with a speculative grade credit rating was $29,000 (noninvestment grade, speculative) and $27,000 (highly speculative or substantial risk and countries without an S&P rating).[63]

---

62 MPI analysis of data from the 2008 American Community Survey indexed to May 2010 Long-Term Sovereign Credit Ratings from Standard and Poor's, www.standardandpoors.com/ratings/sovereigns/ratings-list/en/us/?sectorName=Governments&subSectorCode=39&subSectorName=Sovereigns.

63 Ibid. Includes employed adults aged 18 and older in the civilian labor force.

Figure 1. Sovereign Credit Ratings of Origin Countries of Immigrants to the United States (millions of people)

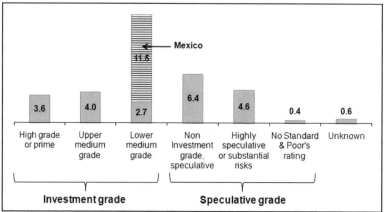

Source: MPI indexing of May 2010 long-term S&P's sovereign credit rating (foreign) to immigrant population estimates from the 2008 American Community Survey; Steven Ruggles, J. Trent Alexander, Katie Genadek, Ronald Goeken, Matthew B. Schroeder, and Matthew Sobek, Integrated Public Use Microdata Series: Version 5.0 [Machine-readable database] (Minneapolis: Univ. of Minnesota, 2010).

Although immigrants from countries with speculative grade ratings appear to have low incomes compared with native-born workers and other immigrants, presumably there is still substantial potential for sovereign debt issues to diasporas in the United States. It is also notable, however, that several developing countries with large diasporas in the United States have not been issued S&P sovereign credit ratings (for instance, Haiti and Ethiopia).

Israel's experience is particularly instructive. Ketkar and Ratha observe that diaspora Jews have historically been extremely willing to purchase diaspora bonds when Israel has come under attack from its neighbors, but have been less forgiving when the country's financial problems are rooted in domestic economic mismanagement.[64] Similarly, in early 2010 Greece mooted the possibility of issuing dollar-denominated bonds as the country faced severe fiscal pressures — presumably targeting Greek diaspora investors in the United States as well as other international investors. In March 2010, the speaker of the Greek Parliament called on the diaspora in the United States, Latin America, Australia, and Europe to contribute to a "Greece Support Fund" to reduce the country's debt.[65] The comments on the diaspora online

---

64 Ketkar and Ratha, *Innovative Financing for Development*, 71.
65 *Greek Reporter*, "Athens May Appeal to Rich Greeks Abroad," March 1, 2010, http://eu.greekreporter.com/2010/03/01/athens-proposal-of-the-president-of-the-parliament-to-create-a-support-fund-for-greece-and-from-greeks-of-the-diaspora/.

forums, however, suggest that many members of the Greek diaspora are receptive, but highly skeptical of such efforts given the widespread perception that Greece's economic problems are due principally to domestic economic mismanagement. As one member of the diaspora commented in an Internet forum, "If they can guarantee the money will go to the country and not some corrupt official's back pocket, I will do it."[66] The underlying lesson is clear: if developing countries wish to tap diaspora wealth, they must be prepared to demonstrate good faith in the investment and be transparent in their accounting and budget allocation practices.

E. Diaspora Mutual Funds

Mutual funds are professionally managed collective investment vehicles that allow individual investors to diversify risk by purchasing shares of a basket of investment products — typically including money market funds, sovereign and corporate bonds, and equities.[67] There is a great deal of flexibility in designing funds, which tend to target specific categories of investments or investors.

Mutual funds allow a broad range of individual investors to diversify risk and have their investments professionally managed without incurring the costs of a personal investment manager. As such, they should appeal to nonexpert diaspora investors interested in investing in their countries of origin but who lack the time and expertise to individually manage the investment. Since few developing country corporations are publicly traded and those that are listed are rarely well known, diaspora funds could also serve a price discovery function. Building upon this logic, members of the Rwandan diaspora recently worked to establish a Rwandan Diaspora Mutual Fund (RDMF). The fund has yet to be formally launched, so it is far too early to draw conclusions, but there is little doubt that it represents an innovative initiative to mobilize savings for investment in Rwanda.

RDMF is as much an initiative of the diaspora as it is an investment vehicle for the diaspora. It was the brainchild of 11 Rwandans residing in Canada, China, Ethiopia, Malaysia, the Netherlands, South Africa, the

---

66 GreekRealm.com, posted on February 28, 2010, at 4:55 pm, www.greekrealm.com/forum/ greek-current-affairs/13220-greece-urges-diaspora-help-debt.html.
67 This section draws on MPI interviews with Robert Kayinamura and Providence Bikumbi Newport of the Rwandan Diaspora Mutual Fund conducted in May 2010 and on Emmanuel Ngomiraronka, "Rwandan Diaspora Mutual Fund: An Investment Initiative of the Rwandan Diaspora," Presentation provided to the MPI, May 2010.

United Kingdom, and the United States. Some, though not all, have professional experience abroad in investment banking and securities law. The initiative has received moral support from the Diaspora Directorate General of the Rwandan Foreign Ministry and technical assistance from the National Bank of Rwanda (the country's central bank) and the Rwandan Capital Markets Advisory Council (the country's securities and exchange regulator).

Once operational (expected in late 2010), the fund will target investors from the Rwandan diaspora as well as the "affinity diaspora" (i.e., friends and associates of Rwandans abroad and others with a personal connection to Rwanda), Rwandans residing in Rwanda, and general foreign investors. In this sense, the diaspora serves not only as an investor base, but also as (1) a conduit for technological transfer and (2) a portal opening up investment opportunities in Rwanda for the outside world. Fund shareholders will be required to maintain a Rwandan franc-denominated account with the Bank of Kigali or an account with one of the bank's foreign affiliates.[68]

The fund is designed to be accessible to small investors in Rwanda as well as in the diaspora. At the time of publication, shares are expected to be priced around 1,000 Rwandan francs (about $2) with two options: (1) a minimum initial purchase of five shares and minimum incremental purchases of three shares thereafter, or (2) a minimum initial purchase of ten shares and incremental purchases of four shares thereafter. In addition, a subscription fee of 5,000 francs (about $10) is assessed to new investors with the fund.

Another example is the proposed Liberian Diaspora Fund — a social investment fund that is owned and managed by Liberians living in the United States and which invests in small businesses in Liberia.[69] The fund focuses on six sectors: agribusiness, fisheries, natural resources, technology, infrastructure development, and health care. Three-quarters of the funding will come from members of the Liberian diaspora, with the remaining quarter coming from multilateral organizations and other social investors. In addition to providing financing, the fund will provide business training and mentoring.

---

68 As of May 2010, the Bank of Kigali had correspondent banks in the European Union, the United States, Kenya, and Burundi.
69 MPI interview with Taa Wongbe, principal, Liberian Diaspora Fund, Washington, DC, July 1, 2010.

F. Unexplored Investment Vehicles

Portfolio investment vehicles targeted at diasporas have focused on sovereign and household debt (diaspora bonds, transnational loans), expanding bank assets (foreign and domestic currency deposits, securitization of remittance flows), and more recently corporate equity (investment funds). But other investment vehicles may also merit consideration:

Subnational debt issues. One largely unexplored avenue for targeting diaspora investors in government debt is at the subnational level (including publicly owned utilities providers). Subnational governments account for an increasing share of public investments across the developing world.[70] For instance, state and local governments finance about half of public investments in countries such as Indonesia and Turkey.[71] In many cases, diasporas maintain strong attachments not only to their country of origin, but also to their state, region, or municipality of origin; often the most powerful bonds among diasporas are local identities — particularly in regions such as West Africa and Central Asia where sovereign states are a recent phenomenon and lack authority as identity-based institutions.

In at least one case, a subnational government has attempted to target debt issues to diaspora investors. Reportedly the government of Kerala (India) attempted to issue a subsovereign diaspora bond, but the Indian federal government did not agree to the plan.[72] Other developing countries with federal systems (e.g., Mexico, Nigeria, Sudan, Ethiopia, Bosnia, and Herzegovina) are strong candidates for subnational debt issues to diasporas.

Diaspora private-equity funds. Private equity provides a vital bridge allowing mid-size companies in developing countries to grow, expand, and innovate. While small and micro-enterprises tend to access financing through accumulated savings or through bank or micro-credit lending, and large companies (even in the developing world) are able to

---

70 The term *subnational* refers to all levels of government and public entities below the federal or central government. It includes states, provinces, autonomous communities, counties, cities, towns, public enterprises, and school districts. Mila Freire, John Petersen, Marcela Huertas, and Miguel Valadez, eds., *Subnational Capital Markets in Developing Countries: From Theory to Practice* (Washington, DC: World Bank, 2004).

71 Otaviano Canuto and Lili Liu, "Subnational Debt Finance and the Global Financial Crisis," World Bank, Poverty Reduction and Economic Management Network, Economic Premise, No. 13, May 2010.

72 MPI communication via e-mail with S. Irudaya Rajan, Center for Development Studies, Trivandrum, Kerala, May 2010.

resort to capital markets, mid-size companies often face greater challenges in securing financing for growth or expansion.[73] Their borrowing needs are typically beyond the capacity of micro-finance lenders yet they often lack the established record of performance that facilitates bank credit and are too small for market listing. Private equity — which combines financial resource mobilization with the deployment of industry-specific and management expertise — is critical to growing companies.

Institutional investors. According to financial economists Cem Kara-cadag, V. Sundararajan, and Kimberly Elliot, one of the most important challenges facing domestic capital markets in developing countries is the need to develop an institutional investor base, including mutual and investment funds and other contractual savings institutions, such as pension funds and insurance companies.[74] As the immigrant population ages — there were 4.5 million immigrants aged 65 and older in the United States in 2007 compared to 2.7 million in 1990 — the pool of immigrants' contractual savings held in pension funds and retirement accounts will increase.[75] These savings potentially represent a powerful pool of resources for development financing. But many institutional investors such as pension funds are prohibited by their charters from investing in subinvestment-grade debt or equity, thereby precluding many developing countries.

Corporate debt and equity. Governments have been far more active than private-sector actors in reaching out to diasporas and engaging them in the political, social, and economic life of their countries of origin.[76] The potential role of diasporas in providing finance to promising emerging and developing country corporations through capital markets has been largely overlooked. A quick examination of data on the immigrant population in the United States and from the Milkin Institute on private-sector access to capital suggest there are several countries with large (and in some cases relatively wealthy) diasporas in the United States that have underdeveloped private-sector capital markets.[77] In some of these countries, high political risk or tensions

---

73 Lael Brainard, ed., *Transforming the Development Landscape: The Role of the Private Sector* (Washington, DC: The Brookings Institution Press, 2006).
74 Cem Karachadag, V. Sundararajan, and Jennifer Elliott, "Managing Risks in Financial Market Development: The Role of Sequencing," in Litan, Pomerleano, and Sundararajan, *The Future of Domestic Capital Markets in Developing Countries.*
75 Aaron Terrazas, "Older Immigrants in the United States," *Migration Information Source,* May 2009, www.migrationinformation.org/USfocus/display.cfm?id=727.
76 For a review of government efforts to engage diasporas, see Dovelyn Agunias, ed., *Closing the Distance: How Governments Strengthen Ties with Their Diasporas* (Washington, DC: MPI, 2009).
77 James R. Barth, Tong Li, Wengling Lu, and Glenn Yago, *Capital Access Index 2009: Best Markets*

between the diaspora and the country-of-origin governments may preclude collaboration (e.g., Iran, Syria) whereas others appear more promising (e.g., Cambodia, Colombia, Ecuador, Ethiopia, Jamaica, Lebanon, Ukraine, and Vietnam).

IV. Conclusions and Policy Options

Capital markets in countries with different levels of development face different challenges. Can diasporas help developing and emerging countries address the twin challenges of attracting sufficient and stable access to international investment?

The potential of diasporas as portfolio investors is less studied than their potential as direct investors. Overall, *there is ample evidence that diasporas hold substantial assets that could potentially be mobilized for portfolio investment in their countries of origin.* The more pressing challenge appears to be devising and marketing investment vehicles to attract this investment, and convincing diasporas of the merits of such investment. Beyond the challenge of marketing, there is clear scope for greater international cooperation to facilitate the transnational mobilization of assets, for instance, through agreements on mutual enforcement of bankruptcy laws (which would enable banks to accept assets held abroad as collateral for lending) and harmonization and sharing of credit scores. Although these fields of cooperation are exceedingly complicated from a technical perspective and face numerous legal and political hurdles, they merit consideration.

It is less clear if portfolio investment inflows from diasporas are more stable than other sources of foreign investment. It is widely accepted that diasporas may have a greater appetite for long-term investment in their countries of origin than other foreign investors. While foreign investors may perceive these investments as high risk, diasporas often view risk differently. Diasporas' perception of investment risk in their countries of origin is often attributed to superior information. But experience in the field of direct investment suggests that diasporas are not necessarily more informed about investment opportunities — particularly since they typically forego expert advice. Rather, the investment decisions of diasporas might be better explained by "home bias" — the idea that investors are more likely to invest in companies in their home countries irrespective of the financial returns

---

for *Business Access to Capital* (Santa Monica, CA: Milkin Institute, 2010).

on the investment.

Both information asymmetries and home bias on the part of the investor are more important for determining direct investment decisions; by contrast, **portfolio managers are the critical actors in portfolio investment decisions.** Indeed, portfolio managers serve as critical intermediaries in promoting diaspora portfolio investment by pooling investors, allocating risk, and actively pursuing investment opportunities.

Some emerging markets — including many in Latin America and East Asia — have well-developed financial markets where diasporas might play a role by contributing to scale (i.e., investing resources), reducing volatility (i.e., investing long term), mainstreaming investments in the country among institutional investors, and expanding access to finance to traditionally excluded borrowers or borrowers in informal markets. In countries where capital markets are less developed, such as in much of Africa and Central America, diasporas might play the role of "first movers" and contribute to innovation and price discovery as well as to scale. In addition, the investment appetite of diasporas varies according to the characteristics of the diaspora. For instance, first-generation diasporas may be particularly interested in direct investment and may be more prone to patriotic discounts. But second- and higher-generation diasporas may find portfolio investment a more accessible and less time-intensive approach.

Diasporas also face many of the same barriers to investing in developing and emerging countries as other international investors. In most developing and emerging economies, capital markets are still small, lack liquidity, face high transaction costs, and suffer from a limited investor base and inadequate information. Is there a role for public policy — and more particularly, for international aid agencies such as USAID — in helping overcome these barriers? If modified or expanded, several existing initiatives within USAID and other US government agencies — such as the Overseas Private Investment Corporation (OPIC), the US Treasury Department's Office of International Affairs, and the US State Department's Office of Development Finance — appear to be particularly promising avenues for promoting diaspora portfolio investment in the countries of origin.

Reducing investment risk: the Development Credit Authority and Overseas Private Investment Corporation. International investment involves a number of risks that can inhibit opportunities for both borrowers and lenders. While diasporas may have a higher risk threshold when it comes to investing in their countries of origin than other international investors, they are also keenly aware of the liabilities involved. Similarly, banks in developing countries are often unwilling to lend to diaspora investors who may lack sufficient domestic assets or credit histories. Two US government agencies — USAID and OPIC — have the potential to support diaspora investment in their countries of origin through risk reduction: USAID by focusing on lenders in the country of origin, and OPIC by focusing on diaspora investors who are US citizens.

Since 2008, DCA has provided partial credit default guarantees to facilitate access to bank credit for Ethiopian diaspora entrepreneurs, although it does not fund loans directly. Rather, the credit guarantee allows USAID's partner banks in Ethiopia to mobilize domestically held assets and savings. (DCA guarantees can also be coupled with USAID's technical assistance to banks, discussed at length below.) DCA guarantees 50 percent of losses in the case of default. Between September 2008 and February 2010, the joint venture guaranteed 37 million birr (about $2.8 million) in loans to ten diaspora businesses, principally in services and agriculture.[78] Similarly, in El Salvador, DCA has facilitated the expansion of transnational micro-lending. However, since the guarantee does not enable banks to mobilize *new* resources — but instead to more efficiently mobilize existing resources — the program clearly has limitations. Moreover, since DCA requests must originate from USAID Country Missions, they typically are not launched unless a diaspora presence is visible in the country of origin.

OPIC offers discounted insurance to US companies investing overseas to protect against several common foreign investment risks, including:

- *Currency risk* (i.e., the possibility that an investor's ability to convert profits or capital from a local currency into US dollars may be limited)

- *Political risk* (i.e., the possibility that an investment will be lost due to war, revolution, insurrection, politically motivated civil strife, terrorism, or sabotage)

- *Expropriation risk* (i.e., the possibility that assets will be seized by a foreign government)

Insurance along similar lines and targeted to diaspora communities (as well as mainstream investors) could promote diaspora investment in the world's more dangerous or risky economies. OPIC has also established and purchased shares of funds that invest in low-income coun-

---

78 Information provided to the MPI by Joseph Obi, EGAT/DC relationship manager, USAID, June 2010.

tries, which is another potential avenue for working with diasporas (for instance, through diaspora mutual funds).

Providing technical assistance: Volunteers for Economic Growth Alliance and the Government Debt Issuance and Management Technical Assistance Program. Although many developing countries are deeply interested in mobilizing diaspora wealth — for instance, through issuing diaspora bonds, expanding transnational loans, and establishing diaspora mutual funds — many of these efforts have been stymied by the technical complexity of accessing international capital markets. Suhas Ketkar and Dilip Ratha (2009) estimate that the fees involved in issuing a diaspora bond (with US registration through the Securities and Exchange Commission) can exceed $500,000, placing these tools beyond the means of most small and mid-size economies.

Multilateral agencies — such as the World Bank, International Monetary Fund, and Bank for International Settlements — may be best placed to provide direct advice on technical questions. But there is also a role for US government agencies such as the US Treasury Department's Office of International Technical Assistance, which oversees a Government Debt Issuance and Management Technical Assistance Program (GDIM) and which could help developing-country governments register and issue sovereign debt bonds to their diasporas in the United States.[79]

Diasporas may also provide technical assistance to their countries of origin. About 606,000 immigrants in the United States work in finance-related occupations and nearly three-quarters are from developing and emerging economies (see Figure 2).[80] If the second-generation, native-born US citizens with immigrant parents are included, the figure is likely to be much higher. Other research in this series has explored the variety of avenues through which diasporas volunteer in their countries of origin and the benefits of institutional support for these efforts; the potential of diaspora financial service volunteers clearly merits further exploration.[81] For instance, as described in this chapter, members of the Rwandan diaspora — including several with expertise in the international financial industry — volunteered time to set up a Rwandan Diaspora Mutual Fund. USAID's Volunteers for Economic Growth Alliance (VEGA) provides an existing framework to mobilize

---

79 See http://treasuryota.us/index.php?option=com_content&task=view&id=30&Itemid=71.
80 MPI analysis of data from the 2008 American Community Survey.
81 See Chapter 6, *Connected through Service: Diaspora Volunteers and Global Development in this volume.*

skilled volunteers for such efforts.[82] Research suggests that the
acteristics and interest of portfolio managers are a key determi
portfolio allocation, so courting diasporas with financial sector _ .
tise through programs such as VEGA would likely have longer-term
spillover effects as well.

Establishing trust: global development alliances. Many diasporas
are eager to contribute to development efforts in their countries of
origin but are deeply skeptical of both risky investment proposals
and the honesty of institutions back home. As the former chairman of
Pakistan's Securities and Exchange Commission observed, in public
perception, financial markets in many developing countries are "run
by brokers for brokers."[83] Diasporas often share this sentiment. Governments and corporations that aim to attract diaspora investments
must have a credible need for foreign investment — and critically — a
plan to put the investment to productive use. Partnerships with USAID
under the aegis of a global development alliance could lend credibility
to specific ventures that demonstrate sound accounting practices,
corporate governance, and transparency in decisionmaking.

Bridging information gaps: private investment needs assessments.
USAID Country Missions reportedly maintain lists of private investment opportunities. These lists could be disseminated to diaspora
communities through partnerships with the country-of-origin consular
networks or USAID headquarters, through online platforms such as
Kiva or Global Giving, or directly to diaspora investment funds where
they exist. Where developing countries maintain strong, independent,
and credible diaspora affairs agencies, these institutions could also
perform similar functions in collaboration with USAID.

---

82 See www.vegaalliance.org/.
83 Cited in Litan, Pomerleano, and Sundararajan, *The Future of Domestic Capital Markets in Developing Countries*, 114.

Figure 2. Immigrants Employed in Finance Occupations, 2008

	Number Employed (thousands)
Financial managers	127
Cost estimators	11
Accountants and auditors	329
Appraisers and assessors of real estate	5
Budget analysts	7
Credit analysts	4
Financial analysts	14
Personal financial advisors	39
Insurance underwriters	6
Financial examiners	1
Loan counselors and officers	34
Tax examiners, collectors, and revenue agents	6
Tax preparers	12
Financial specialists, all others	8
Actuaries	4

Countries of Origin, Income Group

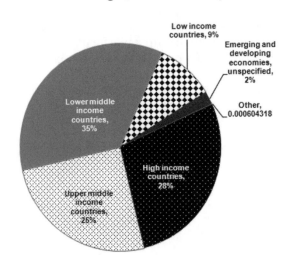

Source: MPI analysis of the 2008 American Community Survey data. Steven Ruggles, J. Trent Alexander, Katie Genadek, Ronald Goeken, Matthew B. Schroeder, and Matthew Sobek, Integrated Public Use Microdata Series: Version 5.0 [Machine-readable database] (Minneapolis: Univ. of Minnesota, 2010). *Note:* Includes employed immigrants aged 18 and older.

The above represent targeted opportunities to expand diaspora participation in the country-of-origin capital markets through existing initiatives rather than more ambitious schemes, although there is clearly merit in the latter as well. On balance, the ongoing global financial crisis has prompted policymakers to reevaluate longstanding assumptions regarding capital flows to emerging and developing countries, which have proven remarkably stable — particularly relative to the financial turmoil of several developed countries.[84] Indeed, a number of developing countries are now concerned about a surfeit of foreign capital rather than a scarcity.[85] In the broader perspective, the assets and investments of diasporas are likely to be small and marginal relative to the wider array of international investors. This is particularly true for the large and open emerging economies that are also associated with large or powerful diasporas — notably China, India, and Mexico. But for the capital markets of smaller or riskier countries outside the limelight of (or even shunned by) international financial markets, there is clearly a larger potential role for diasporas. US government agencies — including USAID, OPIC, and the Treasury Department — are well equipped to facilitate diaspora portfolio investment. ◢

---

84 Institute of International Finance, *Capital Flows to Emerging Market Economies* (Washington, DC: Institute of International Finance, January 2010); Carnegie Endowment for International Peace, "Capital Flows to Emerging Markets Resurgent," *International Economic Bulletin*, November 9–13, 2009, www.carnegieendowment.org/publications/index. cfm?fa=view&id=24116.

85 See Amar Bhattacharya, John Williamson, Arturo Porzecanski, and Uri Dadush, "Managing Capital Flows in the Aftermath of the Global Crisis," Carnegie Endowment for International Peace, International Economics Program, May 26, 2010, www.carnegieendowment.org/ events/?fa=eventDetail&id=2914.

CHAPTER 4

HERITAGE TOURISM AND NOSTALGIA TRADE:
A Diaspora Niche in the Development Landscape

Kathleen Newland and Carylanna Taylor, Migration Policy Institute

Introduction

One of the markers of underdevelopment is weak insertion into the global economy. In general, poor countries benefit less than richer ones from the comparative advantages that come with international trade in goods and services. In addition, their main exports are often primary products with little vertical or horizontal integration in the local economy. Public and private actors alike seek to expand trade in goods with higher local value added and those, like international tourism, that have strong earnings potential. But the barriers to entry are high for nontraditional exports. In particular, it is difficult to introduce and establish unfamiliar goods and new tourist destinations in the international market. In overcoming barriers to entry, diaspora populations can play an important role, acting as a bridge to broader markets.

This chapter explores the development potential of forms of tourism and trade that involve diasporas. We take diasporas to include emigrants and their descendants who retain an active connection to their countries of origin or ancestry.

Diaspora tourism cannot easily be disaggregated from other forms of tourism, but there is little doubt that, overall, tourism is an important source of export earnings (it is treated as a service export, even though it is consumed in the country in which it is provided). Between 2000 and 2008, the number of international tourists visiting developing and emerging countries grew from 259 million to 424 million — far outpacing growth in the number of tourists to advanced economies, which increased more modestly, from 423 million to 495 million.[1] In 2008, international tourism generated $29.9 billion in revenue for African countries, $49.2 billion for the developing and emerging countries of Latin America and the Caribbean, and $75.3 billion for the countries of South and Southeast Asia. While 2009 was a difficult year for the tourist industry, what with the dual crisis of the global economy and the H1N1 pandemic, preliminary data for 2010 suggest a robust recovery: during the first two months of 2010, tourist arrivals increased by 15 percent in South Asia, 10 percent in Southeast Asia, and 8 percent in North Africa. Moreover, 11 developing countries posted double-digit growth in tourist arrivals during the same period: Sri Lanka (50 percent); Vietnam (36 percent); Nepal (30 percent); Egypt (29 percent); Kenya (18 percent); Nicaragua and Seychelles (16 percent); Ecuador, Indonesia, and Morocco (14 percent); and India (13 percent).

In exploring trade in cultural goods from diasporas' countries of origin, this chapter relies heavily on the pioneering work of Manuel Orozco of the Inter-American Dialogue. Orozco refers to these products as "nostalgic goods;" we prefer the terms *nostalgia goods* and *nostalgia trade* but refer to the same phenomena. Orozco demonstrates, through painstaking survey research in the United States, that migrant households are regular and heavy consumers of home-country goods, and that trade in such products earns significant revenue for countries of origin. As with diaspora tourism flows, precise earnings estimates of nostalgia goods are not available because they are not recorded separately in trade statistics. We can safely assume that trade in nostalgia goods is not a major stream of world trade; its importance instead rests on its composition. Nostalgia goods tend to be labor intensive and are often made by local artisans, so earnings from them are likely to be absorbed at the local and household levels. By contrast, revenues from traditional exports of primary products seldom trickle down.

Both nostalgia trade and diaspora tourism occupy niches in a broader market and operate according to distinctive patterns. Migrants often prefer products produced in their home country even when similar products made in their destination country are available at lower cost.[2]

---

1   Data in this paragraph are drawn from the UN World Tourism Organization (UNWTO), *World Tourism Barometer, Interim Update April 2010* (Madrid: UNWTO, 2010), www.unwto.org/facts/eng/pdf/barometer/UNWTO_Barom10_update_april_en_excerpt.pdf.
2   Manuel Orozco, *Tasting Identity: Trends in Migrant Demands for Home Country Goods*

Diaspora tourists often desire different outcomes from visits to their home country than other travelers do, and may spend their money in different ways. They are literally more "at home" when they go to their country of birth or ancestry, and therefore may not demand the kind of insulating intermediaries that are thought to make foreign tourists comfortable.

The governments of countries of migrant origin may try to attract diaspora members as consumers of local products or experiences, as "first movers" to open new opportunities in the international market, as sources of valuable word-of-mouth advertising, and as investors in tourism or export trade. The hoped-for outcome is not simply that more emigrants and their descendants will visit or buy, but that the niche they occupy will attract other, nondiaspora customers and grow into a larger and more profitable market. Development benefits include the employment of local workers and the multiplier effects that their earnings generate in their communities; foreign exchange earnings to support the national balance of payments; and a reinforced relationship with members of the diaspora, including — importantly — the second and subsequent generations.

I. Diaspora Tourism

With the growth of tourism to developing countries obviously robust, why should we be concerned with attracting the diaspora visitor? In the first place, many developing countries have yet to join the roster of tourist destinations, and for those that have, the gains are limited. Often, tourism-targeted infrastructure is either poorly developed or confined to enclaves with little connection to the local economy apart from low-level employment. The enclaves are run by international companies that source many of their supplies externally and repatriate the bulk of their profits. Tourists from the diaspora, however, are more likely than most international tourists to have or make connections with the local economy; to stay in locally owned, smaller accommodations (or with relatives); to eat at local restaurants; and so forth. While they may not spend as much money as foreign tourists, on average, diaspora tourists' expenditures are more likely to go directly into the hands of local businesses. Thus they generally have a different and, in some respects, more positive development impact.

(Washington, DC: US Agency for International Development, 2008).

Diaspora tourism offers two further advantages. First, because it is not necessarily as seasonal as international tourism, it may entail a steadier use of infrastructure throughout the year and provide employment opportunities in off-peak times.[3] Observing how tourism in Cuba reflects winter and summer vacations in the Northern Hemisphere, Jorge Pérez-López offers a number of suggestions for increasing diaspora tourism's potential that could apply to other nations as well. These include promoting festivals, saints' days, and holidays; professional association meetings and conventions; vacations for seniors; and trips for medical treatment. Second, diaspora tourism may result in the geographic expansion of tourism within the country. Pérez-López suggests that diaspora tourists reach less-visited sites than do other international tourists by traveling to see friends and relatives, participating in cultural and sporting events, and visiting secondary or regional sites.

Diaspora tourism seems to occupy an intermediate space between international and domestic tourism. Within it there are two streams of tourists: one is made up of people who are more removed from the origin country and may not be able to call on friends and relatives for food and lodging; the second is composed of more recent emigrants who still have close family in the country of origin. As Regina Scheyvens's case study of Samoa illustrates, visiting emigrants and their families may use the same kinds of facilities that domestic tourists and local residents use — and these facilities are usually cheaper, simpler, and less isolated from the surrounding society than those used by most international tourists.[4] They require less capital to establish and consume fewer resources — especially imported resources — than more mainstream tourist facilities. And because they have lower start-up and running costs, they enable domestic entrepreneurs to enter the tourism sector more easily. As with the Samoan beach huts known as *fale,* these facilities cater to domestic and diaspora tourists, to adventurous, independent (and low-budget) foreign travelers and those in search of an authentic experience of the local way of living.

For new tourist destinations struggling to break into the international market, diaspora tourists may be important first movers. They not only test the waters and spread the word about the attractions of homeland locations but may also invest directly in building new tourist facilities or bringing existing ones up to the standard they have come to expect

---

3   Jorge F. Pérez-López, "The Diaspora as a Commercial Network for Cuban Reconstruction" (Thought Paper for the Association for the Study of the Cuban Economy, 2007), http://146.6.146.2/project/asce/pdfs/volume17/pdfs/perezlopez.pdf.
4   Regina Scheyvens, "Poor Cousins No More: Valuing the Development Potential of Domestic and Diaspora Tourism," *Progress in Development Studies* 7, No. 4 (2007): 307–25.

as a result of their experience abroad.

While educational tours and study-abroad opportunities have long involved a deep engagement with the country visited, such engagement is now becoming mainstream. Since the 1970s, the tourism industry has worked to engage sophisticated travelers whose interests go beyond sun, sea, and sand. For these travelers, going to a foreign-owned, all-inclusive resort or cruise is not enough; they want to experience a country's architecture, religious rituals, cuisine, art, music, and language, and meet local people. Accordingly, tourism marketing campaigns use terms like *authentic, real,* and *responsible* to promote new destinations. The multinational Africa Diaspora Heritage Trail conferences, for example, encourage public and private actors to promote these heritage resources not only among diaspora tourists but also in the fast-growing markets for educational, sustainable, geo-, eco-, and "values" tourism. A segment of this high-value-over-high-volume market also seeks travel experiences tied to philanthropy and volunteerism. Prof. Don Hawkins of George Washington University has explored the development potential of "SAVE" (scientific, academic, volunteer, educational) tourism.

To take advantage of these trends, businesses and tourism authorities are experimenting with offerings such as homestays and cooking and craft lessons that put money directly into the local economy. Some countries are developing certification processes so that these special-ized offerings are indeed authentic and follow good practices (such as working in conjunction with local communities to identify volunteer and philanthropic activities). In many cases these activities support the development of local tourism services and facilities.

Some educational tourism offerings are specifically intended to acquaint members of the diaspora with their ancestral homeland. These are often designed for young people who have little or no direct experience of the country of their ancestors. Interactions between tour participants and their local peers are part of the learning experience. Trips such as those run by the Fund for Armenian Relief and Birthright Israel are intended to foster a durable sense of belonging to the broader nation, which in turn often leads to a sense of obligation to the home-land and a desire to contribute to its development. Other educational tours focus simply on learning the language or history of the homeland.

A. Forms of Diaspora Tourism

The definition of *tourism* is broad. The World Tourism Organization defines tourists as people who "travel to and stay in places outside their usual environment for more than twenty-four (24) hours and not more than one consecutive year for leisure, business and other purposes not related to the exercise of an activity remunerated from within the place visited."[5] This chapter focuses on those forms of tourism dedicated to serving diasporas or where diaspora members play a role in the development of infrastructure and services that support tourism. A number of forms of diaspora tourism are mentioned below, but the discussion focuses on "heritage" tourism — a particularly promising avenue for diaspora-driven development.

Diaspora members' *self-directed visits* to their regions of origin may combine visits to friends and family with conventional tourist or leisure activities like going to the beach or attending cultural events. But many diaspora tourists also engage in activities of a more specialized kind. For example, they may choose to have medical procedures carried out, prospect for business opportunities, or take care of emigration-related logistics. Often, diaspora visitors use country-of-origin passports, which leads to an underestimation of their numbers and of their role in tourism and tourism-related development.[6] Those who enter of "visiting friends and relatives" (VFR) visas are not regarded as tourists by the county of origin — despite the fact that VFR visitors carry funds, values, and ideas (economic and social remittances[7]) that potentially affect local development.

Medical tourism. National tourism campaigns that reach, but do not necessarily target, diasporas promote their countries' medical infrastructure and expertise, as well as the competitiveness of their prices. Of the cases reviewed for this book, the Philippines, India, Taiwan, and Cuba all have strong medical tourism campaigns that show an awareness of diaspora members as potential clients and promoters. As a result, the medical sectors of these countries have benefited from diaspora investment, philanthropy, and volunteerism. Overall, however, diaspora involvement in medical tourism is difficult to gauge — again, because it is not measured separately.

---

5   UNWTO, *UNWTO Technical Manual: Collection of Tourism Expenditure Statistics* (Madrid: UNWTO, 1995), 14, http://pub.unwto.org/WebRoot/Store/Shops/Infoshop/Products/1034/1034-1.pdf. Retrieved 2009-03-26.

6   See Alex Asiedu, "Some benefits of migrants' return visits to Ghana," *Population, Space and Place*, vol. 11 no. 1 (2005): 1-11.

7   See Peggy Levitt, *The Transnational Villagers* (Berkeley, CA: University of California Press, 2001) for a discussion of social remittances among Dominican emigrants.

Business tourism by diaspora groups or individuals has strong development potential. Conference facilities and top hotels are marketed directly to diaspora business people and professional associations through Web sites and as part of VIP tours. In many cases, an introduction to business opportunities is combined with visits to top tourist attractions as countries of origin court high-net-worth diaspora members.

Longer-term return visits can also involve a mix of diaspora tourism and investment. Retirement to the homeland, seasonal migration of seniors from the north to warmer climates, and the building of second homes for prolonged visits all fall under this category. Governments and private-sector companies often promote such offerings to diasporas. For example, the government of the Philippines ran a site called "The Philippines: Live Your Dreams," which marketed homes to the Filipino diaspora.[8]

Heritage tourism centers on history and culture. While the term usually refers to cultural heritage — embodied in historical and archaeological sites, arts, festivals, and pilgrimages — some observers include natural heritage as well, particularly where it is linked to a way of life. Heritage tourism schemes do not exclusively involve the diaspora. The United Nations Economic, Social and Cultural Organization (UNESCO) designates outstanding landmarks as World Heritage Sites, and by doing so attracts many international tourists. Such sites serve as a significant development resource for poor countries since they attract international funds for their restoration and preservation as well as tourism revenue. Some sites are promoted to international tourists as much as or even more than to domestic or diaspora tourists. The Maya Route in Mexico and Central America and Angkor Wat in Cambodia are two examples of this pattern. However, the presentation of local culture to outsiders requires sensitivity and tact so as not to trivialize or denigrate local practices.

Customized tours for diaspora individuals or groups may also be initiated in the country of settlement. Multinational cruises, transnational family reunions, and overland tours of heritage sites certainly fall within the category of diaspora tourism, but their development potential is proportional to the degree to which locally owned and operated resources are used.

---

8   Government of the Philippines, "The Philippines: Live Your Dreams," www.liveyourdreams.ph (accessed June 15, 2010; site now discontinued).

Some forms of heritage tourism exclusively involve diasporas — for example, *genealogy tourism* conducted by those researching their family trees. (Genealogy tourism is also known as "cemetery tourism" for the tendency of visitors to search out their ancestors' final resting places.) Private and public initiatives publicized through national tourism organizations help diaspora members track down documentation and locate graves. The Discover Ireland Web site, for example, suggests relevant information that can be gathered before making a trip (for example, the ancestor's name, date of birth, parish of origin, and religious denomination, and the names of his or her parents or spouse). The Web site also lists genealogical information sources, and links to the Ulster Historical Foundation, "a long-established, highly reputable research and publishing agency" that "offers extensive knowledge on the sources available for tracing Irish and Scots-Irish ancestors. Services include online databases of over 2 million records, genealogy and history books, and personal ancestral research."[9]

Box 1. Genealogy Tourism in India

The Ministry of Overseas Indian Affairs in the states of Uttar Pradesh and Bihar has a project that allows persons of Indian origin to apply to have their roots traced. The goal is to increase both tourism and philanthropy among the Indian diaspora. Those targeted by the campaign are largely descendants of slaves or indentured servants settled in the Caribbean, Mauritius, and Fiji. In an interesting twist, federal and state governments are also actively promoting "cemetery tourism" among British, French, Portuguese, and Dutch people whose ancestors died in India during the colonial period.[10]

Scotland's Homecoming 2009[11] is an example of a very deliberate effort to tap the benefits of diaspora tourism. Scotland dubbed 2009 the year of homecoming and organized a number of events, with a clan gathering as the centerpiece. Widely advertised, the promotion was meant to attract Scots from around the world and increase local tourism both directly, by attracting an influx of foreigners (with an average ten-day stay per participant), and indirectly, by educating Scots to be "better

---

9 Tourism Ireland, "Irish the World Over" (accessed Sept. 27, 2010), www.discoverireland.com/us/ireland-things-to-see-and-do/culture-and-sights/trace-your-ancestry/irish-the-world-over; Tourism Ireland, "The major records repositories in Ireland" (accessed Sept. 27, 2010), www.discoverireland.com/us/ireland-things-to-see-and-do/culture-and-sights/trace-your-ancestry/the-major-repositories-in-ireland.
10 AMN Abdi, "Wooing Tomb Travelers," *South China Morning Post*, July 26, 2009.
11 Moira Birtwistle, "Genealogy Tourism: The Scottish Market Opportunities," in *Niche Tourism,* ed. Marina Novelli (Oxford: Butterworth-Heinemann, 2005) : 59–72.

ambassadors" of a cosmopolitan, modern Scotland, one that has gone beyond kilts, swords, and smokestacks. The popular "I Am a Scot" campaign videotaped those with Scottish roots saying what made them a Scot — and invited write-ins to a dedicated Web site.[12] The campaign encouraged diaspora members to feel that they have a stake in the country's future.

The participants in Scotland's Homecoming 2009 mirrored the extent of the Scottish diaspora: they came from Australia, New Zealand, Canada, Romania, Sweden, Russia, Argentina, Japan, and every US state except North Dakota.[13] The direct development impact was controversial — not as much money came in as had been hoped, and many vendors and service providers went unpaid. A May 2010 government review of the event, however, stated that it had a positive effect on local tourist initiatives. Homecoming 2014 has been confirmed and will coincide with the Commonwealth Games, Ryder Cup, and the 700th anniversary of the Battle of Bannockburn.[14]

African diaspora tourism. A prominent example of heritage tourism is that involving the African diaspora — also known as "roots" tourism, in part because of *Roots*, the 1977 television miniseries (and the book, by Alex Haley, on which it was based), which inspired a generation of African Americans to learn more about their ancestry. The term *slavery tourism* is used by some tourism boards to promote important sites of the slave trade, but it fails to capture the wider cultural and natural environment elements of African diaspora heritage tourism.[15] Numerous tour operators, regional associations, intergovernmental organizations, and individual countries actively develop and promote cultural, historic, and natural heritage sites under the umbrella of African diaspora tourism. UNESCO supports the development of African Diaspora Heritage Trails — an initiative originally proposed by the government of Bermuda to preserve and

---

12 Promotional materials for Homecoming 2009 are a good example of the discourse and logic being used in heritage tourism: "Tend to your Scottish roots. They say a Scotsman carries his country in his heart wherever he may go. And that sense of belonging is passed down through the generations — so that today millions of people worldwide are very proud to be the sons and daughters of Scotland. And visiting Scotland becomes much more than just a trip when you are given the opportunity to retrace your very own ancestral footsteps;" http://cometoscotland.com/what-to-do/search-your-ancestry.

13 Dani Garavelli, "Homeward bound: Scotland's diaspora heads to Edinburgh for the highpoint of the Homecoming celebrations this month," *Scotland on Sunday*, July 5, 2009.

14 Visit Scotland, "Discover your Scottish roots and start planning your ancestral journey to Scotland," www.ancestralscotland.com.

15 Slavery tourism also falls into what some call "dark tourism" — visiting sites to pay honor to those who have suffered from tragedies such as the Holocaust, slave trade, or natural disasters such as Hurricane Katrina.

explain the artifacts of slave life — and commemoration of the slave route, which links sites in Africa and the Americas associated with the slave trade.

Religious or faith tourism. Visits to sites of spiritual significance are increasing around the globe. North Americans alone spend over $10 billion annually on religious tourism, traveling as groups or individuals for pilgrimage, missionary, volunteer, or fellowship purposes. A religious duty to be carried out at least once by every Muslim who is able, the annual Hajj pilgrimage to Mecca in Saudi Arabia is the largest single movement of its kind (about 2 million people took part in 2009). Clingingsmith and others argue that the Hajj promotes shared principles and identity, increasing tolerance and unity among Muslims.[16] Some of the earliest accommodations for personal travel were developed for pilgrims — in Syria for the Hajj, for example, or in the south of France for pilgrims on the *Route Frances* to Santiago de Compostela, Spain.

An estimated 70 million Hindus go to the Ganges River each year in January and February.[17] In 2009, 140,000 pilgrims spent as many as six weeks walking or biking the Camino de Santiago to Santiago de Compostela, site of the tomb of St. James — an estimated 200,000 will make the trip in 2010, a jubilee year. Church officials have granted forgiveness of sins (indulgences) to pilgrims who complete one of the official routes since the Middle Ages. While most pilgrims stay in humble lodges and shelters (some requiring only a voluntary donation), tour agencies are combining pilgrimage and tourism. One offers a ten-day, $2,552 package for this "crown jewel of walking tours," complete with elegant food and lodgings leading up to the simpler fare offered during the last, pilgrimage-dedicated days of the tour. The *Camino*, a UNESCO World Heritage Site, was awarded the Council of Europe's first European Cultural Route status in 1987.

The burgeoning religious tourism industry is not limited to traditional religious routes. Scotland plays up its role in the reformation. A major European travel firm offers tours of Poland exploring the life of Pope John Paul II. Visits to the shrines of local Sufi saints are a major organizing principle of internal travel in Morocco and draw visiting migrants as well.

---

16 David Lawrence Clingingsmith, Asim Ijaz Khwaja, and Michael Kremer, "Estimating the Impact of the Hajj: Religion and Tolerance in Islam's Global Gathering" (HKS Working Paper No. RWP08-022, Harvard University, John F. Kennedy School of Government, April 2008), http://ssrn.com/abstract=1124213.

17 Mary Jordan, "Seeking Answers with Field Trips in Faith," *Washington Post*, June 25, 2007 , www.washingtonpost.com/wp-dyn/content/article/2007/06/24/AR2007062401422.html.

Peak experiences and exposure programs. Birthright programs are designed to bring diasporas into closer contact with their heritage. They tend to operate in countries with a strong sense of national identity, transcending territoriality, and that have a commitment to perpetuating this identity, especially among second and subsequent generations. Exposure programs include study tours for youth, academic exchange programs, and VIP tours for business travelers and government officials. In another variant, Always and Forever, a company based in Portland, Washington, offers specialized tours in which families experience the homeland of their adopted children while the children connect with their birth country.[18]

The development potential of birthright programs and exposure programs is short-term and direct (through funds spent by participants) as well as long-term and indirect (through participants' future contributions as tourists, volunteers, investors, and advocates). The careful construction of these diaspora tours is described by Shaul Kelner as "a form of political socialization that fosters identification with a nation-state and a sense of belonging in a transnational ethnic community."[19]

Box 2. Birthright Israel

Since 1999, hundreds of thousands of young American Jews have visited Israel on an all-expenses-paid ten-day pilgrimage tour known as Birthright Israel. The most elaborate of the state-supported homeland tours that are cropping up all over the world, this tour seeks to foster in the Jewish diaspora a lifelong sense of attachment to Israel based on ethnic and political solidarity. The program is supported by a partnership between private philanthropists acting through the Birthright Israel Foundation, the government of Israel, and Jewish community organizations. Over a half-billion dollars (and counting) has been spent cultivating this attachment, and despite the ongoing Israeli-Palestinian conflict, the tours are still going strong.[20]

Birthright Armenia takes its inspiration from Birthright Israel. It is a nongovernmental organization (NGO) that partners with internship organizations and study-abroad programs to offer young diaspora

---

18 See Always and Forever Adoption Homeland Tours, "Through adoption homeland tours, we help the adoptive families to experience the children's culture of origin, discover their heritage, create positive memories of their birth country and build new friendships," www.alwaysforever.us/home/home.html.

19 Shaul Kelner, *Tours that Bind: Diaspora, Pilgrimage and Israeli Birthright Tourism* (New York, NY: New York Univ. Press, 2010), xvi.

20 Ibid.

members professional internships and community service placements in Armenia, lasting anywhere from eight weeks to a year. Although it is primarily a volunteer project, its promotion of leadership, a shared identity, and cultural ambassadorship make it a good example of how tourism and volunteerism can intersect as forms of diaspora engagement. Program participants returning to their countries of residence participate in alumni and networking programs and act as informal advocates of Armenia. As Kelner notes, birthright programs are becoming increasingly common, often in the form of public-private partnerships. Offering a "peak experience" of intense emotional engagement with the country of origin represents a new, instrumental approach to tourism.

VIP tours are a variation on the peak experience theme, but more focused on specialized adult markets. The Philippines' Department of Foreign Affairs, Department of Tourism, and Department of Trade and Industry run an annual Ambassadors, Consuls General, and Tourism Directors Tour. The goal of the tour is to get second- and third-generation Filipino Americans to see the country not just as the homeland of their parents and grandparents but as a tropical paradise with rich cultural offerings where they will always feel at home — and which they will speak about positively and promote with vigor.[21]

Asia Pacific Philanthropy, a nongovernmental organization, also recommends that the overseas Filipino organizations develop programs to expose their members, especially second-generation Filipinos, to development work in the Philippines. Likewise, in China, sending delegations to diaspora communities and hosting visits from diaspora community members are major avenues for tourism.

Nation branding refers to the process by which national governments create a "competitive identity," actively marketing themselves around a set of core messages and images.[22] Direct media marketing (through TV, radio, print, and the Internet) and social networking sites (Facebook, YouTube) are used to put a "fresh face" on a country and overturn negative perceptions.[23] Diaspora-oriented and nation-branding tourism campaigns such as "Incredible India" highlight iconic images, beauty spots, and colorful festivals such as Holi, with the intention of evoking what Morgan and Pritchard (2002) call an "embodied

---

21 Philippine Department of Tourism, "Philippines: Warmth - Wealth – Wonders" (accessed Sept. 27, 2010), www.experiencephilippines.ph/LM/news/id-1240299764502.html.

22 *Handbook on Tourism Destinations Branding* (Madrid: UNWTO and European Travel Commission, 2009).

23 Christopher Graves of Ogilvy PR China, *PR Week*, October 30, 2009.

empathy" that persuades tourists and emigrants to visit or revisit a particular destination. By appealing to and even fostering diaspora identity, nation branding increases the potential for diaspora engagement of other kinds.

Just as companies or universities do, nations hire public relations firms to guide the branding process. In a recent article, the CEO of one such firm articulated ways in which China could use branding to overcome being seen as a threat to economic security, Western power, and the environment. His recommendations include promoting contemporary art and architecture; sponsoring exchanges of students, thinkers, and artists to build cross-cultural awareness and overturn stereotypes; producing a narrative of forging world-changing technologies; and creating a tourism brand that cherishes regional differences and can be spread by positive word-of-mouth and social media.[24]

The Indian government makes a coordinated effort to incorporate its diaspora into the national tourism industry as tourists and philanthropists. The "Incredible India" campaign works not only to increase the appeal of India as a tourism destination but also to cement national and diaspora identity — and this, in turn, increases the participation of the diaspora in tourism and tourism projects. The campaign is carried out across multiple media platforms, including an international award-winning commercial. A coffee-table book, *Explore Rural India,* promotes the development potential of rural tourism by highlighting UN-funded rural tourism sites. The campaign's YouTube page is young and vibrant, with multiple video clips, including one entertaining series in which a top Bollywood star pleads with resident Indians to remember the ethos of the traditional saying "The guest is God." Comment streams praise the videos and assert pride in being Indian. (The IT-heavy campaign reflects the economic importance of information technology to India's development.)

B. Can Tourism Create a Diaspora Identity?

Arguably, efforts to create national brands to promote tourism have the potential to shape or cement diaspora identities, or even to create diaspora identities where none exist. Evans argues that promoting "Mexicanidad"[25] cements a national identity to motivate tourism and economic development. Giving priority to the Mayan heritage of Mexicans and Central Americans over other indigenous roots — in an

---

24 Ibid.

extremely diverse region — may shape diaspora identity (see Box 3). This is no esoteric matter. In the case of Honduras, for example, it is very difficult to find funding for preservation, research, or development of non-Mayan sites because of the importance that the national government places on Mayan sites for tourism development. Formal education and national and international advertising on television and the Internet reinforce the Mayan identity. When emigrants returning to Honduras seek out their cultural roots, they turn to (the admittedly spectacular) Copan ruins; "secondary" sites rank below the beach, colonial towns, or Lake Yojoa on their itineraries.

Box 3. Privileging Diaspora Identities: The Maya Route and Mundo Maya

The Maya Route traces more than two millennia of the pre-Columbian Mayan civilization through the "Mayan world" of Mexico, Belize, Guatemala, Honduras, and El Salvador. Arguably, these efforts aim to foster a *transborder* identity with which Mexican and Central American emigrants might identify — in a sense creating a regional diaspora identity. Figueroa and others (2010) give an archaeological perspective on how the label "Maya" is being applied to regions with predominantly non-Mayan heritage in an effort to capitalize on private and government tourism funds, such as in Honduras's Bay Islands, which are predominantly Garifuna. Contemporary Mayan people and mestizo descendants do not appear to identify as a Mayan diaspora and, as such, are not directly engaged in tourism development apart from employment in crafts, tourism, or lower-end jobs in hotels, restaurants, and resorts. At the same time, anthropologists have identified a trend toward the Mayanization of native Central American heritage, in which the development of Mayan heritage sites is favored over those of other pre-Columbian groups (for example, the Lenca in Honduras). Fostering identity, therefore, has serious implications for which resources — and which regions — are given priority in tourism development.[26]

---

25 Graeme Evans, "Mundo Maya: From Cancún to City of Culture, World Heritage in Post-Colonial Mesoamerica," *Current Issues in Tourism* 7, No. 3 (2004): 315–29.
26 E. Christian Wells and Karla L. Davis-Salazar, "Environmental Worldview and Ritual Economy among the Honduran Lenca," in *Dimensions of Ritual Economy*, eds. E. Christian Wells and Patricia A. McAnany, (Bingley, UK: Emerald Group Publishing Ltd., 2008): 189-217; Evans, "Mundo Maya: From Cancún to City of Culture."

C. How Do Governments Promote Diaspora Tourism?

Members of diasporas can play a variety of direct and indirect roles related to tourism and development. In addition to being tourists, diaspora travelers can simultaneously be (or later become) direct investors, remitters, philanthropists, volunteers, students, promoters, and/or informal ambassadors. Many of the programs discussed in this chapter are designed to cultivate multiple roles.

National governments (and in some cases state or local governments) and NGOs reach out to diasporas in a variety of ways, including (1) creating programs dedicated to diaspora tourism, (2) offering educational and exchange programs, (3) subsidizing heritage and sporting events, (4) developing a strong Internet presence, (5) marketing carefully crafted national brands across multiple media, and (6) making entry to countries of origin easier and less expensive.

Tourism is widely recognized as an essential industry in many developing countries. In addition to creating jobs — many of which pay relatively well without requiring extensive qualifications — it can promote infrastructure development and generate vital foreign exchange. While recognizing the importance of the tourism sector, most governments do little to take advantage of diaspora ties to promote tourism. There are exceptions, of course, some of which are discussed here. While tourism development projects such as Mexico's *Ruta del Tequila*[27] and the Rose and Saffron routes of Morocco[28] are built around elements of cultural heritage, they are not especially marketed to diaspora groups. Other countries that have barely begun to develop tourism could look to diaspora populations as an entry point into the sector. A country such as Liberia, for example, with its strong historical connection to the US African American population, might market itself as a diaspora destination as it emerges from war — although only a concerted effort might dispel historical tensions between the African American diaspora elite that returned to Liberia in the nineteenth century and the population with no emigrant background.

Once a government has taken the first step of deciding to woo the diaspora tourism market, it can ease travel for emigrants and their descendants. Several countries, including Vietnam and India, have provisions allowing their diasporas to visit without a visa. Filipino Canadians are not required to get visas to visit the Philippines if they travel with a

---

27 *La Ruta del Tequila*/The Tequila Trail, www.rutadeltequila.org.mx.
28 *Tourisme solidaire atlas Maroc*, www.tourisme-atlas.com; Migrations et Développement: www.migdev.org.

Canadian passport. The five members of the East African Community (EAC) — Burundi, Kenya, Rwanda, Tanzania, and Uganda — are reportedly close to agreement on a common visa for foreigners (citizens of the five states can already travel visa-free within EAC), a measure that would greatly facilitate diaspora tourism throughout the region.[29]

Volunteers participate directly in tourism by staging events in host and home countries and by developing information technologies and promotional materials. As with business travelers, those volunteering in countries of origin spend money on hotels and restaurants and may stay on to travel as tourists within the region.

Educational, birthright, and VIP tour programs widely expect that diasporas will promote tourism and the national "brand." In some cases the role is particularly clear: the Executive Committee of Overseas Vietnamese in France is pursuing a campaign to encourage every person in the diaspora community to persuade ten French friends to travel to Vietnam. The initiative supplements major retail and hospitality campaigns designed to meet an ambitious target of 4.2 million international visitors in 2010 — 400,000 more than in 2009, even as government funding of the industry has been reduced.[30] Some evidence supports the expectation that migrants will promote tourism in their countries of origin. A World Bank study found that migrants do indeed give advice to others about vacationing in their home countries. According to this study, "91 percent of New Zealanders, 75 percent of Papua New Guineans, 66 percent of Ghanaians, 56 percent of Tongans and 44 percent of Micronesians have done this. Although our surveys do not permit quantification of the value of new tourism created by such advice, they do show migrants engaging in this type of tourism promotion much more frequently than nonmigrants (with the exception of Micronesia)."[31]

Governments may also encourage diaspora investment in the tourism industry by providing finance or loan guarantees as well as technical assistance and marketing support. Tax breaks or other forms of support for restoring or converting historic buildings to use as hotels or restaurants can increase the attraction of visiting certain areas.

29 Associated Press, "Kenya: Common Visa Favored For 5 East African Nations," *The New York Times*, July 3, 2010, www.nytimes.com/2010/07/03/world/africa/03briefs-VISA.html.
30 Vietnam Net Bridge, "Move to Lure Foreign Tourists," September 3, 2010, www.vietnamopentour.com.vn/vietnam-information/news/move-to-lure-foreign-tourists.html.
31 John Gibson and David McKenzie, "The Economic Consequences of 'Brain Drain' of the Best and Brightest: Microeconomic Evidence from Five Countries" (Working Paper 5394, Development Research Group, Finance and Private Sector Development Team, World Bank, Washington, DC, August 2010).

The restoration of *kasbahs* in Morocco (akin to the restoration of historic buildings as *paradors* in Spain) provides opportunities for creative public-private partnerships as well. Many private investors are returned migrants or the emigrant families of local residents, while country-of-origin governments partner with donor agencies to support tourism development.

Government tourist organizations can make a special effort to reach out to emigrants and their descendants, particularly those that provide travel services in their communities. For example, the African American travel agent Meredith McCleary became a specialist in travel to Botswana and southern African spa destinations after completing a four-day training at an International Destination Expo in South Africa.

Governments should certainly take the lead in mobilizing resources from the private sector, nonprofit organizations and foundations, and multilateral and bilateral donors to preserve and inventory cultural assets that can add value to the tourist experience. The assets may be tangible, such as buildings or monuments, or intangible, such as festivals or exhibitions. Diasporas can be important partners in such efforts.

D. Civil Society Engagement in Diaspora Tourism and Development

The NGO *Migrations et Développement* (M/D) was founded by migrants who had returned to southern Morocco from France with the idea of establishing businesses in their home villages. Poor infrastructure and lack of electricity made successful business development impossible. Through M/D they brought electricity to the region and later improved roads and water services.[32] With the assistance of the Moroccan Social Development Agency and the French Development Agency, M/D turned to fostering tourism. It developed a series of tourism routes organized around the production of saffron, rose oil, and argan oil. Maps for each route also point out lodging and restaurants (many established by M/D members) as well as cultural and natural attractions. The organization's interactive tourism atlas, *www.tourisme-atlas.com,* links directly to rates and descriptions of each hostel. While Moroccans resident abroad are only 10 percent of the clients for these facilities, returned migrants were the crucial first movers who leveraged the creative public-private investment in planning and infrastructure that made

---

32 For more on *Migrations et Développement,* see Natasha Iskander, *Creative State: Forty Years of Migration and Development Policy in Morocco and Mexico* (Ithaca, NY: ILR Press, 2010).

tourism possible. Some migrants invest while remaining abroad and others upon returning to Morocco.

E. Challenges for Diaspora Tourism

Fundamental safety and security. Diaspora members may have better information about potential threats to safety in their countries of origin than other tourists, and may be able to put such threats in perspective more easily. They can distinguish among subregions that have different levels of security, whereas foreign tourists may be more likely to dismiss an entire country because of reports of trouble in one area. However, diaspora travelers are as sensitive as any tourist to the threats posed by armed conflict, lawlessness, pervasive corruption, dangerous transport infrastructure, and so forth. Even the first movers will not move until certain baseline conditions are met for tourism — although they may still feel called upon to travel to the country for other reasons.

Keeping benefits in the target communities/nations. The development potential of tourism depends in part on involvement with the host population. Diaspora tourists are more likely to have the interest, the linguistic skills, the contacts, and the foreknowledge to engage with local people and enterprises. But these inclinations cannot be taken for granted, and they can be easily frustrated by opaque or unwelcoming local services.

Respect for visiting diasporas. It is, unfortunately, fairly common for diaspora tourists to experience different, and less welcoming, treatment in their homelands than that accorded to people perceived as "real" foreigners. Members of diasporas may even be resented for expecting such treatment, as if they were putting themselves above the local residents. Tourist industries that hope to attract diaspora visitors must ensure that they enjoy at least the same level of facilities and services as any other tourist paying the same amount — and it would be smart to treat them especially well in order to earn their loyalty and further involvement with the homeland.

Disposable income. Economic conditions in their countries of current residence and diaspora members' economic success affect their disposable income and time, and thus their travel plans. Travel patterns and spending vary greatly by income level. The country of origin may be a comparatively attractive destination for diaspora members in economic terms, as the hospitality of family and friends may defray some expenses. This potential advantage may be counterbalanced, however, by the obligation to bring presents or make cash gifts to family and friends.

Visa and mobility limitations affect diaspora member's ability to visit their homeland and affect the comparative advantage of nations within regional heritage areas.

Catering to generational differences. Interest in homeland tourism varies by generation, whether within a given diaspora or across diasporas. In some diasporas, especially those that originated in refugee flows, the first generation is alienated from the homeland government and discourages all interaction. Subsequent generations, however, may want to explore their roots and exploit their comparative advantages of linguistic and cultural familiarity in business or other forms of engagement. In other situations, the first generation maintains very close personal ties that diminish in later generations or transform into less personalized cultural interests. Tourist industries must be nimble to track and adjust to generational changes in the level and nature of interest in travel among diasporas.

II. Nostalgia Trade

Solid research supports the conclusion that the presence of an immigrant population leads to larger trade flows between the country of origin and the country of destination. This trend is evident in Spain, where exports to immigrants' countries of origin has increased,[33] and in Canada, where both exports to and imports from origin countries increased.[34] Such findings suggest that diasporas do indeed promote the integration of their countries of origin into the world economy.

Nostalgia trade involves goods produced in the country of origin or ancestry of a migrant group and marketed to that group in the country of destination. The traded goods, often foodstuffs, are distinctive to the country (or region) of origin and are somehow implicated in its culture. In addition to foodstuffs, such goods include films and music, reading material, utensils and dishes, ornaments, textiles and clothing, jewelry,

---

33 Giovanni Peri and Francisco Requena, "The Trade Creation Effect of Immigrants: Evidence from the Remarkable Case of Spain" (Working Paper 15625, National Bureau of Economic Research, December 2009).
34 James Partridge and Hartley Furtan, "Immigration Wave Effects on Canada's Trade Flows," *Canadian Public Policy* 34, no. 2(2008): 193-214.

and ceremonial goods. Nostalgia goods help migrants to maintain a sense of identity and community while living transnational lives.

Interestingly, Manuel Orozco found that commercial distribution networks for nostalgia goods in the United States are well developed and that "most migrants do not use informal mechanisms anymore to buy or bring home country goods."[35] The distribution networks rely primarily on ethnic distributors and small ethnic shops in migrant neighborhoods. The shops specialize in home-country goods and, in many cases, function as informal meeting places for diaspora members. In many cases, they also serve as points of distribution for community information or for the collection of contributions for charitable purposes (in the aftermath of a natural disaster affecting the home country, for example).

In a nationwide survey of 1,200 immigrants from 12 different nationalities across the United States, supplemented by interviews in 50 ethnic shops, Orozco found a very high participation of migrants in the market for home-country goods (see Table 1). Migrants' expenditures on nostalgia products "range up to almost $1,000 per year and may amount to over twenty billion dollars annually" in the United States alone.[36] Orozco also found that nostalgia foodstuffs accounted for a substantial part of migrant households' budgets: in 27 percent of cases, more than half of the diet. The high use of home-country products was also associated with other ways of maintaining connection such as calling home frequently, going on annual trips, and so forth. A January 2010 study by the Honduran Central Bank reinforces Orozco's research with its finding that 75 percent of Hondurans abroad consume nostalgia goods.[37]

---

35 Orozco, *Tasting Identity.*
36 Ibid.
37 Remesas y Desarollo, "Remesas familiares enviadas por hondureños residentes en el exterior y gastos efectuados en el país durante sus visitas," www.remesasydesarrollo.org/documentos/ remesas-familiares-enviadas-por-hondurenos-residentes-en-el-exterior-y-gastos-efectuados- en-el-pais-durante-sus-visitas.

Table 1. Percentage of Immigrants Who Buy Home-Country Goods, by Country of Origin

	Colombia	Ecuador	El Salvador	Guatemala	Guyana	Honduras	Mexico	Nicaragua	Dominican Republic	Bolivia	Jamaica
% who buy home-country goods	81	95	56	50	82	74	76	83	65	70	64

Source: Manuel Orozco, B. Lindsay Lowell, Micah Bump, and Rachel Fedewa, "Transnational Engagement, Remittances and their Relation to Development in Latin America and the Caribbean" (Washington, DC: Institute for the Study of International Migration, Georgetown University, 2005).

A. Moving Beyond the Diaspora Niche Market

While nostalgia goods help to preserve the ethnic and cultural identity of diaspora communities, they also help to integrate the country of origin into the global marketplace. There are challenges, however, in moving beyond the network of ethnic stores into the wider market-place and reaching nondiaspora consumers — or bringing the wider market into ethnic stores. Trade fairs are an important marketing tool for country-of-origin producers, and are often sponsored by their governments. But marketing remains a barrier to entry for many small producers who cannot find distributors to the countries of destination. On a research trip in the Mexican state of Zacatecas in 2009, one of the authors discussed the issue with two small producers who were eager to sell to Mexicans living in the United States. One, a cooperative producing mezcal, found the general market dominated by tequila (the two liquors are virtually identical, but only that produced in the state of Jalisco can be called tequila) and the diaspora market for mezcal saturated by too many small producers. Another found the logisti-cal requirements of selling through large chain stores too costly and demanding for his small enterprise.

Many countries have export promotion agencies such as Pro-Mexico, which was established in 2007 to strengthen Mexico's position in the global marketplace. But few of them promote the artisanal producers who are responsible for a significant proportion of nostalgia goods. And were they to succeed in expanding the market, many artisanal producers might have difficulty keeping up with demand. Producer cooperatives might be better equipped to meet the challenges of going to scale, especially when that involves meeting more elaborate con-sumer protection standards in the importing country. Scale and safety requirements are among the reasons that some nostalgia products succeed in "going mainstream" yet fall short as promoters of development when production shifts to the country of destination. Although salsa has overtaken ketchup in the value of US sales, most salsa production is now US-based.

Table 2. Consumption of Nostalgia Goods in 12 Countries

Country of Origin	Number of Products Bought (#)	Times Bought per Month (#)	Price Paid per Unit ($)	Monthly Expense ($)	Total Paid per Year ($)
Honduras	3	8	4	95	1141
Ethiopia	3	14	3	90	1077
Philippines	3	3	13	99	1020
Ghana	3	7	3	77	919
Paraguay	3	7	3	74	884
Dominican Republic	3	8	3	66	793
Total	3	6	4	64	768
India	4	4	4	58	694
Nigeria	3	6	4	57	683
Colombia	4	5	2	47	564
Mexico	3	3	4	41	494
El Salvador	2	4	4	38	458
Bolivia	2	5	4	34	408

Source: Thomas Debass and Manuel Orozco, "Digesting Nostalgic Trade: A Prequel to a Value Chain Approach" (USAID Breakfast Seminar Series Presentation, Washington, DC, November 20, 2008), http://www.microlinks.org/ev_en.php?ID=29168_201&ID2=DO_TOPIC.

Public- or private-sector donors may play a part in helping nostalgia-goods manufacturers expand their operations to meet demand. In one example, the United States Agency for International Development (USAID) used a credit guarantee scheme to help secure financing for an enterprise in Ethiopia (Etteff Flour Factory and Injera Bakery) that sells teff flour and injera both locally and internationally — including to the United States. Expansion was needed because the factory was to become the sole distributor of injera in Saudi Arabia and other countries in the Middle East.[38]

---

38 United States Agency for International Development (USAID), *DDI Project Quarterly Update, March 31, 2010* (Washington, DC: USAID, 2010).

When Oromo refugees from Ethiopia were unable to find jobs in the United Kingdom, they reached out to the Lorna Young Foundation (LYF). The small charity drew on its experiences with Oromo coffee smallholders and received support from Bolling Coffee (a family-run international coffee importer) to establish the Oromo Coffee Company (OCC). The social enterprise sells its upscale, free-trade, organic coffees to independent delicatessens, ethically aware food stores, corporate purchasers, and faith groups. Income and employment benefits reach producers in Ethiopia and diaspora suppliers in the United Kingdom.

Through OCC and local volunteers, LYF builds skills, experience, and capacity among refugees; fosters income generation and employment opportunities for Oromo both in the United Kingdom and in Ethiopia; and increases UK consumers' respect for fairly traded products and refugees.[39] LYF meets its goal of "helping farmers in developing countries to become more fully empowered and supporting them to shorten the supply chain" through business and enterprise education, marketing, public relations, education on ethical certification, and so on. It partners with a range of individual trustees, commercial ethnic traders (such as Zaytoun and Imani), Coop College UK, Trading Visions, local grassroots campaigners, and community groups.

B. The Value-Chain Approach

Nostalgia goods flow through a multistep process involving manufacturers, home-country distributors, host-country importers, wholesalers, and stores — with a number of middlemen and at least one border crossing along the way (see Figure 1). The potential for policy or project intervention can be found at each step. LYF's activities with OCC demonstrate a multifaceted approach to development that focuses on increasing the value added to a product at each step and, as a result, increasing the overall value of the product.

---

39 Lorna Young Foundation (LYF), "The Oromo Coffee Company and the Lorna Young Foundation" (Information Sheet, 2010); LYF and Oromo Coffee Company, "The Story behind it...The Oromo Coffee Company and the Lorna Young Foundation" (PowerPoint presentation, 2010), www. oromocoffee.org; Andrew Bounds, "Ethiopian refugees discover benefits of coffee," *Financial Times,* May 7, 2009, www.ethiopianreview.com/articles/3989.

Figure 1. Flow of Nostalgic Goods into the United States

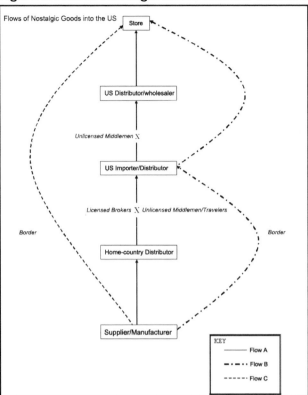

Source: Manuel Orozco, Tasting Identity: Trends in Migrant Demands for Home Country Goods (Washington, DC: US Agency for International Development, 2008).

USAID has adopted such a "value-chain approach" to linking multiple small firms along international, national, and local chains, tapping into economic growth opportunities while "ensuring both the incentives for and the capability to compete in and benefit from market participation."[40] "The focus of the value chain approach is therefore on transforming relationships — particularly between firms linked vertically in the value chain to help stakeholders to: a) become competitive by upgrading their products and distribution, and b) remain competitive by adapting to changes in end-markets, in the enabling environment, or within the chain."[41] A value-chain approach is useful in deciding how to tap the development potential of nostalgia trade in both origin and settlement countries.

---

40 MicroLINKS Wiki, "Value Chain Development" (accessed Sept. 27, 2010), http://apps.develebridge.net/amap/index.php/Value_Chain_Development.

41 MicroLINKS Wiki, "Key Elements of the Value Chain Approach" (accessed Sept. 27, 2010), http://apps.develebridge.net/amap/index.php/Key_Elements_of_the_Value_Chain_Approach.

III. Policy Options and Conclusions

Various combinations of the policy recommendations given below are relevant to most organizations interested in the development potential of diaspora tourism and nostalgia trade. These include governments in countries of origin and residence, donors (bilateral, multinational, and private), private businesses, trade associations, and civil society. All are aimed at "expanding the pie" beyond a handful of sites or companies in order to spread the benefits of tourism and trade to more areas with diaspora ties. Identifying and sharing the lessons learned with other groups is a goal of all the following policy suggestions.

Box 4. USAID-Funded Pakistani-Embroidered Cloth Exports

A three-year, $600,000 project completed in December 2007 integrated rural women into more profitable value chains, increased their economic participation, and enabled greater contribution to household incomes. With funding from USAID, Mennonite Economic Development Associates (MEDA) and the Entrepreneurship and Community Development Institute (ECDI) partnered to successfully train and deploy 213 mobile female sales agents, who unlike traditional middlemen, could conduct face-to-face transactions with sequestered embroiderers. The women sales agents purchased finished fabrics from embroiderers for sale to higher-value urban markets. As part of these transactions, the sales agents embedded product information, quality control, and contemporary designs into their services, reaching a total of 9,425 rural embroiderers. The project also stimulated the supply and demand of commercial design services into the value chain by connecting sales agents to skilled designers. On average, rural embroiderers increased their income by close to 300 percent as a result of project participation. In addition to these economic benefits, producers and sales agents participating in the project also experienced advances in their social conditions — for example, through greater say in household decisions. Program benefits are expected to continue through a number of initiatives aimed at enhancing the sustainability of services provided via the project, namely, a sales agent network association, buying houses, and business development services centers.[42] Some of the production output is sold to "suitcase exporters" — women who purchase suits and sell them to friends and neighbors in the diaspora community when they return to Canada, the United Kingdom, and the United States. Exports are rising as the quality of production improves.[43]

---

42 Mennonite Economic Development Associates (MEDA), "Behind the Veil: Access to Markets for Homebound Women Embroiderers," www.meda.org/WhatWeDo/ProductionMarketing Linkages/WhereWeWork/Longtermprojects/BehindtheVeil.html.

43 E-mail communication between co-author Carylanna Taylor and Alex Snelgrove of MEDA, June 22 and June 24, 2010.

Some general considerations should be kept in mind. Projects need to have good information on the characteristics of the diaspora being targeted — and on the motives, scope, capacity, and manifestations of diaspora-related trade and tourism. Diaspora tourism and nostalgia trade occur across a continuum of emigrant experience ranging from emigrants with a strong primary affiliation to their country of origin, to truly transnational citizens with feet planted in both their countries of origin and of residence, to second- and later-generation descendants who are just beginning to explore their origins.

Donor agencies need to find the intersection between diaspora tourism and trade on the one hand and broader development policy on the other. Questions such as whether a donor government should play a role in promoting a specific industry, product, or value chain, or which organization should be responsible for providing training and technical assistance may be best answered on a case-by-case basis. In most cases, the answers must be determined by the country-of-origin governments, but there may still be points of entry for donors to, for example, support research, training, and capacity building.[44]

Diaspora engagement in tourism and trade can occur in conjunction with or provide an entry point to education, direct investment, philanthropy, and volunteerism. The intersections of these can provide fertile ground for development initiatives. The following subsections draw on existing programs and policies to highlight mechanisms through which stakeholders at all levels can recognize and cultivate the development potential of diaspora tourism and nostalgia trade.

We loosely group suggested interventions in diaspora trade and nostalgia tourism under the following categories:

- Education and training

- The regulatory environment

- Institutional and infrastructure development

- Research and coordination

- Branding and marketing

---

44 For example, supporting civil society and academic efforts to track Jewish heritages back to Jamaica.

A. Education and Training

Foster the interconnections between education and diaspora tourism. Heritage tourism in its many guises offers opportunities for education and cross-cultural understanding among travelers and with local populations. Teaching about national or ethnic heritage in countries of origin helps attract education-minded tourists and students and train local residents involved in tourism.[45] Teaching heritage at schools and universities in countries where diaspora populations reside broadens understanding and may help spur tourism. Offerings such as study tours tied in to university courses or language and culture "camps" may translate interest into actual visits by diaspora members and other tourists.

Educate (and learn from) travel professionals and organizations about offerings, trends, and needs that relate to diaspora tourism, with the aim to better promote cultural and heritage resources and expand diaspora and nondiaspora niche markets amenable to sustainable development.

Promote awareness of the scope and potential of diaspora tourism among local residents, in order to expand offerings and, where necessary, foster equal treatment of diaspora tourists who might otherwise be regarded as less worthy of respect than foreign tourists.[46]

Train entrepreneurs in the technical and business skills necessary to be successful in nostalgia trade and heritage tourism. Alternatively, find ways to *connect those with ideas to those with the specialized training and aptitude* needed to implement them. Organizations in home and host countries may find ways to train potential entrepreneurs, support transfer of knowledge between those receiving training and their partners abroad, and find volunteers/partners in areas of specialized knowledge (exports, health regulations, labeling, developing products suitable to the target market,[47] scaling up production) and/or basic

---

45 One roundtable participant noted that Cape Verde prioritizes technical education (for example, fisheries management). Yet, in a country where there are more Cape Verdeans living outside of the country than inside, heritage and literature offerings would be important educational experiences for visiting second and third generations, galvanizing their future participation in the cultural and economic development of their homeland.

46 India has a television and YouTube campaign that promotes hospitality and features a popular Bollywood actor.

47 Textile artisans from Oaxaca, Ecuador, initially had difficulties selling in the central valley of California because the fabric used for traditional clothing weighed too much. People were not buying even though they liked the product.

business training (human relations, bookkeeping, making a business plan).[48]

Provide critical support for innovation through training and incentives in order to add value to products and retain benefits within the diaspora or home communities. Innovation requires attention. A local community may, for example, be successful producers of agriculture products, but lack the capacity to add value to the products; for example, turning cassava into cassava chips. Diaspora members may be willing to help develop products and marketing channels or volunteer their assistance in projects to move local production up the value chain.

B. The Regulatory Environment: Facilitating the Flow of People and Goods

Make entry easier and less expensive for diaspora visitors. Efforts to waive visas or eliminate entry costs include the Persons of Indian Origin Card, the Overseas Vietnamese Card, and visa waivers for Filipino Canadians traveling to the Philippines under a Canadian passport. Ghana has proposed a "Sankofa stamp" to eliminate the need for visas for African Americans and is considering allowing dual citizenship. The Irish foreign affairs minister has proposed a Certificate of Irish Heritage that would entitle tourists with Irish roots to discounts on tourist facilities.

Share information in order to make diaspora travel safer, easier, and more transparent. Many countries have Web sites that provide information on entry requirements and online visa applications. To answer logistical questions about travel by Mexican nationals and by second- and third-generation emigrants, Mexico's *Programa Paisano* runs a Web site, staffs a 24-hour phone line, and prints more than 1 million booklets each year containing information about entry and exit, imports and exports of personal goods, and about the 3x1 remittance investment program. By increasing transparency and standardization, the effort reduces corruption, empowers migrants, and actively engages Mexico's diaspora.

---

48 Mexico's 3x1 program and Ministry of Agriculture support some nostalgia products, but many do not flourish because they are stuck in fundamentals, such as making a business plan — comment made by a participant at the MPI roundtable on Diaspora Tourism and Nostalgia Trade, Washington DC, June 17, 2010.

Ease transactions for the manufacture, export, import, transport, and distribution of nostalgia goods. For example, delays in smaller ports caused by the practice of searching and x-raying containers add costs and make it difficult for smaller producers to establish sustainable supply chains.[49]

Help producers connect with diaspora markets, gauge the nature and scope of demand, and find ways to strengthen the value chain among diaspora communities and producers in order to retain control of local production. Provide support to diaspora communities working to develop and strengthen distribution networks to allow them to better compete with dominant external distribution networks.

C. Institutional and Infrastructure Development

Involve the local community, including the poor, in tourism development. USAID and other donors can help by encouraging better local governance, increasing awareness of the role of diasporas in tourism, and developing policies and regulations that involve the local community, even at the outset, such as when building permits are granted and the need for labor and skills is assessed. Local governments can provide incentives for hiring local people, and tap into their connections to diaspora communities

Foster production of cultural goods — music, art, and cinema — that would be attractive to tourists and/or consumers in countries of settlement.

Invest in domestic tourism and smaller ventures. By catering only to high-end tourists, many countries fail to engage the much larger pool of lower- and middle-income diaspora visitors and domestic tourists. Large tourism venues, for instance, are generally owned by foreigners or nationals from other parts of the country and tend to invest little in the surrounding community. Developing tourism venues with an eye to domestic and lower- and middle-income visitors supports smaller entrepreneurs with deeper ties to a community's or a region's economy and may have greater multiplier effects than those aimed at higher-income tourists.

---

49 Just Scotland (referring to facilitating imports of jams, marmalades, curries, and chutneys by Eswatini Swazi Kitchen, a Manzini Youth Care project owned and operated in Swaziland), www.justtradingscotland.co.uk.

D. Research and Coordination

Measure the scope and patterns of diaspora visits to friends and relatives, including from within a given region. Determine if diaspora visits to developing countries have helped soften the blow of the global downturn on tourism. If so, identify how economic development policies could take advantage of the relative inelasticity of diaspora members' demand for tourism-related services.

Identify, target, and develop tourism-related areas of interest among diasporas. These may include heritage offerings such as festivals, churches, or historic sites, or social issues such as health care that indirectly support the tourism industry. Different generations within a diaspora may have different priorities. One MPI roundtable participant suggested that recent emigrants place a higher priority on social issues, while second, third, or later generations might be more interested in parks and heritage sites.

Identify products and services with high local value added, going beyond traditional exports of primary or unprocessed products with little value added.

Host conferences and events to promote and share research about diaspora tourism and nostalgia trade. Use these events to identify and build up businesses and attractions that draw diaspora visitors and encourage them to participate in the local economy (hotels, local restaurants, sightseeing companies, arts and crafts vendors). Conferences can also be used to encourage multinational collaboration in researching and documenting diaspora histories and cultivating heritage trails.

Collaborate with and strengthen international government and private trade organizations, such as the UN World Tourism Organization (UNWTO) and the World Travel and Tourism Council (WWTC). Seek out opportunities to collaborate across national borders in order to better appeal to diaspora members whose roots and interests span regions. Support promotional events and tourism-industry training in host countries.

Encourage genealogy tourism by cataloging and facilitating access to birth, death, marriage, residence, baptism, and other public records.

E. Branding and Marketing

Develop and promote a national brand to attract tourists and change foreign public perceptions of a country. Web sites and social networking media may further serve to strengthen a diaspora's identity and ties to the home country.

Generate marketing materials that appeal to and feature both diaspora members and traditional foreign tourists.

Emphasize the quality and uniqueness of home-country goods. Protect national products and brands from infringement by third-party knockoffs, (for example, Thai-grown rice has been marketed in New York and New Jersey as rice grown in Haiti). The Mexican state of Jalisco (tequila), Italy (olive oil, wines), and France (wines, cheeses), among others, have been successful in brand control. Designations like France's *appellation contrôlée* may help to reduce misrepresentation of goods in countries where nostalgia goods are sold.

Pay attention to identity issues. When crafting national brands, take care not to unduly privilege a single regional identity. Members of diasporas can have multiple, mutually reinforcing identities and simultaneously hold strong ties to both home and host country. Careful consideration of how heritage initiatives are funded and national brands are crafted can aid in effective engagement of the widest range of diaspora members.

Aim for high value, not high volume. The diaspora market is an intermediary market that is more connected to the local economy and society rather than enclave tourism, and with lower costs. High value doesn't need to be high cost.

Top Five Recommendations for Strengthening Diaspora Tourism and Nostalgia Trade

- Provide technical support throughout the value chain
- Ease the flow of people and goods across borders
- Support research, training, and policy development for diaspora tourism, trade, and heritage sites
- Support marketing and branding efforts
- Identify opportunities for high-value-added trade and tourism investments with development potential in home and/or diaspora communities.

F. Conclusion

In 2009, the UNWTO reported that tourism had become the fourth largest industry in the world.[50] It was a leading export earner for 83 percent of developing countries.[51] Even as profits often leak out of the local economy, some benefits also leak in, through associated services such as local transportation, guided tours, shopping, and dining. In some cases, tourism also serves as an impetus for promoting environmental protection, as in Costa Rica and Kenya. However, there is widespread recognition that a viable tourist industry requires a minimum level of security and development. Moreover, positive impacts on the local economy are not always realized when a tourist industry is isolated or restricted to secure enclaves. The potential for socially irresponsible tourism with harmful ecological and social externalities is a matter of concern. The observed characteristics of diaspora tourism indicate that it is less susceptible to these negative effects than many other forms of tourism — especially if it is tied to the preservation and enjoyment of cultural heritage.

Trade can, similarly, be a double-edged sword. While it encourages greater efficiency and specialization, it can also undermine the viability of small producers. The diaspora market for nostalgia goods can offer a measure of protection to small or artisanal producers whose products are bought for their quality and symbolic evocation of the homeland rather than for their competitive pricing. Without heavy-handed intervention, governments of countries of origin should promote the distribution and marketing of nostalgia products and encourage cooperative arrangements among small-scale growers and manufacturers who supply the diaspora market.

Nostalgia trade and heritage tourism can involve diaspora populations in transactions that ease the integration of their homeland economies into an increasingly connected global economy, while also helping diasporas to maintain their ties to their countries of origin or ancestry. The governments and societies of those countries would be well advised to cultivate these interactions, and donors to assist them in doing so. ⏎

---

50 UNWTO, *World Tourism Barometer* (Madrid, UNWTO, June 2009).
51 Martha Honey and Raymond Gilpin, "Tourism in Developing Countries: Promoting Peace and Reducing Poverty" (Special Report 233, US Institute of Peace, October 2009).

CHAPTER 5

DIASPORA PHILANTHROPY:
Private Giving and Public Policy

Kathleen Newland, Aaron Terrazas, and Roberto Munster
Migration Policy Institute

Introduction

One of the most familiar, if least understood, aspects of diasporas' engagement with their countries of origin is philanthropy: private resources donated out of an altruistic interest to advance human welfare. Diaspora philanthropy is not a new phenomenon, but as this chapter describes, there are reasons to believe that it is changing. Substantial existing research documents the philanthropic projects of diasporas in their communities of origin, but it often neglects the broader context of diaspora giving in relation to global trends in philanthropy and, critically, understanding of philanthropy's role in development. This chapter aims to bridge some of these knowledge gaps.

Philanthropic contributions are not directed exclusively to the donor's own family and friends, are not intended to generate direct commercial gain for the donor, and are not primarily for the purpose of achieving political power. Many fine lines are drawn when stating whether a resource transfer is or is not philanthropic in nature. For example, in societies organized by clan or tribe, the distinction between one's own family and the larger community may be much less clear-cut than in Westernized settings. Similarly, support for democratization efforts in one's country of origin may bring political benefit to a donor or his/her associates — but if that is the major purpose, it would be inappropriate to characterize such support as philanthropy.

Individual remittances, by far the most prevalent form of diaspora giving, remain within the private sphere.[1] Collective donations (often called collective remittances) — through which migrants combine resources to achieve an impact beyond the reach of an individual acting alone — transcend the private sphere to create the significant new channel of "nonelite" philanthropy in which stakeholders are the major decisionmakers. This is a marked shift from the traditional philanthropy practiced by wealthy individuals, corporations, foundations, and religious or other social institutions.

Philanthropy implies an element of unselfishness or altruism — although the psychic, spiritual, and societal benefits of philanthropic endeavor are an age-old, and by no means disreputable, motivation for giving. In Buddhist teaching, for example, charitable giving is a way for the giver to accumulate merit in the cycle of life, death, and rebirth. Alms-giving is a fundamental obligation of a devout Muslim, and the Christian tradition of tithing, or giving away a tenth of one's income, supports a vast array of faith-based charities. Many societies quite rightly give philanthropists respect and status.

These (and many other) traditions combine with (a) the growth of transnational communities interacting across borders, and (b) the increasingly large sums of money that flow from migrant communities to countries of migrant origin, to generate considerable interest in the nature and potential of what is most commonly called "diaspora philanthropy."

Philanthropic resources flow from diaspora communities in a vast and somewhat bewildering variety of forms. Resources may be monetary or in-kind. Among in-kind contributions, human resources are particularly important and include professional experience, technical expertise, contacts, and direct services. Many members of diasporas visit their countries of origin on a regular basis to teach or apply their skills.[2]

Financial contributions may be small, individual charitable donations or large family fortunes organized into foundations. They may be channeled through small organizations formed for the specific purpose of directing resources to a particular locality in the country of origin

---

1 For a different view of individual remittances, which places them within the philanthropic sphere, see Kathleen Dunn, Diaspora Giving and the Future of Philanthropy, White Paper, The Philanthropic Initiative, May 2004, www.tpi.org/downloads/pdfs/whitepaper-diaspora_giving.pdf.

2 See Chapter 6, "Connected through Service: Diaspora Volunteers and Global Development" in this volume.

(to build a school or a clinic, for example), or through sophisticated and established nonprofit associations working at the national or regional level. In recent years, a number of intermediary organizations have also been created to match donors with projects, to ease communication, and to oversee the use of philanthropic resources.

Box I. A Note on Terminology

Philanthropy is a somewhat controversial term. It has largely replaced the word charity in the realm of organized giving as charity has acquired, perhaps unfairly, a connotation of patronage and conservatism. Charity and philanthropy share similar roots: charity derives from caritas, or loving care for one's fellow beings; "love of man" is the literal meaning of philanthropy. In current usage, however, philanthropy is perceived as more systematic and continuous than charity, with at least the potential to be transformative.

Charitable giving may contribute to the relief of immediate suffering, but in this critical view it does not address the causes of suffering. It not only fails to challenge the status quo that produces suffering, but may indeed reinforce it by applying band-aids to gaping societal wounds.

Some in the donor community are moving toward the use of the term social investment in place of philanthropy to emphasize not only the transformative potential but the transformative intent of their giving. A paper by The Philanthropic Initiative (TPI) defines social investment as the "strategic and systematic investment of private philanthropic resources to address complex, inter-connected manifestations of chronic underdevelopment."[3] In this characterization, social investment is targeted toward issues of poverty, health, the environment, human security, basic education, and so forth — but not necessarily arts and culture, which are both focuses of traditional philanthropy. In the context of diaspora giving, however, arts and culture are often critical to the preservation of identity, and so this chapter continues to use the term philanthropy for disinterested giving, reserving social investment for the slightly narrower category of giving that aims to effect significant change in the status quo.

---

3 Paula Johnson, Global Social Investing: A Preliminary Overview (Boston, MA: The Philanthropic Initiative, May 2001), 4. www.tpi.org/downloads/pdfs/research-global_social_inv.pdf.

I. The New Context of Philanthropy and Development

Philanthropists donate to a wide array of causes, and their impact on international development is not immediately evident. Olga Sulla of the World Bank estimates that about 10 percent of all grants from philanthropic foundations worldwide are targeted toward interntional development — totaling about $800 million in 2005.[4] Meanwhile, international development experts and policymakers are recognizing the importance of a diverse set of private actors, including philanthropists, to sustainable development efforts. At the same time, global philanthropy is evolving: Large donors are becoming more strategic in their giving, while the Internet and social media are making it easier for small donors to group together and to find projects of specific interest. Diasporas are evolving as well: As skilled migration increases, greater numbers of migrants are finding professional and financial success abroad. These migrants are also becoming more self-aware, thanks to the same social media that allow small-scale philanthropists to organize, as well as to greater efforts by countries of origin to engage diasporas.

A. The Emergence of New Development Actors

Over the past decade, an increasingly diverse array of actors — including corporations, grassroots charities, philanthropists, celebrities, faith-based groups, and migrants — have become involved in providing assistance to developing countries. The recent emergence of Internet-based philanthropic aggregators further enlarges this panorama of actors. According to the Hudson Institute's Center for Global Prosperity, of the $64.1 billion that Americans gave to developing countries in 2008, over half ($37.3 billion) was channeled through private philanthropic organizations, and the remainder ($26.8 billion) went through public channels as official development assistance (ODA), (see Table 1).[5] The data are admittedly imperfect: substantial US public assistance to developing countries — with meaningful development impacts — occurs outside the framework of ODA, and a small share of contributions classified as remittances are ultimately directed to private

---

4   Olga Sulla, "Philanthropic Foundations and their Role in International Development Assistance," *World Bank International Finance Briefing Note*, No. 3, February 27, 2007, http://siteresources.worldbank.org/INTRAD/Resources/BackgrounderFoundations).pdf.

5   Hudson Institute, Center for Global Prosperity, *Index of Global Philanthropy and Remittances 2010* (Washington, DC: Hudson Institute, 2010).

philanthropic or voluntary organizations in the recipient countries.[6] Nonetheless, the data provide a compelling portrait of the dynamics shaping Americans' engagement with the developing world.

Table 1. US Economic Engagement with Developing Countries, 2008

	Total Engagement ($ Billions)
US official development assistance	26.8
US private philanthropy	37.3
Foundations	4.3
Corporations	7.7
Private and voluntary organizations	11.8
Volunteerism	3.6
Universities and colleges	1.7
Religious organizations	8.2

Source: Hudson Institute, Center for Global Prosperity, Index of Global Philanthropy and Remittances 2010.

There is growing recognition that each type of actor — the public sector, the private sector, nongovernmental organizations (NGOs), diasporas — brings unique strengths to the development process, and that coordination yields tangible benefits.[7] Official development agencies have access to unrivaled expertise and the resources needed for meaningful impact. But they are often encumbered by bureaucracy and subject to political whims, and — in a period of fiscal austerity throughout the developed world — vulnerable to lasting cuts. The private sector, and private enterprise in particular, leverages unparalleled resources via markets, and thus is the most effective driver of long-term development.[8] However, the fact that its primary responsibility is to shareholders or investors can obstruct the farsighted vision necessary for positive developmental impact. Similarly, private voluntary organizations have the capacity to aggregate resources from

---

6 Some debate whether migrant remittances should be counted as official development assistance (ODA) or private philanthropy; the consensus is that, as intrahousehold transfers, remittances are distinct from both.

7 The arguments in this paragraph are based on the insights in Lael Brainard and Vinca LaFleur, "Making Poverty History? How Activists, Philanthropists, and the Public Are Changing Global Development," and Mark R. Kramer, "Philanthropy, Aid and Investment: Alignment for Impact," in *Global Development 2.0: Can Philanthropists, the Public and the Poor Make Poverty History?* ed. Lael Brainard and Derek Chollet (Washington, DC: Brookings Institution Press, 2008).

8 Commission on Growth and Development, *The Growth Report: Strategies for Sustained Growth and Inclusive Development* (Washington, DC: World Bank, 2008).

many individuals and are not subject to the imperative to make profits or to follow a predetermined public policy line, but face substantial barriers to coordination and collective action. Private philanthropists are often nimble and can make quick or risky decisions aimed at long-term impact. But, except for the very largest, their resource constraints mean that few move beyond a vital role as catalysts and innovators.

From the perspective of official international development agencies, coordination with private donors and migrants is particularly appealing. The development of a strong for-profit sector makes aid agencies' interventions productive and sustainable in the long term. However, in the short to medium term, private philanthropic institutions often undertake high-risk policy innovation and demonstration projects that are not attractive to business and not feasible for government agencies. Diasporas support many of the efforts of both private-sector investors and private philanthropists.

B. The Emergence of New Philanthropists

Philanthropy has a long history in the United States.[9] Touring the United States in the 1830s, the French aristocrat Alexis de Tocqueville observed Americans' ethos of giving and community service in his classic study *Democracy in America*. During the first industrial revolution, highly successful industrialists such as John D. Rockefeller, Henry Ford, and Andrew Carnegie contributed lavishly to social causes, and eventually established large private foundations that remain pillars of US philanthropy today. Some early philanthropists such as Carnegie and Ford envisioned their donations as a means to induce desirable change in communities and government policies. Starting in the 1950s, publicly held corporations began to engage in philanthropy as well. During the information revolution of the 1980s and 1990s, a new generation of philanthropists emerged from the booming finance and information technology industries. In the first decade of the twenty-first century, strong economic growth in emerging economies (particularly in South and East Asia) led to the emergence of new philanthropists with direct ties to the developing world.

---

9   This history of philanthropy in the United States draws on Charles T. Clotfelter and Thomas Ehrlich, eds., *Philanthropy and the Nonprofit Sector in a Changing America* (Bloomington, IN: Indiana Univ. Press, 1999); Gabriel Kasper, *A Legacy of Innovation* (Cambridge, MA: The Monitor Group, 2005), www.futureofphilanthropy.org/files/usPhil_4LegacyofInnovation. pdf; National Philanthropic Trust, *A Chronological History of Philanthropy in the United States* (Jenkinstown, PA: National Philanthropic Trust, 2005); and Lawrence J. Friedman and Mark D. McGarvie, *Charity, Philanthropy, and Civility in American History* (New York: Cambridge Univ. Press, 2002).

A new, more globally aware generation of industrial (and postindustrial) giants has quickly taken up the mantle of socially engaged giving, focusing on core policy issues such as democracy, press freedom, access to education, and economic competitiveness as well as traditional philanthropic concerns such as health, education, and poverty reduction. Their entrepreneurial success has often led them to question the status quo, and many are inclined to donate their wealth to charitable causes. Billionaire philanthropists Bill Gates and Warren Buffet recently recruited 40 wealthy American individuals and families to commit to donating half of their wealth to charitable causes.[10] The list of participants in the Gates-Buffet Giving Pledge includes at least four immigrants to the United States — from South Africa, Sweden, Canada, and France — and at least three second-generation immigrants whose parents were born in Germany, Russia, and Greece.[11]

Philanthropy is not limited to the wealthy. Many middle-income and even relatively poor individuals make meaningful donations to charitable causes as well. For instance, small donations to churches, mosques, temples, and other religious organizations have historically funded substantial relief for the poor and homeless. Immigrant groups in the United States have a long history of donating to organizations that assist compatriots to settle and adapt to life in a new country.[12] Over time this practice has spread to other associations, including those organized around identity (e.g., race, ethnicity, profession) or a particular issue (e.g., environment, education). Indeed, recent research highlighted in *The Economist* suggests that the poor are more likely to make charitable donations than the wealthy; the study also finds that individuals born into poverty but who have achieved financial success are more likely to donate.[13]

---

10 Robert Frank, "More Billionaires Sign the Gates-Buffet Giving Pledge," *Wall Street Journal*, August 4, 2010.

11 Based on MPI analysis of the list available at http://givingpledge.org/#enter. Patrick Soon-Shiong was born in South Africa to Chinese immigrant parents, Pierre Omidyar was born in France of Iranian heritage, Barbro Sachs-Osher was born in Sweden, and Jeff Skoll immigrated to the United States from Canada; George Kaiser's parents fled Nazi Germany, Peter Peterson's parents were Greek immigrants, and Bernie Marcus' parents immigrated to the United States from Russia.

12 See Will Somerville, Jamie Durana, and Aaron Terrazas, *Hometown Associations: An Untapped Resource for Immigrant Integration* (Washington, DC: Migration Policy Institute, July 2008), www.migrationpolicy.org/pubs/Insight-HTAs-July08.pdf.

13 Paul K. Piff, Michael W. Kraus, Stéphane Côté, Bonnie Hayden Cheng, and Dacher Keltner, "Having Less, Giving More: The Influence of Social Class on Prosocial Behavior," *Journal of Personality and Social Psychology* 99, no. 2 (August 2010) cited in *The Economist*, "The Rich are Different from You and Me," July 29, 2010.

Philanthropists have become increasingly engaged with social investment, and many now fund advocacy for policy reforms. Social and economic change — which many socially aware philanthropists support — is inherently political. Meanwhile, new modes of giving have emerged through venture philanthropy initiatives and Internet-based philanthropic aggregators.[14] Venture philanthropists seek to apply the rigorous

---

14 On venture philanthropy, see Christine W. Letts, William Ryan, and Allen Grossman, "Virtuous Capital: What Foundations Can Learn from Venture Capitalists," *Harvard Business Review* (March–April 1997); on Internet-based philanthropic aggregators, see Raj M. Desai and Homi

methods of business investment to philanthropic ventures. They not only put money into their philanthropic "investments," but also take a hands-on approach to training, financial accounting, evaluation, and outcomes; in some cases, they expect the "growth capital" they invest to be paid back into a venture philanthropy fund that can then be used for other social investments. The Indian NGO Dasra — founded by a young Indian American who left Wall Street to return to his country of ancestry to work in philanthropy — operates in this manner, while also advising corporate philanthropies on how best to spend their money in India.[15] These developments may blur the conventional understanding of what constitutes philanthropy, but the donors assert that philanthropy should address the causes as well as the symptoms of poverty and inequality.

C. The New Context of Diaspora Giving

There is little new in the observation that many migrants and their descendants retain meaningful personal and professional ties with their ancestral countries, and that these ties often translate into con-tributions of time and more tangible resources.[16] Substantial existing research (notably by the Harvard University Global Equity Initiative, The Philanthropic Initiative, and the Inter-American Dialogue, among others) maps the financial and in-kind contributions that diasporas make to their countries of origin — particularly in Asia and Latin America.[17]

Kharas, "Do Philanthropic Citizens Behave Like Governments? Internet-based Platforms and the Diffusion of International Private Aid," Wolfensohn Center for Development, Working Paper 12, Brookings Institution, October 2009, www.brookings.edu/~/media/Files/rc/papers/2009/10_kiva_global_giving_kharas/10_kiva_global_giving_kharas.pdf.

15 See www.dasra.org.

16 See generally Kathleen Newland and Erin Patrick, *Beyond Remittances: The Role of Diaspora in Poverty Reduction in their Countries of Origin* (Washington, DC and London: MPI and the UK Department for International Development [DFID], 2004), www.migrationpolicy.org/pubs/Beyond_Remittances_0704.pdf. On donations of time through volunteering, see Chapter 3, *Connected through Service.*

17 See, for instance, Paula Johnson, *Diaspora Philanthropy: Influences, Initiatives and Issues* (Boston, MA: The Philanthropic Initiative and the Global Equity Initiative, 2007); Peter Geith-ner, Lincoln Chen, and Paula Johnson, *Diaspora Philanthropy and Equitable Development in China and India* (Cambridge, MA: Harvard Univ. Press, 2004); Barbara Merz and Lincoln Chen, eds., *New Patterns for Mexico: Observations on Remittances, Philanthropic Giving and Equitable Development* (Cambridge, MA: Harvard Univ. Press, 2005); Adil Najam, *Portrait of a Giving Community: Philanthropy by the Pakistani American Diaspora* (Cambridge, MA: Harvard Univ. Press, 2006); Mark Sidel, "A Decade of Research and Practice of Diaspora Philanthropy in the Asia Pacific Region: The State of the Field," Working Paper, Univ. of Iowa, May 2008; Manuel Orozco and Eugenia Garcia-Zanello, "Hometown Associations: Transnationalism, Philanthropy and Development," *Brown Journal of World Affairs* XV, no. 2 (Spring/Summer 2009): 1–17.

Has this philanthropic impulse among diaspora communities changed over time? There are two reasons to believe that today's diaspora philanthropists may be substantially different from their predecessors:

- **Increasing mobility of talent.** The regulation of human mobility is a controversial issue, but one trend observable across most countries is the extraordinary effort made to attract and ease the admission of talented migrants.[18] Despite widespread limitations on the movement of less-proficient workers, the movement off highly skilled experts, entrepreneurs, artists, athletes, and entertainers is becoming increasingly liberalized. As a result of the growing international migration of accomplished (and often extremely successful) individuals, the number of wealthy and well-connected members of diasporas is on the rise.

- **The organizational revolution.** Communications technologies have revolutionized the way people organize and interact, facilitating philanthropic donations across borders. The Internet, e-mail, and mobile telephony have also made community organizing easier. In the past, middle-income and relatively poor migrants faced enormous barriers to maintaining contact with their communities of origin and their children; second and higher generations often lost contact with their communities of origin entirely. It is now much easier to retain personal relationships across borders and over time.

As a result of these changes, diasporas are increasingly able to contribute toward and actively monitor philanthropic activities in their countries of origin. But important questions remain unanswered. What do diaspora philanthropists aim to achieve and how effective are they in realizing their aims? Are they interested in having a long-term impact, or are they more interested in immediate poverty relief? Do they use high-profile donations to raise their public profile or for political ends? Do their interests align with the development priorities of their countries of origin and of international donors, or do diaspora philanthropists have a different set of priorities? In documenting a wide range of diaspora philanthropic undertakings, the following sections aim to respond to these critical questions.

---

18 Transatlantic Council on Migration, *Talent, Competitiveness and Migration* (Gütersloh, Germany: Bertelsmann Stiftung and MPI, 2009).

II. Experiences of Diaspora Philanthropy

Diaspora philanthropy is characterized by a wide variety of actors with different motivations, objectives, capacities, and impacts. While some donors give directly to beneficiaries or set up their own philanthropic vehicles, others donate through intermediaries such as private foundations, hometown associations, ethnic organizations, professional associations, faith-based groups, and NGOs. These philanthropic intermediaries identify priorities for giving, administer funds (sometimes including due diligence and evaluation), and often aggregate funds from other sources such as nondiaspora donors as well. Internet-based philanthropic aggregators such as Kiva and GlobalGiving help smaller-scale donors identify their giving priorities directly by making it easy for them to select the projects or individuals to whom they wish to give.[19]

Figure 1 categorizes diaspora philanthropists along two critical dimensions: (a) by whether their donation is channeled directly to the beneficiary or via an intermediary (on the horizontal), and (b) by the size of their donation (on the vertical). (Indeed, this categorization is relevant to philanthropic donations not originating from diasporas as well.)

- **Donor aggregation** (horizontal). Whether donors give individually or as a group has profound implications for the impact of their gifts. Individual donors obviously have more flexibility in setting priorities and rapidly identifying emerging issues or opportunities, whereas group priorities typically must be negotiated or specified in advance. Both individual and group donors usually give to causes that have personal resonance — relating, for instance, to challenges they have overcome, experiences that have shaped their life trajectories, or assistance to underprivileged individuals from a similar background. As a result, identity-based organizations are particularly effective at fundraising from groups.

- **Donation size** (vertical). Small donations, whether made by a group or an individual, typically focus on small communities. If well targeted, these donations can have a catalytic impact but are inevitably limited by their small size. Larger donations can achieve greater impact by undertaking more ambitious projects or by reaching larger numbers of beneficiaries (although this potential is not always realized). They can also be encumbered by the challenges of administering large programs with diffuse objectives.

---

19 Strictly speaking, Kiva is a platform for micro-loans. However, as discussed earlier, many micro-loans — in particular those with below-market interest rates — reflect some degree of philanthropic impulse. For a thought-provoking analysis of these Internet-based philanthropic aggregators, see Desai and Kharas, *Do Philanthropic Citizens Behave Like Governments?*

The matrix given in Figure 1 is far from perfect. In many respects the dimensions might be better represented as gradations rather than clear dichotomies. However, it is a useful schematic for thinking about the wide variety of diaspora philanthropists.

Figure 1. Diaspora Philanthropy Matrix

		Donor Aggregation	
		Individual Donor	**Multiple Donors**
Donation Size	**Small**	Some remittances, individual donations	Hometown associations, online platforms, small foundations
	Large	Direct donations from magnates, celebrities, sports stars; large foundations established by such individuals	Professional associations, family foundations, venture philanthropy funds

Source: Authors' elaboration.

The following subsections provide some examples of the range of diaspora philanthropists.

A. Individual Donors

Individual diaspora philanthropists range from small donors who give to specific causes in their communities of origin to migrants who achieve broader success abroad and who are able to donate larger sums. Presumably a small portion of family remittances are ultimately channeled to charitable causes by remittance recipients, but since these donations are allocated from household budgets to which remittances contribute, it is difficult to disaggregate them from domestic giving. That said, the stories of migrants who live humble lives abroad but who save their incomes religiously to donate to community causes in their countries of origin are many. For instance, an article in *The New York Times* in 2000 featured the story of an Indian immigrant to New York City, Om Dutta Sharma, who migrated to the United States in 1974.[20] Working as a taxi driver, Sharma and his wife lived modestly and saved assiduously; over the course of two decades, they donated about $2,000 per year to fund a small rural school in Sharma's home village in northern India. It is clear from the article that the donations implied substantial self-sacrifice by Sharma and his family.

Sometimes, small-scale donors are able to mobilize family and friends

---

20 Celia W. Dugger, "In New York, Just a Cabby. In India, a School's Hero," *New York Times.* January 23, 2000, www.nytimes.com/2000/01/23/world/in-new-york-just-a-cabby-in-india-a-school-s-hero.html?pagewanted=1.

to donate as well. One example is Binh Nguyen, a Vietnamese American from Colorado who, after visiting Vietnam in 1994, contributed over $7,000 to support an orphanage run by Vietnamese nuns. Nguyen then went on to raise $14,000 from family and friends in the United States for the orphanage and later raised funds to open a free clinic and support a private high school as well.[21] Similarly, Dr. Rafael Espada — a Guatemala-born cardiothoracic surgeon who lived for three decades in Houston, Texas, and who was elected Guatemala's vice president in 2007 — donated and raised funds to establish a charity hospital for the indigent in his home country.[22] Espada also volunteered his time to perform surgeries at the hospital.

Many members of diasporas will also make one-time donations in the face of extraordinary needs, such as in the aftermath of a natural disaster. Typhoon Linda in Vietnam in 1997, and floods in 1999, spurred large numbers of donations to relief efforts from Vietnamese communities in the United States — communities that until then had been deeply opposed to any effort that required working with the Vietnamese government.[23] A 1993 earthquake that leveled the ancient Iranian city of Bam drew contributions from Iranian expatriates who had fled after the fall of the shah in 1979 and who remained strongly opposed to the Islamic Republic of Iran.

Meanwhile, the donations of the many migrants who achieve extraordinary professional (and financial) success abroad are numerous and well documented. Celebrities, sports stars, business owners, and magnates have used their fame and influence to promote causes and encourage greater philanthropy to their ancestral countries — and often gained more fame through their philanthropic giving. These individual diaspora donors have a wide variety of interests and objectives. Some aim to effect lasting political or socioeconomic change in their countries (and regions). For instance, George Soros, a Hungarian-born US financier, established the Open Society Institute (OSI) to promote democracy across the developing world and particularly in the former Soviet sphere of influence. More recently, the Sudanese-born British telecommunications magnate Mo Ibrahim established the Mo Ibrahim Foundation, which sponsors an annual $5 million prize to promote good governance throughout Africa.[24]

---

21 Mark Sidel, *Vietnamese-American Diaspora Philanthropy to Vietnam* (Boston, MA: The Philanthropic Initiative and the Global Equity Initiative, 2007).

22 Gobierno de Guatemala, "Dr. Rafael Espada, Vicepresidente," www.vicepresidencia.gob.gt/v2/content/dr-rafael-espada-vicepresidente.

23 Mark Sidel, "Vietnamese-American Diaspora Philanthropy to Vietnam," Paper prepared for The Philanthropic Initiative, Inc, and The Global Equity Initiative, Harvard Univ., May 2007.

24 The Mo Ibrahim Prize is awarded each year to democratically elected former heads of state or

Other diaspora philanthropists — such as Armenian American businessman Mark Kerkorian and Chinese-born Singaporean actor Jet Li — concentrate on humanitarian and community relief efforts in their countries of origin.[25] Recently, an association of Haitian American professional football players received media attention for their work with the National Football League (NFL) to raise funds for relief and recovery efforts in the wake of January 2010's devastating earthquake in Haiti.[26] Similar to smaller-scale donors, some high-profile diaspora philanthropists both donate their own resources and raise funds for their causes. For instance, Wyclef Jean — a Haitian American rap musician — helped establish the Yélé Haiti Foundation, which raised approximately $9.1 million for Haitian earthquake relief efforts in the first half of 2010.[27] (Jean resigned from the foundation in August 2010 after announcing that he would be a candidate for Haiti's presidency; the foundation has also recently been the subject of scrutiny for alleged questionable accounting practices.)

Still other diaspora philanthropists focus on community development initiatives. Colombian-born international pop star Shakira Isabel Mabarak Ripoll (popularly known by her first name) established the US-based Barefoot Foundation (*Fundación Pies Descalzos*) to promote expanded access to childhood education in her native Colombia.[28] A group of Nigerian-origin NFL players in the United States came together under the umbrella of the nonprofit group Athletes in Diaspora Community Interventions (ADCI) to promote the establishment of an athletics-based youth development program in Nigeria.[29] Similarly, Dikembe Mutombo — a well-known US professional basketball player who was born in Zaire, now the Democratic Republic of the Congo (DRC) — established a US-based foundation dedicated to improving the

---

government who "served their term in office within the limits set by the country's constitution and left office during the prior three years." It consists of $5 million over ten years and $200,000 annually for life thereafter. In addition, the Mo Ibrahim Foundation grants $200,000 per year for 10 years toward "public interest activities and good causes espoused by the winner." See www.moibrahimfoundation.org.

25 See The Lincy Foundation, http://lincyinstitute.unlv.edu/lincy.html.
26 National Football League, "NFL Pledges 2.5M to Aid Haiti Earthquake Relief Efforts," Press Release, January 2010, www.nfl.com/news/story?id=09000d5d815bff52&template=with-video-with-comments&confirm=true.
27 Deborah Sontag, "Wyclef Jean Confirms Plans to Run for Haitian Presidency," *The New York Times*, August 4, 2010, www.nytimes.com/2010/08/05/world/americas/05haiti.html?hpw.
28 See the Barefoot Foundation, www.barefootfoundation.com.
29 National Sports Commission of Nigeria, "Athletes in Diaspora to Build Academy of Learning and Sports in Nigeria," www.sportscommission.gov.ng/online/index.php?option=com_content&task=view&id=61&Itemid=27; John Branch, "Four Players Who Came Out of Africa Return to Help," *New York Times*, May 8, 2008, www.nytimes.com/2008/05/08/sports/football/08nigeria.html.

"health, education, and quality of life" of people in the DRC.[30] Brazilian-born international soccer star Ronaldo de Assis Moreira (better known as Ronaldinho) established the Ronaldinho Institute in his hometown of Porto Alegre, Brazil, as a youth development organization.[31]

B. Donations via Intermediaries

While some migrants donate independently with specific projects in mind, many middle-income and relatively poor migrants and members of diasporas cannot directly pursue philanthropic activities in their countries of origin, owing to a lack of resources, time, or expertise. Yet they still retain strong personal and community bonds with their countries of origin and may desire to contribute to charitable activities. Philanthropic intermediaries channel donations from these diaspora members toward initiatives and projects in their countries of origin. Such intermediaries are extremely diverse. They include hometown associations, online-giving platforms, faith-based organizations, professional associations, and diaspora foundations. In general, they provide accessible avenues for individuals to channel donations to their communities of origin. Several types are described in more detail below.

I. Hometown Associations

Hometown associations (HTAs) are among the most familiar (and most studied) migrant organizations. They provide a forum for migrants from the same town, village, state, or region to gather, exchange experiences, and cooperate on issues of common interest. They have been documented among migrants from Mexico, El Salvador, Guatemala, Honduras, Nicaragua, Ecuador, the Dominican Republic, Jamaica, Guyana, Mali, Senegal, Ghana, Nigeria, Cameroon, Burkina Faso, Tanzania, Pakistan, China, the Philippines, and Turkey and probably exist among other groups as well. Occasionally, these associations make collective donations to specific projects — for example, improvements to local infrastructure or the renovation of public spaces and buildings such as churches, schools, and health centers. In fewer instances, these associations have funded educational scholarships for youth in their communities of origin. Mexico has innovated public policies designed to promote these donations through matching grant programs whereby various Mexican government agencies at the federal, state, and local levels match the donations of migrant associations. More recently the so-called Three-for-One program has expanded to include limited

---

30 See the Dikembe Mutombo Foundation, www.dmf.org.
31 See the Instituto Ronaldinho Gaúcho, www.irg.org.br.

donations from the Western Union, a private corporation, and has launched a module to fund educational scholarships for marginalized youth through a similarly designed matching grant program. Governments of diaspora settlement countries such as France and Norway have also contributed to matching grant programs for migrants' philanthropic contributions.

2. Internet-Based Philanthropic Platforms

A variety of Web sites have emerged in recent years allowing individuals to pool resources and give as a group via an online platform. Two of the largest organizations, US-based Kiva and GlobalGiving, have taken different approaches.[32] Kiva allows individuals to lend money for micro-loans through micro-finance institutions in a developing country. The money "invested" in a loan is repaid without interest — in effect, individuals donate the foregone interest. GlobalGiving, on the other hand, allows people to donate directly to a specific project and aggregates their contributions. Both portals are relatively new and their impact is still largely unproven.[33] Online portals such as Kiva and GlobalGiving were not created specifically for diasporas, yet they have the potential to attract diaspora donors. Similar platforms in the United Kingdom (UK) — JustGiving and MyCharityPage — are social networking sites that allow participants to create online pages for fundraising devoted to a particular charity.[34] Since 2000, JustGiving has raised over $712 million for 6,300 charities from 6.5 million donors.[35] (GlobalGiving has also established a UK site.) A smaller platform with a more specific target, Wokai, provides micro-loans to rural Chinese borrowers. The more specific focus of this platform could allow Wokai to better target the Chinese diaspora, although there is no hard evidence of its success in doing so.[36]

3. Faith-Based Groups

Donations made through religious or faith-affiliated organizations have characteristics that distinguish them from other groups. Diaspora congregations in the United States support activities in their countries of origin — and in other countries as well. Faith-based schools and hospitals throughout the developing world draw support from diaspora as well as nondiaspora congregations. One example is a 1,000-member,

---

32 See Kiva, www.kiva.org, and GlobalGiving, www.globalgiving.org.
33 Desai and Kharas, *Do Philanthropic Citizens Behave Like Governments?*
34 See JustGiving www.justgiving.com and My Charity Page, www.mycharitypage.com.
35 Hudson Institute, *The Index of Global Philanthropy and Remittances 2010.*
36 See Wokai, www.wokai.org.

Telugu-language Seventh Day Adventist church in Silver Spring, Maryland, that collects funds from its congregation to support schools, colleges, and medical facilities in Andhra Pradesh, India. The church's members support philanthropic activities in other countries, too, such as earthquake relief in Haiti. The Fund for Armenian Relief (FAR), based in New York City, was founded by the Diocese of the Armenian Church of America after the 1988 earthquake. By 1993, it had reorganized and gained tax-exempt status. In 2008, FAR totaled approximately $1 million in contributions and pledges.[37] FAR fundraises for a variety of causes in Armenia, focusing on five key areas: economic development, child protection, health care, education, and humanitarian aid.[38]

For some communities, religious identity supersedes regional identity. Religious groups are often seen as relatively nonpolitical, and are thus able to operate more easily under the closed regimes of nations such as Laos and Burma.[39] In these countries, religious institutions have well-established networks that have official approval or can circumvent the countries' often restrictive laws on social mobilization. Islamic charitable foundations — many receiving support from diaspora members as well as from the traditional alms-giving of local Muslims — are a major source of welfare spending among the poor in Muslim countries. (After the terrorist attacks of September 11, 2001, US policies significantly restricted donations to religious organizations, especially Islamic ones, as a few were found to be conduits for funding to al-Qaeda.[40]) In many countries, religious groups combine philanthropic work with proselytizing, either directly or simply by setting a good example. Some also have strong political agendas. The Muslim Brotherhood and affiliated charities, for example, have strengthened their political position across the Arab world from Egypt to Morocco by providing welfare services to poor people who get virtually no services from the state.

4. Professional Associations

Some professional associations couple donations of time and resources. In particular, they may donate professional equipment to peers in their countries of origin. For instance, the American Association of

---

37 Fund for Armenian Relief, "2008 Annual Report," http://farusa.org/documents/FAR2008.pdf.
38 See Fund for Armenian Relief, www.farusa.org.
39 Zubair Bhatti, "Pakistan," Paper presented at the Asia Pacific Philanthropy Consortium Conference on Diaspora Giving: An Agent of Change in Asia Pacific Communities? Hanoi, Vietnam, May 21–23, 2008, www.asiapacificphilanthropy.org/conference.
40 John Roth, Douglas Greenburg, and Serena Wille, "Monograph on Terrorist Financing," Staff Report to the 9/11 Commission, 2008, http://counterterrorismblog.org/upload/2008/09/911_TerrFin_Monograph.pdf.

Physicians of Indian Origin (AAPI) brings together 50,000 physicians and medical students of Indian origin. Philanthropy is not a principal objective of the association, but the group undertakes charitable work both in the United States and in India. AAPI mobilized donations of significant resources, notably medical supplies, following a major earthquake in the Indian state of Gujarat in 2006.[41] AAPI members also donate time and resources to support greater access to health care in rural India.[42]

5. Diaspora Foundations

Some diasporas have established foundations to promote philanthropy in their countries of origin. As US-registered nonprofit groups, these foundations are able to raise funds from the diaspora which are tax-deductible from US income. Examples include the American India Foundation, the Ayala Foundation, the Rafik Hariri Foundation, and the Ireland Funds.

- **The American India Foundation** (AIF) is a nonprofit organization that raises funds for philanthropic causes in India. Like many other philanthropic organizations, AIF was founded after a natural disaster (a major earthquake in Gujarat in 2001) and it primarily targets donors from the Indian diaspora in the United States.[43] AIF engages in strategic philanthropy: it actively searches for and selects grant-receiving organizations and is involved in building their capacity, similar to venture philanthropy firms.

- Established in 2000, the **Ayala Foundation USA** (AF USA) is one of the most recognized Filipino diaspora organizations. Its goal is to strengthen and encourage the philanthropy of Filipino Americans and to connect them to well-run nonprofit organizations in the Philippines that work on strategic solutions to poverty. Utilizing tax-deductible donations, AF USA channels in-kind resources and funds to the Philippines via a series of initiatives that include young leader fellowships and capacity- and knowledge-building programs.[44] One such program, Gearing

---

41 Shyamala Shiveshwarkar, *Diaspora Giving: An Agent of Change in Asia Pacific Communities? India (Asia Pacific Philanthropy Consortium*, 2008) and the American Association of Physicians of Indian Origin, http://aapiusa.org/.

42 IndiaInteracts, "The Art of Philanthropy and the Indian Diaspora," http://indiainteracts.in/columnist/2008/01/08/The-art-of-philanthropy-and-the-Indian-diaspora/.

43 See the American India Foundation, www.aifoundation.org; and Johnson, *Diaspora Philanthropy: Influences, Initiatives and Issues.*

44 Victoria Garchitorena, *Diaspora Philanthropy: The Philippine Experience (*Boston, MA: The Philanthropic Initiative and the Harvard Global Equity Initiative, 2007). Migration Policy Institute

up Internet Literacy and Access for Students (GILAS), was started in 2005 to provide computer access to all public high schools. Within its first three years it raised $3.75 million, helping 1,670 public high schools.[45] A large portion of funds donated to AF USA go to education.[46] Between 2003 and 2006, three-quarters of AF USA's donations were in amounts less than $500 — but the much smaller number of larger donations (those averaging $10,000) accounted for almost the same proportion of the total sum of money raised.

- Rafik Hariri — a prominent Lebanese businessman, politician, and philanthropist who twice served as his country's prime minister — established the **Rafik Hariri Foundation** in 1984. (A predecessor group was established in 1979). The foundation's mission is to provide educational opportunities for Lebanese youth. It supports interest-free educational loans for Lebanese students studying abroad. In 1985, the Hariri Foundation established a US-based branch to coordinate efforts with the Lebanese diaspora. The foundation now maintains offices in Paris and London as well.[47]

- *Conexión Colombia* is an innovative hybrid diaspora foundation and online philanthropic platform.[48] It targets the global Colombian diaspora and maintains offices in the United States, Mexico, and Spain. Conexión Colombia also has an extensive online presence. Donors select the project their donation will fund, and can make in-kind donations or volunteer their time and skills. The minimum donation is small — 25,000 Colombian pesos (about $13).

interview with Victoria Garchitorena, Washington, DC, February 18, 2010.

45 Estrella Añonuevo and Augustus Añonuevo, "Philippines," Paper presented at the Asia Pacific Philanthropy Consortium Conference on Diaspora Giving: An Agent of Change in Asia Pacific Communities? Hanoi, Vietnam, May 21–23, 2008, www.asiapacificphilanthropy.org/conference.

46 See Ayala Foundation USA, www.af-usa.org.

47 See Hariri Foundation, www.hariri-foundation.org.lb and Hariri Foundation USA, www.haririfoundationusa.org.

48 See www.conexioncolombia.com. Maria Aysa-Lastra, *Diaspora Philanthropy: The Colombia Experience* (The Philanthropic Initiative and The Global Equity Initiative, Harvard Univ., May 2007) and Migration Policy Institute interview with Angela Escallón, executive director, Conexión Colombia, via telephone, April 2010.

Box 3. The Ireland Funds: Beyond Philanthropy, Beyond the Homeland

The Ireland Funds are a network of diaspora organizations in 12 countries, the first of which was founded in the United States in 1976 to generate support for the island of Ireland (north and south) and its people — at that time among Western Europe's poorest, and mired in a savage conflict in Northern Ireland. In 1987 the American Ireland Fund merged with the American Ireland Foundation to form the largest private body funding constructive change in Ireland. Since 1976 the Ireland Funds have raised over $300 million and have made grants to more than 1,200 organizations in Ireland. The Ireland Funds' three programmatic themes are peace and reconciliation, arts and culture, and education and community development.

The Ireland Funds have also done much to promote the practice of philanthropy in Ireland and the Irish diaspora communities. But the goal is not only to promote philanthropy as a vehicle for political, social, and economic progress but also as a portal for broader diaspora engagement. In the words of the former president and CEO of the Worldwide Ireland Funds, Kingsley Aikins, "Philanthropy can be an effective 'entry point' to engage with Ireland and can lead to more extensive commitments."

With Ireland's rapid growth in the 1990s and early 2000s, the Ireland Funds increasingly supported activities outside of Ireland, drawing upon experience in Ireland. For example, a 1997 grant funded politicians from Northern Ireland, Britain, and the Irish Republic to travel to South Africa to learn from leaders there (including Nelson Mandela) about the conflict resolution process that led to the end of apartheid and the establishment of majority rule to South Africa. The experience, orchestrated by Professor Padraig O'Malley of the University of Massachusetts, led to a communications breakthrough among the Irish participants that contributed to the negotiation of the Good Friday Agreement one year later. Professor O'Malley, with support from the Ireland Funds, has since applied his model of conflict resolution to the conflicts in Iraq, Kosovo, and Cyprus — and succeeded in engaging antagonists who previously refused to speak or even be in the same room together. Although the funds still conduct most of their philanthropic endeavors in Ireland, they also fund social projects in Britain, the United States, other countries of Irish settlement, and in several developing countries.

Source: Kingsley Aikens, Anita Sands, and Nicola White, The Global Irish Making a Difference Together: A Comparative Review of International Diaspora Strategies (Dublin: The Ireland Funds, 2009).

III. Challenges and Lessons Learned

The experiences described in the preceding section confirm that diasporas undertake substantial philanthropic efforts in their countries of origin. In particular, diaspora philanthropists have proven adept at rapidly mobilizing humanitarian relief in the wake of natural disasters or man-made crises, acting as social innovators and change agents with a long-term interest in improving living standards in the developing world, serving as powerful aggregators of issue-based or identity-based giving among diaspora communities, and advocating for country-of-origin causes among mainstream donors.

But diaspora philanthropists also face a number of challenges — some shared with all philanthropists and some unique. Lael Brainard and Derek Chollet point out that all development actors face common challenges, including accountability, the effective deployment of resources, agenda setting, and achieving scale and sustainability; in many developing countries, a lack of basic infrastructure, chronic underinvestment in human capital, and corruption present additional hurdles.[49] Among individual philanthropists, the challenge of achieving scale and sustainability — and convincing institutional actors such as governments of the merit of philanthropic innovation — is particularly challenging. Small-scale philanthropists who donate through aggregators face particularly difficult challenges in agenda setting. Diaspora philanthropists are, in many respects, no different.

But diaspora philanthropists also face several unique and closely interrelated challenges and ambiguities — particularly if donations are to be measured against their impact on development.

A. Agenda Setting and Identifying Priorities

In the case of individual diaspora philanthropists (including individual donors who give directly through Internet-based philanthropic platforms or market-based aggregators), agenda setting is fairly straightforward. But in the case of issue- and identity-based organizations, identifying priorities is more contentious, particularly if the government of the country of origin regards the diaspora with suspicion or even hostility. In some cases, the priorities of diaspora donors do not match those of the intended beneficiaries in the country of origin, which can undermine the effectiveness of projects and jeopardize mutual commitment to cooperation.

---

49 Brainard and Chollet, *Global Development 2.0.*

B. Ambiguous Objectives, Ambiguous Outcomes

As private foundations have professionalized over time, they have increasingly focused on identifying the impact of their donations. This is true for foundations focused on socioeconomic and political change as well as foundations focused on humanitarian relief. Similarly, issue-based NGOs that solicit philanthropic donations from the public are often eager to illustrate concrete impacts to their donors (although the mechanisms for accountability may be less robust). While diaspora donors may benefit from greater insight into needs and how to make limited interventions effective, they may also lack the perspective (and credibility) of an objective outsider. Moreover, diaspora philanthropy is motivated by a much wider range of concerns that may include donors' prestige in the beneficiary community, for example. Not all diaspora philanthropists aspire to have an impact on development or long-term welfare in their countries of origin; many donors limit themselves to short-term humanitarian actions. As Victoria Garchitorena, president of the Ayala Foundation, observes, "Many donors are still content with 'band-aid' programs which may be emotionally satisfying for them but do not result in permanent or systematic improvement."[50]

C. Lack of Trust in the Voluntary and Nonprofit Sector

Among diasporas from poorly governed developing (and developed) countries, a general lack of trust in institutions and a lack of confidence in the nonprofit sector encourages direct giving to individuals — particularly family and friends — and communities, as these provide built-in social accountability mechanisms.[51] As a result, diasporas are more likely to donate to individuals or organizations with whom they are personally familiar, although these recipients may not necessarily reflect the most pressing needs or strategic social investments.

D. Structural Limits on the Impact of Private Philanthropy

Even the most capable diaspora philanthropists and philanthropic institutions are subject to the structural and macroeconomic constraints of the broader economy and society — factors such as low

---

50 Victoria P. Garchitorena, "Diaspora Philanthropy: The Philippine Experience," Paper prepared for The Philanthropic Initiative, Inc. and The Global Equity Initiative, Harvard Univ., May 2007.

51 Johnson, *Diaspora Philanthropy*. Also, Adil Najam in Barbara J. Merz, Lincoln C. Chen, and Peter F. Geithner, eds., *Diasporas and Development* (Cambridge, MA: Harvard Univ. Press).

productivity, poor infrastructure, agricultural subsidies that limit markets for produce from developing countries, and entrenched corruption in both public and private enterprises.

E. Representation

Just as scale is an issue, so is representation. Engaging migrant groups in discussions with multilateral and bilateral donors is tremendously challenging and exceedingly important. The challenges are familiar: which groups are selected to speak on behalf of the diaspora, and do they have broad legitimacy? What kind of influence and power do they have within donor-driven agencies? How do large government agencies ensure a voice for diaspora communities in government-to-government agreements? This last issue becomes especially complex if the diaspora community is the result of a past or percolating conflict; in such cases, diaspora engagement with the home-country government may not be realistic or even safe.

IV. Public Policy Issues

Philanthropy is part of the cultural fabric of many communities and is driven by complex individual and social dynamics. But it is also shaped by public policy. The policy issues surrounding philanthropy are complex and, at times, politically sensitive. Indeed, independence from (and at times competition with) government priorities is a trademark of private philanthropy and an integral part of what makes it a powerful and effective force for change. Yet philanthropy is also inextricably linked to public policy, in particular when philanthropists are strategic in their giving and aim to influence the decisions and actions of policymakers.

Increasingly, philanthropists and governments are joining forces on issues of common concern such as education and international development: For instance, 12 major private foundations have partnered with the US Department of Education to promote innovation in education under the department's Investing in Innovation (i3) Fund.[52] Partnerships between private philanthropists and governments are also increasingly commonplace in the field of international development. The Global Alliance for Vaccines and Immunization (GAVI),

---

52 US Department of Education, Investing in Innovation Fund (i3), www2.ed.gov/programs/ innovation/index.html.

which aims to expand access to immunization in developing countries, is a collaborative among the governments of Australia, Canada, Denmark, France, Germany, Ireland, Italy, Luxembourg, the Netherlands, Norway, the Russian Federation, South Africa, Spain, Sweden, the United Kingdom, the United States, and the European Commission. But the largest single donor to GAVI has been the Bill and Melinda Gates Foundation. The alliance has also received support from the Spanish foundation La Caixa as well as other private donors.[53] (Experience working with smaller donors or donor aggregators is less extensive and is likely more complicated.)

USAID has also been a leader in partnering with private donors. Since 2001, USAID has collaborated with private donors under the aegis of its Global Development Alliance (GDA). GDA was envisioned as a means for USAID to embrace growing US private-sector engagement with the developing world in a partnership to promote sustainable growth and poverty reduction. Collaboration can range from co-funding to in-kind contribution or as little as a "stamp of approval" from USAID. By fiscal year 2007, USAID had partnered with 1,800 entities, including 100 universities and 20 of the top 50 Fortune 500 companies.[54] A recent internal USAID evaluation of GDA found widespread enthusiasm on the part of current and potential private-sector partners as well as significant administrative hurdles.[55] Several high-profile partnerships with philanthropies such as the Gates Foundation highlight the potential benefits of collaboration with private philanthropists.[56]

On balance, the policy issues around philanthropy fall into two categories:

- Policies to encourage (or, indeed, discourage) philanthropy in general and, more specifically, diaspora philanthropy

- Policies to promote strategic philanthropy by diaspora donors and to help these donors be more effective in their giving.

---

53 Global Alliance for Vaccines and Immunizations (GAVI), www.gavialliance.org.
54 USAID, "History of the Global Development Alliance," www.usaid.gov/our_work/global_partnerships/gda/history.html; USAID, Office of the Inspector General, Audit of USAID's Reporting on Global Development Alliances, Audit Report No. 9-000-09-007-P, June 4, 2009, http://pdf.usaid.gov/pdf_docs/PDACO272.pdf.
55 Tom Dewar, Christine Davachi, Katie Swinerton, Chad Bolick, and Karen Kaplan, *Evaluating Global Development Alliances: An Analysis of USAID's Public-Private Partnerships for Development* (Washington, DC: USAID, 2009), www.usaid.gov/our_work/global_partnerships/gda/evaluation.html.
56 For greater detail on USAID's collaboration with the Bill and Melinda Gates Foundation, see www.gatesfoundation.org/livingproofproject/Pages/usaid.aspx.

Of course, there is substantial overlap between the two sets of policies, but both are broadly relevant to governments in donor as well as in developing countries.

A. Policies to Promote (or Discourage) Philanthropic Giving

Most governments view philanthropic giving favorably, at least in principle; few actively discourage philanthropic giving (although some may do so indirectly via high taxation or bureaucratic hurdles). A number of policy areas influence the level of philanthropic giving in any country, but the most obvious — if also among the most delicate — is tax policy.[57]

According to a 2006 study by David Roodman and Scott Standley of the Center for Global Development, among the 21 member countries of the Organization for Economic Cooperation and Development's (OECD's) Development Assistance Committee (DAC), 12 countries allow individuals to deduct charitable contributions from taxable income, six allow partial income tax credits for charitable contributions, and three provide no incentive for charitable giving.[58] Among countries that allow full or partial deductions, three countries have a low ceiling on deductible contributions, 12 have a high ceiling, and three have no ceiling.

In the United States, individual contributions to certain charitable and nonprofit organizations have been exempt from US federal income taxes since income taxes were first implemented in 1917 (corporate charitable contributions first became tax deductible in 1935).[59] Research suggests that the impact of tax policy on charitable contributions varies by the size of the donation: large-scale individual philanthropy is driven by a relatively low tax burden for high earners as well as the dynamism of the US economy, while small-scale philanthropic donations appear less dependent on the tax structure. Economists gen-

---

57 There is an extensive literature on the impact of income taxes on charitable contributions. See, for example, Alice M. Rivlin, director, Congressional Budget Office, Testimony before the Senate Committee on Finance, September 28, 1982, www.cbo.gov/ftpdocs/109xx/doc10917/82-CBO-010.pdf; Congressional Budget Office, The Estate Tax and Charitable Giving (Washington, DC: CBO, July 2004), www.cbo.gov/ftpdocs/56xx/doc5650/07-15-CharitableGiving.pdf.
58 David Roodman and Scott Standley, "Tax Policies to Promote Private Charitable Giving in DAC Countries," Center for Global Development Working Paper No. 82, January 2006, http://cdi.mecon.gov.ar/biblio/doc/cgdev/wp82.pdf.
59 William C. Randolph, "Charitable Deductions," in Joseph J. Cordes, Robert D. Ebel, and Jane G. Gravelle, ed. The Encyclopedia of Taxation and Tax Policy (Washington, DC: The Urban Institute, 1999).

erally agree that tax benefits for charitable giving do not significantly increase donations from small- and medium-scale donors.[60] However, certain types of philanthropy appear more responsive to tax incentives than others (e.g., donations to elementary education versus medical and health-related causes).[61]

The US Congress's Joint Committee on Taxation estimates that tax-deductible contributions amounted to about $36 billion in 2009 — down from around $45 billion in recent years, undoubtedly as a result of the economic recession.[62] In 2008 religious organizations received 35 percent of all donations compared with 9 percent for organizations focusing on human services, 8 percent for public benefit organizations, and 4 percent for organizations focusing on international issues.[63] Between 1995 and 2005, private contributions (including diaspora donations) to US-based charitable organizations that focus on international issues grew faster than any of the other clusters of charitable groups analyzed by the Congressional Research Service.[64]

Generally, foreign charitable organizations must establish a legal presence in the United States in order to solicit tax-deductible contributions from US residents. There are three exceptions to this general rule: Tax treaties allow some charitable contributions to organizations in Mexico, Canada, and Israel to be considered exempt from US income taxes.[65] According to Robert Paine, a leading legal expert in the tax

60 Thomas L. Hungerford, "Tax Expenditures: Good, Bad, or Ugly?" Tax Notes, October 23, 2006; Jane G. Gravelle and Donald J. Marples, *Charitable Contributions: The Itemized Deduction Cap and Other FY2010 Budget Options,* Congressional Research Service Report to Congress R-40518, March 2010.

61 Jerald Schiff, *Charitable Giving and Government Policy: An Economic Analysis* (New York: Greenwood Press, 1990).

62 Joint Committee on Taxation, *Estimates of Federal Tax Expenditures for Fiscal Years 2008–2012,* Staff Report to the House Committee on Ways and Means and the Senate Committee on Finance, October 31, 2008, www.jct.gov/s-2-08.pdf; and Joint Committee on Taxation, *Estimates of Federal Tax Expenditures for Fiscal Years 2009–2013,* Staff Report to the House Committee on Ways and Means and the Senate Committee on Finance, January 11, 2010, www.jct.gov/publications.html?func=startdown&id=3642. Tax revenues lost due to charitable exemptions are estimated to total around $50 billion per year. See Jane G. Gravelle, *Tax Issues Relating to Charitable Contributions and Organizations,* Congressional Research Service Report to Congress RL-34608, August 5, 2008, http://assets.opencrs.com/rpts/RL34608_20080805.pdf.

63 Molly F. Sherlock and Jane G. Gravelle, *An Overview of the Nonprofit and Charitable Sector,* Congressional Research Service Report to Congress R-40919, November 17, 2009, www.fas.org/sgp/crs/misc/R40919.pdf.

64 Other clusters included arts, culture, and humanities; education; environment and animals; health care; human services; other operating public charities; and supporting public charities. Sherlock and Gravelle, *An Overview of the Nonprofit and Charitable Sector,* 21.

65 Internal Revenue Service, Publication 54 (2009), *Tax Guide for US Citizens and Resident Aliens Abroad* (Washington, DC: IRS, 2009): Ch. 5 "Exemptions, Deductions, and Credits," www.irs.gov/publications/p54/.

treatment of international philanthropy, the bilateral tax treaties between the United States and Mexico, Canada, and Israel provide for "reciprocal deductions of cross-border charitable contributions."[66] However, deductions are only allowed against income earned in the country where the deduction is made. For instance, a Mexican immigrant in the United States who donates funds to a charity registered in Mexico cannot deduct the donation against income earned in the United States, only against income earned in Mexico; according to Paine, "if the taxpayer earns no income in Mexico, then a deduction against his US income is not allowed." As a result, the utility of existing tax treaties for diaspora philanthropy is limited.

However, contributions to US-registered charities that then transfer donations overseas are allowed if the US organization retains control over the use of the funds. The trend of recent years, however, has been toward increasing restrictions on charitable contributions abroad due to concerns about terrorist financing.[67] Accordingly, some diaspora philanthropies such as the Ayala and Hariri Foundations have established branches in the United States.

A search of the Internal Revenue Service's *Cumulative List of Organizations described in Section 170(c) of the Internal Revenue Code of 1986* (commonly known as "Publication 78") — the federal government's database of tax-exempt charitable organizations — for groups with the word *diaspora* in their title yielded 51 results, compared with 249 results for groups with the word *migrant* in their title.[68] This is an admittedly crude measure of the size of the formal diaspora-based charitable sector in the United States, but still suggests that it is small compared with other sectors.

Governments typically allow favorable tax treatment of charitable contributions where contributions are considered to ease the burden on government-provided services — for instance, in providing for the indigent or impoverished. According to Robert Paine, the US House of Representatives' Ways and Means Committee concluded in 1938 that contributions to foreign charities do not relieve a government burden and accordingly should not qualify for tax-exempt status.[69] As Paine argues, this is an antiquated view of the US government's obliga-

---

66 Robert Paine, "The Tax Treatment of International Philanthropy and Public Policy," Akron Law Review 19 (2004): 1–24.
67 Roth, Greenburg, and Wille, "Monograph on Terrorist Financing."
68 Internal Revenue Service, *Cumulative List of Organizations described in Section 170(c) of the Internal Revenue Code of 1986* (version updated February 5, 2010), www.irs.gov/charities/article/0,,id=96136,00.html.
69 Paine, "The Tax Treatment of International Philanthropy and Public Policy."

tions — particularly if such contributions were to be sanctioned or promoted by USAID.

Indeed, recent tragedies established a strong legislative precedent for using US tax policy on charitable contributions to promote private donations to foreign relief and development causes. Notably, following the South Asian tsunami in 2004 and the devastating earthquakes in Haiti in January 2010 and Chile in March 2010, the US Congress approved legislation promoting charitable contributions to disaster victims.[70] (Similar legislation was passed following the Hurricane Katrina disaster in Louisiana in 2005.) The Haiti Assistance Income Tax Incentive (HAITI) Act (H.R. 4462), approved on January 20, 2010, allowed charitable contributions to Haitian earthquake victims to count for deductions on 2009 income taxes and allowed deductions for certain contributions to nonprofit relief organizations not registered in the United States.[71] According to the Congressional Research Service (CRS), accelerating deductions can have a quantifiable benefit for donors, although there is substantial debate whether these accelerated deductions influence donations since most charitable contributions in the wake of natural disasters are emotionally charged and are often made before legislation is enacted to allow the deduction.[72]

Although less studied, tax policies in developing countries can also influence trends in diaspora philanthropy. (Of course, tax systems in most developing countries are generally less sophisticated than in developed countries, and developing country governments typically rely less on income and wealth tax revenues.) During the 1970s, the Communist government of Vietnam established a 5 percent tax on all diaspora funds sent back to Vietnam through the banking system, including charitable contributions. The tax was reduced (and eventually removed) in the 1990s as a way of encouraging all kinds of financial flows from Vietnamese abroad — remittances, investment,

---

70 Joint Committee on Taxation, "Technical Explanation of H.R. 4783: A Bill to Accelerate the Income Tax Benefits for Charitable Contributions for the Relief of Victims of the Earthquake in Chile, and to Extend the Period from Which Such Contributions for the Relief of Victims of the Earthquake in Haiti May Be Accelerated," Staff Technical Paper, March 10, 2010, www.jct.gov/publications.html?func=startdown&id=3661.

71 Molly F. Sherlock, *Charitable Contributions for Haiti's Earthquake Victims*, Congressional Research Service Report R41036, January 22, 2010.

72 CRS analyst Molly Sherlock (2010: 4) provides the following example of the financial benefits of accelerating deductions of charitable contributions: "Assuming a marginal tax rate of 35 percent, a taxpayer who made a $1,000 contribution in January 2005 to a charity providing aid to tsunami victims, has a tax deduction for the gift worth $350 if claimed on the 2004 tax return. If the donor waits and claims the tax deduction on their 2005 return, assuming an interest rate of 5 percent, the present value of the future tax deduction is $333. Hence, the taxpayer saved $17 by claiming the charitable contribution on their 2004 tax return."

and philanthropy — and indeed the "Viet Kieu" (overseas Vietnamese) economy in Vietnam grew rapidly after removal of the tax.[73] Similarly, the government of the Philippines, through its embassy and consulates in the United States, familiarizes Filipino Americans with social investment opportunities in the Philippines. One of these is the government-sponsored "Adopt-a-School" program, which encourages diaspora members to support public schools throughout the country. Donations to this particular program are tax deductible by up to 150 percent of their value for income taxes in the Philippines.

Of course, reforms on tax policies are beyond the authority of international development agencies, have a wide range of domestic implications, and are typically subject to extensive deliberations. The tax status of donations to foreign charities raises a number of tricky policy questions, in particular having to do with monitoring and accountability — for instance, around questions of terrorist financing. But beyond tax policies there are a number of more modest ways for donor and developing country governments to promote diaspora philanthropy, including through matching grant programs for philanthropic contributions, the certification and monitoring of nonprofit organizations, and the establishment of Internet-based philanthropic platforms.

As described above, several countries have instituted matching grant programs for diaspora donations to public works projects, and in at least one instance, social welfare initiatives (i.e., Mexico's Three-for-One basic and secondary education scholarships). Matching programs for public works projects have been extensively studied and have been replicated to some degree in El Salvador, West Africa (with French support), and Pakistan (with Norwegian support). But the experience with matching grants for diaspora contributions to educational scholarships is more recent and, accordingly, less well known. Through Mexico's program, migrant associations and federal and state governments contribute to small educational scholarships for underprivileged Mexican youth. This ties in closely with the country's successful conditional cash-transfer program, known as *Oportunidades*," which encourages school completion and health care for underprivileged children.

Another way that donor and developing country governments can work to encourage diaspora philanthropy is by accrediting nonprofit groups or philanthropic initiatives and thus rewarding transparency, effective monitoring, and good accounting practices. Diasporas often hold

---

73 Sidel, "Vietnamese-American Diaspora Philanthropy to Vietnam."

deep-seated mistrust in the nonprofit sector of their countries of origin due to perceptions of corruption or inefficiency. In his seminal study of philanthropy among Pakistani Americans, Adil Najam cites mistrust as one of the most important barriers limiting donations to philanthropic causes in Pakistan.[74] In the Philippines, NGOs have attempted to overcome perceptions of corruption and inefficiency by participating in a government-sanctioned agency that accredits nonprofit organizations, the Philippine Council for NGO Certification (PCNC).[75] The PCNC aims to provide a "seal of good housekeeping" for NGOs, although to date there is little evidence that such efforts are succeeding. USAID has explored the operations and impacts of NGO accreditation and certification bodies; work in this field could have spillover effects well beyond diaspora philanthropy.[76] Support for impact evaluation meant to convince potential diaspora donors of the merits of specific projects could achieve similar objectives.

Finally, Internet-based philanthropic platforms are a relatively new channel of global philanthropy, so it would be premature to draw definitive conclusions regarding their impact. However, early studies suggest both promise — particularly in linking diaspora communities with philanthropic opportunities in their communities of origin — and challenges.[77] It is not clear that diasporas with immediate ties to their countries of origin prefer Internet-based philanthropy to donations via personal contacts; however, the Internet may be an effective tool to promote philanthropy among diasporas with more distant roots in the country of origin.

B. Policies to Build Capacity for Responsible and Strategic Giving

This chapter has argued that diaspora philanthropy is a reality that reflects donors' deep personal ties with their communities of origin, and will take place whether or not governments act to promote it. However, the question of how diaspora philanthropy can contribute to sustainable development efforts is less clear. Of course, not all philanthropy aims to promote development, but available evidence suggests that many philanthropic endeavors by diasporas are well-intentioned

---

74 Najam, *Portrait of a Giving Community.*
75 See www.pcnc.com.ph.
76 Catherine Shea and Sandra Sitar, *NGO Accreditation and Certification: The Way Forward? An Evaluation of the Development Community's Experience*, Report and recommendations to USAID from the International Center for Not-for-Profit Law, 2005, http://pdf.usaid.gov/pdf_docs/PNADB766.pdf.
77 See Desai and Kharas, *Do Philanthropic Citizens Behave Like Governments?*

but amateur, and are often disconnected from broader development strategies. While the decentralized and independent nature of diaspora philanthropy is an advantage in many respects, much good would come from greater mutual awareness (and possible coordination) among diaspora philanthropists, international donors, and country-of-origin governments. Accordingly, a second set of policy interventions revolve around the promotion of responsible and strategic philanthropy — that is, philanthropic giving that meets high financial accounting and transparency standards and aims to have a positive, lasting social and economic impact.

Policies to promote responsible and strategic giving by diasporas fall into two categories: (a) capacity building, and (b) information and knowledge management.

As described above, many high-profile diaspora donors establish foundations or trusts to more systematically pursue their philanthropic objectives, although the institutionalization of giving raises an additional set of challenges. Evidence of the impact of these philanthropic undertakings is limited — many of the initiatives are too new to draw definitive conclusions — and there are some reasons to question their long-term impacts. There is little doubt, however, that the celebrity of their founders and promoters raises general awareness about vital concerns to be found throughout the developing world, and that many individual lives have been changed by their activities. The challenge for many of these efforts is to capitalize on the celebrity of the founders to institutionalize informed and effective giving.

It is clear that many of the foundations established by diaspora celebrities could benefit from trustworthy professional advice and capacity building in areas such as financial management and strategic giving. Of course, smaller diaspora organizations such as HTAs could also benefit from capacity building in these same areas. Some organizations focus on the capacity building of diaspora associations, for instance, the National Alliance of Latin American and Caribbean Communities (NALACC), Oxfam-Novib, and the Florida Association for Volunteer Action in the Caribbean and the Americas (FAVACA).[78] More general efforts to identify good practices in diaspora philanthropy would represent a similar, if more modest, objective for USAID.

---

78 See www.favaca.org and www.enlacesamerica.org/leadership/hometown.html. For a review of Oxfam-Novib's efforts, see Tom De Bruyn, *Evaluation of Oxfam Novib's Capacity Building Programme for Diaspora Organisations* (The Hague: Oxfam Novib, 2008), www.diaspora-centre. org/DOCS/Oxfam_Novib_diaspo.pdf.

In the field of information and knowledge management, there is greater scope for disseminating information about USAID's work and its expertise in country-specific development challenges. However, USAID should be wary of attempts to "sell" projects to diaspora philanthropists. Diaspora donors typically have their own objectives. Rather, donors should engage in dialogue to seek diaspora input on priorities as well as to identify potential areas of mutual interest and collaboration. Of course, such collaborative efforts require diplomacy and political savvy as well as a healthy dose of realism on behalf of both USAID and diaspora groups.

V. Policy Options and Conclusions

The role of public policy in relation to diaspora philanthropy is a delicate one: to support and encourage diaspora efforts with a light hand so that philanthropy belongs to the philanthropists and their partners in social investment. The danger is that government interventions may co-opt, discredit, or seize the initiative from private donors. Instead, public policy should enable and encourage diaspora giving without seeking to control it.

Below, we provide several ideas on how US policymakers might begin to engage the idea of diaspora philanthropy. The ideas presented here require deeper, systematic consideration before moving forward toward implementation. However, they represent an initial step toward meaningful collaboration between the private philanthropic flows generated by diasporas and public authorities in the countries where they reside.

A. Tax Incentives to Promote Diaspora Philanthropy

Extending tax deductions for certain philanthropic contributions to international causes is the most obvious and potentially powerful policy response to promote and enable diaspora philanthropy. However, it is also among the most complex and challenging from a political and administrative perspective. Tax deductions for charitable contributions have long been utilized to subsidize the private provision of public goods (e.g., providing assistance to the homeless and indigent or building research capacity at institutions of higher education).[79]

---

79 Randolph, "Charitable Deductions."

Presumably, there is no reason to limit this to domestic policy; the same rationale would also apply to foreign policy objectives. Moreover, development economists Raj Desai and Homi Kharas of the Brookings Institution have argued that private aid flows better reflect the foreign aid priorities of US taxpayers; diasporas are simply an extension of this argument.[80]

Providing tax incentives to diaspora philanthropists is beyond the mandate of development agencies alone, and overlaps with the responsibility (or is entirely the province) of other government institutions such as, in the United States, the Departments of State and the Treasury (particularly the Internal Revenue Service) as well as Congress. In an era of tightening public finances, any proposal to extend tax deductions would obviously require careful consideration and analysis. The argument that it would be possible to align these contributions with US foreign policy objectives appears tenuous given the independence and autonomy of diaspora donors. One approach to addressing some of these issues might be, for example, to extend tax exceptions for charities registered in a limited subset of developing countries that have large diasporas in the United States, countries that have met a set of predetermined governance indicators (e.g., countries qualifying for Millennium Challenge Account grants), or countries that are of particular priority for USAID (e.g., Haiti).

B. Technical Support for Charity Registration in the United States

There are a number of policy options to facilitate diaspora philanthropy short of extending tax benefits for donations to foreign charities and which may be more practical policy options for development agencies. For instance, USAID could provide technical assistance regarding nonprofit registration in the United States to charities and nonprofit groups whose missions align with USAID objectives; or assist these groups in establishing relationships with diaspora groups in the United States. However, experience suggests that establishing such relationships between diaspora donors and groups or causes in the country of origin is a relatively long-term project that requires sustained investments of time and energies. Reaching out to potential diaspora donors sporadically, without thoughtful planning and evidence of impact can, indeed, be counterproductive and generate mistrust or suspicion.

---

80 See Desai and Kharas, *Do Philanthropic Citizens Behave Like Governments?*

C. Incentive Funds to Promote Social Innovation

Competitive innovation funds are an increasingly popular (if still novel and largely unproven) public policy approach that allows governments to seek new solutions to longstanding and often entrenched challenges. The Obama administration has established innovation funds in a variety of policy fields, including elementary and secondary education (the Education Department's Investing in Innovation Fund) and civic participation and community engagement (the Corporation for National Service's [CNS's] Social Innovation Fund).[81] Similarly, the Group of 20 (G-20) joined forces with the Rockefeller Foundation to launch the G-20 Small and Medium-Size Enterprise Financing Challenge to seek new ideas about financing small and medium-sized businesses in the developing world.[82]

USAID (in partnership with the Western Union Corporation) has experimented with a similar competitive grant program through its African Diaspora Marketplace to promote diaspora entrepreneurship in Africa.[83] The initiative is still being evaluated; while there is little doubt it could be improved, it is clear that the approach is novel. CNS's Social Innovation Fund could be another model that merits consideration and application in the diaspora context.

D. Capacity Building and Advice for Diaspora Donors

As described above, many diaspora philanthropists — both individuals and groups — are amateur philanthropists and often depend on volunteers. Few have professional staff with deep understanding of the technical issues involved in transnational giving or the intricacies of effective development projects. (Admittedly, many manage to do so without expert advice.) The experiences of other bilateral aid agencies, such as Spain's International Development Agency, that have worked

---

81 The Investing in Innovation (i3) fund for elementary and secondary education was established by the American Recovery and Reinvestment Act of 2009; see www2.ed.gov/programs/innovation/index.html. The Social Innovation Fund was funded by the 2009 Edward M. Kennedy Serve America Act. Corporation for National and Community Service, "Social Innovation Fund," www.nationalservice.gov/about/serveamerica/innovation.asp.

82 See www.changemakers.com/SME-Finance.

83 See www.diasporamarketplace.org/.

with migrant associations suggest that diaspora projects are often plagued by an underuse of professional advice.[84]

Some international donors and nonprofit groups have experimented with providing technical assistance on these issues to diaspora groups. The Ford Foundation, for example, supported the formation and first meetings of the Vietnamese NGO network VANGO. Training and capacity building in diaspora organizations can also benefit from donor support, which would probably be most effective if provided through umbrella organizations such as federations of Mexican and other HTAs, AFFORD in the United Kingdom, or the Center for Diaspora and Development in the Netherlands. Identifying the specific needs of diaspora groups and the specific challenges of working in their country of origin are critical to making such training workshops productive. USAID missions in diasporas' countries of origin could play an instrumental role in providing insight into the challenges of undertaking development projects in specific countries.

E. Responsible Giving Forums for High-Profile Diaspora Donors

High-profile diaspora donors — including celebrities, sports stars, magnates, and professionals — have unique advantages, but also face unique challenges. Similar to smaller-scale donors, many are fiercely independent and have clear ideas regarding their giving priorities and expected impacts. Others are less focused and can encounter challenges in the administration of individual foundations or trusts. USAID could consider establishing a forum for these high-profile diaspora donors to become acquainted with the development challenges in their countries of origin (from the perspective of policymakers), learn about giving strategies and the administration of development projects, and to network among themselves as well as with policymakers from donor and perhaps origin countries. Of course, attracting input and active participation from such high-profile members of diasporas would require USAID (or other US government partners) to identify policymakers with sufficient gravitas and name recognition — for instance, the USAID administrator — and to invest in establishing and maintaining these relationships.

---

84 Maribel Rodríguez, ed., *Cooperación para el desarrollo, migraciones y economías locales* (Madrid: Fundación Carolina CeALCI, March 2010), www.fundacioncarolina.es/es-ES/publicaciones/documentostrabajo/Documents/DT40.pdf.

F. Information, Outreach, and Knowledge Management

On a more basic level, USAID could make a greater effort to inform diasporas in the United States of its work in their countries of origin and to consult diasporas on needs and priorities for USAID. Reaching out to diaspora associations, professional groups, and consular official from diasporas' countries of origin who often maintain extensive ties with diasporas could represent initial steps to this end. *↲*

CHAPTER 6

CONNECTED THROUGH SERVICE:

Diaspora Volunteers and Global Development

Aaron Terrazas, Migration Policy Institute

Introduction

Nearly 1 million Americans spend time volunteering abroad each year, including about 110,000 immigrants residing in the United States and about 76,000 second-generation immigrants.[1,2] Indeed, researchers at the Center for Social Development (CSD), which studies volunteering, recently found that immigrants are 46 percent more likely than native-born US citizens to volunteer internationally.[3] (Immigrants and their descendants also represent a substantial portion

---

1 The US Census Bureau defines the foreign born as individuals who had no US citizenship at birth. The foreign-born population includes naturalized citizens, lawful permanent residents, refugees and asylees, legal nonimmigrants (including those on student, work, or other temporary visas), and persons residing in the country without authorization. The terms *foreign born* and *immigrant* are used interchangeably. The term *second-generation* immigrant refers to native-born US citizens with at least one foreign-born parent. There is no consensus on the term *diaspora* but for the purposes of this report we consider include immigrants and their descendants who self-identify as members of a geographically dispersed kinship group.

2 Migration Policy Institute (MPI) analysis of data from a pooled sample of data from the 2004 to 2008 September Volunteering Supplements to the US Census Bureau's Current Population Survey (CPS). The CPS is a monthly sample survey of about 60,000 US households conducted by the US Census Bureau. Since 2004, the September administration of the CPS has included a supplemental survey on the volunteer work of US residents. The results reported here average data from the September CPS administered from 2004 to 2008. The analysis is limited to the population aged 16 and older.

3 Amanda Moore McBride and Benjamin J. Lough, "Access to International Volunteering," Center for Social Development Working Paper No. 08-30, George Warren Brown School of Social Work, Washington Univ., Saint Louis, 2008, http://csd.wustl.edu/Publications/Documents/WP08-30.pdf.

of volunteers who donate time to efforts within the United States.)
These donations — of time, energy, and often more tangible resources
as well — reflect the meaningful personal and community ties that
Americans of all national origins have developed and maintain around the
world. The data used to calculate the number of international volunteers do not specify precisely where the volunteer work is performed
abroad (see footnote 2). But it is safe to assume that a substantial
portion of voluntary work performed abroad by immigrants — including, to a lesser extent, second- and higher-generation immigrants — is
undertaken in their countries of origin.

Extensive — if often scattered — evidence documents how diasporas
spend time working on community development projects and providing
pro bono professional advice and training to institutions in their countries of origin.[4] Many more spend time in their country of residence
volunteering for causes related to their country of origin or raising
funds for philanthropic activities there. Often diaspora volunteers have
the contacts and the capacity to undertake volunteer work outside
of formal programs. But diasporas also volunteer in their countries
of origin through a wide range of nonprofit and community-based
organizations, including ethnic community-based groups, hometown
associations, professional associations, alumni networks, and religious
organizations. Other members of diasporas volunteer through corporate or government volunteer programs. Some of these programs are
specifically targeted toward immigrants and their descendants, while
others are more broadly focused but still attract significant numbers of
diaspora members.

On balance, there is little doubt that diaspora volunteers make valuable
contributions to both national and community development objectives
in the countries where such work is undertaken and that such activities
often have a positive spillover effect in their countries of residence as
well. Yet despite the proliferation and contributions of diaspora volunteers, there has been (to our knowledge) no systematic analysis of the
volunteer work undertaken by diasporas in their countries of origin
— certainly not from a policy perspective. Many questions remain
unanswered, and it is not immediately evident what policymakers can
or should do to foster this phenomenon. This chapter represents an
initial attempt to survey how diasporas volunteer in their countries of

---

4   See Manuel Orozco and Rebecca Rouse, "Migrant Hometown Associations and Opportunities
for Development: A Global Perspective," *Migration Information Source*, February 2007, www.
migrationinformation.org/feature/display.cfm?ID=579 and Will Somerville, Jamie Durana,
and Aaron Terrazas, *Hometown Associations: An Untapped Resource for Immigrant Integration?*
(Washington, DC: MPI, 2008), www.migrationpolicy.org/pubs/Insight-HTAs-July08.pdf.

origin, to identify their impact where possible, and to weigh the potential merits and limitations of policy interventions.

The chapter is divided into three principal sections. First it discusses the impact of international volunteers and identifies common motivations for greater inclusion of diasporas in formal volunteer programs. In its second section, this chapter maps out a range of programs that offer volunteer opportunities for diasporas, both intentionally and inadvertently. Some of these programs were started and are operated by community organizations and diaspora-led nonprofit groups, while others were founded and are run by larger identity-based organizations such as professional associations and religious groups, national governments, or international agencies. In some cases, governments have partnered with community- or identity-based organizations. A third section draws lessons from the experiences described in the preceding section and discusses potential policy implications.

This study does not attempt a comprehensive evaluation of the impact or effectiveness of these programs, many of which are too small and too recently launched to be judged on the basis of random sampling, sound experimental design, or baseline assessment. The fact that many programs are the product of long-standing unstructured efforts by individuals and community organizations further complicates impact assessment. Moreover, diasporas may differ from development agencies or mainstream volunteer organizations in their view of what constitutes a desirable development impact. But based on available — often anecdotal — evidence as well as interviews with key stakeholders and program participants, we draw informed conclusions and identify promising practices that merit further inquiry. Still, readers should bear in mind that more research is needed to evaluate specific programmatic outcomes.

I. International Volunteering: Definitions, Motivations, and Impacts

Volunteering is an intuitive but conceptually elusive concept. The *Oxford English Dictionary* considers a volunteer anyone who "of his own free will takes part in any enterprise." This definition, however, may be too broad, as it makes no reference to motivations for participation and could include normal paid labor (as in a volunteer army). The *Merriam-Webster Collegiate Dictionary* frames the term more narrowly as "one who renders a service or takes part in a transaction while having no legal concern or interest." But this definition also fails to recognize that individual motivations for most activities are complex, multifaceted, and often impossible to isolate. As Jacqueline Copeland-Carson observes, "good intentions and self-interest coexist, albeit sometimes quite uncomfortably, through the world's philanthropy."[5] The same can be said for the world's volunteer work.

Conceptions of community service and giving vary dramatically across countries and cultures. Nevertheless, there are several widely accepted elements that can contribute to a common working understanding of what exactly constitutes volunteer work. After reviewing the official definitions of volunteer used by the statistics offices of the United Kingdom, Canada, Denmark, the United States, Mexico, and the United Nations, the International Labor Organization (ILO) proposed five essential features of volunteer work. The following features are drawn from ILO's 2008 *Manual on the Measurement of Volunteer Work.*[6]

- *Volunteer work must involve work.* Volunteer work produces something of potential economic value for a recipient.

- *Volunteer work is noncompulsory or nonobligatory.* Volunteer activity must involve a significant element of choice. People engage in these activities willingly, without being legally or institutionally obligated or otherwise coerced to do so. Social obligations such as peer pressure, parental pressure, or expectations of social groups do not make an activity compulsory.

- *Volunteer work can occur informally or through formal organizations.* Individuals can volunteer directly with other individuals or through nonprofit or other types of organizations.

- *Volunteer work is unpaid.* While there is general consensus that volunteer work is without monetary pay or compensation, the issue of remuneration of volunteer work is particularly complicated. Volunteers may receive nonmonetary benefits from volunteering in the form of skills development, social connections, job contacts, social standing, or psychosocial rewards. Some volunteers may receive reimbursement for out-of-pocket expenses of the volunteer assignment (e.g., travel, equipment)

---

5   Jacqueline Copeland-Carson, *Kenyan Diaspora Philanthropy: Key Practices, Trends and Issues* (The Philanthropic Initiative and the Global Equity Initiative, Harvard Univ., March 2007), www.tpi.org/downloads/pdfs/Kenya_Diaspora_Philanthropy_Final.pdf.

6   International Labor Organization (ILO), International Conference of Labor Statisticians, *Manual on the Measurement of Volunteer Work*, Room document prepared for the 18th International Conference of Labor Statisticians, November 2008, 12—13, www.ilo.org/global/What_we_do/ Statistics/events/icls/lang--en/docName--WCMS_100574/index.htm.

and living allowances or stipends to cover lodging. Compensation, however, cannot be "significant," is largely symbolic, and is not contingent upon market rates or the quantity or quality of the work. Whether compensation is considered "significant" is highly subjective and depends on a range of individual and community perceptions.

- **Volunteer work does not include work done for members of one's household or immediate family**. For obvious reasons, household work and unpaid work in family businesses are not considered volunteering.

Even ILO's precise definition may fail to take into account important gradations between voluntary and paid work on two fronts: discounted services and skills development. For instance, should providing services at a discounted rate with partial philanthropic or voluntary impulses be considered volunteering? What about volunteer work that offers the volunteer nonpecuniary rewards such as training or skills development? These commitments of time clearly represent some degree of voluntary impulse but do not fall within ILO's definition of volunteering, as compensation will likely surpass the "significant" threshold. Still, they might be considered partial donations if the compensation is far below the volunteer's normal remuneration.

Changes in the labor force in recent decades have also contributed to blurring the distinction between voluntary and paid work on the one hand, and education and training on the other. ILO's definition accepts that volunteer work can contribute to skills development if volunteers are unpaid or receive only symbolic compensation or expense reimbursement. In the past an apprenticeship might have fallen under this definition, although it is intuitively not volunteer work. In the context of a modern service economy, it is not clear if internships or fellowships — which can have altruistic motivations but are also typically considered career-building activities — should be considered volunteer work.

In practice, it is often difficult to draw a clear distinction between volunteer work and other types of work. This chapter does not attempt to resolve these ambiguities, but simply recognizes their existence. Ultimately, unified definitions are not a prerequisite for good policymaking. Volunteers in all forms and degrees of commitment are an unavoidable reality, and many make meaningful contributions to development efforts worldwide. The Johns Hopkins University Comparative Nonprofit Sector Project estimates that volunteers contribute $400 billion to the global economy each year.[7]

---

7   Lester M. Salamon, S. Wojciech Sokolowski, and Regina List, *Global Civil Society: An Overview* (Baltimore, MD: Johns Hopkins Center for Civil Society Studies, 2003).

There are also many nonmonetary benefits of volunteering — both to individuals and to communities at large. According to ILO, volunteer work has many positive side effects, such as the following:[8]

- Providing employment training and a pathway into the labor force

- Contributing to the global fight against poverty and addressing the Millennium Development Goals (MDGs)

- Providing services not easily provided by paid workers, such as mentoring

- Enhancing social solidarity, social capital, political legitimacy, and quality of life

- Serving as a means of social inclusion and integration of minority or excluded communities

- Providing a sense of personal satisfaction, fulfillment, well-being, and belonging to persons who volunteer

In addition to these benefits identified by ILO, an emerging body of evidence suggests that international volunteer service has a positive impact on individual volunteers, the host communities where the volunteer work is performed, and in many instances, volunteers' communities of origin. The preliminary results of a major study by Washington University in St. Louis' CSD suggests that international volunteer work broadens the global perspective of international volunteers, orients their career prospects, and contributes to building human links across countries.[9] Ongoing research by CSD is examining the impact of international volunteers on health and education outcomes in host communities.

International volunteers take their experiences home as well. As generations of Peace Corps volunteers have powerfully illustrated, youth who spend a formative period of their lives volunteering abroad often engage in a lifetime of volunteer work both domestically and internationally; many Peace Corps volunteers also pursue professions in public service or medicine. From a more narrowly focused strategic perspective, international volunteering is a vital tool of US

---

8   ILO, *Manual on the Measurement of Volunteer Work.*
9   Amanda Moore McBride, Benjamin J. Lough, and Margaret Sherrard Sherraden, *Perceived Impacts of International Service on Volunteers: Interim Results from a Quasi-Experimental Study* (Washington, DC: Brookings Institution of Global Economy and Development and Washington Univ. in Saint Louis Center for Social Development, May 25, 2010).

soft power. The Peace Corps' Office of Strategic Information, Research and Planning recently reported that Peace Corps volunteers improve the image of the United States abroad. "By living and working within local communities, Peace Corps Volunteers foster positive relationships with host country nationals, dispel myths about Americans, provide a broader context for understanding stereotypical American characteristics (e.g., being hard working)," the report concluded. "During their service, Volunteers share and represent the culture and values of the American people, and in doing so, earn respect and admiration for the United States among people who otherwise may have limited contact or exposure to Americans and American culture."[10]

II. What Role for Diasporas?

Extensive anecdotal evidence suggests that diasporas are an important subset of international volunteers. For instance, writing for Harvard University's Global Equity Initiative, Nick Young and June Shih describe how Chinese diaspora physicians in the United States, Hong Kong, Taiwan, and Southeast Asia independently travel to China to provide pro bono, hands-on training to Chinese doctors.[11] Similarly, a recent report from the German Agency for Technical Cooperation (GTZ) cites examples of Afghan physicians residing in Germany and Italy who operate clinics in Jalalabad, Mazar-e-Sharif, and the Chewa refugee camp, and of Ethiopian university professors who spend their summers teaching courses at Ethiopian universities.[12]

Much of this volunteer work takes place outside organized international volunteer programs. Diasporas often have connections in the communities, understand local needs, can easily enter and leave the country, and are not afraid of traveling alone in their countries of origin. As a result, they often do not require organizational support and their international volunteer work occurs under the radar of

---

10 Janet Kerley and Susan Jenkins, *The Impact of Peace Corps Service on Host Communities and Host Country Perceptions of Americans* (Washington, DC: Peace Corps, Office of Strategic Information, Research and Planning, June 2010).

11 Nick Young and June Shih, "Philanthropic Links between the Chinese Diaspora and the People's Republic of China," in *Diaspora Philanthropy and Equitable Development in China and India*, ed. Peter F. Geithner, Paula D. Johnson, and Lincoln C. Chen (Cambridge, MA.: Harvard Univ. Press, 2004).

12 Tatjana Bauralina, Michael Bommes, Heike Daume, Tanja El-Cherkeh, and Florin Vadean, *Egyptian, Afghan, and Serbian Communities in Germany: How Do They Contribute to Their Countries of Origin* (Eschborn, Germany: Deutsche Gesellschaft für Technische Zusammenarbeit, 2006) and Nathalie Schlenzka, *The Ethiopian Diaspora in Germany: Its Contributions to Development* (Eschborn, Germany: Deutsche Gesellschaft für Technische Zusammenarbeit, 2009).

public attention. Many of these extraordinarily committed individuals are motivated by genuine voluntary impulses, community ties, and a deep understanding of on-the-ground needs. Indeed, the independent, spontaneous, and needs-driven nature of many diaspora volunteers is part of the allure of the concept of diaspora volunteering.

But individual diaspora volunteering initiatives can also be chaotic and unorganized, and have unintended consequences. While the decentralized nature of diasporas' voluntary initiatives may be a benefit in some circumstances as it directs attention and resources to traditionally underserved communities, there are doubtless benefits from greater coordination (or at least mutual awareness) among volunteer initiatives. As the literature on diaspora entrepreneurship suggests, a desire to engage with the country of origin does not always translate into effective or sustainable engagement. Support structures may be particularly necessary for diasporas without immediate personal ties to the country — such as historic diasporas (e.g., the Armenian and Jewish diasporas) or the descendants of immigrants. Over the years a number of arguments have been forwarded as to why diasporas deserve particular focus in international volunteering programs. Below, we outline these arguments and discuss their merits.

A. Diasporas Provide Discounted Technical Advice

In the 1970s, many developing countries believed that the costs associated with hiring international development experts were unnecessarily high and represented a misuse of foreign development assistance. Thus, as the migration of highly skilled workers increased, some of these countries looked to their diasporas for discounted expertise and the first diaspora volunteer programs emerged. This concept of a "patriotic discount" is well documented — for instance, diasporas have invested in and lent money to their countries of origin at a discounted rate, although it is often less than expected.[13] Presumably, the diaspora discount operates for services as well as for finance. But a 2003 United States Agency for International Development (USAID) report concluded that the expenses associated with international volunteer programs are not always less than the cost of directly hiring a consultant.[14] As this chapter discusses later, the diaspora discount for volunteers may

---

13 Suhas Ketkar and Dilip Ratha, eds., *Innovative Financing for Development* (Washington, DC: World Bank, 2008).

14 Jill Keesbury, *The Value of International Volunteerism: A Review of Literature on International Volunteer-Sending Programs*, Report, US Agency for International Development (USAID) Development Information Services, July 1, 2003, http://pdf.dec.org/pdf_docs/Pnacw574.pdf.

apply only in the long term — that is, if and when volunteers remain active after the mission ends.

B. Diasporas' Linguistic and Cultural Familiarity Makes Aid More Effective

A second, widely accepted line of argument claims that incorporating diaspora volunteers into development projects increases the effectiveness of development aid by capitalizing on diasporas' cultural and linguistic familiarity with their countries of origin. International agencies operating in dangerous, war-torn, or volatile regions — such as Somalia and the Caucasus — have long employed members of the diaspora both directly and as intermediaries because of their language skills and ability to easily blend into the general population. An early review of diaspora volunteers in Turkey found that 24 out of 30 host organizations considered diaspora volunteers more effective than other foreign volunteers.[15] Interviews conducted for this chapter with several programs that recruit diaspora volunteers suggest that members of diasporas typically require less-intensive predeparture and postarrival orientation. Moreover, some programs encourage diaspora volunteers to lodge with family members or friends, further reducing costs.[16]

The argument that diaspora volunteers' cultural familiarity and linguistic skills make them more effective than other volunteers is often overstated, though. Migrants who have been away from their countries of origin for extended periods of time — and to an even greater extent, second- or higher-generation immigrants — may have only basic linguistic and cultural knowledge. As a number of the diaspora volunteer programs described here have learned, it may be counterproductive to require that volunteers speak the language of the ancestral country or to assume that volunteers will adjust seamlessly to life there. Bob Awuor of the UK-based African Community Development Foundation notes that "diaspora distractions," or personal or family concerns, can sometimes consume diaspora volunteers while on assignment.[17] In an early review of diaspora volunteers, Solon Ardittis of ILO points to the potential for patronage and favoritism in diaspora volunteer programs that allow host organizations to select volunteers based on personal

---

15   Solon Ardittis, *Le retour assisté des migrants qualifies dans leur pays d'origine: Les programmes multilatereaux du PNUD et du CIM* (Geneva: ILO 1984), 26.
16   MPI interview with Tedla W. Giorgis, founder, Network of Ethiopian Professionals in the Diaspora (NEPID) and Visions for Development, Inc., Washington, DC, January 27, 2010.
17   MPI interview via telephone with Bob Awuor, executive director, African Community Development Foundation, January 26, 2010.

connections rather than merit.[18]

C. Diaspora Volunteers Counter the Effects of "Brain Drain"

The argument that diaspora volunteerism can compensate for perceived development losses stemming from "brain drain" has been advanced for decades. But it remains controversial. Several high-profile initiatives target highly skilled and technical professionals from the diaspora for short- or medium-term consultancies in their countries of origin — often as volunteers. These programs grew out of the 1970s concern that the departure of highly skilled individuals represented a substantial human resource loss for many developing countries.

More recently, debates about the development implications of highly skilled migration have become more balanced, although they have certainly not disappeared. Scholars and policymakers have come to recognize three important points:

- Many skilled migrants continue to contribute to and maintain ties with their countries of origin after departure ("brain circulation").[19]

- Had their migration options been restricted, fewer people would have been able to develop their skills.[20]

- The prospect of increased opportunities for skilled migrants may influence the educational decisions of youth in some developing countries, yielding higher overall educational outcomes and a more skilled domestic workforce ("brain gain").[21]

It is impossible to completely dismiss concerns about the human resource and development implications of skilled migration. A systemic scarcity of highly skilled and technologically savvy workers likely impedes research and innovation in the developing world (although

---

18 Ardittis, *Le retour assisté des migrants qualifies dans leur pays d'origine*, 27.

19 Michael A. Clemens, *Skill Flow: A Fundamental Reconsideration of Skilled-Worker Mobility and Development*, Human Development Research Paper 2009/08, United Nations Development Programme, April 2009, http://hdr.undp.org/en/reports/global/hdr2009/papers/HDRP_2009_08.pdf.

20 See generally United Nations Development Programme (UNDP), *Overcoming Barriers: Human Mobility and Development* (New York: UNDP, 2009), http://hdr.undp.org/en/reports/global/hdr2009/.

21 Oded Stark, Christian Helmenstein, and Alexia Prskawetz, "A Brain Grain with a Brain Drain," *Economics Letters* 55, no. 2 (1997): 227—34.

the net effect is probably small relative to broader trends in international trade and investment shaping the developing world's economic prospects).[22] Even in the context of typically weak labor markets resulting from the global financial crisis that began in late 2007, employers across the developing world — including Argentina, Costa Rica, Mexico, Peru, Poland, Romania, and South Africa — consistently cite challenges in finding skilled workers.[23] (The economic crisis has proved to be far less severe in the developing world than in industrialized countries.) But this phenomenon may be limited to the short term — particularly in some important sectors, such as education and health care, which suffer from the effects of emigration in so many developing countries. In the longer term, concerns about brain drain may be misguided.

D. Volunteering Is an Entry Point to Long-Term Engagement

Some programs promote diaspora volunteering in the country of origin to increase volunteers' long-term engagement with their homeland via diplomacy, advocacy, investment, entrepreneurship, or even permanent return. These programs are justified in terms of the country of origin's long-term interests rather than its immediate development needs.

Emerging, but still largely anecdotal, evidence does indeed suggest that volunteer programs that aim to create a formative experience in the country of origin for diaspora youth may contribute to long-term interest in, commitment to, and engagement with the ancestral country. For instance, a former Peace Corps volunteer of Armenian ancestry whom the Peace Corps allowed to serve in Armenia eventually established an independent program to facilitate shorter-term volunteer opportunities in Armenia for the diaspora. Similarly, one Indian American youth volunteer who served in Indicorps — a yearlong community-based

---

22 The concept of a labor shortage is notoriously imprecise and complex. Shortages presume an undersupply of labor relative to demand. But as Ruhs and Anderson (forthcoming 2010) point out, there is a "dynamic and mutually conditioning" relationship between labor demand and supply. "Employer demand for labor is malleable, aligning itself with supply, as labor supply adapts to the requirements of demand. Moreover, these relations are situated within regulatory systems that may themselves be equally flexible," they write. Admittedly, this analysis is primarily concerned with labor shortages in developed countries, but it also holds particular relevance for discussions on the implications of skilled migration for developing countries. See Martin Ruhs and Bridget Anderson, eds., *Who Needs Migrant Workers? Labor Shortages, Immigration and Public Policy* (London: Oxford Univ. Press, forthcoming 2010).

23 Manpower Research Center, *2009 Talent Shortage Survey Results* (Milwaukee, WI: Manpower Inc., 2009), http://files.shareholder.com/downloads/MAN/817822014x0x297372/dab9f206-75f4-40b7-88fb-3ca81333140f/09TalentShortage_Results_USLetter_FINAL_FINAL.pdf.

service fellowship for Indian diaspora youth — paired a passion for education (fostered while working for Teach for America in the United States) with a passion for India and now works with Teach for India, that country's equivalent of the well-known US education reform movement. Another Indian American who volunteered in India in 2001 through the American India Foundation's (AIF) William J. Clinton Fellowship now serves as a political officer in the US embassy in New Delhi.

E. Overcoming Coordination and Collective Action Challenges

A final argument for including diaspora volunteers in organized volunteer programs revolves around the challenges of coordination and collective action. The focus of spontaneous efforts by diaspora volunteers may differ substantially from the priorities of national development authorities and/or foreign aid agencies. Without passing judgment on which priorities should take precedence — diasporas may have a better understanding of local needs whereas foreign aid agencies and national governments may have a broader perspective — working together can achieve some alignment of objectives and better allocation of resources. To this end, formal volunteer organizations should work to form true partnerships with diaspora community-based organizations. The experience of the US Department of Health and Human Services' Office of Refugee Resettlement and its various community-based partner organizations provides an instructive case of how productive such relationships can be.[24] The Mexican government's experience working with diaspora community-based organizations under the Three-for-One program is another good example of such cooperation.[25]

---

24 We are indebted to Tedla W. Giorgis for this point. For further information on the Office of Refugee Resettlement's work with community-based organizations, see Kathleen Newland, Hiroyuki Tanaka, and Laura Barker, *Bridging Divides: The Role of Ethnic Community-Based Organizations in Refugee Integration* (Washington, DC: MPI and the International Rescue Committee, 2007), www.migrationpolicy.org/pubs/Bridging_Divides.pdf.
25 See Francisco Javier Aparicio, and Covadonga Meseguer, "Collective Remittances and the State: The 3x1 Program in Mexican Municipalities," Working Paper, Centro de Investigación y Docencia Económica, Mexico City, 2008.

III. The Mechanics of Diaspora Volunteering

In this section we review the experiences of over a dozen volunteer programs that provide volunteer opportunities for diasporas, intentionally or otherwise. The aim is not to generate an exhaustive list of volunteer opportunities for the diaspora but rather to compile a range of examples that offer important lessons for policymakers or merit further study.

The experiences of diaspora volunteer programs are incredibly diverse. But there appear to be four "clusters" of programs, each one focused on a different type of diaspora volunteer.

- The first cluster includes programs that target subgroups of highly skilled volunteers — including those with expertise in entrepreneurship and business growth, public health, postconflict relief and recovery, higher education, and public policy advice and capacity building. These diaspora volunteers often resemble discounted consultants in providing expert insight (and occasionally services) and the missions are relatively short although occasionally repeated.

- The second cluster includes programs that target youth volunteers from the diaspora for a period of community-based service work in their ancestral countries. The terms of service for diaspora volunteers in these programs are typically longer and aim to provide a formative experience for the volunteers and a transformative interaction for the host communities.

- Another third cluster of diaspora volunteer programs are "multipurpose" in that they aim to attract a wide range of diaspora volunteers including both youth and highly skilled diaspora volunteers.

- Finally, a fourth cluster includes volunteer programs that do not explicitly targeted to diaspora volunteers, but that rely heavily on diaspora volunteers as a matter of reality and diasporas participate heavily in the programs.

A. Highly Skilled Diaspora Volunteer Programs

Many of the most familiar diaspora volunteer programs target highly skilled migrants and there is a rich and diverse policy experience with these programs at the international, national, and community levels. Skilled diaspora volunteers provide advice to business and entrepreneurs, build public health capacity, assist in postconflict relief and recovery, contribute expanding access to and improving higher education, and provide public policy advice in their countries of origin. Some of these experiences are described below.

1. The International Executive Service Corps and the Volunteers for Economic Growth Alliance

The International Executive Service Corps (IESC) was established in 1964 to mobilize American business expertise and private sector acumen for international development efforts.[26] The brainchild of Chase Manhattan Bank president David Rockefeller, Xerox Corporation chairman Sol Linowitz, and Senator Vance Hartke of Indiana, IESC is a private, not-for-profit organization that works closely with USAID. Since 1964, IESC has completed over 25,000 technical and managerial assistance consultancies in over 130 countries; it currently maintains a database of 8,500 volunteer experts.

Several members of IESC's staff are part of diasporas, and the organization actively recruits diaspora volunteers for its programs in Ethiopia, Lebanon, and Sudan. For instance, since 2006 IESC has partnered with USAID's Volunteers for Economic Growth Alliance (VEGA) to recruit Ethiopian American business owners to provide technical assistance and mentoring to Ethiopian businesses wishing to market export-oriented products. The initiative also provides technical assistance to Ethiopian banks, helping them understand US credit ratings as part of a USAID initiative to expand bank lending to Ethiopian diaspora entrepreneurs.[27] Similarly, IESC's Access to International Markets through Information Technology initiative in Lebanon aimed to develop that country's information and communications technology (ICT) sector by linking Lebanese ICT companies with global markets. Following the Comprehensive Peace Agreement ending the war between Sudan and Southern Sudan in 2005, IESC worked to create a database of skilled Sudanese expatriates in North America who might be able to volunteer their time toward the reconstruction and redevelopment of Southern Sudan (again in partnership with VEGA). IESC's partners have also registered and mobilized Sudanese expatriates living in other African

---

26 The information presented in this section is based on the Web site of the International Executive Service Corps (IESC), www.iesc.org as well as MPI interviews with Tarek Nabhan, vice president for global program operations, IESC; Sujeewa de Alwis, senior director of program operations, IESC; David Hartingh, senior director of program development; and Erin Spinnell, senior global program manager, IESC, March 25, 2010.
27 For further details, see Chapter 3, "Diaspora Investment in Developing and Emerging Country Capital Markets: Patterns and Prospects," in this volume.

countries such as Egypt, Uganda, Tanzania, and South Africa — a rare example of south-south migration and development efforts.

While many of IESC's efforts to work with diaspora volunteers have been successful, others have faced obstacles. First, business owners in developing countries may question the credibility of advice from diaspora volunteers more than that offered by nondiaspora members. Second, populating databases of skilled expatriates is a daunting challenge, as is keeping the databases updated. (Contracting members of the diaspora community as recruiters to populate the databases is among the more successful methods.) Third, there must be buy-in from the country of origin. In the case of its database of Southern Sudanese diaspora professionals, IESC eventually handed the database over to the government of Southern Sudan, which then lost the data.

2. American International Health Alliance HIV/AIDS Twinning Center and the Network of Ethiopian Professionals in the Diaspora

The American International Health Alliance (AIHA) is a nonprofit organization based in Washington, DC, that relies on volunteer health professionals — including nurses, physicians, hospital administrators, educators, allied health professionals, and public health experts — to build sustainable health-care capacity in developing countries.[28, 29] The HIV/AIDS Twinning Center is an AIHA program that pairs organizations in developed and developing countries that are working on similar or related issues in the global effort to improve services for people living with or affected by HIV/AIDS.[30] The Twinning Center's Volunteer Healthcare Corps (VHC) currently operates in Ethiopia, Tanzania, and South Africa and is piloting programs in Mozambique and Botswana. It provides volunteers with coach airfare; vaccinations and other preventative medical treatments when necessary; visa and work permits; travel, accident, and medical evacuation insurance; basic housing or a housing allowance; a modest stipend; and preassignment orientation and in-country support.[31] Volunteers are not recruited or

28 The information presented in this section is based on interviews with Tedla Giorgis on January 27, 2010, and Aazamina Rangwala, project associate, American International Health Alliance (AIHA) and HIV/AIDS Twinning Center, Washington, DC, January 27, 2010.
29 AIHA receives in-kind and financial support from USAID; the US Department of Health and Human Services (DHHS); the Health Resources and Services Administration (HRSA); the World Health Organization (WHO); the Global Fund to Fight AIDS, Tuberculosis and Malaria (GFATM); and the German Society for Technical Cooperation (GTZ). More information on AIHA can be found on its Web site at www.aiha.com.
30 HIV/AIDS Twinning Center, "Twinning against HIV/AIDS," www.twinningagainstaids.org.
31 American International Health Alliance (AIHA) and HIV/AIDS Twinning Center, "The VHC Program," www.twinningagainstaids.org/vhc_overview.html.

placed on a preestablished cycle; rather, the Twinning Center works with individual volunteers and host institutions to develop a program that meets both needs. Table 1 provides basic administrative data on the five programs.

Table I. Volunteer Health Corps Missions

Country	Program Inception	Number of Volunteers Placed	Number of Placement Sites	Total In-Kind Professional Time Volunteered (days)
Ethiopia	Sept. 2006	44	30+	14,434
Tanzania	May 2007	18	14	4,525
South Africa	Feb. 2008	14	15	2,977
Mozambique†	Feb. 2009	3	1	266
Botswana†	Sept. 2009	4	4	816

Notes: Only the Ethiopian program actively recruits diaspora volunteers. Data current as of July 31, 2010.
†Indicates that the program is in the pilot phase.
Source: Courtesy of the AIHA, HIV/AIDS Twinning Center

In 2006, the Twinning Center partnered with the Network of Ethiopian Professionals in the Diaspora (NEPID), a nonprofit association, to recruit diaspora volunteers with health-care expertise to work on VHC programs in Ethiopia.[32] (It is currently exploring opportunities to launch similar diaspora volunteer programs for Nigeria and Tanzania.[33]) NEPID is responsible for the outreach, recruitment, and selection of volunteers using its extensive networks among the Ethiopian diaspora. Particularly in countries with volatile political environments, it is important to select volunteers dedicated to the program's specific mission rather than to broader political or personal agendas in the country of origin. NEPID's part in selecting such candidates appears to be essential. NEPID also assists in identifying promising partner institutions in Ethiopia.

Since its launch, the partnership has placed 36 diaspora volunteers in Ethiopia. Although the majority of participants have been Ethiopian Americans, the volunteer program has also included members from the Ethiopian diaspora residing in Australia, France, and the United Kingdom. The partnership has found that diaspora volunteers require less orientation and case management upon arrival in the country of

---

32 NEPID is a project of Visions for Development, Inc., a private consultancy.
33 Current as of January 2010.

origin and generally take responsibility for their own lodging. Tedla Giorgis, founder of NEPID, also argues that diaspora volunteers may lead to more sustainable capacity building because they are more likely than other volunteers to develop relationships that continue beyond the volunteer program.

The Twinning Center is supported by the President's Emergency Plan for AIDS Relief (PEPFAR), the US government's multi-billion-dollar global effort to combat HIV/AIDS, tuberculosis, and malaria.[34] In the past, VHC has also worked with Volunteers for Prosperity (VfP), a presidential initiative launched in 2003 to encourage international voluntary service by highly skilled Americans in support of US foreign assistance priorities, particularly in the areas of global health and development.[35] VfP provides limited assistance in disseminating volunteer opportunities. Although VHC is supported through PEPFAR — a federally funded foreign assistance program — the Diaspora Volunteer initiative was the brainchild of NEPID and its founder, Tedla Giorgis.

3. Canadian University Service Overseas and Voluntary Service Overseas: Canada's Emerging Diaspora Volunteer Programs

In 2007, the Canadian University Service Overseas and Voluntary Service Overseas Canada (CUSO-VSO) launched a much smaller diaspora volunteer program than VSO-UK's Diaspora Volunteering Initiative, with support from the International Development Research Center (IDRC) and local diaspora associations in Canada.[36] (CUSO-VSO receives general operating support from the Canadian International Development Agency [CIDA] and is currently exploring the possibility of expanding its work with diasporas.[37]) As of January 2010, CUSO-VSO was piloting three diaspora volunteer programs, in Ethiopia, Guyana, and the Philippines, While CUSO-VSO's work with the Filipino diaspora

---

34 President's Emergency Plan for AIDS Relief (PEPFAR) was first approved by Congress in 2003 and was reauthorized in 2008 at a funding level of $48 billion over the period 2008 to 2013.

35 In addition to PEPFAR programs, Volunteers for Prosperity (VfP) volunteers support the African Global Competitiveness Initiative, the Water for the Poor Initiative, the Digital Freedom Initiative, the Middle East Partnership Initiative, the Millennium Challenge Account, and the President's Malaria Initiative. Executive Order 13317 of September 25, 2003, available at www.volunteersforprosperity.gov/news/eo13317.htm.

36 Canadian University Service Overseas and Voluntary Service Overseas Canada (CUSO-VSO) was formed in 2008 from the merger of two Canadian volunteer development agencies. CUSO was established in 1961 and VSO-Canada was established in 1995. CUSO-VSO also directly recruits volunteers from the United States and indirectly from India (through IVO), Ireland (VSO-Ireland), Uganda (VSO-Jitolee), and Australia (AVI).

37 MPI telephone interview with Rosa Candia, diaspora volunteering program coordinator, CUSO-VSO, January 19, 2010.

is still in the developmental stages and has yet to produce concrete plans, the group's experiences in Ethiopia and Guyana provide several lessons.[38]

In collaboration with VSO-Ethiopia and the Ottawa-based nonprofit Academics for Higher Education and Development (AHEAD), which focuses on "mobilizing and channeling resources and expertise available within the Ethiopian diaspora in Canada," CUSO-VSO launched an 18-month pilot and feasibility study on recruiting, selecting, and training volunteers from the Ethiopian diaspora in Canada to support the development of the health-care sector in Ethiopia. As originally envisioned, volunteers would work for up to six months in Ethiopia to train Ethiopian physicians and medical students in specialist topics. But in its early stages, the program failed to attract the expected interest from the Ethiopian diaspora in Canada, so CUSO-VSO had to recalibrate its expectations for the program. Program Coordinator Rosa Candia believes many prospective volunteers felt the duration of the missions was too long.

CUSO-VSO has had more success working with the Guyanese diaspora in Canada. A pilot project is to build on the work of a community association of retired teachers of Guyanese origin, the Canada-Guyana Teacher Education Project (CGTEP). Since the 1980s, CGTEP has been organizing teachers of Guyanese origin residing in Canada to undertake summer volunteer work to train teachers and expand educational opportunities in rural areas of Guyana. CUSO-VSO's initiative aims to identify longer-term volunteer placements.

4. The United Nations Development Programme's Transfer of Knowledge through Expatriate Nationals Initiatives

The United Nations Development Programme (UNDP) Transfer of Knowledge through Expatriate Nationals (TOKTEN) is arguably the oldest formal program aimed at facilitating diaspora volunteerism. It organizes short-term volunteer consultancies by expatriates in their countries of origin; these consultancies typically last anywhere from three weeks to six months. According to an early review of TOKTEN by Solon Ardittis, then at ILO, the program initially had four principal objectives:[39]

---

38 CUSO-VSO, "Diaspora Volunteering," www.cuso-vso.org/about-cuso-vso/how-we-work/diaspora-volunteering.asp; CUSO-VSO, "Promoting Volunteering from within the Ethiopian Diaspora in Canada," Proposal submitted by the Academics for Higher Education and CUSO-VSO to the International Development Research Centre (IDRC), provided to the MPI by CUSO-VSO.
39 Ardittis, *Le retour assisté des migrants qualifiés dans leur pays d'origine.*

- To lower the cost of technical advice

- To allow developing countries to gain access to consultants who would be more effective than other consultants due to their linguistic or cultural competencies

- To seed potential return of skilled expatriates or their long-term engagement with their country of origin

- To depoliticize development-oriented volunteer work as the aegis of UNDP allows political autonomy.

TOKTEN was launched in 1977 in Turkey with a focus on scientists, technology experts, and managers of Turkish origin residing abroad, and has since expanded to at least 50 other developing countries.[40] On balance, government interest in TOKTEN appears to have peaked in the 1980s and then gradually waned.

The program is administered by UNDP offices in participating countries with support from the United Nations Volunteers program (UNV) and the governments of participating countries, as well as third-party donors and, in some cases, the private sector.[41] As a result, the national programs vary substantially in their organization, management, and outcomes.[42] But all share a basic framework and key operating proce-

---

40 There is no centralized information source on the range of national Transfer of Knowledge through Expatriate Nationals (TOKTEN) programs. The following list of national TOKTEN projects was compiled by a comprehensive search of existing national TOKTEN documents and is accurate to the best of our knowledge. Argentina, Armenia, Afghanistan, Bangladesh, Benin, Bosnia and Herzegovina, Brazil, Cambodia, Central African Republic, Cape Verde, China, Czech Republic, Dominica, Dominican Republic, Egypt, Ethiopia, Ghana, Greece, Grenada, Guinea-Bissau, Guyana, India, Iran, Kyrgyzstan, Latvia, Lebanon, Liberia, Mali, Madagascar, Moldova, Morocco, Nepal, Nigeria, Pakistan, the West Bank and Gaza, Philippines, Poland, Rwanda, Saint Lucia, Senegal, Sri Lanka, Somalia, Sudan, Syria, Trinidad and Tobago, Ukraine, Uzbekistan, and Vietnam. Many of the national programs are no longer in operation.

41 International donors to recent TOKTEN programs in Mali and the Palestinian territories have included the governments of France, Japan, and Norway, as well as the European Union (EU) and United Nations Educational, Scientific and Cultural Organization (UNESCO). (In Mali TOKTEN volunteers contributed to projects funded by USAID although the agency did not fund the volunteers directly.) TOKTEN programs in Lebanon, Rwanda, and Sudan examined for this report were largely funded by UNDP and governments of the countries receiving volunteers. Mali's TOKTEN program has also received funding from the online philanthropic aggregator platform, GlobalGiving. TOKTEN programs in Afghanistan have been funded through Rapid Deployment Facility funds provided for Afghanistan by the governments of Belgium, Japan, Luxembourg, and Germany. The international development agencies of the Netherlands, the United Kingdom, and Canada have supported Sudan's TOKTEN program.

42 International coordinating meetings for the various national TOKTEN programs have been held in Istanbul, Turkey (1978), Islamabad, Pakistan (1982), Cairo, Egypt (1985), New Delhi, India (1988), and Manila, Philippines (1991). The sixth meeting was held in Beijing, China, in 2000 hosted by the government of China and UNDP. It included representatives from 13 TOKTEN program countries and aimed to exchange lessons learned and best practices of TOKTEN implementation, to assess the achievements of TOKTEN, and to explore future

dures. Standard features include the following:

- **Establishing, populating, and maintaining a dat/
tial volunteers.** All start-up TOKTEN programs fa͟ᴄ͟
of creating a current database of potential diaspora vo͟ɪ͟
Although this task has become substantially easier with the
advent of the Internet and new communication technologies,
it continues to require substantial outreach. Through consular
networks, community and professional associations, and university alumni associations, members of the diaspora are invited to
submit their curricula vitae to the database. As a result, a strong
online presence is now an essential component of any TOKTEN
program.

- **Volunteer requirements.** Volunteers must typically be expatriate nationals (i.e., individuals born in the developing country
and residing permanently and legally abroad; the program is not
open to second- or higher-generation expatriates), over age 25,
with at least a bachelor's degree, a record of excellence in their
field, and a minimum of five years of relevant work experience.
They must also display a genuine interest in contributing to the
development of their countries of origin.

- **Identification and prioritization of volunteering needs.** Agencies
requesting a volunteer typically provide terms of reference to
the TOKTEN management detailing the services being requested
and minimum qualifications. A committee composed of representatives of UNDP and government agencies approve projects.
(The precise composition of the committee varies by country.)
Programs may aim to support a recovery from war or disaster
(e.g., Sudan, Afghanistan) or may seek longer-term improvement in living standards (e.g., Mali, Rwanda). In some programs
the requesting agencies are allowed to access the database to
select a volunteer; in others, the TOKTEN management gives the
requesting agencies several volunteer options.

- **Completing the TOKTEN consultancy.** The TOKTEN program
provides volunteers with roundtrip airfare, lodging, and a
stipend during their consultancy. Upon completing their consultancy, both the TOKTEN volunteer and the requesting agencies
draft brief reports on the experience and submit them to the
TOKTEN management. TOKTEN guidelines require that stipends
to volunteers be substantially below remuneration levels for
comparable international experts. UNV-Ghana estimates that because their services are volunteered, TOKTEN experts typically
cost programs 50—75 percent less than international technical
experts.[43] But some evidence also suggests that the fees of even
TOKTEN experts remain at or above local wage rates in many
developing countries.

directions for the project. To the authors' knowledge, no publicly available evaluations or
guidelines resulted from the meeting and no subsequent meetings have since been held.
43 United Nations Volunteers (UNV) — Ghana, "TOKTEN Programme," http://ghana.unv.org/
how-to-volunteer/in-ghana/tokten-programme.html.

its early years, TOKTEN was guided by the philosophy that (1) volunteers should complement national development plans rather than direct development objectives, (2) consultancies should be purely temporary in nature without obligation for permanent return, and (3) remuneration for TOKTEN projects should be substantially below salaries in developed countries and in line with standard rates for comparable consultancies by private firms or international organizations in developing countries.[44] But experience suggests that some TOKTEN programs deviated from these founding objectives over time.

Ardittis documents how in the case of TOKTEN-Egypt the program became a much more active promoter of services than originally envisioned, violating TOKTEN's original mission to provide technical support rather than be a policy development program.[45] Similarly, the program is ostensibly neutral regarding permanent returns, but many of the national programs appear to view permanent return as a favorable (if unintended) outcome: about one-third of volunteers in Rwanda's program in 2006 returned permanently, and about one-fifth of TOKTEN volunteers in the Palestinian territories ultimately settled there.[46]

The question of remuneration is particularly complex: insufficient stipends or cost reimbursement could hinder recruitment of some (although certainly not all) highly skilled expatriate volunteers, but at the same time, unnecessarily generous stipends undermine the program's raison d'être and can cause friction between volunteers and local workers concerned about displacement. For instance, a 2006 evaluation of Sudan's TOKTEN program notes that the daily living allowance provided to volunteers is "extremely high" in some parts of the country and suggests that the stipend be adjusted to the local cost of living. Other TOKTEN programs, such as in Rwanda, have already adjusted the allowance to local costs of living.[47] It is important to

---

44 Rastam Lalkaka, *Transfer of Knowledge for Development through International Volunteerism* (New York: UNDP, 1987) cited in Bernard I. Logan, "An Assessment of the Potential Application of the Transfer of Knowledge through Expatriate Nationals (TOKTEN) Programme in Sub-Saharan Africa," *Applied Geography* 10, no. 3 (July 1990): 223—36.

45 Ardittis, *Le retour assisté des migrants qualifiés dans leur pays d'origine*, 52.

46 Katim S. Touray, *Final Evaluation of the Support Project to the Implementation of the Rwanda TOKTEN Volunteer Program*, Final Report to the UNDP, March 2008; Sari Hanafi, "Physical Return, Virtual Return: The Palestinian Diaspora and the Homeland," in *The Palestinian Diaspora in Europe: Challenges of Dual Identity and Adaptation*, ed. Abbas Shiblak (Jerusalem and Ramallah: Institute of Jerusalem Studies and the Shaml Palestinian Refugee and Diaspora Center, 2005).

47 Gopi K. Sedhain, *Assessment of Preparatory Assistance Phase Implementation Process: Transfer of Knowledge through Expatriate Nationals*, Report submitted to UNDP Sudan, Khartoum, November 23, 2006, www.sd.undp.org/doc/prodocs/dg3%20TOKTEN/Doc.26-35.pdf.

recognize that providing diaspora volunteers with stipends above local wage rates is sometimes justified, notably when their skills are truly scarce (or nonexistent) in the developing country or when they provide unique insights or global connections. But moving too far in this direction risks diluting the distinction between volunteers and paid consultants who would best be recruited in standard markets.

On balance, there is some evidence that volunteer hosts do receive a substantial discount on the services that TOKTEN consultants provide. Citing the case of TOKTEN-Palestine, UNV-Ghana estimates that the average TOKTEN volunteer costs about $3,000 per month — roughly one-quarter the cost of an international expert in the Palestinian territories.[48] UNDP-Sudan estimates that the average cost for each volunteer assignment of one and a half months was $7,357.[49] Estimates vary according to the length of the assignment, but there is little doubt that the cost is less than that of a similarly qualified international expert (though international assignments are inevitably expensive due to the cost of international flights and lodging). Individual TOKTEN programs have innovated two approaches to ensure that program costs are minimized without sacrificing the quality of volunteers: Focusing exclusively on high-value-added volunteers, and encouraging volunteers to build upon their missions and establish deeper institutional relationships

- **Targeting high-value-added volunteers.** Lebanon's TOKTEN program distinguishes between "junior" and "senior" volunteers.[50] Junior volunteers are required to have at least five years of active experience and "important" professional achievements. By contrast, senior volunteers are required to have at least ten years of active experience with "outstanding" achievements in their field of specialty. According to the director of TOKTEN-Lebanon, the program is increasingly focusing on attracting and placing senior volunteers to meet the needs of a developing country with comparatively high levels of education.[51] These highly skilled and experienced volunteers typically contribute strategic analysis and planning support rather than direct service. The program recruits most from the diaspora residing in North America and Europe (rather than in the developing world) since these individuals are more likely to be at the top of their

---

48 Ibid.
49 Sedhain, *Assessment of Preparatory Assistance Phase Implementation Process.*
50 Further discussion of Lebanon's TOKTEN program can be found in Paul Tabar, *Immigration and Human Development: Evidence from Lebanon*, UNDP Human Development Research Paper 2009/35, August 2009, http://hdr.undp.org/en/reports/global/hdr2009/papers/HDRP_2009_35.pdf.
51 MPI interview via telephone with Ariane Elmas, director, TOKTEN-Lebanon, January 8, 2010.

fields and have access to state-of-the-art technology. Yet, as noted by the director, the diaspora in the developing world might also have specific expertise necessary for Lebanon's development. She cited the example of a Lebanese engineer residing in northern Iraq with expertise designing urban traffic systems for cities in emerging countries.

- **Promoting long-term relationships.** In some cases TOKTEN merely provides a platform for members of the diaspora to leverage outside funding for volunteer work they are eager to undertake. For instance, one TOKTEN-Mali volunteer coupled his TOKTEN work in Mali with research funded by a US university and later used the consultancy to establish a joint research project between that university and the University of Bamako. Similarly, a TOKTEN volunteer in Lebanon collaborated over the course of two years on a joint project between a US-based medical research institution and the Lebanese government to develop chemotherapy treatment standards for Lebanon. Clearly, these arrangements — whereby volunteer service leads to more substantive institutional cooperation — have the greatest long-term development potential but are limited by their dependence on the efforts of extraordinary individuals. Longer volunteer missions may be a key determinant of whether a volunteer engages in a broader undertaking. An evaluation of Rwanda's TOKTEN program finds that one of the greatest constraints on the program's effectiveness is the relatively short term of assignments, which averaged less than two months.[52]

5. The International Organization for Migration's Migration for Development in Africa Program

In addition to TOKTEN, another initiative that aims to facilitate short-term volunteer work among highly educated diasporas is the International Organization for Migration's (IOM's) Migration for Development in Africa (MIDA) in the Great Lakes region of Africa. (MIDA Great Lakes is one of several MIDA programs launched by IOM starting in 2001.[53]) It is much smaller and more narrowly targeted than TOKTEN, but it is similarly structured.[54]

---

52 Touray, *Final Evaluation of the Support Project to the Implementation of the Rwanda TOKTEN Volunteer Program.*

53 Migration for Development in Africa (MIDA) grew out of the International Organization for Migration's (IOM's) Return of Qualified African Nationals (RQAN) initiative in the 1980s, which aimed to assist African expatriates return permanently to their countries of origin. On the origins of the MIDA programs, see IOM, Office of the Inspector General, *Evaluation of the Migration for Development in Africa Initiative as an Illustration of IOM's Approach to Making Migration Work for Development,* Final Report, Geneva, August 2007. Other MIDA projects are generally considered to have been failures. See for example, IOM, Office of the Inspector General, *Evaluation of the MIDA Italy Project* (Final report, Geneva, May 2005).

54 Another IOM program based upon a similar model and with similar results is the Temporary

The MIDA Great Lakes project was launched by IOM's Brussels office in 2001 with support from the Belgian Federal Ministry of Foreign Affairs, International Trade, and Development Cooperation.[55] A formal evaluation of the program was requested by the 2007 Global Forum on Migration and Development, hosted by the Belgian government. This discussion draws the formal evaluation's outcomes.

The project sought to involve the Rwandan, Burundian, and Congolese (from the Democratic Republic of the Congo, DRC) diasporas in three categories of transfers that the project's designers considered essential for development in the Great Lakes region of Central Africa: (1) physical transfers via temporary returns to the country of origin to engage in volunteer work, (2) skill transfers through long-distance volunteering, and (3) financial transfers, namely in the form of investment. The volunteers focused on three sectors: higher education, health, and rural development. Under the MIDA Great Lakes program, IOM's Brussels office developed and maintained a database of skilled Rwandans, Burundians, and Congolese residing abroad. This database eventually grew to include over 1,000 individuals. Local IOM offices would advertise the program and collect volunteer requests. A local advisory committee (whose composition varied in each of the three countries) would then review the requests and prioritize needs. IOM Brussels would then prescreen candidates and provide between two and five options to the requesting agency.

The project's third phase — between 2005 and 2006 — supported 160 volunteer missions: 49 in the DRC, 15 in Burundi, and 14 in Rwanda. Among all volunteers in the three countries, over two-thirds (67 percent) worked in universities and higher education, 14 percent worked in ministries and public sector agencies, 10 percent in NGOs, 9 percent in hospitals, and the remaining 3 percent in the private sector. Project funds supported travel and a small stipend for volunteers. The entire process — from the initial volunteer request to the arrival of the expert — typically took about six months, which the evaluation criticizes as unnecessarily protracted. The missions varied in length from four to 190 days; the average mission was 55 days long. A 2008 independent evaluation of the program estimated that each placement cost about 10,321 euros (about $15,000) compared to about 15,000 euros (about

Return of Qualified African Nationals to Sierra Leone program. See Robyn Joanne Mello, *Reaping What's Been Sown: Exploring Diaspora-Driven Development for Sierra Leone*, thesis submitted to the faculty of the Univ. of Delaware in partial fulfillment of the requirements for the degree of bachelor of arts (honors) in sociology with distinction, spring 2009, http://dspace. udel.edu:8080/dspace/bitstream/19716/4237/3/Mello,%20Robyn_2009_Thesis.pdf.
55   This discussion of the MIDA project draws on Société d'Études et d'Évaluation sarl., *Evaluation du Programme MIDA Grands Lacs, Phase III*, Final Report to IOM, Luxembourg, August 2008.

$22,000) per volunteer for TOKTEN-Rwanda.[56] The final evaluation of the first phase of the TOKTEN-Rwanda project (for the funding period December 2005 to December 2007) does not include direct estimates of program costs per volunteer.[57] But data available in the report suggest that 52 missions were conducted over the course of three years with a total available budget of $592,000, of which $557,000 was spent. This yields an estimated cost per TOKTEN volunteer of $10,711 (about 7,320 euros) — half the estimate cited in the MIDA Great Lakes evaluation. Differences between the two programs in the average time spent volunteering as well as currency fluctuations account for some of the difference. On balance, MIDA's claim of cost savings is probably overstated and the cost difference between the two programs is likely minimal.

Overall, the 2008 independent evaluation of the MIDA Great Lakes program pointed to disappointing results: the virtual skill and financial transfer components of the project evoked little interest from the diasporas, and capacity to support the virtual volunteers was extremely limited. For instance, attempts to launch several distance courses taught by instructors from the diaspora suffered from limited access to computer technologies and patchy Internet access in the Great Lakes region. Similarly, plans by one diaspora physician to provide online anesthesiology instruction to medical students and professionals at the University of Lubumbashi (DRC) were hampered by insufficient medical facilities and supplies. The evaluation of the skilled-diaspora volunteer component of the project was more positive, though it was suggested that the program increase volunteer terms and improve coordination with development priorities.

Another MIDA program — MIDA in the Horn of Africa — aimed to recruit members of the Somali diaspora living in Finland for medical and public health volunteer missions in Somaliland and Puntland.[58] With support from the Finnish Foreign Ministry; the Association of Somali Healthcare Professionals in Nordic Countries; and IOM offices in Helsinki, Hargeisa, and Bossaso, the program placed 22 volunteer missions ranging from 3.5 weeks to 3 months between August 2008 and December 2009. IOM estimates that about 500 doctors, hospital nurses, laboratory technicians, nursing and medical students, and about 1,000

---

56 Euro-dollar conversions are calculated at average daily interbank exchange rates in 2008, the year of the evaluation: about 1.47 euros per dollar and $0.68 dollars per euro.

57 Touray, *Final Evaluation of the Support Project to the Implementation of the Rwanda TOKTEN Volunteer Program.*

58 This paragraph draws on Thomas Lothar Weiss, ed., *Migration for Development in the Horn of Africa: Health Expertise from the Somali Diaspora in Finland* (Helsinki: IOM, Regional Office for the Nordic and Baltic States, 2009). We are also indebted to Frantz Celestin of the IOM Office for North America and the Caribbean for bringing this initiative to our attention.

patients in Somaliland and Puntland benefited from the volunteers.

6. The Advisory Council of the Institute for Mexicans Abroad

Some developing countries have mobilized diasporas to serve on volunteer public policy advisory councils.[59] In a groundbreaking study on the institutions developing countries have established to maintain ties with their diasporas, Dovelyn Agunias of MPI recently identified a number of such advisory bodies, the most notable of which is the Advisory Council of the Institute for Mexicans Abroad — CCIME by its Spanish acronym.[60] The council is composed of members of the Mexican diaspora elected to represent various consular jurisdictions and to provide public policy advice on issues of concern both in Mexico and across the diaspora.

7. USAID Efforts to Mobilize Diaspora Volunteers for Postconflict Relief and Recovery

Admittedly, not all diaspora volunteer programs are successes. Over the past decade, USAID has undertaken two extremely small projects to encourage diaspora volunteers in their countries of origin. Both projects described here were framed in terms of promoting diaspora volunteers as a means to building relief-and-recovery capacity in the country of origin. The limited publicly available information on the two programs suggests that neither was particularly successful in promoting diaspora volunteers.

Starting in 2001, the nonprofit development group America's Development Foundation (ADF) partnered with USAID to launch the Community Revitalization through Democratic Action (CRDA) Program in the Vojvodina region of eastern Serbia. The program leveraged over $50 million in public and private resources over six years to promote agriculture development projects, small- and medium-size enterprise creation, trade promotion and market access, tourism development, economic infrastructure expansion, and a variety of other targeted interventions.[61] As part of the program, ADF attempted to recruit

---

59 We are grateful to José Borjón of the Embassy of Mexico in Washington, DC, for this point. See José V. Borjón, "Volunteering in the Diaspora: The Case of Mexico," essay provided to MPI, March 2010.
60 Dovelyn Agunias, ed., *Closing the Distance: How Governments Strengthen Ties with Their Diasporas* (Washington, DC: MPI, 2009).
61 America's Development Foundation (ADF), *Community Revitalization through Democratic Action Economy Program*, Final report to USAID under agreement 169-A-00-01-00124-00, October 2007, www.adfusa.org/content/document/detail/812/.

skilled volunteers from the Serbian diaspora residing in the United States. In 2005, ADF advertised volunteer opportunities via a variety of ethnic media — including newspapers and Serbian-language television — and at community centers. Volunteer opportunities were flexible both in terms of placement and duration, and ADF expressed willingness to adapt the mission to the particular needs of the individual volunteer. But after several months of advertising, only two diaspora volunteers had been identified, and the initiative was terminated.[62] ADF officials suspect that the relative lack of interest among the Serbian diaspora relates to an inability to sacrifice several months of paid work in the United States to undertake volunteer work in Serbia.

USAID undertook a second project to work with diaspora volunteers in 2006 and 2007. The Diaspora Skills Transfer Program for South Sudan, which was implemented by the Academy for Educational Development (AED), was more narrowly targeted at mobilizing diaspora expertise to support reconstruction efforts in South Sudan following the Comprehensive Peace Agreement signed in 2005. The program aimed to select up to 150 highly skilled members of the South Sudanese diaspora to provide technical support for reconstruction and redevelopment efforts at the Southern Sudanese ministries of education and health.[63] The program was open to South Sudanese expatriates residing around the world; between February 2006 and the program's termination in early 2007, 88 volunteers were sent to 25 locations in Southern Sudan for one- to eight-month assignments.[64] The coordinating agency — in this case AED — undertook the tasks of identifying priority volunteer opportunities, compiling a database of potential volunteers, and selecting and placing volunteers.[65]

B. Diaspora Youth Volunteer Programs

Volunteer programs designed to attract diaspora youth are a more recent phenomenon and the policy experience is much thinner. Most of these volunteer programs are managed my community organizations based in the country of origin. Three experiences are described below.

---

62 This description of the Serbian diaspora volunteer program is taken from an MPI interview via telephone with Marina Cukic, office manager, ADF, February 1, 2010.
63 This summary is based on information available on the Academy for Educational Development's (AED's) Web site at http://cit.aed.org/forecast_sudan_faq.htm. To our knowledge, no formal evaluation of the program was undertaken.
64 Academy for Educational Development (AED), "Program Volunteer Alumni," http://cit.aed.org/forecast_sudan_program%20alumni.htm.
65 To the author's knowledge, no final evaluation of the project was conducted. No response was received from several attempts to contact AED staff.

1. Indicorps: Targeting Diaspora Youth Volunteers for Community-based Development Work

Established in 2002 by US-born siblings Anand, Sonal, and Roopal Shah, Indicorps is a nonprofit organization based in Ahmedabad, India, that encourages diaspora Indians to actively participate in India's development.[66] It places youth from the Indian diaspora with grassroots community organizations across India, generally for one-year fellowships (though some fellows decide to extend their term by an additional year and others have more recently held shorter fellowships over the summer). The fellowships are strongly rooted in traditional Gandhian precepts — particularly in the ideas that the fellow should strive to "be the change that you want to see in the world" and that service is a two-way process of mutual learning. It is expected that fellows will both culturally enrich and learn from their host communities, as well as gain invaluable personal experience, strengthen their ties with India, and deepen their sense of civic responsibility both at home and within the global Indian diaspora.[67] The program aims to "engage the most talented young Indians from around the world on the frontlines of India's most pressing challenges" and "nurture a new brand of socially conscious leaders with the character, knowledge, commitment, and vision to transform India and the world."[68]

Indicorps is a small program, with only 26 fellows in 2009—10 (up from four in the program's first year). The intensive application process — involving the submission of a résumé, several essays, and letters of recommendation, as well as an interview — results in an applicant pool that is highly motivated. Most of the fellows have been recent college graduates (the oldest thus far was 31), and although the majority of them have hailed from the United States, some were first-, second-, and higher-generation migrants whose ancestors had settled in Australia, Canada, Ghana, Guyana, Hong Kong, Saudi Arabia, Singapore, South Africa, the United Arab Emirates, the United Kingdom, and the Virgin

---

66 This description on Indicorp's guiding philosophy, work, and experience is drawn from Indicorp's Web site, www.indicorps.org, as well as an MPI interview with Roopal Shah, executive director of Indicorps in Washington, DC, on October 30, 2009; Indicorps, *Perspectives: Indicorp's 2008—2009 Reflections on Change*, program brochure provided to the authors; and MPI interviews with several former Indicorps volunteers, including Neil Jain, Aazamina Rangwala, Priya Jindal, Sheela Prasad, Sahil Chaudry, Ashish Gupta, Chetan Shenoy, and Pulkit Agrawal.

67 Indicorps publications cite the following quote, which is attributed to Australian Aboriginal activist Lila Watson, to describe their idea of service work: "If you have come here to help me, you are wasting your time. But if you have come because your liberation is bound up with mine, then let us work together."

68 Indicorps, *Perspectives: Indicorp's 2008—2009 Reflections on Change*.

Islands.[69] (More recently Indicorps has begun accepting a limited number of applications from urban youth within India who wish to volunteer in India's rural regions.) Over half (75 of 121) were female, and all had at least a university-level education.[70] Some had traveled to India frequently and were familiar with the country, while others were the first of their families to return to India in several generations. To facilitate travel to India, volunteers are normally required to have nonresident Indian cards, which serve as multientry visas and grant work authorization.

Among the 121 Indicorps fellows placed between 2002 and early 2010, most did their service in rural areas. Some appeared to be interested in careers in international development and likely viewed their volunteer work as similar to an internship; others likely viewed it as an escape from routine life in the United States (for instance, several volunteers left jobs in finance or consulting to spend time volunteering). Still others had more personal motivations (for instance, one volunteer was inspired to work with the blind in India because of his own Indian-born grandfather's blindness).

Indicorps fellows are expected to live simply. Fellows pay for their own airfare and health insurance, and the partner organizations with which the fellows work provide housing. Indicorps itself runs a month-long training and orientation session upon fellows' arrival in India, including language training when necessary. Fellows receive a small monthly stipend of about 2,000 rupees (about $43). Indicorps' annual budget of about $75,000 is drawn from individual donations; the group relies on volunteers for some strategic planning work. During their volunteer placements Indicorps fellows abstain from alcohol and tobacco and are prohibited from engaging in intimate personal relationships with members of the communities they serve. In interviews, current fellows and former fellows said that they largely adhered to these rules; however, many recognize that this is likely a function of the small size of the program, the intense application and orientation processes, and a system of mutual accountability whereby fellows are in regular contact with their peers as well as former volunteers.

Fellows typically work on specific, localized projects — for instance,

---

69 The 1.5 generation was born in the country of origin but immigrated before age 12 and was accordingly raised and had formative life experiences in the destination country. The second generation was born in the destination country to one or more foreign-born parent. See Ruben Rumbaut and Alejandro Portes, *Ethnicities: Children of Immigrants in America* (New York: Russell Sage Foundation, 2001).

70 These data are derived from MPI analysis of fellow profiles available on the Indicorps Web site (www.indicorps.org/ourfellows.php).

helping orphans in rural Gujarat, forming an Ultimate Frisbee league for urban children in Ahmedabad, or developing literacy curricula for the children of migrant workers in Maharashtra. These small projects likely have a large impact in the host communities, but are not necessarily connected to broader development objectives. Other Indicorps assignments are more closely aligned with the program's mission of applying the brightest young minds from the diaspora to India's pressing development challenges. For instance, one fellow helped the city of Hyderabad improve the accessibility of its metropolitan bus system. Thanks to Indicorps' partnership with the Grassroots Development Laboratory (GDL) based in Bagar, Rajasthan — a small village in northern India — other fellows innovate small-scale demonstration projects for solutions to problems such as potable water access, sewage and sanitation, and enterprise development that, if successful, could be more broadly replicated across India (see Box 1).[71]

Indicorps has not undertaken any evaluation of its fellows' impact on the communities where they serve, but anecdotal evidence gleaned from interviews with former volunteers suggests that the program is a formative experience in the lives of most fellows. In some respects, the program is designed to have a long-term rather than an immediate effect on development in India. Although it is still too early to draw definitive conclusions about Indicorps' long-term impact, some early evidence suggests that former Indicorps volunteers continue to be engaged with India. One example is Sheela Prasad, who discovered a passion for education during an Indicorps fellowship. After working with Teach for America, she eventually returned to India to work for Teach for India, the group's Indian equivalent.[72] Other former Indicorps volunteers recently launched a series of "Engage in Change" events in the United States to promote a culture of grassroots activism and community engagement within the Indian American community.

2. The Armenian Volunteer Corps and Birthright Armenia

The Yerevan-based Armenian Volunteer Corps (AVC) was established in 2000 to promote volunteering in Armenia by the diaspora.[73] AVC grew

---

71 Grassroots Development Laboratory (GDL) is the initiative of the Piramal Foundation, a philanthropic initiative of the Piramal family, a prominent Indian industrialist family.
72 On Teach for America, see www.teachforamerica.org. On Teach for India, see www.teachforindia.org.
73 The information presented here is drawn from the Web site of the Armenian Volunteer Corps (AVC), www.armeniavolunteer.org and from MPI interviews via telephone with Sharistan Melkonian, executive director of AVC, on January 26, 2010; with Rev. Fr. Hovnan Demerjian (formerly Jason Demerjian), cofounder of AVC, on February 26, 2010; and with Thomas J. Samuelian, cofounder of AVC, on March 2, 2010.

Box 1. Indicorps' Partnership with the Grassroots Development Laboratory in Bagar, Rajasthan

Indicorps aims to create opportunities for socially aware diaspora youth to serve India by using their skills, time, and resources to advance grassroots projects and sustainable strategies for change in India. The partnership between Indicorps and GDL in Bagar, Rajasthan, is a powerful example of how the energies of diaspora youth can be mobilized to address development challenges.

GDL is a project of the Piramal Foundation — the philanthropic initiative of the Piramal family, a prominent Indian industrialist family — and focuses on implementing small-scale social enterprises to address the development challenges of rural India. It is located in the village of Bagar, Rajasthan (about 10,000 residents), which faces many developmental challenges including access to basic health care, potable water, solid waste management, and employment.

The partnership operates with a team of Indicorps fellows, other international volunteers, interns, and local staff. GDL volunteers identify rural development needs and then develop market-based, sustainable solutions. GDL teams must thoroughly research project proposals and write detailed plans with specific goals, progress benchmarks, and budgets.

Indicorps fellows have been instrumental in launching three social enterprises in recent years (two of which have since evolved into independent companies), including the following:

A vocational training institute that provides the industry-focused computer literacy skills demanded by employers yet not included in basic education curricula

A rural business process outsourcing (BPO) company, Source for Change, that provides employment for rural women

A purified water distribution business, Sarvajal ("water for all"), which has developed a model to reduce barriers to entry in the drinking water distribution business

Further information about GDL, Source for Change, and Sarvajal can be found at www.piramal.org.in, www.sourceforchange.in, and www.sarvajal.com, respectively.

Sources: Grassroots Development Laboratory (www.piramal.org.in) and Migration Policy Institute (MPI) interview with Ashish Gupta, Indicorps fellow 2006—07, via telephone, March 9, 2010.

out of the experience of Rev. Fr. Hovnan Demerjian (formerly Jason Demerjian), who first arrived in Armenia as a Peace Corps volunteer in 1996. Initially the Peace Corps had declined to place Demerjian in Armenia, upholding its policy of not placing diaspora volunteers in their countries of origin, but in this case the group responded to lobbying on Demerjian's behalf and eventually sent him to Armenia, where he developed the idea of creating a more accessible way for diaspora Armenians to volunteer in their homeland. AVC was launched with initial funding from the Fund for Armenian Relief, an Armenian American charity established in the aftermath of the devastating earthquake of 1988.

Unlike most Indicorps volunteers, who are typically second-generation (in some instances first-generation) immigrants and have active roots in India, most AVC volunteers have much more distant roots in Armenia, dating to the early twentieth century. Moreover, most diaspora Armenians in the West trace their roots to historic Western Armenia rather than the modern Armenian state directly to its east. (Historic Western Armenia was located in the modern states of Turkey, Syria, Iraq, and Iran.) As a result, few diaspora Armenians are willing to undertake volunteer work in Armenia outside the framework of an organized program.

As of December 2009, the AVC had helped about 300 volunteers work in about 150 community organizations throughout Armenia. AVC is more broadly focused than Indicorps, accepting applicants aged 21 years or older (most of the volunteers are in their 20s and 30s) for service projects (in schools, nonprofit groups, churches, and the private sector) that range from one month to one year. A primary focus is providing English-language instructors to rural Armenian schools. AVC does not provide stipends, but does provide housing for placements outside of Yerevan. There is no language requirement (although Eastern Armenian language courses are encouraged) and the program is not officially limited to individuals of Armenian ancestry, although almost all participants have been from the Armenian diaspora.

Although AVC's program is not explicitly targeted to the Armenian diaspora, its partnership with Birthright Armenia offers special services and support to diaspora Armenians who volunteer with the program. Birthright Armenia is a nonprofit group that promotes ties between diaspora youth and Armenia. It offers a limited number of fellowships for diaspora youth who choose to volunteer or intern in Armenia. Participants must be high school graduates between the ages of 20 and 32, must be of Armenian heritage (defined as having at least one Armenian-born grandparent), and cannot previously have participated in any Birthright Armenia programs. First-generation immigrants are not eligible for participation, although the 1.5 generation (i.e., former Armenian citizens who emigrated before age 12) may participate. Birthright Armenia participants must commit to a minimum eight-week stay in Armenia — of which at least four weeks must be for volunteer work.

Through the partnership, AVC places volunteers while Birthright Armenia provides Armenian language courses and arranges for lodging with an Armenian family. Participants must commit to at least 30 hours of volunteer work per week and participate in community meetings. As of late 2009, volunteers with Birthright Armenia came overwhelmingly from the United States (68 percent), and to a lesser extent from Canada (12 percent), Europe (11 percent), the Middle East (5 percent), South America (3 percent), and Australia (1 percent).[74] They served mainly in nonprofit community groups (44 percent), but also in government agencies (26 percent), the private sector (16 percent), and international organizations (14 percent).[75]

Birthright Armenia asks participants who have completed the program to contemplate their future engagement with the country. According to the program's Web site, "The experience in Armenia is meant to serve as a basis for life-long commitment to Armenian affairs. In that context, each participant must submit a 1—2 page proposal on how he/she intends to stay continually involved in Armenia affairs, whether in Armenia or in the Diaspora. The proposal must be a realistic, sustainable, and achievable roadmap for the volunteer's post-experience phase."[76] There is little concrete evidence that these commitments translate into measurable outcomes, and the program's lifespan and scale is likely too small for meaningful inquiry into these concerns.

3. Ayala Foundation's Filipino American Youth Leadership Program

Between 2004 and 2006, the Ayala Foundation, one of the Philippines' largest philanthropic organizations, operated a youth volunteer program for second- and third-generation Filipino American youth between the ages of 18 and 25.[77] The Chevron Corporation and the

---

74 Birthright Armenia, "Participant Statistics," www.birthrightarmenia.org/pages. php?al=statistics.

75 Ibid.

76 Birthright Armenia, "How it All Works: The Experience," www.birthrightarmenia.org/pages. php?al=how_works.

77 The information presented here is based on a review of Ayala Foundation annual reports between 2004 and 2006 (www.phildev.org/site/PageServer?pagename=about_annual_report)

corporate social responsibility branch of the Luzon Brokerage Corporation, a Filipino-owned and California-based shipping conglomerate, supported the initiative. The program aimed to help outstanding Filipino American youth rediscover their roots, better understand the social challenges facing the Philippines, and "become global advocates of the Philippines in the United States."[78]

Over its three-year term, the program placed 21 Filipino American youth with grassroots nonprofit organizations in the Philippines for six to eight weeks. The volunteers worked in areas such as health care, livelihood (economic subsistence) counseling, and education, as well as in the community organization of indigenous peoples. Volunteers were expected to cover some of the costs of the program, including airfare and transportation, although need-based scholarships (both full and partial) were available.

The Ayala Foundation eventually terminated the program because it found the process of identifying volunteer opportunities, selecting and matching volunteers, and monitoring the volunteer program too time intensive (and the impact not sufficiently significant). But according to the Ayala Foundation president, Vicky Garchitorena, Filipino American families remain eager for opportunities for diaspora youth to volunteer in the Philippines, and many are willing to fund travel and lodging independently. The Philippines has a long history of volunteer work — particularly through religious institutions such as the Jesuit Volunteer Corps and the University of the Philippines' Pahinguhod Volunteer Program — and the foundation is exploring avenues to link members of the diaspora with these existing volunteer programs.[79]

---

and MPI interviews with Vicky Garchitorena, president, Ayala Foundation USA.
78 Ayala Foundation USA, *Annual Report 2005* (Redwood City, CA: Ayala Foundation USA, 2005), www.phildev.org/site/PageServer?pagename=about_annual_report.
79 More information on the University of the Philippines' Pahinguhod Volunteer Program is available at http://pahinungod.org/aboutus.htm.

C. Multipurpose Diaspora Volunteer Programs

In at least one instance that we are aware of, a mainstream international volunteering and development organization — Voluntary Service Overseas (VSO) — has partnered with a national aid agency to focus on recruiting diaspora volunteers through a wide variety of volunteer programs that target both highly skilled and youth volunteers. The experience is described below.

DFID's Diaspora Volunteering Program

In recent years, VSO and DFID have pioneered a program that aims to involve diasporas in community-based volunteer work in their ancestral countries. VSO, an international nongovernmental organization (NGO), was established in 1958 in the United Kingdom to promote independent volunteering; it has since expanded to include branches in Canada, the Netherlands, the Philippines, and Kenya. As it has expanded abroad, VSO's mission has increasingly focused on improving living standards and reducing poverty through volunteer work in the developing world.

VSO volunteers have diverse origins; however, research conducted in 2004—05 for VSO-UK found that participation by immigrant and ethnic minority communities in VSO programs was low despite significant interest from these populations in volunteer work.[80] Moreover, the study found that immigrants and ethnic minorities felt excluded from traditional volunteer opportunities and wanted to have their own volunteer programs rather than be integrated in mainstream programs. They also tended to have development priorities that differed from those of mainstream development organizations, based on their own personal experiences and interaction with friends and family members abroad.[81]

VSO took the idea of a diaspora-specific volunteer program to DFID,

---

80 Ethnicity in the United Kingdom is a multifaceted concept that relates to country of birth, nationality, language spoken at home, parent's country of birth in conjunction with country of birth, skin color, national/geographic origin, racial group, and religion. For a variety of historical and sociological reasons, ethnic minority communities are traditionally conceived of as including non-European immigrants and their descendants. See UK Office of National Statistics, *Ethnic Group Statistics: A Guide for the Collection and Classification of Ethnicity Data* (Newport: HM Statistics Office, 2003), www.ons.gov.uk/about-statistics/measuring-equality/ethnic-group-statistics/index.html.

81 Dee Jethwa, *International Volunteering and the Asian Community (UK): Views, Attitudes, Barriers, Needs*, final report to Voluntary Service Overseas (VSO) from the Asian Foundation for Philanthropy (AFP), March 2006.

and in 2006 the UK government's White Paper for DFID proposed to "expand opportunities for . . . diaspora communities to volunteer in developing countries."[82] This commitment was reaffirmed in 2009.[83] DFID's commitment to diaspora volunteering was framed in terms of promoting awareness of international development concerns in the United Kingdom. Accordingly, VSO-UK's diaspora program was launched with multiple objectives: to encourage volunteering among ethnic minority communities in the United Kingdom while at the same time raising the awareness of international development among all members of the UK populace. VSO also recognized the risks inherent in skilled migration such as perceived effects of the brain drain and the benefits that diaspora volunteers potentially bring with them in terms of language skills and cultural competencies.[84] The diaspora volunteer program is supported by a three-year GBP £3 million (about $5.6 million) grant from DFID for the period 2008 to 2011. It has also received a five-year grant of about GBP £485,000 (about $730,000) from the United Kingdom's national lottery fund and recently received support from the European Commission (EC) to support Dutch efforts on diaspora volunteering. (The UK government is currently implementing deep budget cuts across all government agencies in an effort to reduce the country's budget deficit following elections in May 2010. During the campaign the new government pledged to protect overseas development assistance from budget cuts and initial budget proposals appear to do so, although it is not clear if it will continue to do so.)

For the purpose of the program, diasporas are broadly defined to include anyone who self-identifies as such, including those with current connections to or distant origins in a country other than the United Kingdom as well as those with emotional, family, or financial links with a country or continent of origin.[85] This expansive definition includes first- and second-generation immigrants, the spouses of immigrants, or anyone with substantive personal links to a developing country; the term is not considered to be synonymous with race or ethnicity.

Through the Diaspora Volunteering Program, VSO-UK provides support to community-based diaspora organizations in five main areas:

---

82 Department for International Development (DFID), *Eliminating World Poverty: Making Governance Work for the Poor* (London: DFID White Paper, July 2006).
83 DFID, *Eliminating World Poverty: Building our Common Future* (London: DFID White Paper, July 2009).
84 VSO (Voluntary Service Overseas), *The DFID Diaspora Volunteering Programme in Partnership with VSO* (London: VSO, 2008), www.vso.org.uk/volunteer/diaspora-volunteering.
85 Ibid.

- Assisting community-based diaspora organizations to conduct research on the needs of partner community organizations in their focus country, including research visits and the implementation of pilot volunteer programs

- Developing and implementing volunteer management systems — including monitoring and evaluation of partners; placement; volunteer recruitment and assessment; and volunteer orientation and training

- Training and supporting fund raisers to ensure that the programs are sustainable

- Providing in-country support from DFID and VSO offices

- Raising the awareness of international development issues in the United Kingdom

Box 2 describes in detail the process through which community-based diaspora organizations partner with VSO. VSO-UK established several criteria to ensure the good governance and accountability of community-based diaspora organizations. Among other requirements, these include having clear links with a diaspora from Africa, Asia, Latin America, or any non-European Union (non-EU) developing country outside these regions; having a clear focus on addressing disadvantage or poverty; being a registered charity or nonprofit group in the United Kingdom; having a functioning board of directors or other governing structure that meets regularly; and producing annual financial reports.[86] These requirements reflect many of the common challenges that governments face in working with community organizations. However, as of March 2010, VSO-UK had identified 20 partner diaspora organizations working in Bangladesh, Burkina Faso, Cameroon, Ethiopia, Ghana, Guyana, India, Malawi, Nepal, Nigeria, Rwanda, Sierra Leone, Sri Lanka, Tanzania, and Zimbabwe[87] and had placed 329 volunteers. The program aims to place a total of 600 volunteers through its partner organizations by the end of the DFID grant period in 2011.[88]

VSO-UK's Diaspora Volunteering Program is a relatively recent innovation, so drawing definitive conclusions about its impact would be premature. However, a close examination of one VSO-UK partner, the Asian Foundation for Philanthropy (AFP), reveals some promising early

---

86 VSO-UK, "Diaspora Volunteering Program: Partnership Criteria," www.vso.org.uk/images/ diaspora-volunteering-partnership-criteria_tcm79-23688.pdf.

87 MPI communication with Matt Lesslar, deputy program manager, Development Awareness Team, Communications Division, DFID, March 4, 2010.

88 For a full list of VSO-UK partner organizations, see www.vso.org.uk/volunteer/diaspora-volunteering/diaspora-volunteering-alliance.asp.

results. Formally established in 2005, AFP grew out of community efforts in 2001 to mobilize humanitarian aid from the Indian diaspora in the United Kingdom following devastating earthquakes in Gujarat. AFP has several programs that involve the South Asian diaspora in the United Kingdom, including its volunteer initiative, the *"Paropkaar" Program.*[89]

Box 2. VSO-UK Support of Community-Based Diaspora Organizations

Partnerships between VSO-UK and community-based diaspora organizations to coordinate diaspora volunteers evolve following five steps:

1. A diaspora organization expresses interest in partnering with VSO

2. VSO assesses the diaspora organization's eligibility and capacity to engage in the program.

3. A partnership agreement is signed.

4. VSO works to help develop the partner diaspora organization's skills and knowledge in areas such as volunteer programs, volunteer management, organizational development, strategic planning, HR policies and practice, work management skills, governance, and UK development awareness.

5. The partner diaspora organization has the opportunity to apply for grants for research, piloting, and/or implementation of volunteer programs and development awareness activities:

   a. Research grants. Grants to perform overseas needs analysis, partnership and placement development, risk assessment, and UK research, for example, to assess the supply of volunteers. Such grants are awarded after a capacity-building baseline has been attained.

   b. Pilot grants. Grants that give organizations the opportunity to pilot programs with a small number of volunteers and to then review the work and capacity-building plans before implementation.

   c. Implementation grants. Grants that allow partners to run full volunteer programs, maintain clear program area plans, tighten monitoring and evaluation systems, and formulate strategies for fund-raising and expansion.

   d. Development awareness grants. Diaspora organizations and returned volunteers undertake activities in the United Kingdom to raise general awareness of international development issues, known as "development awareness." (VSO-UK describes development awareness as activities undertaken in the United Kingdom that "increase people's understanding of global issues and encourage them to take action.")

Note: The above description is an overview of the partnership process from beginning to end. If an organization is already a partner or has advanced organizational skills, it may enter the process at a later stage.
Source: VSO-UK 2008.

---

89 For more information on AFP's work, visit www.affp.org.uk.

When it became a VSO partner, AFP began an exhaustive review of potential partner organizations in the four places where most of the United Kingdom's Indian diaspora originate: Delhi and the states of Gujarat, Karnataka, and Uttar Pradesh.[90] The research — which took place over the course of about five months and was conducted by AFP's director, Bala Thakrar, and a lecturer from the Delhi School of Economics — ultimately identified 12 partner community organizations in India that focus on education, young child and maternal health, disabled persons, and livelihood strategies (employment and entrepreneurship). AFP works with the partner organizations to identify precisely where volunteers could be used and continues to monitor the partner organizations once volunteer placements have begun.

Once volunteer opportunities had been identified, AFP accepts applications from potential volunteers. Volunteers typically learn of AFP's work via word of mouth. The group has discovered that returned volunteers are among the program's most effective recruiters. About 25 volunteers are selected each year, and each must participate in predeparture orientation. The orientation is designed to prepare volunteers for the inevitable cultural adjustment that occurs upon arrival in India. Although diaspora volunteers are commonly perceived to have deeper familiarity with the culture and language of the developing countries in which they volunteer, AFP's experience suggests that there are gaps in their knowledge. For instance, AFP's orientation warns volunteers about living conditions and linguistic differences (many volunteers speak Hindi or other regional languages but may be unfamiliar with local dialects). In addition, AFP has learned that it is essential to work with the families of volunteers — particularly when the volunteers are second- or higher-generation immigrants. Diaspora volunteers' parents may have left the country of origin under traumatic circumstances or may harbor negative stereotypes; such conditions can be a significant impediment to mission completion.

The 70 volunteers that AFP placed over the course of its first three years brought a wide range of experience to their volunteer work. Their ages ranged from 18 to 73, but on average they were in their early 30s. Most had university-level educations, although AFP's director recognizes the value of life experience and is adamant about selecting volunteers from across the socioeconomic spectrum, including those without formal language skills or education. She cites the example of one middle-aged female volunteer without a postsecondary education

---

90 This description of AFP's work was compiled from a review of AFP's Web site and annual reviews (www.affp.org.uk/resources?location=All&type=22&topic=all) and an MPI interview via telephone with Bala Thakrar, founder and director, AFP, October 7, 2009.

but who had extensive experience setting up small corner stores. This particular volunteer's mission focused on working with underprivileged women to establish their own corner stores.[91] With support from VSO, AFP is able to assist volunteers in paying for international flights, training, and in situ support, but volunteers are also expected to contribute financially toward the mission.

Upon their return to the United Kingdom, *Paropkaar* volunteers are encouraged to become involved with the foundation's Jagruti — or development awareness — program. Through seminars, conferences, exhibitions, community talks, and business networking events, the *Jagruti* program aims to raise awareness in the United Kingdom and among ethnic minority communities of the MDGs, development issues in India and South Asia, and the UK's international development policy. *Jagruti* events are designed to be accessible to a nontechnical audience. More recently, AFP and DFID have developed two specific projects within the *Jagruti* program: the *Sudarshan* project and the *Naitika* project. Translated as "leading by example," the *Sudarshan* project promotes social responsibility among Asian-owned small and medium-size businesses, while the *Naitika* ("ethical") project promotes development awareness among ethnic minority youth groups in the United Kingdom, particularly with respect to clothing and fashion. All of VSO-UK's partners are encouraged to facilitate development awareness programs among returned volunteers. These programs appear to be particularly effective at working with diasporas to raise consciousness about international development concerns in the developed world through person-to-person interaction.

AFP's *Paropkaar* program is the flagship initiative within VSO's diaspora volunteer program. Other partner organizations are diverse, ranging from small community groups with narrow objectives to larger associations that grew out of student movements or promote human rights. Compared with AFP, volunteer work appears to be less central to the missions of these larger groups, which tend to focus on broader development challenges.

D. "De Facto" Diaspora Volunteer Programs

Many programs not aimed at diasporas still support (and occasionally rely heavily on) first-, second- and higher-generation immigrants to volunteer in their ancestral countries. Data on diaspora

---

91 For a review of diaspora entrepreneurship, see Chapter 2, "Mobilizing Diaspora Entrepreneurship for Development," in this volume.

participation in these general volunteer programs are spotty, since diaspora involvement is rarely advertised and data on the origins of volunteers is almost never collected. As a result, the only available evidence comes from individual examples the authors were able to locate and the impressions of program managers. With these caveats in mind, we highlight several cases of diasporas volunteering through broadly focused youth, professional, and faith-based volunteer programs.

In some cases, diasporas may choose to volunteer through programs that are not diaspora based because they are unaware of diaspora-specific programs; because no diaspora-specific programs exist; or because they are strongly anchored in alternative identities including generational, professional, religious, regional, or corporate identities.

- **Youth.** The American India Foundation's (AIF's) William J. Clinton Fellowship for Service in India is designed to facilitate ten months of grassroots volunteer work in India for young Americans. The program aims to "serve as an exchange of technical skills and intellectual resources which aims to build the capacity of Indian NGOs while developing American leaders with an understanding of India." AIF provides training and technical support to fellows; ongoing supervision; and a stipend to cover housing, food, travel, transportation, and supplemental health insurance. In 2008-09, as many as 12 of the 23 fellows were of South Asian origin despite the fact that the program does not specifically target diaspora youth.[92]

- **Professionals.** The Vermont-Oxford Network is a professional association of neonatal medical specialists.[93] Launched in 2009, the Network's Black Lion Project sends professional volunteers for three to four weeks twice a year to support neonatal care at the Black Lion Hospital, Ethiopia's largest urban hospital. A former Peace Corps volunteer who served in Ethiopia and who has maintained personal contacts in the country launched the project. It has also attracted at least two neonatologists from the Ethiopian diaspora in the United States.

- **Faith based.** Some faith-based nonprofit groups have served as a conduit for diasporas to volunteer in their countries of origin. For instance, through its network of universities and hospitals across the world, the Adventist Development and Relief Agency (ADRA) places skilled volunteers as needs emerge. (Missions are

---

92 AIF (American India Foundation), "Serve in India," http://www.aifoundation.org/programs/signature/fellowship.htm.

93 Information provided by Georgis Kefale, associate neonatologist, Fairfax Neonatal Associates and Volunteer, Vermont Oxford Network Black Lion Project, interview via telephone with MPI, March 3, 2010. For more information, see www.vtoxford.org/about/about.aspx.

entirely demand driven.) Reportedly, diasporas can play a role in these programs and utilize their language skills and cultural familiarity, although a specific national origin is clearly not requisite.[94] The worldwide network of Adventist universities also provides a platform for diaspora academics to teach courses, on a volunteer basis, in their countries of origin. For instance, the Massachusetts-based nonprofit organization Here and Home, Inc., provides a conduit for African diaspora academics to lead courses in Adventist universities throughout Africa.[95] (Although the focus is on recruiting diaspora professionals, non-Africans who have ties to Africa through missionary or humanitarian work also volunteer through the program.) According to the president of Here and Home, Inc., Issumael Nzamutuma, the idea for the diaspora volunteer program grew out of a religious duty for missionary work and a personal desire to contribute to his country of origin, Rwanda.[96]

- **Regional.** The Florida Association of Voluntary Agencies in the Caribbean and the Americas (FAVACA) is a private, nonprofit organization established in 1982 by then Florida governor Bob Graham.[97] FAVACA's Florida International Volunteer Corps enjoys statutory authority under Florida state law and receives an annual appropriation from the state to send about 200 skilled volunteers per year to Latin America and the Caribbean. (FAVACA was established largely in response to the growing presence in Florida of immigrants from the Caribbean region and a desire among state authorities to help address the root causes of immigration from the region.) Most of the association's work is project based and placements are demand driven. FAVACA then works with the requesting party to develop focused terms of reference for the volunteer and identifies skilled volunteers from its volunteer database and community networks across Florida. While the organization does not track the origins of its volunteers, many are members of diaspora communities. As Florida's demographics have evolved over the past two decades, increasing numbers of skilled immigrants and their descendants are volunteering through FAVACA, according to FAVACA's director of development, Rebecca Reichert.

---

94 Based on MPI communication with Tricia Hayes, associate director for recruitment, Adventist Development and Relief Agency (ADRA).

95 This information is drawn from Here and Home, Inc.'s Web site, www.hereandhome.org, as well as an MPI interview with Issumael Nzamutuma, president, on March 11, 2010.

96 According to Nzamutuma, Here and Home, Inc., also believes that successful immigrants are better placed to contribute to their countries of origin. As a result, the organization is launching a summer mathematics tutorial program for African diaspora youth in the United States with support from Atlantic Union College.

97 This information is drawn from the Florida Association of Voluntary Agencies in the Caribbean and the Americas (FAVACA's) Web site, www.favaca.org, as well as an MPI interview via telephone with Rebecca Reichert, director of development, on March 5, 2010.

Although the author was unable to locate specific examples, we suspect similar trends may be observable in corporate volunteer programs.[98] In particular, members of diasporas may act as catalysts within corporations, identifying volunteer opportunities in their countries of origin that are in line with corporate social responsibility objectives and then promoting these opportunities among nondiaspora colleagues.

IV. Lessons Learned and Policy Conclusions

This chapter has surveyed the range of organized programs that provide opportunities for diasporas to volunteer in development projects in their countries of origin. Although they are, for the most part, small-scale and it is impossible to draw comprehensive conclusions, a number of them demonstrate promising approaches to attaining development goals. On balance, however, no clear models emerge from the review. Rather, the individual programs demonstrate strengths and liabilities, and the different approaches appear more or less suitable for different circumstances and different ends. We discuss some of the principal challenges and unresolved questions below:

A. Lessons Learned

I. Development Impact

It is difficult (if not impossible) to measure the development impact of many of these programs. Most development projects are measured by little more than a summary of financial accounting. Yet individual volunteers, program organizers, and development agencies may have different ideas about what constitutes a successful programmatic outcome. Some diaspora volunteer programs attempt to address immediate development challenges directly — such as programs that recruit professionals in hopes of mitigating "brain drain" — while others take a longer-term perspective by connecting highly motivated diaspora youth with community-based volunteer opportunities in the country of origin. This latter group of programs aims to facilitate a formative

---

98 For a review of corporate volunteer programs, see Greg Hills and Adeeb Mahmud, *Volunteering for Impact: Best Practices in International Corporate Volunteering* (Boston: FSG Social Impact Advisors and Pfizer, Inc., September 2007), www.brookings.edu/~/media/Files/rc/papers/2007/09volunteering/Volunteering_for_Impact.pdf.

experience for diaspora youth that will serve as the basis for a lifetime of meaningful engagement.

2. Balancing Priorities

A common criticism of the volunteer work undertaken by diasporas is it is often haphazard, unprofessional, and insufficiently coordinated with broader development objectives. These critiques are not always justified, but there is little doubt that there are benefits from aligning the development priorities of diaspora volunteers with the priorities of other actors. But even alignment can create challenges, especially when it is between development agencies (both from developed and developing countries) and community groups. In these cases, whose priorities should volunteers address? In light of their personal ties, diasporas may be more attuned to community-level challenges whereas national authorities may have a better appreciation of the macro perspective. A simplistic view is to cede authority to whomever contributes the lion's share of resources, but the experiences of other collaborative efforts between governments and community organizations suggests that true stakeholder buy-in is essential.

3. Matching Volunteer Demand and Supply

The challenges faced by all international volunteer programs — of which diaspora volunteer programs form a subset — are to (1) identify community needs, and then (2) match individuals with volunteering opportunities in an efficient and timely manner. The digitization of personnel databases has doubtlessly facilitated the matching process, yet populating these databases remains a challenge. Partnering with diaspora organizations can substantially facilitate the identification of potential volunteers. But these relationships can also complicate program management since many diaspora community organizations are themselves volunteer based with limited capacity. Conflicting priorities may complicate the volunteer placement process. The risks of these partnerships increase when diasporas are highly politicized. Identifying needs remains a complex undertaking that technology has not yet been able to fully resolve. The highest demand is generally for the most skilled volunteers, but experience suggests the value of evaluating both demand and volunteer characteristics more closely. As an early report on USAID's Diaspora Skills Transfer for Southern Sudan project concluded, "there are hundreds of graduates and experienced South Sudanese in the Diaspora who may be willing to come back. Realistically however, there are few positions requiring highly skilled personnel in the public sector available for them to fill at present.

Unfortunately, as of yet, there is also no enabling environment in the private sector to encourage them as entrepreneurs."[99]

4. Structuring Programs

The programs reviewed for this chapter suggest a variety of organizational structures for diaspora volunteer programs. Some — such as the partnership of DFID, VSO, and diaspora community organizations in the United Kingdom — build the capacity of organizations to recruit volunteers and manage programs with technical support from VSO, which has substantial expertise in managing international volunteer programs. DFID provides a broad framework for program objectives and allows diaspora organizations substantial autonomy in targeting volunteers. Other programs — such as the partnership between the HIV/AIDS Twinning Center and NEPID — similarly pair expertise in volunteer management with an in-depth knowledge of the diaspora and health challenges in Ethiopia. This occurs within the narrowly framed objectives of PEPFAR. Still other programs, such as TOKTEN, leverage the development expertise (and, perhaps more importantly, operational autonomy) of international organizations such as UNDP. While UNDP may lack expertise in volunteer management (though it receives some support from UN volunteers) or access to grassroots diaspora networks, its autonomy is clearly important in countries such as Lebanon, where the diaspora is politically divided and may lack confidence in government. The community-based organizational structure of youth volunteer programs like Indicorps and Birthright Armenia allows these programs the flexibility to make long-term investments in meaningful relationships with highly motivated diaspora youth, while also helping to meet short-term development needs. Finally, a reliance on independent community organizations can facilitate volunteer placements in especially dangerous or volatile countries such as Somalia.

5. Cost Effectiveness

International volunteer programs bear the high costs of international travel, lodging, and coordination across countries. (Even facing the competitive pressures of the private sector, many businesses have been unable to reduce the costs of short-term assignments overseas.) Indeed, a 2003 USAID report concluded that the expenses associated with an international volunteer are not significantly less than those for a

---

99 Lynne Cogswell, Richard Hailer, Robert Holm, James Purcell, and Don Smith, *Training and Capacity Development Needs Assessment for the USAID Sudan Field Office*, report to USAID, Development Associates, Inc., Arlington, VA, February 2005.

consultant.[100] These costs, however, need not be prohibitive — individual programs have explored a number of ways to make diaspora volunteer assignments more cost-effective without sacrificing quality. These include both strategic innovations — such as targeting higher-value-added volunteers — with operational changes such as encouraging (or even requiring) longer-term placement and volunteer contribution toward transportation and lodging. The focus on diaspora volunteers is also often considered a cost-saving measure as diasporas are assumed to have superior cultural and linguistic knowledge, which means they require less orientation and can "hit the ground running." While valid, this case is often overstated. There is little doubt that a common language facilitates volunteer work, but the true benefit may not be cost savings but rather the more meaningful relationships that diaspora volunteers are able to develop with their counterparts. Accordingly, a more realistic case could highlight diasporas' greater likelihood of long-term engagement based on personal connections with peers in the country of origin.

6. Scalability

In recent years it has become clear that a perpetual challenge for development policymakers is how to replicate successful demonstration projects. As former World Bank president James Wolfensohn has stated, "We have to discover how we move from our feel-good successes, how to scale up these initiatives to a depth and breadth where we can really have an impact of poverty."[101] On this issue, many questions about the development potential of diaspora volunteer programs remain outstanding. Among all programs, the most promising appear to be led by dynamic, motivated, committed, and savvy individuals. Many require the exhaustive review of candidates and opportunities, and then the labor-intensive matching of the two. It is unclear whether and under what conditions these programs can be scaled — or if it is even advisable to do so. The optimal size of diaspora volunteer programs may be small, in which case it will be important to consider whether the various models can be replicated or if their central concepts can be exported to other countries. The one case of a diaspora volunteer program that has been widely replicated is TOKTEN, but the experience has been mixed. A limited number of programs appear to have taken root while the majority of programs have failed to attract more than a handful of volunteers.

---

100 Keesbury, The Value of International Volunteerism.
101 James D. Wolfensohn, "Foreword," in Reducing Poverty on a Global Scale, ed. Blanca Moreno-Dodson (Washington, DC: World Bank, 2005).

B. Implications for US Government International Volunteering and Diaspora Engagement Programs

Over the past half-century, the United States has promoted a wide range of international volunteer programs as a means to advance its foreign policy goals. These goals ranged from containment during the Cold War to democracy promotion and counterterrorism since September 11, 2001.[102] But development assistance has been the most common and omnipresent justification for most international volunteer programs. In some cases the US government has designed and managed international volunteering programs (include the most well known, the Peace Corps). In other cases it has partnered with civil society groups (for instance, through Volunteer for Prosperity). Some have promoted international volunteering in general, but the most have been more targeted toward specific issues or objectives (e.g., Farmer-to-Farmer Volunteers and the HIV/AIDS Twinning Center Volunteer Health Corps).

US-government-sponsored international volunteering programs tend to target two categories of volunteers:

- Experienced professionals (i.e., "highly skilled" volunteers) for short-term technical assistance missions

- College-educated youth (often considered "less skilled") for longer missions (volunteer programs for less-educated youth, such as AmeriCorps, tend to be domestically focused)

Highly skilled international volunteers — for instance, those that work through the Farmer-to-Farmer program, IESC, and Financial Service Volunteer Corps — typically aim for immediate development impact and transfer of knowledge or technology (although they often develop long-term relationships as well). By contrast, youth volunteers abroad — for instance, through the Peace Corps — typically carry out routine or frontline development work and often develop lasting relationships with the communities they serve, leading to lifelong engagement.

As the experiences described in this chapter suggest, there is little doubt that diasporas constitute a significant pool from which to draw volunteer manpower and talent for international development efforts, and that many are already engaged in such efforts, whether by their own initiative or through civil society groups. This may be particularly true for skilled members of the diaspora who have active professional, academic, and personal networks in the country of origin. But several

---

102 For a summary of this view, see Lex Rieffel and Sarah Zalud, "International Volunteering: Smart Power," Brookings Institution, Policy Brief No. 155, June 2006.

questions remain. Where do diasporas fit into USAID international volunteer programs? How might USAID more actively promote diaspora volunteering in development projects? Two complementary approaches appear particularly promising: encouraging greater diaspora participation in existing international volunteer programs, and partnering with civil society groups (such as diaspora-community-based organizations, professional associations, and faith-based groups) to promote new volunteer opportunities for diasporas. Admittedly, in some instances, this will require minor policy changes such as a greater willingness by the Peace Corps to place diaspora youth in their ancestral countries.

The experiences described here suggest that USAID initiatives often rely (intentionally or inadvertently) on diaspora volunteers. USAID and other international development agencies have extensive experience working with international volunteers. In many respects, diasporas are no different from other volunteers: They typically require some sort of remuneration — although this is often psychic rather than monetary or substantially below market rates—and the benefits are more likely to be substantial if the volunteer remains engaged long after the volunteer mission ends. But diasporas also differ from other volunteers in many ways. And the informal role of diasporas in US government volunteer programs is not well understood or documented. USAID- and PEPFAR-funded programs have experimented with recruiting highly skilled diaspora volunteers for specific projects. These efforts led to considerable success in some instances (e.g., the HIV/AIDS Twinning Center's VHC) but evinced little interest in other cases (e.g., Serbian Diaspora Volunteers). The most successful examples of recruiting diasporas for international skilled volunteer programs appear to be the result of partnerships between agencies with expertise in placing international volunteers and with an on-the-ground presence in developing countries (e.g., USAID, VSO) and organizations with deep community roots in the diaspora (e.g., some ethnic community-based organizations, professional networks, faith-based groups).

While USAID has extensive experience working with nongovernmental partners, this discussion does not aim to address the entire range of good practices for development partnerships. Diasporas are, however, distinct from typical partners for several important reasons. First, they are rarely impartial outsiders; rather, they have complex relationships with their countries of origin. Part of their advantage as international volunteers is their unique ability to carefully balance insider credibility with outsider perspective. Reliable partners help navigate these complex politics. Second, as is typically the case, partnerships allow USAID projects to leverage greater resources since they imply community buy-in. But the selection of partners is a particularly sensitive process of which governments must be aware to avoid fully dependent relationships. Third, diaspora partners may have different development priorities than USAID. Attempts to redirect diaspora volunteers toward support of USAID objectives are unlikely to succeed unless there is meaningful consultation. A more fruitful strategy may be to identify successful initiatives launched by NGOs that align with USAID objectives and build upon these programs or to offer incentives for NGOs with a record of success in promoting international volunteering to expand into strategic sectors. Finally, it is necessary to recognize that partnering with individual diaspora organizations may make sense where diasporas have sufficient critical mass. But where diasporas are small — as remains the case for many African diasporas in the United States — greater participation in existing programs may be the most realistic option.

Often, the critical barrier to recruiting diaspora volunteers is identifying them. Databases of skilled expatriates with a desire to volunteer must be populated and maintained, and matched with volunteer needs. USAID country missions have the capacity to identify volunteer opportunities but it may prove necessary to partner with community groups or, in some cases, country-of-origin governments to establish databases of potential volunteers. To this end, developing countries' consular networks in the United States or alumni associations from universities may prove particularly valuable. Of course, the collection and maintenance of data on individual members of the diaspora requires careful safeguarding and privacy protection.

The programmatic experience with diaspora youth volunteers is much less extensive. The Peace Corps typically shies away from placing diaspora youth in their ancestral countries (or entertaining any specific request for placement) although it has done so in at least once instance. In that case, the Peace Corps mission served to catalyze a much deeper level of engagement between the volunteer and the country of origin, eventually leading to the founding of AVC. The experiences of NGOs — such as AVC, Indicorps, and AIF — with diaspora youth volunteers suggest that community service work by diaspora youth often leads to a lifetime of engagement with the country of origin.

Americans of all national origins undertake international volunteer work and diasporas are an important — if discrete — subset of these volunteers. Without unduly privileging diaspora communities, international volunteer programs cannot afford to overlook this constituency, particularly in light of the unavoidable demographic shift underway in the United States. In the coming decades, a growing share of the US youth (and eventually adult) population will be second-generation immigrants: Between 1990 and 2008, the number of native-born US citizen children with at least one foreign-born parent doubled from 6.3 to 13.9 million (or from 10 to 20 percent of all children under age 18).[103] In 2008, about 12.7 million children — over 90 percent of children with immigrant parents and about 18 percent of all US children — had a parent born in a developing country.[104] As these children age into young adulthood, the pool of potential diaspora youth volunteers with proximate roots in the developing world will only increase. And contrary to claims that there is a trade-off between community engagement in the country of origin and the country of residence,[105] the two seem to complement each other. Extensive interviews with former Indicorps volunteers conducted for this chapter suggests that Indian American youth volunteers are equally concerned about community involvement in India and in the United States. ⏎

---

103 MPI Data Hub, "Children Age 17 and under in Immigrant and Native Families by State: 1990 to 2008," www.migrationinformation.org/datahub/historicaltrends.cfm.
104 MPI analysis of 2008 American Community Survey data.
105 In particular, Stanley A. Renshon of the Center for Immigration Studies suggests that it would be preferable if immigrant and second-generation youth volunteered in domestic volunteer programs such as Teach for America rather than perform volunteer work in their countries of origin. Our research suggests that the perceived trade-off between community service work in the country of origin and the country of residence is overly simplistic and that there are in fact complementarities between the two. For instance, this report highlights the example of one Indicorps volunteer whose service in India led to involvement with both Teach for America and Teach for India. See Stanley A. Renshon, *Reforming Dual Citizenship in the United States: Integrating Immigrants into the American National Community* (Washington, DC: Center for Immigration Studies, September 2005), www.cis.org/articles/2005/dualcitizenship.pdf.

CHAPTER 7

VOICE AFTER EXIT:
Diaspora Advocacy

Kathleen Newland, Migration Policy Institute

Introduction

In Albert Hirschman's classic book on social choice, *Exit, Voice, and Loyalty*, Hirschman describes three choices that "consumers" (whether of products or political systems) have when they are discontented: change to another "product," voice their discontent in the hope of stimulating change, or put up with the status quo.[1] Emigrants, in a sense, already exercised the first of these options when they left their countries of origin and settled in another; however, along with their descendants, they show a commitment to continuing "voice" when they engage in advocacy on issues concerning their country of origin or ancestry.

Diaspora communities, organizations, and individuals are increasingly vocal and influential in their countries of origin and of settlement. While government is their primary target, they also seek to influence international organizations, the media, the private sector, nongovernmental organizations (NGOs), and other actors.

Diaspora advocacy has become at once more immediate and more abundant in the era of electronic communications, as the ease of organizing diaspora members across distances and national

---

1   Albert O. Hirschman, *Exit, Voice, and Loyalty: Responses to Decline in Firms, Organizations, and States* (Cambridge, MA: Harvard Univ. Press, 1970).

boundaries has removed old constraints. Web sites, discussion groups, and social networks of diaspora members have proliferated, resulting in a multiplication of the organizational potential of groups and even individuals.[2]

Of the roles that diasporas play in development, advocacy is among the least studied. This study surveys a range of cases to identify forms of diaspora advocacy, the primary concerns targeted, and the means through which diasporas advance their causes. It gives an overview of diaspora advocacy by presenting examples that, taken together, address five questions:

- Who participates in diaspora advocacy and diplomacy?

- Who or what are the "targets" of their efforts?

- What means do they use to advance their causes?

- What are the issues on which they focus?

- How effective are they?

Diaspora engagement in countries of origin is so varied as to defy generalization. The analysis that follows identifies patterns of advocacy and illustrates them with examples relating to each question. While it is by no means comprehensive, the study attempts to provide a framework for thinking about the topic. The examples presented below suggest some answers to our opening questions.

I. Who Participates in Diaspora Advocacy?

Diaspora advocates are members of diaspora communities with grievances, ambitions, and/or agendas that they promote by enlisting the support of other actors. Although diasporas are communities that maintain active links to their communities of origin, not all members of these communities engage in advocacy on behalf of their countries of origin. Moreover, some immigrants and their descendants choose complete assimilation in their countries of settlement and abandon all ties with their countries of origin. (This does not necessarily prevent people in destination countries from identifying them as members

---

2   Jennifer M. Brinkerhoff, *Digital Diasporas: Identity and Transnational Engagement* (Cambridge: Cambridge Univ. Press, 2009).

of a diaspora and imputing to them an agenda that, in fact, does not interest them.) Active membership in a diaspora is a matter of individual choice, although social pressure surely plays a role in that choice. Engagement in advocacy is a further choice.

Diaspora organizations are enormously diverse. Advocates are drawn from ethnic affinity groups, associations of migrants originating from the same locality, alumni associations, religious organizations, professional associations, charitable organizations, development NGOs, investment groups, affiliates of political parties, protest movements, humanitarian relief organizations, schools and clubs for the preservation of culture, virtual networks, and federations of associations.

A. Representation and Legitimacy

Emigrants and their descendants who choose to engage in advocacy and diplomacy face issues of representation and legitimacy as soon as they claim to represent a broader public interest. Who is entitled to speak for whom? One of the first questions decisionmakers must ask when confronted with diaspora advocates is, "Who are these people and whom do they represent?"

Many diasporas are fragmented and fractious; competing factions advocate for competing agendas. Some diaspora groups and individuals make no claims to represent anyone but themselves, advocating on the strength of their ideas, the justice of their cause, or their access to resources. But many others advocate on the basis of particular political, religious, ethnic, territorial, or historical agendas. A priority of many diaspora organizations, therefore, is to gain recognition from the "targets" of their advocacy — whether these are the governments of origin or destination countries, the public in these countries, donors, mass media, or others.

The targets of diaspora advocacy, especially public authorities, also have an interest in the legitimacy of their diaspora partners. If the diaspora organizations they work with are not recognized as genuinely representative in the source community, public authorities may be charged with naïveté, cynicism, or playing favorites.

The government of Mexico is one that has tried to address the question "Who speaks for the diaspora?" by sponsoring the Consultative Council of the Institute for Mexicans Abroad (CCIME), composed primarily of *elected* leaders from diaspora communities.[3] The council makes recommendations to the government about its policies toward the diaspora and helps set the agenda of the Institute for Mexicans Abroad (IME), a branch of the Foreign Ministry. The council freely criticizes and disagrees with government positions when it feels called upon to do so, which — paradoxically perhaps — bolsters the confidence of both parties that disagreement does not mean alienation. The fact that most of IME's members are elected (although the election procedure is far from perfect) goes some way toward protecting the government of Mexico from charges that its diaspora policy is arbitrary or purely self-serving.[4]

Competing claims to representativeness and legitimacy are most stark in situations of civil conflict, as in Sudan, Iraq, Sri Lanka, and many other countries. Emigrants often replay the conflicts of their homelands in diaspora and try to enlist the governments and civil society institutions of the settlement country in their cause. Diaspora groups whose origin is in a refugee flow often remain bitterly hostile to the government of their country of origin, even after a degree of reconciliation has been achieved in that country. In the case of Armenia, discussed below, diaspora objections have slowed reconciliation with Turkey at a time when both official and popular opinion in Armenia has seemed to favor it.

Decades of war, repression, and dysfunctional institutions leave many societies with a legacy of mistrust that makes cooperation among diaspora groups difficult to achieve. For example, the Haitian diaspora in the United States has been deeply divided and has achieved little in terms of increasing attention to Haiti's needs, in the United States or internationally — although the 2010 earthquake seems to have instilled a greater sense of unity, at least temporarily. The Tibetan diaspora, by contrast, has generated enormous support for Tibetan human rights, cultural survival, and political autonomy worldwide. With the Dalai Lama at the helm, the Tibetans' espoused causes enjoy almost universal recognition and legitimacy within the diaspora and among its supporters.

---

3   Institute for Mexicans Abroad / *Instituto de los Mexicanos en el Exterior* (IME), "Consejo Consultivo," www.ime.gob.mx/.
4   There have been rifts within Mexican diaspora groups based on one group's feeling that another was too close to the government or the majority political party — which were virtually one and the same in the days of the Institutional Party of the Revolution's (PRI) 70-year monopoly on power. See Heather Williams, "From Visibility to Voice: The Emerging Power of Migrants in Mexican Politics," Global Migration and Transnational Politics (Working Paper no. 4, George Mason Univ. Center for Global Studies, March 2008).

A. Motives for Engaging in Advocacy

Referring in particular to advocacy pertaining to conflict in home countries, Jennifer Brinkerhoff of George Washington University and Robin
Cohen of Oxford University have separately identified a number of
motivations that lead members of diasporas to take action: to express
their identities, to acquire power or resources, to assuage feelings of
guilt as they seek to reconcile their preferences for the adopted country
with their allegiance to a suffering homeland, to maintain a collective
memory/myth about the homeland, to express a strong ethnic group
consciousness, and to keep alive the expectation of a future return.[5]
Diasporas also advocate for changes in policies or practices in order to
bring about conditions more conducive to development.

Diasporas that have a strong sense of injustice or existential threat
are highly motivated to advocate for their homelands. The American
Israel Public Affairs Committee (AIPAC), along with other Jewish
organizations, has been famously effective in lobbying the US Congress
to "ensure that Israel remains strong militarily and economically, and
endures as a national homeland for Jews."[6] Advocacy on the part of the
Armenian diaspora is stimulated by the memory of mass killings in
Turkey at the end of the Ottoman Empire and the desire to have them
recognized as genocide. Greek Americans — many only a generation
or two away from the forced relocation of their ancestors from what is
now Turkey — formed more than 20 new lobbying organizations after
Turkey invaded Cyprus in 1974. Their chief purpose was to advocate
for a ban on US military assistance to Turkey. The Greek diaspora in the
United States had not been very politically active before the invasion
and in fact was divided in attitudes toward the then-ruling military
junta in Greece. But Turkish aggression in Cyprus (even though it was
provoked by an attempted coup in Cyprus instigated by the Greek
junta) and the displacement of more than 200,000 Greek Cypriots by
the Turks' division of the island brought unprecedented unity and
activism to the diaspora.[7]

That same sense of injustice motivates many diaspora groups to
advocate *against* their countries of origin. Tibetan and Uighur
advocates of greater autonomy for their regions have very little scope

---

5   Jennifer M. Brinkerhoff, "Digital Diasporas and Conflict Prevention: The Case of
    Somalinet.com," *Review of International Studies*, 32 (January 2006): 25–47.
    Robin Cohen, *Global Diasporas: An Introduction* (Seattle: Univ. of Washington Press, 1997).
6   Morris S. Solomon, "The Agenda and Political Techniques of the American Israel Public
    Affairs Committee (AIPAC)" (Washington, DC: The Industrial College of the Armed Forces,
    1993).
7   "New Lobby in Town: The Greeks," *Time Magazine*, July 14, 1975.

to press their demands inside China, but externally they are active in calling for condemnation of human rights abuses visited upon these national minorities.

More positive motives for diaspora advocacy center on efforts to strengthen bilateral relations between the countries of origin and settlement, generally or in one particular area such as trade relations. Diaspora groups in the United States have spoken out both for and against the North American Free Trade Agreement (NAFTA), the Central American Free Trade Agreement, and other bilateral trade agreements.

II. Who or What Are the Primary Targets of Diaspora Advocacy?

Diasporas direct their advocacy efforts primarily at the governments of origin and settlement countries, but they also engage with international organizations, mass media, businesses, and other potential allies such as labor unions, churches, and NGOs. In turn, diasporas gain strength when governments and other organizations court their support.

Mexican emigrants and their descendants in the United States, for example, have lobbied both the US and Mexican governments for an extension of their political rights. In the United States, they have called for immigration legislation that would create a path to legal status for unauthorized immigrants, among other provisions. They have lobbied the executive branch and members of the legislature in Mexico to extend voting rights and dual citizenship to Mexicans abroad.

Homeland governments are the most common objects of diaspora advocacy among first-generation migrants. As immigrants and their descendants become more thoroughly integrated into their countries of settlement, they are more likely to include destination-country governments in their advocacy sights.

Higher levels of understanding of how the political system works in settlement countries also lead advocates to reach out to other nodes of influence on decisionmakers, broadening the reach and power of their advocacy. For example, Mexican farm workers in the United States formed coalitions with US labor unions (e.g. the United Farm Workers), with churches in rural American communities, and with NGOs to draw attention to and address frequent violations of farm workers' labor and human rights in both Mexico and the United States.[8]

The Importance of the Political Framework

Both a diaspora's ability to influence policy and the scope and form such advocacy take depend heavily on the political system of the "target" country. In authoritarian political systems, influence is most likely to be exerted successfully through personal contacts, economic pressure, or external intervention. In representative systems, diasporas can take part directly (in the countries where they are citizens) or indirectly in the electoral process. In parliamentary systems, where elected representatives are subject to party discipline, politicians may be less responsive to direct contact with diaspora advocates — although in systems with proportional representation, small groups of diaspora citizens may have outsize influence on smaller parties in coalition governments. Federal systems often give greater voice to diaspora groups in electoral districts where diasporas are concentrated than to those in areas with smaller concentrations. The United States, with its long-established system of interest-group pluralism, gives ample scope for diaspora groups, even if small in number, to exert influence on elected representatives.

As the case of China illustrates, opposition to an authoritarian or semi-authoritarian government may come to be centered in diaspora communities because opposition from within the country may invite harsh reprisals. The government may also effectively control the media at home, so that diaspora communities become the only effective platform for advocacy. Often the actions and demands of the diaspora are relayed back to the country of origin through foreign news media or through Web-based communications. In such settings, the diaspora may target its advocacy indirectly, through external actors such as international news and social media, human rights organizations, or corporations that do business in the country of origin. The anti-apartheid movement, much of it operating from exile, had great success in building alliances with businesses, as well as international sporting federations (most of which excluded South Africa from international competition), the entertainment industry, university students, human

---

8 Gaspar Rivero-Salgado, "Mixtec activism in Oaxacalifornia: Transborder Grassroots Strategies," *American Behavioral Scientist*, 42, no. 9 (1999): 1439–58.

rights groups, churches, and the media, as well as the governments of their countries of destination.

III. What Means Do Diasporas Use to Advance Their Causes?

Diasporas employ a variety of means to influence governments in their countries of origin and settlement, international organizations, mass media, and potential allies. Their strategies include direct lobbying, media campaigns, fundraising, demonstrations, electronic communication, and electoral participation. The effectiveness of these efforts is tempered by the strength of personal contacts and transnational social networks, and by the resonance that advocates' goals have within the broader diaspora and key interest groups in their home and/or host countries.

A. Lobbying and Direct Participation in Government

Lobbying — the effort to persuade policymakers to act in a manner favorable to one's interests — is an important method of many of the diaspora advocacy efforts discussed in this study, be they around issues of development, commerce, or conflict. In some cases, organizations develop with a primary goal of appealing to policymakers; in others, lobbying becomes necessary as a way to advance their interests. Working within and across national borders, diaspora groups network with and lobby government agencies and legislatures in their countries of residence and origin, international agencies, and influential nonprofits (e.g., Amnesty International).

Intense lobbying efforts by Indian Americans, both through the US India Business Council and through lobbying firms hired by the Indian government, were instrumental in persuading the US Congress to pass the 2008 Indo-US Civilian Nuclear Agreement, meant to overcome India's energy crisis and place civil nuclear facilities under the authority of the International Atomic Energy Agency (IAEA). (The agreement was controversial because of India's status as a nuclear weapons state that has not signed the Nuclear Non-Proliferation Treaty, which under prior US law barred cooperation with India on nuclear issues or trade in nuclear fuel or equipment.) Indian Americans reached out to the 43-member Congressional Black Caucus and 20-member Hispanic

Caucus to expand legislative support for the agreement. The main lobbying group, the US India Political Action Committee (USINPAC),[9] created a strong foundation by reaching out to Indian Americans settled in various regions of the United States, creating a youth committee to perpetuate the new vision of Indian American leadership, and starting a national outreach program to bring together different Indian American viewpoints. USINPAC solicited donations from members directly and through its Web site, who then wrote letters to congressional representatives urging them to support the deal. USINPAC tracked the agreement's progress closely, making campaign contributions to 22 members of the House of Representatives and nine senators in areas with significant Indian American populations and leveraging the support of other congressional delegations.[10] USINPAC also followed the progress of the deal in Congress by tracking which representatives were already in favor of it and which ones needed to be targeted for further attention. When progress on the deal stalled in India, USINPAC met with senior leaders of the Congress Party, parties on the left, and the right-wing *Bharatiya Janata Party* (BJP) to understand their differing perspectives on the issue.[11]

B. Lawsuits

Vietnamese Americans have greatly influenced US policy toward Vietnam through most of the advocacy techniques discussed in this study. The Vietnamese diaspora was one of the first to use litigation in their campaigning. In March 1994, 250 Vietnamese Americans sued the State Department to force it to review the US immigration applications of Vietnamese boat people held in Hong Kong rather than repatriating them and compelling them to reapply to immigrate. The involvement of Vietnamese Americans has also been instrumental in US pressure, ultimately successful, to persuade the government of Vietnam to release thousands of political prisoners.

---

9 US India Political Action Committee, "Indian-American Community Welcomes Congressional Passage of the Us India Civil Nuclear Agreement," www.usinpac.com/nuclear_deal/index. html.

10 Allison Freedman, "USINPAC and the U.S.-India Nuclear Deal: Lasting Influence or One Shot Victory?" CUREJ – College Undergraduate Research Electronic Journal, Univ. of Pennsylvania, College of Arts and Sciences, 2009, http://repository.upenn.edu/cgi/viewcontent. cgi?article=1119&context=curej.

11 As of July 2010, the deal had been signed but not implemented and remained a subject of US-India negotiations. "Indo-US nuclear deal moving forward, says SM Krishna" *Daily Times*, June 3, 2010, www.dailytimes.com.pk/default.asp?page=2010\06\03\story_3-6-2010_ pg7_35.

C. Fundraising

Diaspora advocates have long used fundraising as a tool for causes in home or host countries. Diasporas raise funds at a range of levels and through a variety of mechanisms. Events are usually organized by diaspora groups rather than by individual diaspora members (in part so that the groups can assert their credibility among their target populations). However, many individual diaspora members donate money to causes and candidates that they believe are worth supporting. Mechanisms to raise funds have diversified in recent decades as online fundraising has gained traction. Common methods of solicitation include contributions at charity events or through auctions and sales, membership dues, online donations in response to email campaigns, and direct person-to-person contributions.

Often, advocating for home-country policies means raising money for political parties. Political parties from many origin countries have created party organizations at the municipal and regional level in migrant communities, including the Mexican *Partido de la Revolución Democrática* (PRD), the Dominican *Partido Revolucionario Dominicano* (PRD), the Brazilian *Partido dos Trabalhadores* (PT), the Armenian *Dashnak Party*, and India's BJP. Dominicans in New York have gained considerable political leverage in the Dominican Republic by raising hundreds of thousands of dollars for candidates during election cycles, much of it through $150-a-plate dinners.[12] A single fundraising dinner in Houston, Texas, in 2007, organized by supporters of Ghana's main opposition leader (and former president) Jerry Rawlings and his National Democratic Congress, reportedly raised $700,000 from members of the Ghanaian diaspora located in at least nine major cities across the United States and Canada.[13]

After natural disasters and during wars, origin-country governments have set up fundraising accounts and diaspora advocates have collected large sums to contribute to government-run funds. For example, during the Ethiopian-Eritrean war, money for the war effort flowed from the Eritrean diaspora to a national defense bank account advertised on

---

12 Adrian D. Pantoja, "Transnational Ties and Immigrant Political Incorporation: The Case of Dominicans in Washington Heights, New York," *International Migration* 43, no. 4 (2005): 123–146.

13 World Bank, *Concept Note: Mobilizing the African Diaspora for Development* (Washington, DC: Capacity Development Management Action Plan Unit [AFTCD], Operational Quality and Knowledge Services Department, September 7), http://siteresources.worldbank.org/INTDI-ASPORA/General/21686696/conceptnote.pdf.

www.dehai.org, a diaspora Web site.[14] Out of political and defense concerns, donor governments considering supporting or working with a diaspora organization should evaluate the role that diaspora funds and fundraising have played in supporting home-country conflicts. Fundraising in the diaspora by the Tamil Tigers, for example, often bordered on extortion, and the Tigers were declared a terrorist organization in the United States and elsewhere.

Diaporas have, even more frequently, raised funds for disaster relief and channeled them through NGOs or religious institutions. In some cases, the government of the country of destination has encouraged diasporas to organize themselves and establish charitable institutions to handle contributions. US President Bill Clinton is said to have approached Indian diaspora leaders in the United States after the Gujarat earthquake in 2001, starting a conversation that led to the creation of the American India Foundation (AIF), a nonprofit organization that works to advance India's social and economic development. Not only does AIF raise funds for projects in India; it also engages in what might be called "demonstration advocacy:" "demonstrating innovations in areas which the government can then adopt and scale up with their far greater resources."[15] Diaspora contributions for relief efforts and development projects often build bonds of trust with the origin-country government that enable the diaspora to be more effective advocates when more contentious issues arise.

D. Electoral Politics and Direct Participation in Government

In addition to fundraising for political candidates, an increasing number of countries allow their citizens abroad to vote in domestic elections. As a result, diaspora communities are increasingly likely to host political candidates from their home countries on the campaign trail. This was the case in July 2010, when Peruvian presidential candidate Keiko Fujimori visited Paterson, New Jersey — home to one of the largest concentration of Peruvians outside of Peru — to court diaspora

---

14 "Since independence, Eritreans in the wider diaspora have been asked by the government to pay 2 percent of their income to the state, as a 'healing tax'; during the recent conflict with Ethiopia even greater demands were made of the diaspora, and their contributions paid for much of the conflict's costs." Nicholas Van Hear, "Refugee Diasporas, Remittances, Development, and Conflict," *Migration Information Source*, June 2003, www.migrationinformation.org/feature/display.cfm?ID=125; See also Victoria Bernal, "Eritrea On-line: Diaspora, Cyberspace, and the Public Sphere," *American Ethnologist* 32, no. 4 (2005): 660–75, 671.

15 American India Foundation, "Why AIF?" on the AIF Web site at www.aifoundation.org/aboutUs/whyAif.htm. consulted October 18, 2010.

votes in advance of the April 2011 election. Fujimori promised her audiences that she would push for congressional representation of the diaspora in Peru's congress.[16] Dominican politicians have long courted votes as well as campaign contributions from the Dominican diaspora in New York City.

Returning diaspora members in some cases play a large part in home-country politics, shaping domestic agendas with views and ties formed abroad. Returning Somalis are a significant presence in the government of Somaliland, a province of Somalia whose declaration of independence is largely unrecognized but that functions autonomously nonetheless: as of 2009, ten ministers in a cabinet of 29, leaders of two out of three political parties, the head of one of two legislative chambers, and 30 members of the 82-member House of Representatives were returnees.[17] The president of Liberia, Ellen Johnson-Sirleaf, worked at the World Bank in Washington, DC, for many years and developed close ties with the African American diaspora.

Home-country ministries and agencies are often staffed with returning diaspora members who built experience and networks while working or studying abroad. Many of the technocrats returning to Afghanistan after the removal of the Taliban government were educated in the West or had worked with Western aid agencies and NGOs in Pakistan as refugees. Returning diaspora members may experience resentment among those who never left, as was the experience of many of the Afghans returnees in relation to Islamist and traditional elites. Diaspora experience and support are no substitute for a domestic power base. Without that, diasporas may be seen as agents of a foreign power, lacking legitimacy in the affairs of the country of origin.[18]

These cases illustrate how "domestic" politics are made transnational by diaspora involvement. It should no longer surprise anyone, for example, that "political campaigns in Liberia are shaped by transnational networks that link Monrovia with communities in New Jersey, Providence, and Minneapolis."[19]

---

16 Associated Press, "Peruvian Presidential Candidate to Stump in Paterson," July 22, 2010, www.nj.com/news/index.ssf/2010/07/peruvian_presidentail_candidat.html. Elizabeth Llorente, "Peruvian Candidate Fujimori Courts Votes in North Jersey," *The Bergen Record*, July 22, 2010, www.northjersey.com/news/072210_Peruvian_candidate_Fujimori_pushes_for_congressional_seat_in_North_Jersey_stop.html.

17 United Nations Development Programme (UNDP), *Somalia's Missing Million: The Somali Diaspora and its Role in Development* (Somalia: UNDP, March 2009), www.so.undp.org/index.php/Somalia-Stories/Forging-Partnerships-with-the-Somali-Diaspora.html.

18 Jonathan Goodhand and Mark Sedra, "Who Owns the Peace? Aid, Reconstruction, and Peace Building in Afghanistan," *Disasters*, ODI (London), published online in March, 2009.

19 Terrance Lyons and Peter Mandaville, "Global Migration and Transnational Politics: A Concep-

E. Making Use of Media for Advocacy: From Postcards to Online Posts

Diasporas use the Internet in general and social networking sites in particular to keep in touch and promote their causes. Using media for diaspora advocacy dates far back before blogs and Facebook posts to tried-and-true methods such as letter-writing campaigns, newspaper op-eds and radio interviews, and demonstrations staged with an eye to the TV camera.

The multifront information-sharing of African Americans seeking the end of the Italo-Ethiopian war (1936–41) remains an example of old-fashioned — but not outdated — media advocacy. The African American press reported regularly on the crisis, examining the conflict from a racial angle and spreading dispatches from the Associated Negro Press in London, Paris, and Geneva. African American scholarly publications provided vital sources of anti-fascist, anti-racist information and news. "It was through these sources that African Americans learned of the critical events surrounding the conflict and informed one another of efforts to support Ethiopia," writes Sharon Gramby-Sobukwe.[20] She adds that the Ethiopian Research Council (ERC), collaborating with a large network of organizations, "published analyses of conditions in Ethiopia, maps, the constitution, and fact sheets on Ethiopian history. This information was sold at churches, lodges, NAACP meetings and rallies, social and study groups, from door-to-door, and on street corners." [21] The efforts to change US policy were unsuccessful, but resource mobilization within African American communities and among African representatives served to provide aid to the sick and wounded as well as food and clothing to refugees.

Diaspora members commonly pressure their host or home-country governments to support or denounce a particular issue by sending letters, collecting signatures, or petitioning members of congress. These efforts range from small-scale to huge. For example, during the Ethiopian-Eritrean war (1998–2000), Eritreans in Somerville, Massachusetts, sent 120 letters to US senators from Massachusetts and Rhode Island on behalf of relatives arrested in Ethiopia, hoping to persuade Congress to put pressure on Ethiopia to cease such actions.[22] At the other end

---

tual Framework" (Working paper no. 1, George Mason Univ. Center for Global Studies, Project on Global Migration and Transnational Politics, March 2008), http://cgs.gmu.edu/publications/gmtpwp/gmtp_wp_1.pdf.

20 Sharon Gramby-Sobukwe, "Africa and U.S. Foreign Policy: Contributions of the Diaspora to Democratic African Leadership," *Journal of Black Studies* 35, no. 6 (2005): 779–801, 789.

21 Gramby-Sobukwe, "Africa and U.S. Foreign Policy," 779–801, 788.

22 Victoria Bernal, "Eritrea On-line: Diaspora, Cyberspace, and the Public Sphere," *American*

of the spectrum, the Armenian Assembly of America (AAA) and the Armenian National Committee of America (ANCA) cooperated to send 150,000 postcards to then–President Clinton to protest the 1997 visit of Azerbaijan's then–President Gaidar Aliyev. The mass mailing supplemented demonstrations by AAA and ANCA that focused attention on Aliev's human rights record.[23] The Armenian diaspora, widely considered to be one of the most effective ethnic lobbies in Washington, uses media campaigns alongside individual communications to legislators and participation in electoral campaigns.

Similarly, members of diasporas and their political allies often write opinion pieces in major newspapers, blogs, and news-related Web sites to express their opinion as well as advocate for a certain position. Kofi A. Boeteng, a leading advocate for external voting rights for Ghanaians, regularly wrote informational and opinion articles on www.moderng-hana.com to build support in the diaspora base and among resident Ghanaians.

The Internet has become an important tool for both formal and informal connections among diaspora networks, individuals, and policymakers. It provides a transnational platform for advocates to communicate issues to people living all over world. Organizations such as US Copts Association, a diaspora organization representing native Egyptian Christians, incorporate interactive use of information technology in efforts to advance their political agendas.[24] More than other advocacy measures such as lobbying or demonstrating, the Internet offers individuals and small, dispersed groups a chance to voice their beliefs through chat rooms, forums, and blogs. Through Web sites, advocates can quickly disseminate information about their work to the general public, governments, and NGOs that might be willing to help them in their cause.

The Internet provides a forum for factions within diasporas to present their arguments, reach out to potential allies, and even engage in direct debate. In the wake of the 2009 coup in Honduras, a number of Web sites cropped up where journalists and researchers shared informa-

---

Ethnologist 32, no. 4 (2005): 660–675, 665.
23 Rachel Anderson Paul, "Grassroots Mobilization and Diaspora Politics: Armenian Interest Groups and the Role of Collective Memory," *Nationalism and Ethnic Politics* 6, no. 1 (2000): 24–47, 31.Armenian Assembly of America. "Home of the Armenian Assembly of America," www.aaainc.org. Armenian National Committee of America, "Armenian National Committee of America | Home," www.anca.org.
24 Jennifer M. Brinkerhoff, "Digital Diasporas and Governance in Semi-Authoritarian States: The Case of the Egyptian Copts," *Public Administration and Development* 25, no. 3 (2005): 193–204, 197.

tion not available through major newspapers or CNN with those in the diaspora.[25] Associated blogs and comment streams provided a way to circulate information and document human rights abuses. Diaspora members used the material to call for censure of the "transition" government, including a motion condemning the coup, passed through electronic voting by the American Anthropological Association,[26] even as other diaspora members used the Internet to argue the constitutional basis of the regime change.

One example of a news-based site used by diasporas is www.dehai. org.[27] In order to pay for network resources, the site charges a US$20 yearly membership fee, waived for residents of Africa. During the 1998–2000 border war between Eritrea and Ethiopia, dehai.org reached a peak membership of over 2,000 subscribers, dispersed across several countries in Europe and North America.[28] Meanwhile, the Eritrean government used the site to dispense information and raise funds. As with other forms of advocacy, governments of origin or destination may have a strong influence on diaspora-run Internet sites, be it overt as in the case of dehai.org or deliberately obscured.

While online communication is broadly accessible, it is not universally so. Costs of setting up and maintaining Web sites must be borne by someone; a number of the sites visited during research for this study had not been updated in years, or were no longer available because the owners could not pay server costs. There is an inherent bias against economically disadvantaged, rural populations and others without regular, affordable Internet access or sufficient computer skills or literacy. Moreover, Web sites do relatively little to capture the attention of those not already interested in following a particular issue. Often, another medium must be used to draw attention to a topic before people outside a narrow community of interest will visit Internet sites devoted to it. The Internet is companion to, not a substitute for, more traditional advocacy methods.

25 Honduras Coup 2009, http://hondurascoup2009.blogspot.com. Vos el Soberano, http://vosel-soberano.com.

26 American Anthropological Association (AAA), "Proposed AAA Statement in Support of Hondurans Resisting Military Dictatorship," http://blog.aaanet.org/2009/12/17/aaa-honduras-resolution-vote-jan-xx.

27 Eritrean Community Online Network, DEHAI. "Dehai News-Mailing List Archive," http://dehai.org.

28 Victoria Bernal, "Eritrea On-line: Diaspora, Cyberspace, and the Public Sphere," *American Ethnologist* 32, no. 4 (2005): 660–675, 665.

F. Promoting (and Protesting) Countries of Origin Through Art and Media

Diasporas share the heritage of their countries of origin through art, music, films, literature, photography, cuisine, crafts, and other cultural artifacts. Actively promoting these — and at times using them as tools of protest — is a form of cultural diplomacy or advocacy. Exposure to the culture of a country through its diaspora may serve as a portal through which people in a host country develop a broader interest in the diaspora's homeland — including its political and economic circumstances.

Country-of-origin governments often promote culture as a way of raising the profile and burnishing the reputation of their country. Diaspora members may cooperate in these efforts or pursue them independently. For instance, through GhanaExpo, a US-based Ghanaian family provides a Web-based platform for sharing and discussing news, movies, music, live FM radio, photos, market information, and even audio versions of the Bible and the Quran. [29]

Diaspora groups also use cultural products such as films or exhibits to advocate for social change. For instance, in June 2010, Truth and Reconciliation for the Adoption Community of Korea (TRACK) mounted an exhibition in Seoul that incorporated 90,000 price tags, each representing an adopted child, to protest the commercialization of adoption and discrimination against unwed mothers and children born out of wedlock.[30] TRACK is led by the "adoption diaspora" — Korean-origin adults who were adopted and grew up outside of Korea. Together with adoptive families and unwed mothers in Korea, they advocate for equal access to social benefits for unwed mothers and seek to diminish the harsh social stigma that leads many to abort or give up children for adoption. The exhibit was followed by a BBC radio documentary, "Korea's Lost Children." The movement has had some success: according to TRACK, the government of South Korea is committed to changing domestic law to provide equal income subsidies to unwed mothers.

G. The Power of the Image

Sophisticated diaspora groups have long since learned the power of visual images to create powerful impressions. There are few more

---

29 GhanaExpo, http://ghanaexpo.com.
30 Truth and Reconciliation for the Adoption Community of Korea (TRACK), "Setting the Record Straight," http://justicespeaking.wordpress.com.

effective tools for advancing a cause than to give it a human face. During the Nigerian civil war of 1967–70, arguably the most powerful weapon of the outmanned and outgunned Biafran secessionists was a London-based fax machine that spewed images of starving children and other civilians.[31] In retrospect, some have argued that the enormous international humanitarian response to the needs of the Biafran population was manipulated by Ibo secessionists abroad and the governing forces in Biafra, with the effect of prolonging the war. Diasporas both respond to and use images of suffering to mobilize humanitarian relief within their own communities and to press governments and other organizations in their countries of settlement to respond generously to humanitarian needs.

Diaspora groups also use images to promote a modern and progressive image of their country of origin as a desirable partner in economic and political undertakings. The India of high-tech industry, Bollywood films, and diligent, English-speaking workers is competing with and perhaps slowly replacing the ancient images of bullock carts and ragged children, not least through the efforts of the Indian diaspora.

H. Demonstrations

When the quieter means of advocacy prove insufficient, diaspora advocates turn to protest. Following the 1999 capture of Kurdish leader Abdullah Ocalan, Kurds participated in organized mass demonstrations in dozens of localities, particularly in Western Europe, bringing Kurdish issues to worldwide attention and generating pressure on Turkey to improve its treatment of its Kurdish population. In spring 2006, tens of thousands of Latino immigrants and citizens of Latino descent demonstrated in cities across the United States in favor of comprehensive immigration reform. Persistent demonstrations against the apartheid regime in South Africa helped to turn governments away from "constructive engagement" policies with the regime and increase the pressure for political change.

---

31 For examples of the photographs that were used at the time, see www.westafricareview.com/vol2.2/biafra/bpic.htm.

IV. What Are the Main Focuses of Diaspora Advocacy?

The issues that diaspora advocates take up cover a wide range, but can be roughly divided among issues that (1) affect the status of the members of the diaspora in their countries of origin or destination, (2) affect the homeland, and (3) have bilateral implications between the countries of origin and settlement. Citizenship, migration status, and voting rights are some of the prominent issues in the first category; human rights, good governance, and political participation are among the most common in the second; and trade policy, humanitarian relief, and development policy fall into the third. Below, we explore examples from each category.

A. Advocating for Overseas Voting Rights and Dual Nationality

One of the most consistent demands that diaspora populations make to their countries of origin is the right to vote and to retain their original citizenship even if they adopt the citizenship of the country in which they have settled. In pursuing these demands, they have had considerable success. About 115 countries allow nonresident citizens to vote, and 11 countries reserve seats in their legislatures for the diaspora. Migrants return home to participate in elections (Israel and Turkey), vote at overseas embassies (Indonesia and Algeria), vote by mail (Spain, Italy, Portugal) or vote via the Internet (France). More and more countries are allowing their expatriates to participate in the electoral process. Some recognize dual citizenship or do not actively seek to strip citizens of their status if they acquire citizenship in another country.

At the same time, nonresident voting rights remain controversial. India refuses to permit nonresidents to vote, although it gives them other privileges. Armenia accepted the idea of nonresident voting and then reversed its decision. The Philippines requires overseas Filipinos who wish to vote to sign a statement that they will be returning to reside in the country within three years. Some argue that diasporas may unduly influence electoral results, whose consequences they do not have to bear, and that their preferences differ from those of resident citizens. This has indeed been shown to be true, for example, in Croatia and Armenia. In some cases, including Mexico and Iraq, far fewer voters than eligible have turned out for elections, despite intensive campaigns to get out the vote. Diasporas have learned from others' experiences: as

Ghanian diaspora members lobbied the Ghana government for the right to vote abroad and for dual citizenship, the Diaspora Vote Committee (DVC) drew on Filipino and Senegalese laws and experience.[32]

Citizens of Ecuador were among the earliest diaspora populations to advocate for nonresident voting rights and dual citizenship, starting with a petition in 1967. It took 28 years and many disappointments before the Ecuadorean legislature finally approved dual nationality, with voting rights for expatriates, in 1995. Emigrants from Colombia achieved success more quickly, as their initial appeal for dual citizenship and voting rights occurred just as constitutional reform was getting under way in Colombia. An amended constitution, approved in 1991, included the desired political rights for Colombians abroad. Not coincidentally, the overseas voting procedures finally agreed to in Ecuador bore a close resemblance to those adopted by Colombia.

Members of the Dominican diaspora, particularly in the United States, have also been advocating for overseas voting since the 1970s. Organized into hometown associations and political clubs, they lobbied members of the Dominican Congress and contributed money to the campaigns of candidates who supported their objectives.[33] The Dominican government set up a commission after the presidential elections of 2000 to study the options for voting by Dominicans abroad, with the goal of making it possible for emigrants to vote in the 2004 presidential election. After a series of discussions and consultations in the country and abroad, the commission set up procedures for voting abroad. Diaspora voter participation in that election was 66.8 percent — very high when compared with the less than 25 percent participation rates of the Iraqi and Mexican diasporas in the United States.[34]

Hungary's far-flung diaspora was quick to ask for voting rights after the end of Communist rule, but encountered marked ambivalence from its new political class. A 2004 referendum on providing dual citizenship to ethnic Hungarians in neighboring countries failed when low turnout invalidated the bare majority in favor. Despite a strong media campaign sponsored by the World Congress of Hungarians and the major center-right political parties, voter apathy and concern about the impact of nonresident voting on economic and political stability in the

---

32 World Bank, *Concept Note: Mobilizing the African Diaspora for Development,* 20.

33 Adrian D. Pantoja, "Transnational Ties and Immigrant Political Incorporation: The Case of Dominicans in Washington Heights, New York," *International Migration* 43, no. 4 (2005): 123–46, 128.

34 Michael Jones-Correa, "Under Two Flags: Dual Nationality in Latin America and Its Consequences for Naturalization in the United States," *International Migration Review* 35, no. 4 (2001): 997–1029, 1002–3.

neighborhood combined to derail the process. A number of countries with minority populations in neighboring countries, or substantial immigration from them, have shown reluctance to adopt dual nationality and, in some cases, nonresident voting.[35] India, for example, accepts dual nationality with a group of high-income countries including the United States and the United Kingdom, but not with its impoverished neighbors. It makes no provision for nonresident voting, however, despite diaspora enthusiasm for it.

Diaspora members feel that they deserve political representation in part because their remittances are so important to their countries of origin, often keeping the national accounts afloat. Michael Jones-Correa, writing about Latin America, argues that "immigrants have been able to translate their economic muscle into political leverage, winning concessions from political parties and legislatures in their countries of origin, regularizing their status as citizens, allowing dual nationality, ownership of land and easy access when returning, among other things."[36] There remain important exceptions to that generalization in other parts of the world, however — leaving aside those countries of origin where no one votes.

B. Advocating for Caste, Ethnic, and Religious Rights

Many of the diaspora organizations discussed here advocate for fair treatment and representation of their nations or ethnicities. USINPAC[37] has created Indian caucuses in the House of Representatives and Senate, with enough leverage to derail the career of former Virginia governor and senator George Allen for insulting his opponent's Indian American volunteer with the slur *macaca*.[38] Recognizing the potential leverage to be gained from vote-seeking public officials, the Web site of the Pakistani-American Public Affairs Committee (PAKPAC) offers a set of guidelines to obtain the votes of the 7-million-strong American

---

35 Mayra A. Waterbury, "From Irredentism to Diaspora Politics: States and Transborder Ethnic Groups in Eastern Europe" (Working paper no. 6, George Mason Univ., Global Migration and Transnational Politics, July 2009).

36 Michael Jones-Correa, "Under Two Flags: Dual Nationality in Latin America and Its Consequences for Naturalization in the United States," 997–1029, 1001.

37 USINPAC, "US India Political Action Committee | Indian American Community," www.usinpac.com.

38 A *macaca* is a kind of monkey, and the term was used as a pejorative epithet among French colonialists in the Congo. Allen may have heard it from his mother, who grew up in Tunisia under French colonial rule. Tom Curry, "Gaffe Underscores Indian-American Clout: Sen. Allen's Blunder Puts Focus on Growing Group of Donors and Voters," *MSNBC.com*, August 17, 2006, www.msnbc.msn.com/id/14395449/.

Muslim community.[39]

Some diaspora organizations that advocate against discrimination based on caste, ethnicity, and religion collaborate with human rights organizations to increase their credibility and visibility. For instance, the US-based NGO Nepali-America Society for Oppressed (NASO)[40] Community advocates for the rights of the Dalit community in Nepal, which still faces discrimination. NASO has organized several seminars in the United States to discuss ways to incorporate Dalit rights into Nepal's new constitution.[41]

Religiously based diasporas have formed advocacy organizations to increase awareness of their religion and advocate for their right to worship as they choose. The Baha'i community worldwide has mobilized opinion against the government of Iran, which has branded them apostates and subjected them to persecution. The Falun Gong movement emerged in exile as a major critic of the Chinese Communist Party (CCP) after the movement was banned in China in 1999. Its followers criticize the CCP for human rights abuses against Falun Gong practitioners and lobby Western governments to put pressure on China to honor freedom of religion.

Diaspora groups that have not been involved in advocacy may turn to it out of concern about events in their home country. The aftermath of violent riots targeting Muslim neighborhoods in Gujarat, India, in February and March 2002 (after a Muslim attack on a train carrying Hindu pilgrims) revealed the contribution of diaspora activists to ethnic and religious tensions in the country. Extremist Hindu organizations such as the Vishwa Hindu Parishad (World Hindu Congress), with strong diaspora support (as well as close ties with the Hindu-influenced Indian government then in office), put all the blame on the initial attack that set off the riots, while other diaspora constituencies such as Gujarati Muslims in the United Kingdom demanded accountability from government officials who looked away from or even encouraged the violence in which the great majority of the victims were Muslims.[42]

---

39 Pakistani American Public Affairs Committee, "For Candidates," www.pakpac.net/Candidate.asp.

40 "NASO Community," http://nasocommunity.com/default.aspx.

41 The Advocacy Project, "Nepali-American Society for Oppressed Community (NASO)," www.advocacynet.org/page/naso.

42 Ajay Gandhi, "The Indian Diaspora in Global Advocacy," *Global Networks* 2, no. 4 (2002): 357–62, 360.

C. Advocating for Development and Disaster Relief

As other studies in this volume show, diaspora members play numerous roles in home-country development, including through philanthropy, volunteering, and investment. As advocates, they may support development programs and policies by lobbying the governments of their countries of residence and origin, appealing to international institutions, or working to raise awareness among broader populations.

The African Foundation for Development (AFFORD) seeks to expand and enhance the contribution of African diasporas by connecting organizations working for development in Africa from outside the continent with organizations on the continent working toward the same goals.[43] It also advocates in favor of specific development goals and approaches, working with the British Department for International Development (DFID), international development agencies, other donors, and NGOs. Each year, it sponsors a day of interaction among nine UK-based, African-led development organizations and donors. Each annual meeting focuses on a particular theme; the 2004 theme was especially relevant to diaspora advocacy — "transforming the local everywhere" — with a focus on how Africans in the United Kingdom promote change both there and in their regions of origin.[44]

Diasporas can also serve as bridges. Mexico's hometown associations are perhaps best known for their social investment in the 3x1 Program, but their role as mediators makes them worth mentioning as an example of diaspora advocacy. Under the Program for Mexican Communities Abroad, begun in 1990, hometown associations became the principal interlocutors between the Mexican government and Mexican-American civil society.[45] While Mexican hometown associations are the most numerous and well established, the Ghanaian, Salvadoran, Mauritanian, Senegalese, and Malian diasporas all have analogous institutions throughout the world, mostly in North America and Europe. Many of these organizations play a role as interlocutors with their governments, a role that is most effective when individual associations combine into federations that have a wider network of constituents, greater resources, and more impact.

---

43 African Foundation for Development, "AFFORD-UK," http://afford-uk.org.
44 African Diaspora and Development Day (AD3) 2004, "Theme: 'Transforming the local everywhere: Africa here, there, Africa everywhere'" MyAfrica, May 30, 2004, http://myafrica.ru/addinfo/data.php?id1=189.
45 Will Somerville, Jamie Durana, and Aaron Matteo Terrazas, *Hometown Associations: An Untapped Resource for Immigrant Integration?* (Washington, DC: MPI, 2008), www.migrationpolicy.org/pubs/Insight-HTAs-July08.pdf.

According to a 2008 Migration Policy Institute (MPI) report,[46] Mexican hometown associations have become significant political actors in the United States (the country of destination for 90 percent of Mexican migrants) on controversial immigration issues. At the state and regional levels, as the authors point out, "One of the earliest civic mobilizations of Mexican HTAs [hometown associations] in Southern California was in response to Proposition 187, a hotly contested 1994 referendum that aimed to exclude unauthorized immigrants from access to a wide range of public services including education and health care. More recently, California HTAs have mobilized against California Assembly efforts to limit the use of consular identification cards and in favor of comprehensive immigration reform." Most Mexican hometown associations in the United States multiply their clout by acting through federations composed of HTAs whose members come from the same state in Mexico.

In response to the devastating January 2010 earthquake, Haitian diaspora groups enlarged their focus from directly providing money and services to lobbying governments, international organizations, and corporations for disaster-relief funding, supplies, and eased travel restrictions. Despite sending substantial remittances (more than $1.3 billion in 2008 alone), the fractious Haitian diaspora was once shunned for "abandoning" its homeland — and elements of it were seen to pose a political threat to whatever government was in power. Through sharing human and financial resources and lobbying donor governments, diaspora members and organizations became an invaluable postearthquake conduit for Creole-speaking doctors, nurses, project managers, and advisers, and even reconstruction planners. Some were also able to mobilize funds. The US-based nonprofit National Organization for the Advancement of Haitians (NOAH), for example, secured a $100,000 donation from AT&T in July 2010 for a relief project to ensure a safe, potable supply of water for Haitians in remote areas.[47]

As part of the reconstruction process, members of the diaspora and groups such as the Haitian Diaspora Unity Congress are lobbying for eased travel and greater political and economic participation in Haiti (a campaign already started before the earthquake). Their lobbying succeeded in getting the Organization of American States (OAS) to hold a special meeting of Haitian diaspora groups in March 2010 "to map out plans for reconstruction and to ensure that the Haitian diaspora is included, not only by the government but also by contractors and

---

46 Ibid.
47 "AT&T Makes $100,000 Contribution to Haitian Earthquake Relief Effort" *PRNewswire,* July 9, www.noahhaiti.org/index.php?option=com_content&view=frontpage&Itemid=1.

nongovernmental organizations."[48] The diaspora has a continued role to play in leveraging funds for and carrying out development projects.

D. Advocating for Commerce

In order to improve business climates, facilitate better market access, and generate entrepreneurial opportunities, diaspora members and networks may advocate for international, regional, and local business partnerships and trade agreements. Such "commercial diplomacy" potentially generates economic development within home and host communities. It may also foster economic liberalization and financial literacy in the home country.

NAFTA exemplifies diaspora engagement in "commercial diplomacy." Patricia Hamm argues that Mexican Americans involved in the negotiation of NAFTA were motivated more by business interest and concern for the broader Hispanic American community than altruistic support of the homeland.[49] NAFTA was strongly supported by the Hispanic Alliance for Free Trade. This business-oriented coalition included the Latino Business Association, US Hispanic Chamber of Commerce, Texas Association of Mexican Chambers of Commerce, the League of United Latin American Citizens, and members of the Congressional Hispanic Caucus including US Representatives Eligio "Kika" De La Garza (Texas) and Bill Richardson (New Mexico). More conditional support came from The Latino Consensus on NAFTA, a coalition of civil rights groups, including the National Council of La Raza. They hoped for nonmaterial gains such as greater visibility and recognition of Hispanic Americans, a platform for voicing grievances, and political empowerment on both sides of the border. Community interests led to the allocation of funds through the North American Development Bank for investment in US-Mexico border infrastructure, environmental mitigation, and sustainable development in areas where NAFTA causes job loss.

---

48 Shaila Dewan, "Scattered Émigrés Haiti Once Shunned Are Now a Lifeline" *New York Times*, February 3, 2010, www.nytimes.com/2010/02/04/us/04diaspora.html?_r=1&pagewanted=all.
49 Patricia H. Hamm, "Mexican-American Interests in U.S.-Mexico Relations: The Case of NAFTA," (Working paper no. 4, Univ. of California–Irvine, Center for Research on Latinos in a Global Society, 1996), www.escholarship.org/uc/item/3wx2g9f2.

> **Box 1. Diaspora Organizations Responding to Changed Needs**
>
> The Haitian case shows that the focus of diaspora and diaspora associations can change over time. Expanded mandates attest to diaspora organizations' ability to respond quickly to origin-country needs. Once a "fun-loving social organization" of doctors who came together to invite singers and poets from Pakistan, the Pakistan-American Public Affairs Committee (PAKPAC) grew into a nationwide political lobbying nonprofit to improve US-Pakistan relations and media representation of Pakistanis and Pakistani Americans.[50] Originally formed to support schools and mosques in Bangladesh, provide scholarships for students, and assist in disaster relief, the Bianibazar Association of London and the Baniachang Association of East End in the United Kingdom now provide leadership on voting rights and racial discrimination.[51] The London-based Tamil Solidarity Movement (TSM) is an advocacy group that was founded after the military defeat of the Tamil Tigers in 2009 ended their struggle for an independent Tamil state in Sri Lanka. The TSM retains the goal of an independent state but rejects violence. It relies instead on advocacy, starting with members of the British parliament and companies that do business in Sri Lanka.[52]

V. Conclusions and Policy Options

The examples above give some indication of the characteristics of effective diaspora advocacy. Success is rooted in unity, commitment, and focus. The advocacy "targets" of a highly factionalized diaspora will find it difficult to know to whom they should listen — and thus find it easy to choose, cynically, those whose message is most convenient for the receivers. If unity is out of reach, then at least mutual tolerance and some coordination of effort is desirable. The Armenian Assembly of America and the Armenia National Committee of America are rivals for funds and influence — but on important issues they collaborate, as we have seen. The commitment of members is the diaspora advocacy effort's fuel cell. No person or institution on the receiving end of advocacy can be expected to expend political or financial capital on behalf

---

50 Ali Eteraz, "Pride and the Pakistani Diaspora" *Dawn*, February, 14, 2009, www.dawn.com/wps/wcm/connect/dawn-content-library/dawn/news/pakistan/Pride-and-the-Pakistani-Diaspora..

51 Somerville, Durana, Terrazas, *Hometown Associations*.

52 Shyamantha Asokan, "War by Other Means," *Financial Times*, October 17-18, 2009.

of a constituency that seems lukewarm about its objectives. In other words, the target cannot be expected to care about an issue more than its proponents do. A diaspora advocacy group that has too many objectives risks confusing its interlocutors about what is really important. Successful advocates are consistent in their priorities and will negotiate on lesser issues in order to achieve the most important goals.

Effective diaspora advocates must also command resources and have a strategy to deploy them for maximum impact. Money (or fundraising prowess) may be the most important resource, but it is not the only one. Alliances are invaluable, as are deep connections with influential people in both countries of origin and destination. Of course, money will help pave the way for achieving both of these. It is notable that in 2004, one in five of AIPAC's board members were top fundraisers for either the Republican or Democratic presidential candidates. AIPAC's influence in the US Congress and administration stems largely from campaign contributions by its wealthy members, supplemented by its ability to mobilize highly motivated voters. Moral stature may not be bankable, but diaspora organizations that have the support of figures like the Dalai Lama, Nelson Mandela, and Amartya Sen gain immeasurable credibility. Sophistication in the use of mass media is also a critical resource. It is hard to imagine a successful advocacy campaign that does not make use of either traditional or new media — and preferably both.

Finally, a diaspora group's connectedness is a good predictor of its ability to succeed in advocacy. Effective diaspora advocates are likely to be well integrated in their settlement countries and to maintain their networks both there and in their countries of origin. Lack of partisanship is an asset for sustainable influence, although tying the advocacy group's fortunes to a single party or faction may produce short-term gains. Finally, it is essential for diaspora advocates to cultivate a thorough understanding of the institutions they are trying to influence. The effectiveness of US-based Jewish organizations in lobbying for Israel has inspired many other diasporas to emulate them. The American Jewish Committee, for example, has trained diaspora organizations from India, Mexico, and Nigeria, among others, in how the US political system works and how to be effective lobbyists.

Should Donors Support Diaspora Advocacy?

Diasporas conduct advocacy on a wide range of topics, only a few of which are discussed above. Many of the topics raise questions about the role of governments in supporting and encouraging diaspora advocacy. Development agencies have an interest in diaspora advocacy because, as we have seen throughout this volume, diasporas are important actors and stakeholders in development in their countries of origin. They are only one kind of voice among many interest group voices, but one with particular expertise and insight into development. Advocating for projects, fundraising, identifying needs, debating priorities, and contributing expertise all bring diaspora advocates directly into the development territory familiar to USAID and other donor organizations. Listening to diaspora advocates is a matter of self-interest for donors, but it requires a discriminating ear. Each diaspora group has its own constituencies and agendas. Understanding the relationships of diasporas with institutions and communities in their countries of origin is a prerequisite to intelligent diaspora engagement.

Support for diaspora advocacy carries dangers for both diaspora members and donors. Donor support may open diaspora members to charges of cooptation by the targets of their advocacy, and thus erode their legitimacy. For the donors, support to diaspora organizations may look like an attempt to manipulate the diaspora and twist its priorities to those of the donor. It may also seem to reward the emigrant over the development actors within the country of origin — including the government. Both parties need to be on guard against such distortions.

For donors, an enabling framework is the best approach to diaspora advocacy, capable of encouraging the voice of diaspora members without rewarding their exit. Some of the ways that this approach can be pursued include the following:

- **Listen** to less well-organized and financed diasporas, so that the donor gets a more representative picture of diaspora views. Inclusive forums open to all diaspora voices will expose donors to those that have capabilities or ideas to contribute to a development partnership.

- **Support the right to organize** across borders. In regularizing diaspora policies, European institutions have established norms that help decrease potential tensions.[53] The Organization for

---

53 Mayra A. Waterbury, "From Irredentism to Diaspora Politics: States and Transborder Ethnic Groups in Eastern Europe" (Working paper no. 6, George Mason Univ., Global Migration and Transnational Politics, July 2009).

Security and Cooperation in Europe (OSCE) office of the High Commissioner on National Minorities, for example, asserts as a matter of principle that, "persons belonging to national minorities should be able to establish and maintain free and peaceful contacts across State borders to develop cultural and economic links."[54]

- **Train** diaspora groups in how development agencies work, so that such groups may develop their capacities to advocate realistically.

- **Evaluate** specific programs of diaspora engagement (such as USAID's African Diaspora Marketplace) so that best practices can be identified and built upon. Replicating best practices should be an advocacy target in itself.

- **Consult** diaspora advocates in the policymaking process in order to understand what coincidence there is between the donor's goals and those of the diaspora.

- **Share information** on policy goals with diasporas, so they can identify common goals and advocate with country-of-origin governments around those goals.

While working to enable diaspora groups to engage effectively in advocacy, donors should be strengthening their own capacities to listen and respond (when appropriate) to diaspora advocacy. This capacity should reside in overseas offices of the donor agencies as well as in headquarters. Indeed, it should infuse all parts of governments that deal with diaspora issues, from foreign policy and national security to immigration and civil rights. Diaspora advocates can be allies of donor governments, but should never be treated instrumentally as mere "tools" in development policy. They should neither be overlooked nor taken for granted. ⤴

---

54 Organization for Security and Cooperation in Europe (OSCE) High Commissioner on National Minorities, "The Bolzano/Bozen Recommendations on National Minorities in Inter-State Relations and Explanatory Note," 2008, www.osce.org/item/33388.html?ch=1189.

WORKS CITED

Chapter 1. Six Studies and a Road Map: Diasporas as Partners in Development

Agunias, Dovelyn Rannveig 2009. Institutionalizing Diaspora Engagement within Migrant-Origin Governments. In *Closing the Distance: How Governments Strengthen Ties with Their Diasporas*, ed. Dovelyn Rannveig Agunias. Washington, DC: Migration Policy Institute.

Altai Consulting. 2006. *An Evaluation of the EU-RQA Program for the International Organization for Migration and the European Commission.* Kabul: International Organization for Migration.

European Commission-UN Joint Migration and Development Initiative. Undated. Mainstreaming Migration in Development Planning—Key Actors, Key Strategies, Key Actions. Background Paper 1.2, Global Forum on Migration and Development.

Gonzalez Gutierrez, Carlos. 2009. The Institute of Mexicans Abroad: An Effort to Empower the Diaspora. In *Closing the Distance: How Governments Strengthen Ties with Their Diasporas*, ed. Dovelyn Rannveig Agunias. Washington, DC: Migration Policy Institute.

Kharas, Homi. 2007. *The New Reality of Aid.* Washington, DC: Wolfensohn Center for Development, Brookings Institution.

Natsios, Andrew. 2010. The Clash of the Counter-Bureaucracy and Development. Essay, Center for Global Development, July 2010.

Severino, Jean Michel, and Olivier Ray. 2009. The End of ODA: Death and Rebirth of a Global Public Policy. Working Paper 167, Center for Global Development, March 2009.

Sheffer, Gabriel. 1986. A New Field of Study: Modern Diasporas in International Politics. *Modern Diasporas in International Politics*, ed. Gabriel Sheffer. London: Croom Helm, 1986. Quoted in Koser, Khalid. 2003. New African Diasporas: An Introduction. In *New African Diasporas*, ed. Khalid Koser. London: Routledge.

United States Agency for International Development (USAID). 2009. Global Diaspora Networks Alliance Framework. Draft briefing paper, unpublished.

Chapter 2. Mobilizing Diaspora Entrepreneurship for Development

Ács, Zoltán J. 2006. "How is Entrepreneurship Good for Economic Growth?" *Innovations* (Winter 2006): 96–107. www.mitpressjournals.org/doi/pdf/10.1162/itgg.2006.1.1.97?cookieSet=1.

Ács, Zoltán J., and Attila Varga. 2005. "Agglomeration, Entrepreneurship and Technological Change." *Small Business Economics* 24 (3): 323–34

Ács, Zoltán J., and Laszlo Szerb. 2007. "Entrepreneurship, Economic Growth, and Public Policy." *Small Business and Economics* 28 (2–3): 109–22.

Ács, Zoltan J., David B. Audretsch, and Robert J. Strom, eds. 2009. *Entrepreneurship, Growth, and Public Policy*. Cambridge, United Kingdom: Cambridge Univ. Press.

AFFORD. *Connecting UK-based African Organizations with Mainstream NGOs*. London, United Kingdom. www.afford-uk.org/documents/DownloadArea/connecting_ukbaco_with_ngos.pdf.

African Diaspora Marketplace (ADM). "2009 Finalists." www.diasporamarketplace.org/sites/default/files/adm2009_finalists.pdf.

———. 2010. "U.S.-Based African Diaspora Entrepreneurs to Spur Job Growth in Their Native Countries with Innovative Business Plans." Press Release, January 13, 2010. www.diasporamarketplace.org/sites/default/files/African_Diaspora_Marketplace_Winners_Release_1-13-10_0.pdf.

Armenia 2020. "News." Press Release, October 23, 2007.

———. "News." Press Release, July 31, 2007.

Basch, Linda G., Nina Glick-Schiller, and Cristina Szanton Blanc. 1994. *Nations Unbound: Transnational Projects, Postcolonial Predicaments, and De-territorialized Nation-States*. Amsterdam, The Netherlands: Gordon and Breach.

Baumol, William J., Robert E. Litan, and Carl J. Schramm. 2007. *Good Capitalism, Bad Capitalism and the Economics of Growth and Prosperity*. New Haven, CT: Yale Univ. Press.

Begley, Thomas M. and Wee-Liang Tan. 2001. "The Socio-Cultural Environment for Entrepreneurship: Comparison between East Asian and Anglo-Saxon Countries." *Journal of International Business Studies* 32 (3): 537–53.

BiD Network. "BiD Network Results." www.bidnetwork.org/page/92869/en.

———. "How to Use the BiD Network." www.bidnetwork.org/page/820/en.

———. "SMEs Matched via BiD Network." www.bidnetwork.org/page/121645.

Chaco, Elizabeth, and Marie Price. 2009. *The Role of the Diaspora in Development: The case of Ethiopia and Bolivian immigrants in the USA*. Washington, DC: George Washington Univ. http://iussp2009.princeton.edu/download. aspx?submissionId=92786.

Chile Global. "¿Quiénes Somos?" www.chileglobal.org/quienes-somos.

Development Marketplace for African Diaspora in Europe. 2009. "The Development Marketplace for African Diaspora in Europe: Promoting Diaspora Investment Projects and Innovative Entrepreneurial Activities in Africa." www.dmade.org/admindb/ docs/D-MADE_CompetitionGuidelinesweb.pdf.

Doing Business Project. www.doingbusiness.org.

Ethiopia Commodity Exchange (ECX). "About Us." www.ecx.com.et/CompanyProfile. aspx#AU.

Fontaine, Thomson. 2006. "Tracing the Diaspora's Involvement in the Development of a Nation: The Case of Dominica." Paper prepared for the George Washington University's Research Workshop and Edited Book Project on the Role of Diasporas in Developing the Homeland. www.thedominican.net/articles/diasporaPaper.pdf.

Fundación Chile. "I'm an Investor: Invest in Your Dreams." http://ww2.fundacionchile.cl/ portal/web/guest/inversionista.

Gillespie, Kate, Liesl Riddle, Edward Sayre, and David Sturges. 1999. "Diaspora Interest in Homeland Investment." *Journal of International Business Studies* 30 (3): 623–35.

GlobalScot. 2009. *GlobalScot: Building International Business Networks for Scotland*. Glasgow, Scotland: Scottish Enterprise. www.globalscot.com/web/FILES/ GlobalScot_Brochure_2009.pdf.

Gubert, Flore, and Christophe J. Nordman. 2009. "Return Migration and Small Enterprise Development in the Maghreb." Presentation at the World Bank Conference on Diaspora for Development, Washington, DC, July 14. http://siteresources.worldbank.org/INTPROSPECTS/Resources/ 334934-1110315015165/Gubert_Nordman.pdf.

Hamm, Steve. 2007. *Bangalore Tiger: How Indian Tech Upstart Wipro is Rewriting the Rules of Global Competition*. New York, NY: McGraw-Hill.

International Organization for Migration (IOM). "Migration for Development in Africa (MIDA)." www.iom.int/jahia/Jahia/mida-africa/.

Kapur, Devesh. 2001. "Diasporas and Technology Transfer." *Journal of Human Development* 2 (2): 265–86. www2.ssc.upenn.edu/about/Diasporas and Technology Transfer.pdf.

———. 2002. "The Causes and Consequences of India's IT Boom." *India Review* 1 (2): 91–110.

Klapper, Leora, and Juan Manuel Quesada. 2007. *Understanding Entrepreneurship: Influences and Consequences of Business Creation*. Washington, DC: World Bank.

Klapper, Leora, Raphael Amit, Mauro F. Guillén, and Juan Manuel Quesada. 2007. *Entrepreneurship and Firm Formation across Countries*. Washington, DC: World Bank Group. http://knowledge.wharton.upenn.edu/papers/1345.pdf.

Kloosterman, Robert, and Jan Rath, eds. 2003. *Immigrant Entrepreneurs: Venturing Abroad in the Age of Globalization.* Oxford, United Kingdom and New York, NY: Berg.

Kurata, Phillip. 2008. "Ethiopia Launches Commodity Exchange to Develop Agriculture." *America.gov*, October 31. www.america.gov/st/econ-english/2008/October/20081031174240cpataruk0.134823.html.

———. 2009. "African Migrants Invest in Their Home Countries." *America.gov*, November 9. www.america.gov/st/develop-english/2009/November/20091106173018cpataruk0.2806055.html;

Kuznetsov, Yevgeny. 2005. "Por que ChileGlobal? Red de Talentos en el Exterior para Desarrollo Tecnologico de Chile." Presentation at the first meeting of ChileGlobal, San Francisco, June 10. http://info.worldbank.org/etools/docs/library/201209/ChileDiaspora.pdf.

Kuznetsov, Yevgeny, and Charles Sabel. 2006. "International Migration of Talent, Diaspora Networks, and Development: Overview of Main Issues." In *Diaspora Networks and the International Migration of Skills: How Countries Can Draw on Their Talent Abroad*, ed. Yevgeny Kuznetsov. Washington, DC: World Bank.

Leblang, David. 2009. "Another Link in the Chain: Migrant Networks and International Investment." Presentation at the World Bank Conference on Diaspora and Development, Washington, DC, July 14. http://siteresources.worldbank.org/INTPROSPECTS/Resources/334934-1110315015165/Leblang.pdf

Levitt, Peggy. 2001. *The Transnational Villagers.* Berkeley, CA: Univ. of California Press.

Lubkemann, Stephen C. 2008. "Remittance Reflief and Not-Just-for-Profit Entrepreneurship: The Case of Liberia." In *Diasporas and Development: Exploring the Potential*, ed. Jennifer M. Brinkerhoff. Boulder, CO: Lynne Rienner Publishers, Inc.

MacRae, Mairi, with Martin Wight. 2006. "A Model Diaspora Network: The Origin and Evolution of Globalscot." In *Diaspora Networks and the International Migration of Skills: How Countries Can Draw on Their Talent Abroad*, ed. Yevgeny Kutznetsov. Washington, DC: World Bank.

Madsen, Henning, Helle Neergaard, and John P. Ulhøi. 2008. "Factors Influencing the Establishment of Knowledge Intensive Ventures." *International Journal of Entrepreneurial Behavior and Research* 14 (2): 70–84.

Migration for Development in Africa (MIDA). 2008. "The MIDA Italy Experience." Presentation, given at the Conference on International Migration and Development: Continuing the Dialogue Legal and Policy Perspectives, New York, January. www.un.int/iom/MIDA%20Rome.pdf.

Nayeck, Joyker. 2009. "Circular Migration — The Case for Mauritius." Presentation at the International Conference on Diaspora for Development at the World Bank, Washington, DC, July 14. http://siteresources.worldbank.org/INTPROSPECTS/Resources/334934-1110315015165/Nayeck.pdf.

Ndiaye, Ndioro. 2009. "The MIDA Experience and Beyond." Presentation given at the World Bank Conference on Diaspora and Development, Washington, DC, July 13. http://siteresources.worldbank.org/INTPROSPECTS/Resources/334934-1110315015165/Ndiaye.pdf.

Newland, Kathleen, with Erin Patrick. 2004. "Beyond Remittances: The Role of Diasporas in Poverty Reduction in their Countries of Origin." A Scoping Study for the Department for International Development, United Kingdom, July. www.migrationpolicy.org/pubs/Beyond_Remittances_0704.pdf.

Paglayan, Agustina S., and Mariano Lafuente. 2008. *Mendoza Emprende: Enhancing Youth Entrepreneurship in Argentina by leveraging its Diaspora*. Washington, DC: World Bank. http://siteresources.worldbank.org/INTARGENTINA/Resources/Mendoza-EmprendeDisseminationReport.pdf.

———. 2009. "Reversing the Brain Drain: The Role of the Argentine Diaspora in Building the Entrepreneurial Skills of Argentine Youth." Presentation given at the World Bank Conference on Diaspora and Development, Washington, DC, July 14. http://siteresources.worldbank.org/INTPROSPECTS/Resources/334934-1110315015165/Paglayan_Lafuente.pdf.

Papademetriou, Demetrios G., Will Somerville, and Hiroyuki Tanaka. 2009. "Talent in the 21st Century." In *Talent, Competitiveness and Migration*. Eds. Bertelsmann Stiftung and Migration Policy Institute. Guetersloh: Bertelsmann Stiftung.

Programme Migrations et Initiatives Economiques (PMIE). "The Economic Initiatives and Migration Programme." www.pseau.org/outils/ouvrages/pmie_presentation_ve.pdf.

Qadeer, Mohammad A. 1983. *Urban Development in the Third World: Internal Dynamics of Lahore, Pakistan*. New York, NY: Praeger.

Quek, Tracy. 2010. "China's Not-so-little talent blueprint," *Straits Times,* Sept. 26, 2010, http://wanderingchina.wordpress.com/2010/09/26/chinas-not-so-little-talent-blueprint-straits-times/.

Ramamurti, Ravi. 2004. "Developing Countries and MNEs: Extending and Enriching the Research Agenda." *Journal of International Business Studies* 35 (4): 277–85.

Saxenian, AnnaLee. 2006. "International Mobility of Engineers and the Rise of Entrepreneurship in the Periphery." Research Paper No. 142, United Nations Univ., Tokyo, Japan. www.wider.unu.edu/publications/working-papers/research-papers/2006/en_GB/rp2006-142/_files/78091822234994961/default/rp2006-142.pdf.

———. 2006. *The New Argonauts: Regional Advantage in a Global Economy*. Cambridge, MA: Harvard Univ. Press.

Schumpeter, Joseph Alois. 1974. *Capitalism, Socialism and Democracy*. 4th ed. London, United Kingdom: Unwin.

Scottish Enterprise. 2009. "GlobalScot." Press Release, October 15.

———. "What We Do." http://www.scottish-enterprise.com/about-us/se-whatwedo.aspx.

Sheikh, Hassan, and Sally Healy. 2009. *Somalia's Missing Million: The Somali Diaspora and its Role in Development*. New York, NY: United Nations Development Programme. www.so.undp.org/index.php/View-document-details/70-Forging-Partnerships-with-the-Somali-Diaspora.

The African Network. "What is the Africa Network." www.theafricannetwork.org/.

The Indus Entrepreneurs (TiE). "Overview." www.tie.org/chapterHome/about_tie/
OverView200706189912181967/viewInnerPagePT.

United Nations Conference on Trade and Development (UNCTAD). 2001. *Investment Policy Review: Mauritius.* New York and Geneva: UNCTAD. www.gov.mu/portal/sites/ ncb/mac/nlibrary/efiles/dig4.pdf.

United States Agency for International Development (USAID). 2008. *Global Diaspora Networks Alliance Framework.* Washington, DC: USAID.

———. 2008. *Diaspora Networks Alliance: Leveraging Migrant Resources for Effective Development.* Washington, DC: USAID.

Wadhwa, Vivek, AnnaLee Saxenian, Richard Freeman, Gary Gereffi, and Alex Salkever. 2009. *America's Loss is the World's Gain: America's New Immigrant Entrepreneurs, Part IV.* Kansas City, MO: Kauffman Foundation.

Waldinger, Roger. 1986. *Through the Eye of the Needle: Immigrants and Enterprise in New York's Garment Trades.* New York, NY: New York University Press.

Waldinger, Roger, Howard Aldrich, and Robin Ward. 1990. *Ethnic Entrepreneurs: Immigrant Business in Industrial Societies.* New York, NY: Sage Publications.

Watkins, Alfred, and Natalia Agapitova. 2004. *Creating a 21st Century National Innovation System for a 21st Century Latvian Economy.* Washington, DC: World Bank. www-wds.worldbank.org/servlet/WDSContentServer/WDSP/IB/2004/12 /07/000012009_20041207121312/Rendered/PDF/WPS3457.pdf.

Watson, Robert, Kevin Keasey, and Mae Baker. 2000. "Small Firm Financial Contracting and Immigrant Entrepreneurship." In *Immigrant Businesses: The Economic, Political and Social Environment,* ed. Jan Rath. Basingstoke, United Kingdom and New York, NY: Macmillan and St. Martin's.

World Bank. 2009. "Quick Query Selected from World Development Indicators." In *World Development Indicators.* Washington, DC: World Bank.

Chapter 3. Diaspora Investment in Developing and Emerging Country Capital Markets: Patterns and Prospects

Aggarwal, Reena, Asli Demirgüç-Kunt, and Maria Soledad Martinez Peria. 2005. *Do Workers' Remittances Promote Financial Development?* Washington, DC: World Bank.

Agunias, Dovelyn Rannveig, ed. 2009. *Closing the Distance: How Governments Strengthen Ties with Their Diasporas.* Washington, DC: Migration Policy Institute (MPI).

Agunias, Dovelyn Rannveig, and Aaron Terrazas. 2008. "Leveraging Diaspora Investment for Development: Lessons from the Housing Sector," Unpublished draft, Migration Policy Institute, September.

Andrade, Sandro C., and Vidhi Chhaochharia. 2010. "Information Immobility and Foreign Portfolio Investment." *The Review of Financial Studies* 23 (6): 2429–63.

Ball, Steffan G. 2008. *Stock Market Participation, Portfolio Choice and Pensions over the Life-Cycle*. Washington, DC: Federal Reserve Board, Finance and Economics Discussion Series, Divisions of Research and Statistics and Monetary Affairs, November.

Barranco, Alberto. 2010. "Sigue Su Casita." *El Universal*, June 17.

Barth, James R., Tong Li, Wenling Lu, and Glenn Yago. 2010. *Capital Access Index 2009: Best Markets for Business Access to Capital*. Santa Monica, CA: Milken Institute.

Beck, Thorsten, Asli Demirgüç-Kunt, and Ross Levine. 2004. "Finance, Inequality, and Poverty: Cross-Country Evidence." National Bureau of Economic Research, Working Paper 10979, December. Cambridge, Massachusetts.

Bhattacharya, Amar, John Williamson, Arturo Porzecanski, and Uri Dadush. 2010. "Managing Capital Flows in the Aftermath of the Global Crisis." Presentations, Carnegie Endowment for International Peace, International Economics Program, May 26. Washington, DC. www.carnegieendowment.org/events/?fa=eventDetail&id=2914.

Birks, J. S., and C. A. Sinclair. 1978. "Human Capital on the Nile: Development and Migration in the Arab Republic of Egypt and the Democratic Republic of the Sudan." International Labor Organization, World Employment Program, Working Paper 2-26/WP 27, May. Geneva.

Börsch-Supan, Axel, ed. 2003. *Life-Cycle Savings and Public Policy: A Cross-National Study in Six Countries*. Amsterdam and Boston: Academic Books.

Brainard, Lael, ed. 2006. *Transforming the Development Landscape: The Role of the Private Sector*. Washington, DC: The Brookings Institution Press.

Canuto, Otaviano, and Lili Liu. 2010. "Subnational Debt Finance and the Global Financial Crisis." World Bank Poverty Reduction and Economic Management Network, Economic Premise, No. 13, May. Washington, D.C.

Carnegie Endowment for International Peace. 2009. "Capital Flows to Emerging Markets Resurgent." *International Economic Bulletin*, November 9–13. www.carnegieendowment.org/publications/index.cfm?fa=view&id=24116.

Castillo, Nancy, Landen Romei, and Manuel Orozco. 2010. *Toward Financial Independence: Financial Literacy for Remittance Senders and Recipients*. Washington, DC: Inter-American Dialogue, June. www.thedialogue.org/page.cfm?pageID=32&pubID=2400.

Central Bank of the Republic of Turkey. "FX Deposit Accounts." www.tcmb.gov.tr/iscidvz/iscidozengyeni.htm.

———. 2010. *Balance of Payment Statistics and International Investment Position*. Ankara: Central Bank of Turkey, March. www.tcmb.gov.tr/yeni/eng/.

Chami, Ralph, Connel Fullenkamp, and Sunil Sharma. 2009. *A Framework for Financial Market Development*. IMF Working Paper WP/09/156, International Monetary Fund, Washington, DC, July.

Chishti, Muzaffar A. 2007. *The Phenomenal Rise in Remittances to India: A Closer Look*. Washington, DC: MPI. www.migrationpolicy.org/pubs/MigDevPB_052907.pdf.

Commission on Growth and Development. 2008. *The Growth Report: Strategies for Sustained Growth and Inclusive Development*. Washington, DC: World Bank.

————. 2010. *Post-Crisis Growth in Developing Countries: A Special Report of the Commission on Growth and Development on the Implications of the 2008 Financial Crisis.* Washington, DC: World Bank.

Consultative Group to Assist the Poor (CGAP). 2009. *Financial Access 2009.* Washington, DC: CGAP.

Dow Jones. 2010. "China Minsheng Bank 2009 Net Profit Soars 53%." April 19.

Durdu, Ceyhun Bora, and Serdar Sayan. 2008. "Emerging Market Business Cycles with Remittance Fluctuations." International Finance Discussion Paper No. 946, Board of Governors of the Federal Reserve System, September. Washington, D.C.

Dustmann, Christian, and Josep Mestres. 2010. "Savings, Asset Holdings, and Temporary Migration." Center for Research and Analysis of Migration, Discussion Paper No. 05/10. www.econ.ucl.ac.uk/cream/pages/CDP/CDP_05_10.pdf.

Dziunda, Wioletta, and Jordi Mondria. 2009. "Assymetric Information, Portfolio Managers and Home Bias." AFA 2010 Atlanta Meeting Paper, February. http://papers.ssrn.com/sol3/papers.cfm?abstract_id=1359280&rec=1&srcabs=1344880.

The *Economist*. 2010. "Earthbound." March 27.

————. 2010. *A Special Report on Banking in Emerging Market Economies.* May 15.

Freire, Mila, John Petersen, Marcela Huertas, and Miguel Valadez, eds. 2004. *Subnational Capital Markets in Developing Countries: From Theory to Practice.* Washington, DC: World Bank.

Ghana Ministry of Finance and Economic Planning. "Golden Jubilee Savings Bond." www.mofep.gov.gh/gj_bond.htm.

Ghosh, Swati R. 2010. "Dealing with the Challenges of Capital Inflows in the Context of Macrofinancial Links." World Bank Economic Premise No. 19, June. Washington, D.C.

Glen, Jack, and Ajit Singh. 2003. "Capital Structure, Rates of Return and Financing Corporate Growth: Comparing Developed and Emerging Markets, 1994–00." ESRC Centre for Business Research, Univ. of Cambridge Working Paper No. 265, June.

Grant, George. 2009. "Can a Diaspora Bond Help Grenada?" October 4. www.caribbeannetnews.com/article.php?news_id=22475.

Greek Reporter. 2010. "Athens May Appeal to Rich Greeks Abroad." March 1. http://eu.greekreporter.com/2010/03/01/athens-proposal-of-the-president-of-the-parliament-to-create-a-support-fund-for-greece-and-from-greeks-of-the-diaspora/.

Grinblatt, Mark, and Matti Keloharju. 2001. "How Distance, Language, and Culture Influence Stockholdings and Trades." *The Journal of Finance* 56, no. 3 (June): 1053–73.

Guiliano, Paola, and Marta Ruiz-Arranz. 2006. "Remittances, Financial Development and Growth." IZA Discussion Paper No. 2160, June. Berlin.

Gupta, Sanjeev, Catherine Pattillo, and Smith Wagh. 2007. "Impact of Remittances on Poverty and Financial Development in Sub-Saharan Africa." IMF Working Paper WP/07/38, International Monetary Fund, Washington, DC, February.

Hall, Joan. 2010. *Diez años de innovación en remesas: Lecciones aprendidas y modelos para el futuro.* Washington, DC: Multilateral Investment Fund, Inter-American Development Bank, January.

Hatchondo, Juan Carlos. 2007. "Assymetric Information and the Lack of International Portfolio Diversification." Federal Reserve Bank of Richmond Working Paper No. 05-07, September. http://www.richmondfed.org/publications/research/working_papers/2005/pdf/wp05-7.pdf.

Häusler, Gerd, Donald J. Mathieson, and Jorge Roldos. 2003. "Trends in Developing-Country Capital Markets Around the World." In *The Future of Domestic Capital Markets in Developing Countries,* ed. Robert E. Litan, Michael Pomerleano, and V. Sundararajan. Washington, DC: The Brookings Institution, 21–44.

Institute of International Finance. 2010. *Capital Flows to Emerging Market Economies.* Washington, DC: Institute of International Finance, January.

Karachadag, Cem, V. Sundararajan, and Jennifer Elliott. 2003. "Managing Risks in Financial Market Development: The Role of Sequencing." In *The Future of Domestic Capital Markets in Developing Countries,* ed. Robert E. Litan, Michael Pomerleano, and V. Sundararajan. Washington, DC: Brookings Institution.

Kaul, Inge, and Pedro Conceição, eds. 2006. *The New Public Finance: Responding to Global Challenges.* New York and Oxford: Oxford Univ. Press.

Kempf, Alexander, and Peer C. Osthoff. 2007. "The Effect of Socially Responsible Investing on Portfolio Performance." *European Financial Management* 13, no. 5 (November): 908–22.

Ketkar, Suhas, and Dilip Ratha, eds. 2009. *Innovative Financing for Development.* Washington, DC: World Bank.

Kubo, Koji. 2007. "Do Foreign Currency Deposits Promote or Deter Financial Development in Low-Income Countries? An Empirical Analysis of Cross-Country Data." Institute for Development Studies Discussion Paper No. 87, January. London.

Lambert, Frederic, and Matteo Pignatti. 2008. "Saving Behavior over the Life-Cycle Does Not Differ across Countries. Portfolio Choices Do." Working Paper, Banque de France, August. Paris.

Leblang, David. 2009. "Diaspora Bonds and Cross Border Capital." Working Paper, Univ. of Virginia, Department of Politics.

Litan, Robert E., Michael Pomerleano, and V. Sundararajan. 2003. *The Future of Domestic Capital Markets in Developing Countries.* Washington, DC: The Brookings Institution.

Massey, Douglas S., and Emilio Parrado. 1994. "Migradollars: The Remittances and Savings of Mexican Migrants to the USA." *Population Research and Policy Review* 13, no. 1 (March): pp. 3-30.

McCauley, Robert, and Eli Remolona. 2000. "Size and Liquidity of Government Bond Markets." *Bank for International Settlements Quarterly Review,* November. Basel.

Moss, Todd, Vijaya Ramachandran, and Scott Standley. 2007. "Why Doesn't Africa Get More Equity Investment? Frontier Stock Markets, Firm Size, and Asset Allocation of Global Emerging Market Funds." Center for Global Development Working Paper No. 112, February. Washington, DC. www.cgdev.org/content/publications/detail/12773.

National Bank of Ethiopia. 2004. "Directive No. FXD/25/2004, Amendment to Directive No. FXD/24/2004, Establishment and Operation of Foreign Currency Account for Non-Resident Ethiopians and Non-Resident Ethiopian Origin." July 12. www.mfa.gov.et/Ethiopians_Origin_Abroad/Services.php?page=Home.htm.

Negash, Minga. 2009. "Ethiopian Diaspora Investment Potential and EEPCO's Millennium Bond." Working Paper, Univ. of Witwatersrand, March. http://papers.ssrn.com/sol3/papers.cfm?abstract_id=1370515.

Newland, Kathleen, and Erin Patrick. 2004. *Beyond Remittances: The Role of Diaspora in Poverty Reduction in Their Countries of Origin.* Washington, DC and London: MPI and the UK Department for International Development (DFID).

Newland, Kathleen, and Hiroyuki Tanaka. 2010. "Mobilizing Diaspora Entrepreneurs for Development." In Kathleen Newland, ed. *Diasporas: New Partners in Global Development Policy.* Washington, DC: MPI.

Ngomiraronka, Emmanuel. 2010. "Rwandan Diaspora Mutual Fund: An Investment Initiative of the Rwandan Diaspora." Presentation provided to the MPI, May. Kigali.

Orozco, Manuel. 2010. "Financial Access among Remittance Senders." Presentation at the Inter-American Dialogue, Washington, DC, June 14.

Osili, Una Okonkwo. 2007. "Remittances and Savings from International Migration: Theory and Evidence Using a Matched Sample." *Journal of Development Economics* 83 (2): 446–65.

Ratha, Dilip, Sanket Mohapatra, and Ani Silwal. 2010. *Outlook for Remittance Flows 2010–11.* Washington, DC: World Bank.

Razin, Assaf, Efraim Sadka, and Chi-Wa Yuen. 1999. "Excessive FDI Flows under Assymetric Information." Federal Reserve Bank of San Francisco Working Paper No. 27-99, August. www.frbsf.org/economics/conferences/990923/papers/razin_sadka_yuen.pdf.

Reinhart, Carmen, and Guillermo Calvo. 2000. "When Capital Inflows Come to a Sudden Stop: Consequences and Policy Options." In *Reforming the International Monetary and Financial System,* ed. Peter Kenen and Alexandre Swoboda. Washington, DC: IMF.

Reserve Bank of India. "Features of Various Deposit Schemes Available to Non-Resident Indians." www.rbi.org.in/scripts/FAQView.aspx?Id=69.

———. 2010. "NRI Deposits — Outstandings and Inflows(+)/Outflows(-)." *RBI Bulletin,* May 12. www.rbi.org.in/scripts/BS_ViewBulletin.aspx.

Reuters. 2007. "China's Minsheng Bank to buy into UCBH." October 8. www.reuters.com/article/idUSSHA20222420071008.

Rios Avila, Fernando, and Eva Schlarb. 2008. "Back Accounts and Savings — The Impact of Remittances and Migration: A Case Study of Moldova." Kiel Institute for the World Economy Working Paper No. 448, May. Kiel, Germany.

Ruggles, Steven, J. Trent Alexander, Katie Genadek, Ronald Goeken, Matthew B. Schroeder, and Matthew Sobek. 2010. *Integrated Public Use Microdata Series: Version 5.0* [Machine-readable database]. Minneapolis: Univ. of Minnesota.

Scotia Capital. 2000. *A Securitization Primer.* Toronto: Scotia Capital. www.securitization.net/pdf/lin_primer.pdf.

Senterfitt, Akerman. 2006. *A Primer on Securitization.* New York: World Services Group, October. www.hg.org/articles/article_1723.html.

Shane, Scott. 2008. *The Illusions of Entrepreneurship: The Costly Myths that Entrepreneurs, Investors, and Policy Makers Live By.* New Haven, CT: Yale University Press, 99.

Statman, Meir. 2000. "Socially Responsible Mutual Funds." *Financial Analysts Journal* 56, no. 3 (May/June): 30–39.

Terrazas, Aaron. 2009. "Older Immigrants in the United States." *Migration Information Source*, May. www.migrationinformation.org/USfocus/display.cfm?id=727.

———. 2010. *Connected through Service: Diaspora Volunteers and Global Development.* In Kathleen Newland, ed. *Diasporas: New Partners in Global Development Policy.* Washington, DC: MPI.

Terrazas, Aaron, and Jeanne Batalova. 2009. "Frequently Requested Statistics on Immigrants and Immigration in the United States." *Migration Information Source*, October. www.migrationinformation.org/USFocus/display.cfm?ID=747.

Williamson, John. 2005. *Curbing the Boom-Bust Cycle: Stabilizing Capital Flows to Emerging Markets.* Washington, DC: Peterson Institute for International Economics.

Wong, Paul. 2003. "Leveraging the Jamaican Diaspora for Development." Washington, DC: USAID Office of Development Credit, November. www.tcgillc.com/tcgidocs/Jamaica031124.pdf.

Yasin, Jehad. 2007. "Demographic Structure and Private Savings: Some Evidence from Emerging Markets." Working Paper, Department of Economics, Population Studies Center, Fort Valley State University.

Yewondwossen, Muluken. 2009. "Ethiopia — EEPCo and Diaspora to Bond with Agents." Nazret.com, August 3. http://nazret.com/blog/index.php?title=ethiopia_eepco_and_diaspora_to_bond_with&more=1&c=1&tb=1&pb=1.

Chapter 4. Heritage Tourism and Nostalgia Trade: A Diaspora Niche in the Development Landscape

Asiedu, Alex. 2005. "Some Benefits of Migrants' Return Visits to Ghana." *Population, Space and Place* 11 (1): 1–11.

Associated Press. 2010. Kenya: Common Visa Favored For 5 East African Nations. *The New York Times*, July 3, 2010. www.nytimes.com/2010/07/03/world/africa/03briefs-VISA.html.

Birtwistle, Moira. 2005. "Genealogy Tourism: The Scottish Market Opportunities." *Niche Tourism*, ed. Marina Novelli. Oxford: Butterworth-Heinemann, 59–72.

Bounds, Andrew. 2009. Ethiopian refugees discover benefits of coffee. *Financial Times*, May 7, 2009, www.ethiopianreview.com/articles/3989.

Clingingsmith, David Lawrence, Asim Ijaz Khwaja, and Michael Kremer. 2008. "Estimating the Impact of the Hajj: Religion and Tolerance in Islam's Global Gathering." HKS Working Paper No. RWP08-022, Harvard University John F. Kenedy School of Government. http://ssrn.com/abstract=1124213.

Debass, Thomas and Manuel Orozco. 2008. "Digesting Nostalgic Trade: A Prequel to a Value Chain Approach." USAID Breakfast Seminar Series Presentation, Washington, DC, November 20, 2008. www.microlinks.org/ev_en.php?ID=29168_201&ID2=DO_TOPIC.

Evans, Graeme. 2004. "Mundo Maya: From Cancún to City of Culture. World Heritage in Post-Colonial Mesoamerica." *Current Issues in Tourism* 7 (3): 315–29.

Garavelli, Dani. 2009. Homeward bound: Scotland's diaspora heads to Edinburgh for the highpoint of the Homecoming celebrations this month. *Scotland on Sunday*, July 5, 2009.

Gibson, John, and David McKenzie. 2010. "The Economic Consequences of 'Brain Drain' of the Best and Brightest: Microeconomic Evidence from Five Countries." Working Paper 5394, Development Research Group, Finance and Private Sector Development Team, World Bank, Washington, DC.

Honey, Martha and Raymond Gilpin. 2009. "Tourism in Developing Countries: Promoting Peace and Reducing Poverty." Special Report 233, US Institute of Peace, October 2009.

Iskander, Natasha. 2010. *Creative State: Forty Years of Migration and Development Policy in Morocco and Mexico.* Ithaca, NY: ILR Press.

Jordan, Mary. 2007. Seeking Answers with Field Trips in Faith, *Washington Post*, June 25, 2007, www.washingtonpost.com/wp-dyn/content/article/2007/06/24/AR2007062401422.html.

Kelner, Shaul. 2010. *Tours that Bind: Diaspora, Pilgrimage and Israeli Birthright Tourism.* New York, NY: New York University Press.

Levitt, Peggy. 2001. *The Transnational Villagers.* Berkeley, CA: University of California Press.

Lorna Young Foundation (LYF). 2010. "The Oromo Coffee Company and the Lorna Young Foundation." Information sheet. www.lyfe.ac/en_GB/ventures.html.

LYF and Oromo Coffee Company. 2010. "The Story Behind it . . .The Oromo Coffee Company and the Lorna Young Foundation." PowerPoint Presentation. www.oromocoffee.org.

Orozco, Manuel. 2008. *Tasting Identity: Trends in Migrant Demands for Home Country Goods.* Report commissioned by the US Agency for International Development, Washington, DC.

Orozco, Manuel, B. Lindsay Lowell, Micah Bump, and Rachel Fedewa. 2005. *Transnational Engagement, Remittances and their Relation to Development in Latin America and the Caribbean.* Washington, DC: Institute for the Study of International Migration, Georgetown University, http://isim.georgetown.edu/Publications/LindsayPubs/Rockefeller%20Report.pdf.

Partridgee, James and Hartley Furtan. 2008. "Immigration Wave Effects on Canada's Trade Flows." *Canadian Public Policy* 34 (2): 193-214.

Pérez-López, Jorge. 2007. "The Diaspora as a Commercial Network for Cuban Reconstruction." Thought Paper for the Association for the Study of the Cuban Economy. http://146.6.146.2/project/asce/pdfs/volume17/pdfs/perezlopez.pdf.

Peri, Giovanni and Francisco Requena. 2009. "The Trade Creation Effect of Immigrants: Evidence from the Remarkable Case of Spain." Working Paper 15625, National Bureau of Economic Research.

Scheyvens, Regina. 2007. "Poor Cousins No More: Valuing the Development Potential of Domestic and Diaspora Tourism." *Progress in Development Studies* 7 (4): 307–25.

United Nations World Tourism Organization (UNWTO). 1995. *UNWTO Technical Manual: Collection of Tourism Expenditure Statistics*, 14. Madrid: UNWTO. http://pub.unwto.org/WebRoot/Store/Shops/Infoshop/Products/1034/1034-1.pdf.

———. 2010. *World Tourism Barometer, Interim Update April 2010*. Madrid: UNWTO. www.unwto.org/facts/eng/pdf/barometer/UNWTO_Barom10_update_april_en_excerpt.pdf.

United States Agency for International Development (USAID). 2010. *DDI Project Quarterly Update, March 31, 2010*. Washington, DC: USAID.

Vietnam Net Bridge. 2010. Move to Lure Foreign Tourists, September 3, 2010. www.vietnamopentour.com.vn/vietnam-information/news/move-to-lure-for-eign-tourists.html.

Wells, E. Christian and Karla L. Davis-Salazar. 2008. "Environmental Worldview and Ritual Economy among the Honduran Lenca." *Dimensions of Ritual Economy*, eds. E. Christian Wells and Patricia A. McAnany. Bingley, UK: Emerald Group Publishing Ltd., 189-217.

Chapter 5. Diaspora Philanthropy: Private Giving and Public Policy

Aikens, Kingsley, Anita Sands, and Nicola White. 2009. *The Global Irish Making a Difference Together: A Comparative Review of International Diaspora Strategies*. Dublin: The Ireland Funds.

African Development Bank. 2008. *Migrant Remittances a Development Challenge*. Tunis: African Development Bank. www.afdb.org/fileadmin/uploads/afdb/Documents/Publications/70000012_EN_Transfert%20des%20fonds%20ANG.pdf.

Anand, Priya. 2004. "Hindu Diaspora and Religious Philanthropy in the United States." Paper presented at the Sixth International Society for Third Sector Research, Toronto, Canada.

Añonuevo, Estrella, and Augustus Añonuevo. 2008. "Philippines." Paper presented at the Asia Pacific Philanthropy Consortium Conference, "Diaspora Giving: An Agent of Change in Asia Pacific Communities?" Hanoi, Vietnam, May 21–23. www.asiapaci-ficphilanthropy.org/conference.

Asian Development Bank. 2006. *Workers' Remittance Flows in Southeast Asia*. Manila: Asian Development Bank.

Aysa-Lastra, Maria. 2007. *Diaspora Philanthropy: The Colombia Experience.* The Philanthropic Initiative and the Global Equity Initiative, Harvard Univ.

Bhatti, Zubair. 2008. "Pakistan." Paper presented at the Asia Pacific Philanthropy Consortium Conference, "Diaspora Giving: An Agent of Change in Asia Pacific Communities?" Hanoi, Vietnam, May 21–23. www.asiapacificphilanthropy.org/conference.

Bishop, Matthew. 2008. "Who Will Be Relevant in 2020?" *Global Development 2.0: Can Philanthropists, the Public and the Poor Make Poverty History?* ed. Lael Brainard and Derek Chollet. Washington, DC: Brookings Institution Press.

Branch, John. 2008. "Four Players Who Came Out of Africa Return to Help." *New York Times,* May 8. www.nytimes.com/2008/05/08/sports/football/08nigeria.html.

Brill, Betsy. 2004. "A World of Philanthropic Opportunity: A Global Perspective on Giving." *Journal of Practical Estate Planning* 6, no. 2 (April/May): 19.

Brinkerhoff, Jennifer M. 2008. "Diaspora Philanthropy in an At-Risk Society: The Case of Coptic Orphans in Egypt." *Nonprofit and Voluntary Sector Quarterly* 37, no. 3 (September 2008): 411–33.

De Bruyn, Tom. 2008. *Evaluation of Oxfam Novib's Capacity Building Programme for Diaspora Organisations.* The Hague: Oxfam Novib. www.diaspora-centre.org/DOCS/Oxfam_Novib_diaspo.pdf.

Burgess, Katrina. 2005. "Migrant Philanthropy and Local Governance." *New Patterns for Mexico: Observations on Remittances, Philanthropic Giving, and Equitable Development,* ed. Barbara Merz. Cambridge, MA: Harvard Univ. Press.

Clotfelter, Charles T. 1985. *Federal Tax Policy and Charitable Giving.* Chicago: Univ. of Chicago Press.

Clotfelter, Charles T., and Thomas Ehrlich, eds. 1999. *Philanthropy and the Nonprofit Sector in a Changing America.* Bloomington, IN: Indiana Univ. Press.

Commission on Growth and Development. 2008. *The Growth Report: Strategies for Sustained Growth and Inclusive Development.* Washington, DC: World Bank.

Congressional Budget Office (CBO). 2004. *The Estate Tax and Charitable Giving.* Washington, DC: CBO. www.cbo.gov/ftpdocs/56xx/doc5650/07-15-CharitableGiving.pdf.

Copeland-Carson, Jacqueline. 2007. *Kenyan Diaspora Philanthropy: Key Practices, Trends and Issues.* Boston, MA: The Philanthropic Initiative and the Global Equity Initiative.

Corporation for National and Community Service. "Social Innovation Fund." www.nationalservice.gov/about/serveamerica/innovation.asp.

Deeney, John. 2005. "A Neglected Minority in a Neglected Field: The Emerging Role of Chinese American Philanthropy in US-China Relations." *Expanding Roles of Chinese Americans in US-China Relations: Transnational Networks and Trans-Pacific Interactions,* ed. Peter Koehn and Xiao-huang Yin. Brunswick, NJ: East Gate Publishers.

Desai, Raj, and Homi Kharas. 2009. *Do Philanthropic Citizens Behave Like Governments? Internet-Based Platforms and the Diffusion of International Private Aid.* Wolfensohn Center for Development, Brookings Institution.

Dewar, Tom, Christine Davachi, Katie Swinerton, Chad Bolick, and Karen Kaplan. 2009. *Evaluating Global Development Alliances: An Analysis of USAID's Public-Private Partnerships for Development*. Washington, DC: US Agency for International Development. www.usaid.gov/our_work/global_partnerships/gda/evaluation.html.

Dugger, Celia W. 2000. "In New York, Just a Cabby. In India, a School's Hero." *New York Times*, January 23. www.nytimes.com/2000/01/23/world/in-new-york-just-a-cabby-in-india-a-school-s-hero.html?pagewanted=1.

Dunn, Kathleen. 2004. *Diaspora Giving and the Future of Philanthropy*. Boston, Mass.: The Philanthropic Initiative.

Fajnzylber, Pablo, and Humberto López, eds. 2008. *Remittances and Development: Lessons from Latin America*. Washington, DC: World Bank.

Fernández de Castro, Rafael, Rodolfo García Zamora, and Ana Vila Freyer, eds. 2006. *El Programa 3x1 para Migrantes: ¿Primera Política Transnacional en México*. Mexico City: Miguel Ángel Porrúa, Universidad Autónoma de Zacatecas, and Instituto Tecnológico de Monterrey.

de Ferranti, David, and Anthony J. Ody. 2007. "What Can Remittances and Other Migrant Flows Do for Equitable Development?" *Diasporas and Development*, ed. Barbara J. Merz, Lincoln C. Chen, and Peter F. Geithner. Cambridge, MA: Harvard Univ. Press.

Friedman, Lawrence J., and Mark D. McGarvie. 2002. *Charity, Philanthropy, and Civility in American History*. New York: Cambridge Univ. Press.

Garchitorena, Victoria. 2007. *Diaspora Philanthropy: The Philippine Experience*. Boston, MA: The Philanthropic Initiative and the Harvard Global Equity Initiative.

Gravelle, Jane G. 2008. *Tax Issues Relating to Charitable Contributions and Organizations*. Congressional Research Service Report to Congress RL-34608, August 5. http://assets.opencrs.com/rpts/RL34608_20080805.pdf.

Gravelle, Jane G., and Donald J. Marples. 2010. *Charitable Contributions: The Itemized Deduction Cap and Other FY2010 Budget Options*. Congressional Research Service Report to Congress R-40518, March.

Geithner, Peter, Lincoln Chen, and Paula Johnson. 2004. *Diaspora Philanthropy and Equitable Development in China and India*. Cambridge, MA: Harvard Univ. Press.

Gobierno de Guatemala. "Dr. Rafael Espada, Vicepresidente." www.vicepresidencia.gob.gt/v2/content/dr-rafael-espada-vicepresidente.

De Haas, Hein. 2006. *Engaging Diasporas: How Governments and Development Agencies Can Support Diaspora Involvement in the Development of Origin Countries*. Oxford, UK: International Migration Institute.

Hudson Institute, Center for Global Prosperity. 2010. *Index of Global Philanthropy and Remittances 2009*. Washington, DC: Hudson Institute.

Hungerford, Thomas L. 2006. "Tax Expenditures: Good, Bad, or Ugly?" *Tax Notes*, October 23.

IndiaInteracts. "The Art of Philanthropy and the Indian Diaspora." http://indiainteracts.in/columnist/2008/01/08/The-art-of-philanthropy-and-the-Indian-diaspora/.

Internal Revenue Service (IRS). 2009. *Publication 54 (2009), Tax Guide for US Citizens and Resident Aliens Abroad.* Washington, DC: IRS. www.irs.gov/publications/p54/.

_____. 2010. *Cumulative List of Organizations Described in Section 170(c) of the Internal Revenue Code of 1986.* Version updated February 5, 2010. www.irs.gov/charities/article/0,,id=96136,00.html.

Johnson, Paula. 2001. *Global Social Investing: A Preliminary Overview.* Boston, MA: The Philanthropic Initiative.

_____. 2003. *Global Giving, Making a World of Difference.* Boston, MA: The Philanthropic Initiative.

_____. 2007. *Diaspora Philanthropy: Influences, Initiatives and Issues.* Boston, MA: The Philanthropic Initiative and the Global Equity Initiative.

Johnson, Paula, and Stephen Johnson. 2005. *Tools for Good: A Guide to Vehicles for Philanthropy and Charitable Giving.* Working Paper, International Network of Strategic Philanthropy, January.

Johnson, Paula, Stephen Johnson, and Andrew Kingman. 2004. "Promoting Philanthropy: Global Challenges and Approaches." Working Paper, International Network on Strategic Philanthropy, December.

Joint Committee on Taxation. 2008. *Estimates of Federal Tax Expenditures for Fiscal Years 2008–2012.* Staff Report to the House Committee on Ways and Means and the Senate Committee on Finance, October 31. www.jct.gov/s-2-08.pdf.

_____. 2010. *Estimates of Federal Tax Expenditures for Fiscal Years 2009–2013.* Staff Report to the House Committee on Ways and Means and the Senate Committee on Finance, January 11. www.jct.gov/publications.html?func=startdown&id=3642.

_____. 2010. "Technical Explanation of H.R. 4783: A Bill to Accelerate the Income Tax Benefits for Charitable Contributions for the Relief of Victims of the Earthquake in Chile, and to Extend the Period from which Such Contributions for the Relief of Victims of the Earthquake in Haiti May Be Accelerated." Staff Technical Paper, March 10. www.jct.gov/publications.html?func=startdown&id=3661.

Kasper, Gabriel. 2005. *A Legacy of Innovation.* Cambridge, MA: The Monitor Group. www.futureofphilanthropy.org/files/usPhil_4LegacyofInnovation.pdf.

Letts, Christine W., William Ryan, and Allen Grossman. 1997. "Virtuous Capital: What Foundations Can Learn from Venture Capitalists." *Harvard Business Review* (March–April).

Lubkemann, Stephen. 2008. "Remittance Relief and Not-Just-for-Profit Entrepreneurship: The Case of Liberia." *Diasporas and Development: Exploring the Potential,* ed. Jennifer M. Brinkerhoff. Boulder, CO: Lynne Rienner Publishers.

Mansoor, Ali, and Bryce Quillen, eds. 2006. *Migration and Remittances: Eastern Europe and the Former Soviet Union.* Washington, DC: World Bank.

Merz, Barbara, and Lincoln Chen, eds. 2005. *New Patterns for Mexico: Observations on Remittances, Philanthropic Giving and Equitable Development.* Cambridge, MA: Harvard Univ. Press.

Najam, Adil. 2006. *Portrait of a Giving Community: Philanthropy by the Pakistani American Diaspora.* Cambridge, MA: Harvard Univ. Press.

National Football League (NFL). 2010. "NFL Pledges 2.5M to Aid Haiti Earthquake Relief Efforts." Press Release, January. www.nfl.com/news/story?id=09000d5d815bff 52&template=with-video-with-comments&confirm=true.

National Philanthropic Trust. 2005. *A Chronological History of Philanthropy in the United States*. Jenkinstown, PA: National Philanthropic Trust.

National Sports Commission of Nigeria. No date. "Athletes in Diaspora to Build Academy of Learning and Sports in Nigeria." www.sportscommission.gov.ng/online/index.php?option=com_content&task=view&id=61&Itemid=27.

Newland, Kathleen, and Erin Patrick. 2004. *Beyond Remittances: The Role of Diaspora in Poverty Reduction in their Countries of Origin*. Washington, DC and London: Migration Policy Institute and the UK Department for International Development. www.migrationpolicy.org/pubs/Beyond_Remittances_0704.pdf.

Newland, Kathleen, and Hiroyuki Tanaka. 2010. "Mobilizing Diaspora Entrepreneurship for Development." In Kathleen Newland, ed. *Diasporas: New Partners in Global Development Policy*. Washington, DC: MPI.

Opiniano, Jeremiah. 2005. *Good News for the Poor: Diaspora Philanthropy by Filipinos*. Quezon City: Association of Foundations.

Orozco, Manuel, and Eugenia Garcia-Zanello. 2009. "Hometown Associations: Transnationalism, Philanthropy and Development." *Brown Journal of World Affairs* XV, no. 2 (Spring–Summer): 1–17.

Paine, Robert. 2004. "The Tax Treatment of International Philanthropy and Public Policy." *Akron Law Review* 19: 1–24.

Piff, Paul K., Michael W. Kraus, Stéphane Côté, Bonnie Hayden Cheng, and Dacher Keltner. 2010. "Having Less, Giving More: The Influence of Social Class on Prosocial Behavior." *Journal of Personality and Social Psychology* 99, no. 2 (August) cited in *The Economist*, "The Rich are Different from You and Me," July 29, 2010.

Randolph, William C. 1999. "Charitable Deductions." *The Encyclopedia of Taxation and Tax Policy*, ed. Joseph J. Cordes, Robert D. Ebel, and Jane G. Gravelle. Washington, DC: The Urban Institute.

Rignall, Karen, Jeanette Mansour, Taleb Salhab, and Karin Tice. 2006. *Insights on Arab-American Giving: A Report from the Collaborative of Arab-American Philanthropy*. A Project of the National Network for Arab-American Communities and the Arab Community Center for Economic and Social Services, October 20. www.centeraap.org/pdf/Insights%20Arab-American%20Giving.pdf.

Rivlin, Alice M. 1982. Testimony before the Senate Committee on Finance. September 28. www.cbo.gov/ftpdocs/109xx/doc10917/82-CBO-010.pdf.

Rodríguez, Maribel, ed. 2010. *Cooperación para el desarrollo, migraciones y economías locales*. Madrid: Fundación Carolina. www.fundacioncarolina.es/es-ES/publicaciones/documentostrabajo/Documents/DT40.pdf.

Roodman, David, and Scott Standley. 2006. "Tax Policies to Promote Private Charitable Giving in DAC Countries." Center for Global Development Working Paper No. 82, January. http://cdi.mecon.gov.ar/biblio/doc/cgdev/wp82.pdf.

Roth, John, Douglas Greenburg, and Serena Wille. 2008. "Monograph on Terrorist Financing: Staff Report to the Commission." National Commission on Terrorist Attacks upon the United States. www.9-11commission.gov/staff_statements/911_TerrFin_Monograph.pdf.

Rusdiana, Dede, and Zaim Saidi. 2008. "Indonesia." Paper presented at the Asia Pacific Philanthropy Consortium Conference, "Diaspora Giving: An Agent of Change in Asia Pacific Communities?" Hanoi, Vietnam, May 21–23. www.asiapacificphilanthropy.org/conference.

Sacks, Eleanor. 2006. *Community Foundations: Symposium on Global Movement.* Brussels: Worldwide Initiatives for Grantmaker Support.

Schiff, Jerald. 1990. *Charitable Giving and Government Policy: An Economic Analysis.* New York: Greenwood Press.

Shea, Catherine, and Sandra Sitar. 2005. *NGO Accreditation and Certification: The Way Forward? An Evaluation of the Development Community's Experience.* Report and recommendations to USAID from the International Center for Not-for-Profit Law. http://pdf.usaid.gov/pdf_docs/PNADB766.pdf.

Sherlock, Molly F. 2010. *Charitable Contributions for Haiti's Earthquake Victims.* Congressional Research Service Report R41036, January 22.

Sherlock, Molly F., and Jane G. Gravelle. 2009. *An Overview of the Nonprofit and Charitable Sector.* Congressional Research Service Report to Congress R-40919, November 17. www.fas.org/sgp/crs/misc/R40919.pdf.

Shiveshwarkar, Shyamala. 2008. "India." Paper presented at the Asia Pacific Philanthropy Consortium Conference, "Diaspora Giving: An Agent of Change in Asia Pacific Communities?" Hanoi, Vietnam, May 21–23. www.asiapacificphilanthropy.org/conference.

Sidel, Mark. 2007. *Vietnamese-American Diaspora Philanthropy to Vietnam.* Boston, MA: The Philanthropic Initiative and the Global Equity Initiative.

_____. 2008. "A Decade of Research and Practice of Diaspora Philanthropy in the Asia Pacific Region: The State of the Field." Univ. of Iowa, Working Paper, May.

Somerville, Will, Jamie Durana, and Aaron Terrazas. 2008. *Hometown Associations: An Untapped Resource for Immigrant Integration.* Washington, DC: Migration Policy Institute, July. www.migrationpolicy.org/pubs/Insight-HTAs-July08.pdf.

Sontag, Deborah. 2010. "Wyclef Jean Confirms Plans to Run for Haitian Presidency." *The New York Times,* August 4. www.nytimes.com/2010/08/05/world/americas/05haiti.html?hpw.

Sulla, Olga. 2007. "Philanthropic Foundations and their Role in International Development Assistance." World Bank International Finance Briefing Note, No. 3, February 27. http://siteresources.worldbank.org/INTRAD/Resources/BackgrounderFoundations).pdf.

Terrazas, Aaron. 2010. "Connected through Service: Diaspora Volunteers and Global Development." In Kathleen Newland, ed. *Diasporas: New Partners in Global Development Policy.* Washington, DC: Migration Policy Institute.

Transatlantic Council on Migration. 2009. *Talent, Competitiveness and Migration.* Gütersloh, Germany: Bertelsmann Stiftung and Migration Policy Institute.

US Agency for International Development (USAID), Office of the Inspector General. 2009. *Audit of USAID's Reporting on Global Development Alliances.* Audit Report No. 9-000-09-007-P, June 4. http://pdf.usaid.gov/pdf_docs/PDACO272.pdf.

_____. No date. "History of the Global Development Alliance." www.usaid.gov/our_work/global_partnerships/gda/history.html.

Chapter 6. Connected through Service: Diaspora Volunteers and Global Development

Published and Unpublished Resources

Academy for Educational Development (AED). No date. "Program Volunteer Alumni." http://cit.aed.org/forecast_sudan_program%20alumni.htm.

Agunias, Dovelyn Rannveig, ed. 2009. *Closing the Distance: How Governments Strengthen Ties with Their Diasporas.* Washington, DC: Migration Policy Institute (MPI).

America's Development Foundation (ADF). 2007. *Community Revitalization through Democratic Action Economy Program.* Final report to the US Agency for International Development (USAID) under agreement 169-A-00-01-00124-00. www.adfusa.org/content/document/detail/812/.

American India Foundation (AIF). "Serve in India." www.aifoundation.org/programs/signature/fellowship.htm.

American International Health Alliance (AIHA) and HIV/AIDS Twinning Center. No date. "The VHC Program." www.twinningagainstaids.org/vhc_overview.html.

Aparicio, Francisco Javier, and Covadonga Meseguer. 2008. "Collective Remittances and the State: The 3x1 Program in Mexican Municipalities." Working Paper, Centro de Investigación y Docencia Económica, Mexico City.

Ardittis, Solon. 1984. *Le retour assisté des migrants qualifiés dans leur pays d'origine: Les programmes multilatéraux du PNUD et du CIM.* Geneva: International Labor Organization (ILO).

Ayala Foundation USA. Various years. *Annual Reports.* Redwood City, CA: Ayala Foundation USA. www.phildev.org/site/PageServer?pagename=about_annual_report.

Bauralina, Tatjana, Michael Bommes, Heike Daume, Tanja El-Cherkeh, and Florin Vadean. 2006. *Egyptian, Afghan, and Serbian Communities in Germany: How Do They Contribute to Their Countries of Origin.* Eschborn, Germany: Deutsche Gesellschaft für Technische Zusammenarbeit.

Birthright Armenia. "Participant Statistics." www.birthrightarmenia.org/pages.php?al=statistics.

Borjón, José V. "Volunteering in the Diaspora: The Case of Mexico." Essay provided to the Migration Policy Institute, March 2010.

Canadian University Service Overseas—Voluntary Service Overseas (CUSO-VSO). No date. "Diaspora Volunteering." www.cuso-vso.org/about-cuso-vso/how-we-work/diaspora-volunteering.asp.

————. No date. "Promoting Volunteering from within the Ethiopian Diaspora in Canada." Proposal submitted by the Academics for Higher Education and CUSO-VSO to the International Development Research Centre, provided to the Migration Policy Institute by CUSO-VSO.

Caprara, David, Kevin F. F. Quigley, and Lex Rieffel. 2009. *International Volunteer Service: A Smart Way to Build Bridges, Recommendations on How to Enhance U.S. Volunteer Efforts.* Policy Brief 2009—01, Global Economy and Development, Brookings Institution, Washington, DC. www.brookings.edu/~/media/Files/rc/papers/2009/06_volunteering_caprara/06_volunteering_caprara.pdf.

Clemens, Michael A. 2009. "Skill Flow: A Fundamental Reconsideration of Skilled-Worker Mobility and Development." Human Development Research Paper 2009/08, United Nations Development Programme, April. http://hdr.undp.org/en/reports/global/hdr2009/papers/HDRP_2009_08.pdf.

Cogswell, Lynne, Richard Hailer, Robert Holm, James Purcell, and Don Smith. 2005. *Training and Capacity Development Needs Assessment for the USAID Sudan Field Office.* Report to USAID, Development Associates, Inc., Arlington, VA.

Copeland-Carson, Jacqueline. 2007. *Kenyan Diaspora Philanthropy: Key Practices,Trends and Issues.* The Philanthropic Initiative and the Global Equity Initiative, Harvard University. www.tpi.org/downloads/pdfs/Kenya_Diaspora_Philanthropy_Final.pdf.

Department for International Development (DFID). 2006. "Eliminating World Poverty: Making Governance Work for the Poor." DFID White Paper, July. http://webarchive.nationalarchives.gov.uk/+/http://www.dfid.gov.uk/wp2006/whitepaper-printer-friendly.pdf.

————. 2009. "Eliminating World Poverty: Building our Common Future." DFID White Paper, July. www.dfid.gov.uk/documents/whitepaper/building-our-common-future-print.pdf.

Geithner, Peter F., Lincoln C. Chen, and Paula D. Johnson, eds. 2005. *Diaspora Philanthropy and Equitable Development in China and India.* Cambridge, Mass.: Harvard Univ. Press.

Hanafi, Sari. 2005. "Physical Return, Virtual Return: The Palestinian Diaspora and the Homeland." *The Palestinian Diaspora in Europe: Challenges of Dual Identity and Adaptation*, ed. Abbas Shiblak. Jerusalem and Ramallah: Institute of Jerusalem Studies and the Shaml Palestinian Refugee and Diaspora Center.

Hills, Greg, and Adeeb Mahmud. 2007. *Volunteering for Impact: Best Practices in International Corporate Volunteering.* Boston: FSG Social Impact Advisors and Pfizer, Inc. www.brookings.edu/~/media/Files/rc/papers/2007/09volunteering/Volunteering_for_Impact.pdf.

HIV/AIDS Twinning Center. "Twinning against HIV/AIDS." www.twinningagainstaids.org.

International Labor Organization (ILO), International Conference of Labor Statisticians. 2008. "Manual on the Measurement of Volunteer Work." Room document prepared for the 18th International Conference of Labor Statisticians. Geneva. November 24 to December 5, 2008. www.ilo.org/global/What_we_do/Statistics/events/icls/lang--en/docName--WCMS_100574/index.htm.

International Organization for Migration (IOM), Office of the Inspector General. 2007. *Evaluation of the Migration for Development in Africa Initiative as an Illustration of IOM's Approach to Making Migration Work for Development*. Final report, Geneva.

———. 2005. *Evaluation of the MIDA Italy Project*. Final report, Geneva, May.

Jethwa, Dee. 2006. *International Volunteering and the Asian Community (UK): Views, Attitudes, Barriers, Needs*. Final report to Voluntary Service Overseas from the Asian Foundation for Philanthropy.

Keesbury, Jill. 2003. *The Value of International Volunteerism: A Review of Literature on International Volunteer-Sending Programs*. Report, USAID Development Information Services, July 1. http://pdf.dec.org/pdf_docs/Pnacw574.pdf.

Kerley, Janet, and Susan Jenkins. 2010. *The Impact of Peace Corps Service on Host Communities and Host Country Perceptions of Americans*. Washington, DC: Peace Corps, Office of Strategic Information, Research and Planning.

Ketkar, Suhas, and Dilip Ratha, eds. 2008. *Innovative Financing for Development*. Washington, DC: World Bank.

Ky, Abdoulaye, and Moctar Sow. 2008. *Evaluation du Projet TOKTEN, 1998 à 2007*. Final report submitted to the Ministry of Secondary and Higher Education and Scientific Research, the University of Bamako, and UNDP-Mali, Bamako.

Lalkaka, Rastam. 1987. *Transfer of Knowledge for Development through International Volunteerism*. New York: UNDP. Cited in Bernard I. Logan. 1990. "An Assessment of the Potential Application of the Transfer of Knowledge through Expatriate Nationals (TOKTEN) Programme in Sub-Saharan Africa." *Applied Geography* 10, no. 3 (July): 223—36.

Manpower Research Center. 2009. *2009 Talent Shortage Survey Results*. Milwaukee, WI: Manpower Inc. http://files.shareholder.com/downloads/MAN/817822014x0x297372/dab9f206-75f4-40b7-88fb-3ca81333140f/09TalentShortage_Results_USLetter_FINAL_FINAL.pdf.

Mello, Robyn Joanne. 2009. *Reaping What's Been Sown: Exploring Diaspora-Driven Development for Sierra Leone*. Thesis submitted to the Faculty of the Univ. of Delaware in partial fulfillment of the requirements for the degree of Bachelor of Arts (Honors) in Sociology with distinction, Spring. http://dspace.udel.edu:8080/dspace/bitstream/19716/4237/3/Mello,%20Robyn_2009_Thesis.pdf.

Moore McBride, Amanda, and Benjamin J. Lough. 2008. "Access to International Volunteering." Center for Social Development Working Paper No. 08-30, George Warren Brown School of Social Work, Washington University in Saint Louis. http://csd.wustl.edu/Publications/Documents/WP08-30.pdf.

Moore McBride, Amanda, Benjamin J. Lough, and Margaret Sherrard Sherraden. 2010. *Perceived Impacts of International Service on Volunteers: Interim Results from a Quasi-Experimental Study*. Washington, DC: Brookings Institution of Global Economy and Development and Washington Univ. in Saint Louis Center for Social Development.

Newland, Kathleen, and Hiroyuki Tanaka. 2010. "Mobilizing Diaspora Entrepreneurship for Development." In Kathleen Newland, ed. *Diasporas: New Partners in Global Development Policy*. Washington, DC: MPI.

Newland, Kathleen, Hiroyuki Tanaka, and Laura Barker. 2007. *Bridging Divides: The Role of Ethnic Community-Based Organizations in Refugee Integration.* Washington, DC: Migration Policy Institute and the International Rescue Committee. www.migrationpolicy.org/pubs/Bridging_Divides.pdf.

Orozco, Manuel, and Rebecca Rouse. 2007. "Migrant Hometown Associations and Opportunities for Development: A Global Perspective." *Migration Information Source*, February. www.migrationinformation.org/feature/display.cfm?ID=579.

Rieffel, Lex, and Sarah Zalud. 2006. "International Volunteering: Smart Power." Brookings Institution, Policy Brief No. 155, June.

Rumbaut, Ruben, and Alejandro Portes. 2001. *Ethnicities: Children of Immigrants in America.* New York: Russell Sage Foundation.

Renshon, Stanley A. 2005. *Reforming Dual Citizenship in the United States: Integrating Immigrants into the American National Community.* Washington, DC: Center for Immigration Studies. www.cis.org/articles/2005/dualcitizenship.pdf.

Ruhs, Martin, and Bridget Anderson, eds. 2010 forthcoming. *Who Needs Migrant Workers? Labor Shortages, Immigration and Public Policy.* London: Oxford Univ. Press.

Salamon, Lester M., S. Wojciech Sokolowski, and Regina List. 2003. *Global Civil Society: An Overview.* Baltimore, MD: Johns Hopkins Center for Civil Society Studies.

Schlenzka, Nathalie. 2009. *The Ethiopian Diaspora in Germany: Its Contributions to Development.* Eschborn, Germany: Deutsche Gesellschaft für Technische Zusammenarbeit.

Sedhain, Gopi K. 2006. *Assessment of Preparatory Assistance Phase Implementation Process: Transfer of Knowledge through Expatriate Nationals.* Report submitted to UNDP-Sudan, Khartoum. www.sd.undp.org/doc/prodocs/dg3%20TOKTEN/Doc.26-35.pdf.

Société d'Études et d'Évaluation sarl. 2008. *Evaluation du Programme MIDA Grands Lacs, Phase III.* Final report to the International Organization for Migration, Luxembourg.

Somerville, Will, Jamie Durana, and Aaron Terrazas. 2008. *Hometown Associations: An Untapped Resource for Immigrant Integration?* Washington, DC: Migration Policy Institute. www.migrationpolicy.org/pubs/Insight-HTAs-July08.pdf.

Stark, Oded, Christian Helmenstein, and Alexia Prskawetz. 1997. "A Brain Grain with a Brain Drain." *Economics Letters* 55 (2): 227—34.

Tabar, Paul. 2009. "Immigration and Human Development: Evidence from Lebanon." United Nations Development Programme Human Development Research Paper 2009/35. New York. http://hdr.undp.org/en/reports/global/hdr2009/papers/HDRP_2009_35.pdf.

Terrazas, Aaron. 2010. "Diaspora Investment in Developing and Emerging Country Capital Markets: Patterns and Prospects." In Kathleen Newland, ed. *Diasporas: New Partners in Global Development Policy.* Washington, DC: MPI.

TOKTEN-Mali. 2009. *Transfer des connaissances à travers les expatriés nationaux.* Internal document provided to the authors by TOKTEN-Mali, December.

Touray, Katim S. 2008. *Final Evaluation of the Support Project to the Implementation of the Rwanda TOKTEN Volunteer Program.* Final Report submitted to UNDP-Rwanda, Kigali.

United Kingdom Office of National Statistics. 2003. *Ethnic Group Statistics: A Guide for the Collection and Classification of Ethnicity Data*. Newport: HM Statistics Office. www.statistics.gov.uk/STATBASE/Product.asp?vlnk=11040.

United Nations Development Programme (UNDP). 2009. *Overcoming Barriers: Human Mobility and Development*. New York: UNDP. http://hdr.undp.org/en/reports/global/hdr2009/.

UNDP-Sudan. 2008. *TOKTEN Sudan Annual Progress Report, January to December 2007*. Khartoum.

————. 2009. *TOKTEN Sudan Annual Progress Report, January to December 2008*. Khartoum.

United Nations Volunteers (UNV) — Ghana. No date. "TOKTEN Programme." Accessed June 2010. Web site no longer active. http://ghana.unv.org/how-to-volunteer/in-ghana/tokten-programme.html.

Voluntary Service Overseas — United Kingdom (VSO-UK). 2008. *The DfID Diaspora Volunteering Programme in Partnership with VSO*. London: VSO-UK. www.vso.org.uk/volunteer/diaspora-volunteering.

————. No date. "Diaspora Volunteering Program: Partnership Criteria." www.vso.org.uk/images/diaspora-volunteering-partnership-criteria_tcm79-23688.pdf.

Weiss, Thomas Lothar ed. 2009. *Migration for Development in the Horn of Africa: Health Expertise from the Somali Diaspora in Finland*. Helsinki: IOM, Regional Office for the Nordic and Baltic States.

Wolfensohn, James D. 2005. "Foreword." *Reducing Poverty on a Global Scale*, ed. Blanca Moreno-Dodson. Washington, DC: World Bank.

Young, Nick, and June Shih. 2004. "Philanthropic Links between the Chinese Diaspora and the People's Republic of China." *Diaspora Philanthropy and Equitable Development in China and India*, ed. Peter F. Geithner, Paula D. Johnson, and Lincoln C. Chen. Cambridge, Mass.: Harvard Univ. Press.

Interviews

Adan, Abdikarim Abdi. Director, Wales Somaliland Communities Link. Via telephone. January 26, 2010.

Agrawal, Pulkit. Indicorps fellow, 2008—09. Via telephone. January 29, 2010.

Anjum, Maher. Diaspora volunteering alliance consultant. Via telephone. March, 15, 2010.

Awuor, Bob. Executive director, The African Community Development Foundation. Via telephone. January 26, 2010.

Bagayoko, Diola. Former volunteer, TOKTEN Mali and Southern University System Distinguished Professor of Physics, Southern University at Baton Rouge. Via telephone. January 7, 2010.

Candia, Rosa. Diaspora volunteering program coordinator, Canadian University Service Overseas-Voluntary Service Overseas. Via telephone. January 19, 2010.

Chaudry, Sahil. Indicorps fellow, 2009—10. Via telephone. February 9, 2010.

Cukic, Marina. Office manager, America's Development Foundation. Via telephone. February 1, 2010.

Demerjian, Rev. Fr. Hovnan (formerly Jason Demerjian). Pastor, St. Hagop Armenian Church and Cofounder, Armenian Volunteer Corps. Via telephone. February 26, 2010.

Diakité, Oumarou. Project coordinator, TOKTEN-Mali. Via telephone. January 7, 2010.

Elmas, Ariane. Project manager, TOKTEN-Lebanon. Via telephone. January 8, 2010.

Garchitorena, Vicky. President, Ayala Foundation USA. Washington, DC. February 18, 2010.

Giorgis, Tedla W. Founder, Network of Ethiopian Professionals in the Diaspora and Visions for Development, Inc. Washington, DC. January 27, 2010.

Gupta, Ashish. Indicorps fellow, 2006—07. Via telephone. March 9, 2010.

Heljeberg, Judith. Fundraising capacity builder, Diaspora Volunteering Program, Voluntary Service Overseas United Kingdom. Via telephone. October 9, 2009.

Jain, Neil. Indicorps fellow, 2008—09. Via telephone. December 7, 2009.

Jindal, Priya. Indicorps fellow 2006—07. Via telephone. February 18, 2010.

Kefale, Georgis. Associate neonatologist, Fairfax neonatal associate and volunteer, Vermont-Oxford Network Black Lion Project. Via telephone. March 2, 2010.

Kleibo, Mounir. Former director, TOKTEN-Palestine. Via telephone. January 6, 2010.

Lesslar, Matt. Deputy program manager, Development Awareness Team, Communications Division, UK Department for International Development. Via telephone. March 4, 2010.

Lough, Benjamin. Research associate, Center for Social Development, Washington University in Saint Louis. Via telephone. October 1, 2009.

Melkonian, Sharistan. Executive director, Armenian Volunteer Corps. Via telephone. February 4, 2010.

Nzamutuma, Issumael. President, Here and Home, Inc. Via telephone. March 11, 2010.

Rangwala, Aazamina. Program associate, American International Health Alliance HIV/AIDS Twinning Center. Washington, DC. January 27, 2010.

Reichert, Rebecca. Director of development, Florida Association for Volunteer Action in the Caribbean and the Americas. Via telephone. March 5, 2010.

Samuelian, Thomas J. Cofounder, Armenian Volunteer Corps. Via telephone. March 2, 2010.

Shah, Roopal. Executive director, Indicorps. Washington, DC. October 30, 2009.

Shenoy, Chetan. Indicorps fellow, 2008—09. Via telephone. February 5, 2010.

Thakrar, Bala. Founder and director, Asian Foundation for Philanthropy. Via telephone. October 7, 2009.

Trecartin, Homer. Director, Adventist Volunteer Service. Via telephone. March 26, 2010.

The authors would also like to thank the following individuals for providing access to evaluation reports, program information, and interview contacts: Dovelyn Agunias (MPI), John Ajawin (UNDP-Sudan), Solon Ardittis (Eurasylum), Lakshmi Eassey (Indicorps), Priyanjana Ghosh (AIF), Ganiyu Ipaye (UNDP-Sudan), Jean Paul Rwabuyonza (UNDP-Rwanda), and Ron Skeldon (University of Sussex). Migration Policy Institute fall 2009 intern Jessica Dwyer provided research assistance for an earlier version of this paper.

Programs Referenced

Adventist Development and Relief Agency, www.adra.org/site/PageServer.

Advisory Council of the Institute for Mexicans Abroad, www.ime.gob.mx/ccime/ccime.htm.

American India Foundation, William J. Clinton Fellowship for Service in India, www.aifoundation.org/programs/signature/fellowship.htm.

American International Health Alliance, HIV/AIDS Twinning Center, Health Volunteer Corps, www.twinningagainstaids.org/volunteers.html.

Armenian Volunteer Corps, www.armenianvolunteer.org/.

Asian Foundation for Philanthorpy, Paropkaar Diaspora Volunteers, www.affp.org.uk/what-we-do/paropkaar-programme-international-volunteering.

Ayala Foundation Filipino-America Youth Leadership Program, www.phildev.org/site/PageServer.

Birthright Armenia, www.birthrightarmenia.org/.

Canadian University Service Overseas and Voluntary Service Overseas Canada, Diaspora Volunteering, www.cuso-vso.org/about-cuso-vso/how-we-work/diaspora-volunteering.asp.

Florida Association of Voluntary Agencies in the Caribbean and the Americas, www.favaca.org/.

Grassroots Development Laboratory, www.piramal.org.in/main/index.php?option=com_content&task=view&id=1&Itemid=10.

Here and Home, Inc., www.hereandhome.org/.

Indicorps, www.indicorps.org/.

International Executive Service Corps, www.iesc.org/.

Migration for Development in Africa, Grands Lacs, http://mida.belgium.iom.int/.

Migration for Development in Africa, Horn of Africa, http://iom.fi/content/view/212/8/.

Network of Ethiopian Professionals in the Diaspora, www.nepid.org/.

Transfer of Knowledge through Expatriate Nationals, Lebanon, www.toktenlebanon.org/.

Transfer of Knowledge through Expatriate Nationals, Mali, www.tokten-mali.org/.

Transfer of Knowledge through Expatriate Nationals, Rwanda, www.undp.org.rw/Poverty_Project2.html.

Transfer of Knowledge through Expatriate Nationals, Sudan, www.sd.undp.org/projects/tokten%20work.htm.

UK Department for International Development, Diaspora Volunteering Program, www.dfid.gov.uk/working-with-dfid/funding-opportunities/individuals/dvs/.

Vermont-Oxford Network, Black Lion Project, www.vtoxford.org/home.aspx.

Voluntary Service Overseas, Diaspora Volunteering Program, www.vso.org.uk/volunteer/diaspora-volunteering/.

Volunteers for Economic Growth Alliance, www.vegaalliance.org/.

Chapter 7. Voice after Exit: Diaspora Advocacy

African Diaspora and Development Day (AD3). 2004. "Theme: Transforming the Local Everywhere: Africa Here, There, Africa Everywhere." MyAfrica, May 30. http://myafrica.ru/addinfo/data.php?id1=189.

African Foundation for Development (AFFORD). AFFORD-UK. http://afford-uk.org.

American Anthropological Association (AAA). 2009. "Proposed AAA Statement in Support of Hondurans Resisting Military Dictatorship." http://blog.aaanet.org/2009/12/17/aaa-honduras-resolution-vote-jan-xx/.

American India Foundation (AIF). "Why AIF?" www.aifoundation.org/aboutUs/whyAif.htm.

Armenian Assembly of America. "Home of the Armenian Assembly of America." www.aaainc.org.

Armenian National Committee of America. "Armenian National Committee of America." www.anca.org.

Asokan, Shyamantha. 2009. "War by Other Means." *Financial Times,* October 17–18.

Associated Press. 2010. "Peruvian Presidential Candidate to Stump in Paterson." July 22. www.nj.com/news/index.ssf/2010/07/peruvian_presidentail_candidat.html.

Bernal, Victoria. 2004. "Eritrea Goes Global: Reflections on Nationalism in a Transnational Era." Cultural Anthropology 19 (1): 3–25.

———. 2005. "Eritrea On-line: Diaspora, Cyberspace, and the Public Sphere." American Ethnologist 32 (4): 660–75.

Brinkerhoff, Jennifer M. 2005. "Digital Diasporas and Governance in Semi-Authoritarian States: The Case of the Egyptian Copts." *Public Administration and Development* 25 (3): 193–204.

———. 2006. "Digital Diasporas and Conflict Prevention: The Case of Somalinet.com." *Review of International Studies* 32: 25–47.

———. 2009. *Digital Diasporas: Identity and Transnational Engagement.* Cambridge: Cambridge Univ. Press.

Cohen, Robin. 1997. *Global Diasporas: An Introduction.* Seattle: Univ. of Washington Press.

Curry, Tom. 2006. "Gaffe Underscores Indian-American Clout: Sen. Allen's Blunder Puts Focus on Growing Group of Donors and Voters." *MSNBC.com,* August 17. www.msnbc.msn.com/id/14395449/.

Dewan, Shaila. 2010. "Scattered Émigrés Haiti Once Shunned Are Now a Lifeline." *New York Times,* February 3. www.nytimes.com/2010/02/04/us/04diaspora.html?_ r=1&pagewanted=all.

Eritrean Community Online Network, DEHAI. "Dehai News-Mailing List Archive." http://dehai.org/.

Eteraz, Ali. 2009. "Pride and the Pakistani Diaspora." *Dawn,* February 14. www.dawn. com/wps/wcm/connect/dawn-content-library/dawn/news/pakistan/ Pride-and-the-Pakistani-Diaspora.

Freedman, Allison. 2009. "USINPAC and the U.S.-India Nuclear Deal: Lasting Influence or One Shot Victory?" *CUREJ — College Undergraduate Research Electronic Journal,* Univ. of Pennsylvania, College of Arts and Sciences. http://repository.upenn. edu/cgi/viewcontent.cgi?article=1119&context=curej.

Gandhi, Ajay. 2002. "The Indian Diaspora in Global Advocacy." *Global Networks* 2 (4): 357–62.

GhanaExpo. Home. http://ghanaexpo.com/.

Goodhand, Jonathan, and Mark Sedra. 2009. "Who Owns the Peace? Aid, Reconstruction, and Peacebuilding in Afghanistan." *Disasters* 10 (4): S78–S102.

Gramby-Sobukwe, Sharon. 2005. "Africa and U.S. Foreign Policy: Contributions of the Diaspora to Democratic African Leadership." *Journal of Black Studies* 35 (6): 779–801.

Hamm, Patricia H. 1996. "Mexican-American Interests in U.S.-Mexico Relations: The Case of NAFTA." Working Paper no. 4, Univ. of California, Center for Research on Latinos in a Global Society, Irvine. www.escholarship.org/uc/item/3wx2g9f2.

Hirschman , Albert O. 1970. *Exit, Voice, and Loyalty: Responses to Decline in Firms, Organizations, and States.* Cambridge, MA: Harvard Univ. Press.

Honduras Coup. 2009. http://hondurascoup2009.blogspot.com/.

Institute for Mexicans Abroad/Instituto de los Mexicanos en el Exterior (IME). "Consejo Consultivo." www.ime.gob.mx/.

Jones-Correa, Michael. 2001. "Under Two Flags: Dual Nationality in Latin America and its Consequences for Naturalization in the United States." *International Migration Review* 35 (4): 997–1029.

Llorente, Elizabeth. 2010. "Peruvian Candidate Fujimori courts Votes in North Jersey." *The Bergen Record*, July 22, 2010. www.northjersey.com/news/072210_Peruvian_candidate_Fujimori_pushes_for_congressional_seat_in_North_Jersey_stop.html.

Lyons, Terrance, and Peter Mandaville. 2008. "Global Migration and Transnational Politics: A Conceptual Framework." Working Paper no. 1, George Mason Univ., Center for Global Studies, Project on Global Migration and Transnational Politics, March. http://cgs.gmu.edu/publications/gmtpwp/gmtp_wp_1.pdf.

Nepali America Society for Oppressed Community (NASO). "NASO Community." http://nasocommunity.com/default.aspx.

Organization for Security and Cooperation in Europe (OSCE) High Commissioner on National Minorities. 2008. "The Bolzano/Bozen Recommendations on National Minorities in Inter-State Relations and Explanatory Note." www.osce.org/item/33388.html?ch=1189.

Pakistani American Public Affairs Committee. "For Candidates." www.pakpac.net/Candidate.asp.

Pantoja, Adrian D. 2005. "Transnational Ties and Immigrant Political Incorporation: The Case of Dominicans in Washington Heights, New York." *International Migration* 43 (4): 123–46.

Paul, Rachel Anderson. 2000. "Grassroots Mobilization and Diaspora Politics: Armenian Interest Groups and the Role of Collective Memory." *Nationalism and Ethnic Politics* 6 (1): 24–47.

PRNewswire. 2010. "AT&T Makes $100,000 Contribution to Haitian Earthquake Relief Effort." PRNewswire, July 9. www.noahhaiti.org/index.php?option=com_content&view=frontpage&Itemid=1.

Reuters. 2010. "Indo-US Nuclear Deal Moving Forward, Says SM Krishna." *Daily Times*, June 3. www.dailytimes.com.pk/default.asp?page=2010\06\03\story_3-6-2010_pg7_35.

Rivero-Salgado, G. 1999. "Mixtec Activism in Oaxacalifornia: Transborder Grassroots Strategies." *American Behavioral Scientist* 42 (9): 1439–58.

Solomon, Morris S. 1993. *The Agenda and Political Techniques of the American Israel Public Affairs Committee (AIPAC)*. Washington, DC: The Industrial College of the Armed Forces.

Somerville, Will, Jamie Durana, and Aaron Matteo Terrazas. 2008. *Hometown Associations: An Untapped Resource for Immigrant Integration?* Washington, DC: Migration Policy Institute (MPI). www.migrationpolicy.org/pubs/Insight-HTAs-July08.pdf.

The Advocacy Project. "Nepali-American Society for Oppressed Community (NASO)." www.advocacynet.org/page/naso.

Time Magazine. "New Lobby in Town: The Greeks." July 14, 1975.

Truth and Reconciliation for the Adoption Community of Korea (TRACK). "Setting the Record Straight." http://justicespeaking.wordpress.com.

United Nations Development Programme (UNDP). *Somalia's Missing Million: The Somali Diaspora and its Role in Development.* Somalia: UNDP. www.so.undp.org/index.php/Somalia-Stories/Forging-Partnerships-with-the-Somali-Diaspora.html.

US India Political Action Committee (USINPAC). "Indian-American Community Welcomes Congressional Passage of the Us India Civil Nuclear Agreement." www.usinpac.com/nuclear_deal/index.html.

———. "US India Political Action Committee/Indian American Community." www.usinpac.com.

Van Hear, Nicholas. 2003. *Refugee Diasporas, Remittances, Development, and Conflict.* Washington, DC: Migration Policy Institute. www.migrationinformation.org/feature/display.cfm?ID=125.

Vos el Soberano. http://voselsoberano.com.

Waterbury, Mayra A. 2009. "From Irredentism to Diaspora Politics: States and Transborder Ethnic Groups in Eastern Europe." Working Paper no. 6, George Mason Univ., Center for Global Studies, Project on Global Migration and Transnational Politics, Arlington, VA, July.

Williams, Heather. 2008. "From Visibility to Voice: The Emerging Power of Migrants in Mexican Politics." Working Paper no. 4, George Mason Univ., Center for Global Studies, Project on Global Migration and Transnational Politics, Arlington, VA.

World Bank. 2007. "Concept Note: Mobilizing the African Diaspora for Development." Capacity Development Management Action Plan Unit (AFTCD), Operational Quality and Knowledge Services Department, World Bank, Washington, DC. http://siteresources.worldbank.org/INTDIASPORA/General/21686696/conceptnote.pdf.

ACKNOWLEDGMENTS

This volume is the final product of a matching grant from the US Agency for International Development's (USAID) Office of Poverty Reduction, Diaspora Networks Alliance, to the Migration Policy Institute's (MPI) Migrants, Migration, and Development Program. The match to USAID's grant was made by MPI from funding for its migration and development work provided by the John D. and Catherine T. MacArthur Foundation.

I extend my thanks to Yvon Resplandy of USAID and Renee Gifford of The QED Group for their diligence, insight, and enthusiasm for the collaborative MPI-USAID initiative which led to the production of this volume. Thomas Debass, formerly Senior Advisor for Diaspora and Remittances at USAID, initially conceived this project and deserves credit for his leadership and foresight in framing the DNA project. Karen D. Turner, Director of the Office of Development Partners at USAID, has been an immensely helpful and steadfast supporter of the project.

Finally, I would like to thank my colleagues at MPI without whose tireless efforts this book would not have been possible, chief among them Policy Analyst Aaron Terrazas, whose sophisticated research, penetrating analysis, fluid writing, and organizational skills have contributed enormously to the realization and quality of this volume. Michelle Mittelstadt, MPI's Director of Communications, oversaw the editing and production of the manuscript on a punishing schedule and stepped in to suggest crucial improvements at every stage. April Siruno's skills in design and production gave the book its elegant format. Other MPI colleagues who contributed to this work were: Dovelyn Agunias, Lisa Dixon, Gale Gearhart, and Hiroyuki Tanaka. Three chapters in the book benefited from research and writing support from two outstanding research interns, Roberto Munster and Carylanna Taylor; Dhriti Bhatta and Phoram Shah provided additional research assistance. And Fayre Makeig edited and greatly improved our prose.

The project as a whole and these chapters in particular benefited from the insight and expertise of an extraordinary group of policymakers, practitioners, scholars, business persons, and diaspora leaders who participated in the seven roundtable discussions organized to inform and refine each of the chapters in this volume. In many cases, they pointed us to new sources or examples. We are grateful to all of them for taking time away from their extremely demanding work to become our partners in this effort to understand and reinforce the myriad arenas in which diasporas can and do take part in the development of their countries of origin. They are:

Yilma Adamu (US Patent and Trademark Office)

Carol Adelman (Hudson Institute)

Kingsley Aikins (The Irelands Funds)

Kedi Ali (Ethiopian Ministry of Capacity Building)

Erika Alvarez (Embassy of the Dominican Republic in Washington, DC)

Kofi Anani (The World Bank)

Luis Aparicio (Embassy of El Salvador in Washington, DC)

Michael Ardovino (USAID)

Raquel Artecona (Economic Commission for Latin America and the Caribbean)

Andre Berg (Fund for Armenian Relief)

Providence Bikumbi (Rwandan Diaspora Mutual Fund)

Rafic Bizri (Hariri Foundation USA)

Jose Vicente Borjon Lopez-Coterilla (Embassy of Mexico in Washington, DC)

Jennifer Brinkerhoff (The George Washington University)

Geneive Brown-Metzger (Consulate General of Jamaica in New York)

Hope Bryer (USAID)

Richard Cambridge (The World Bank)

Ana Maria Carillo Soubic (Institute for Mexicans Abroad)

Frantz Celestin (International Organization for Migration)

Bruno Cornelio (USAID)

Uri Dadush (Carnegie Endowment for International Peace)

Kris Dasgupta (American India Foundation)

Sujeewa de Alwis (International Executive Service Corps)

Thomas Debass (Overseas Private Investment Corporation)

Paula Doherty Johnson (The Philanthropic Initiative, Inc.)

Joseph Domask (US State Department)

Angela Escallon (Conexion Colombia)

Richard Foltin (American Jewish Committee)

Thomson Fontaine (International Monetary Fund)

Olga Frolova (USAID)

Victoria Garchitorena (Ayala Foundation USA)

Tedla Giorgis (Visions for Development, Inc.)

Leni Gonzalez (League of United Latin American Citizens)

Andrea Gorog (US State Department)

Mark Hannafin (USAID)

Maria Luisa Hayem (Multilateral Investment Fund)

Gaynelle Henderson (African Diaspora Heritage Trails Movement)

Rockfeler Herisse (USAID)

Martha Honey (Center for Responsible Travel)

John Hurley (US Treasury Department)

Natasha Iwegbu (Inno Product Development Group, LLC)

Jeffrey Jackson (USAID)

Nadine Jalandoni (Independent Sector)

Garrett Johnson (US Senate Committee on Foreign Relations)

Ozlenen Eser Kalav (Turkish Philanthropy Funds)

Robert Kayinamura (Rwandan Diaspora Mutual Fund)

Georgis Kefale (Fairfax Neonatal Associates)

Sara Kefe-Heltner (US Treasury Department)

Suhas Ketkar (Vanderbilt University)

Saliha Loucif (US Department of Commerce)

Stephen Lubkemann (The George Washington University)

Terrence Lyons (George Mason University)

Soheyla Mahmoudi (The World Bank)

Peter Mandaville (George Mason University)

Molly Mattessich (National Peace Corps Association)

Jocelyn McCalla (JMC Strategies, LLC)

Morgan Miller (US Institute of Peace)

Tatiana Munteanu (Embassy of the Republic of Moldova in Washington, DC)

Tarek Nabhan (International Executive Service Corps)

Kate Nahapetian (Armenian National Committee of America)

Andy Neustaetter (Peace Corps)

Rachel O'Hara (US State Department)

Manuel Orozco (Inter-American Dialogue)

Egbe Osifo-Dawodu (The World Bank Institute and Association of Nigerian Physicians in the Americas)

Borany Penh (USAID)

Sonia Plaza (The World Bank)

Sofia Porres (Embassy of Guatemala in Washington, DC)

Kevin F.F. Quigley (National Peace Corps Association)

Venkatesh Raghavendra (American India Foundation)

Aazamina Rangwala (American International Health Alliance)

Liesl Riddle (The George Washington University)

Ana Gloria Rivas-Vasquez (Hispanics in Philanthropy)

Neil Ruiz (The World Bank)

Leonard Saxe (Brandeis University)

Scott Schirmer (USAID)

Steve Silcox (USAID)

Sanjay Sinho (American India Foundation)

Enilson Solano (Embassy of El Salvador in Washington, DC)

Barbara Span (Western Union)

Afeefa Syeed (USAID)

Karen Turner (USAID)

John Wasielewski (USAID)

Patricia Weiss Fagan (Institute for the Study of International Migration, Georgetown University)

Jill Wheeler (Inter-American Foundation)

Although we benefited greatly from the involvement of the people named above, the views expressed in the chapters do not necessarily reflect their views or those of their organizations, and responsibility for any errors remains with the authors alone.

Kathleen Newland
Washington, DC
November 2010

ABOUT THE EDITOR

 **Kathleen Newland** is Co-Founder of the Migration Policy Institute and directs MPI's programs on Migrants, Migration, and Development and Refugee Protection. Her work focuses on the relationship between migration and development, governance of international migration, and refugee protection. Previously, at the Carnegie Endowment for International Peace, she was a Senior Associate and then Co-Director of the International Migration Policy Program (1994-2001). She sits on the Board of the International Rescue Committee and is a Chair *Emerita* of the Women's Commission for Refugee Women and Children. She is also on the Boards of the Foundation for the Hague Process on Migrants and Refugees and Kids in Need of Defense (KIND).

Prior to joining the Migration Program at the Carnegie Endowment in 1994, Ms. Newland worked as an independent consultant for such clients as the UN High Commissioner for Refugees (UNHCR), the World Bank, and the office of the Secretary-General of the United Nations. From 1988-1992, Ms. Newland was on the faculty of the London School of Economics. During that time, she also co-founded (with Lord David Owen) and directed Humanitas, an educational trust dedicated to increasing awareness of international humanitarian issues. From 1982 to 1988, she worked at the United Nations University in Tokyo, Japan. She began her career at Worldwatch Institute in 1974.

Ms. Newland is a graduate of Harvard University and the Woodrow Wilson School at Princeton University. She did additional graduate work at the London School of Economics.

ABOUT THE AUTHORS

Roberto Munster is a consultant at the World Bank, where he works in private sector development for the Latin America and Caribbean region. Mr. Munster has master's of Public Policy and bachelor's degrees in Finance and Economics from the University of Maryland.

Hiroyuki Tanaka is a student at Tsinghua University and former Associate Policy Analyst at the Migration Policy Institute, where he worked between 2006 and 2010, specializing in transatlantic migration and global mobility security issues. He has published numerous book chapters, reports, and articles including: *Transatlantic Information Sharing: At a Crossroads* (2010), *Hybrid Immigrant-Selection Systems: The Next Generation of Economic Migration Schemes* (2009), and *North Korea: Understanding Migration to and from a Closed Country* (2008).

Mr. Tanaka holds a BA with honors from Princeton University, where he majored in the Woodrow Wilson School of Public and International Affairs and earned certificates in European Politics and Society and French. He also studied at the Institut d'Etudes Politiques in Paris as a member of a task force on immigration policy in Europe.

Carylanna Taylor is pursuing her doctoral degree in Applied Anthropology at the University of South Florida (USF). She was a Research Intern for the Migration Policy Institute's program on Migrants, Migration, and Development in summer 2010.

Her research has focused on international development, globalization, environmental conservation, and natural resource management with a geographic focus in Latin America. She has worked in Chile, Ecuador, and Honduras, where she conducted research on the globalization of environmental knowledge. Her dissertation research focused on how the flow of funds and ideas within transnational families stretching from a Honduran village to New York and Florida affect the ways in which Honduran households and communities manage their farms and natural resources. The project was funded by the USF Department of Anthropology, USF Institute for the Study of Latin America and the Caribbean, and the National Science Foundation (NSF). Her most recent publication is *Taking Emigration and Remittances into Account in Conservation and Development Policy* (2009).

Ms. Taylor holds a bachelor of science in Latin American Studies and Economics from Penn State University and a master of science in Development Sociology from Cornell.

 **Aaron Terrazas** is a Policy Analyst at the Migration Policy Institute, where he focuses on the linkages between migration and development in migrants' countries of origin, the role of immigrants in the workforce, and more recently, how immigrants have fared over the economic crisis.

Mr. Terrazas studied international affairs at the Edmund Walsh School of Foreign Service at Georgetown University and at the Institut d'Etudes Politiques in Paris. His recent publications include *Recovering from the Recession: Immigrants in the Transatlantic Economy* (co-authored), *The Binational Option: Addressing America's Chronic Shortage of English as a Second Language Instructors* (co-authored), *Immigrants and the Current Economic Crisis: Research Evidence, Policy Challenges, and Implications* (co-authored), and *Learning by Doing: Experiences of Circular Migration* (co-authored). He is a frequent contributor to the Migration Information Source.

THE MIGRATION POLICY INSTITUTE'S MIGRANTS, MIGRATION, AND DEVELOPMENT PROGRAM

Governments, multilateral agencies, and development specialists have recently rediscovered the connections between migration and development. Increasing volumes of research are focusing on the actual and potential contributions of migrant communities to sustainable development or the reduction of poverty in their countries of origin.

The findings have not been systematically translated into policy guidance, however, and important topics remain under-investigated. One result is that little coherence is to be found between the development policies and the migration policies of governments in either countries of destination or countries of origin. The Migration Policy Institute (MPI) has begun to address the paucity of policy analysis through its Migrants, Migration, and Development program launched in 2004.

MPI is deeply engaged in efforts to encourage a multilateral discussion and exchange of experience through participation in the annual Global Forum on Migration and Development and other high-level meetings, as well as through its own events and publications.

MPI's work in migration and development has two major strands:

- Drawing out the policy implications of a voluminous and rapidly expanding body of literature, much of which is primarily theoretical or descriptive, and evaluating whether it implies a major revision of conventional understandings of migration-and-development linkages.

- Producing new research findings on diaspora engagement in countries of origin and on the migration-related development policies of countries of origin as well as donor countries and institutions.

In conjunction with its research and analysis, MPI convenes discussions with important stakeholders, in particular policymakers and migrant leaders, to enrich its findings with their views and agendas in the process of developing practical policy implications.

THE US AGENCY FOR INTERNATIONAL DEVELOPMENT'S DIASPORA NETWORKS ALLIANCE

The United States hosts more international migrants than any other country and is also home to millions of hyphenated Americans who trace their lineages to every corner of the world. An estimated 25 percent or more of all the capital that flows abroad from the United States is in the form of recorded remittances, which makes them second only to private capital flows like foreign direct investment.

The strategic approach taken by the US government towards diaspora community engagement is thus becoming an increasingly important focus for both foreign policy and development needs. Such an engagement and outreach will enable the US government to leverage resources, increase development impact, and further foreign policy objectives.

Although diaspora community engagement with home countries is sizeable, the developmental potential for this group remains largely untapped. To unleash this potential, the US Agency for International Development (USAID) has launched a flagship public-private initiative called the Diaspora Networks Alliance (DNA).

DNA is a framework that enables partnerships between USAID, the private sector, other donor organizations, and diasporas that are built on knowledge generation, engagement, and operational work with the purpose of promoting economic and social growth in the countries of origin. One of the DNA partnerships is with the Migration Policy Institute (MPI), and through this partnership, MPI conducted a number of studies, included in this volume, in the areas of advocacy and diplomacy, capital markets, entrepreneurship, philanthropy, trade and tourism, and volunteerism.

USAID is taking a leadership role in the development community by innovating and fostering partnership models to deepen and scale diasporas' engagement in home-country development. Such engagements are inherently sustainable as diasporas' connection to their homeland is unbreakable (hence the acronym, DNA) and also promote inclusiveness in development policy planning and cooperation.

Strategies

Look at what others are doing:

in US -

⎣→ Youth volunteers from D. to work / teach in COO + COD — eg "teach for America" + Teach for In~ — complementary rather than competing interests

[COD] ⎣→ promote D volunteering in dev't projects?
COO → cld discuss c̄ COD HOW to do that!! — eg have dev't agencies cld wcl. D in existing int'l tech prog~s +/or partner c̄ CS groups

DEV'T ASSIST~ED HAS BEEN THE MOST COMMON JUSTIF'N FO[R]
INT'L VOLUNTEERING PROGM'S
⎣→Dev't agencies have extensive exper'ce c̄ volunteer[s]
→ D are no diff't from other volunteers.
Best examples of rec~ → skilled D volunteers appear to be p't'ssc̄ exper'ce in placing volunt~ + connect'~s c̄ on the ground org~s +c̄ deep community roots in the D. (faith-based, eth~ community-based, profess'l n'works)
*⎣
CRITICAL BARRIERS? → data on the D
→ D grps c̄ insuff't # ɯ till mass (small-per A)w groups in USA

KNOW YOUR DIASPORA
→ How well are they organizing 'selves?
DAY, websites, discuss groups + social n'works
→ D members have proliferated, ~~resulting~~
~ expanded the organiz'e potential of
groups + indiv'ls.

→ Who is speaking + on whose behalf?
~ico has addressed this by sponsoring the
~onsultative Council of the Amst for Mexicans
~broad (CCIME) composed of elected leaders
~om D. communities
~he Council advises gov't on D policies +
~elps set the agenda for the IME (MFA) & partners
This assures representativeness + legitimacy
is a vis the D. + the gov't(s).

HUS - EXAMPLE - What ~ D have? - create path
→ lobbied USG for ~ing policies to ~give
~ legal status for ~Ms.
→ lobbied GOM to give voting rights + dual
~itiz'ip to D. abroad.

Joint action groups + committees can also
~ely on issues of mutual CO O/COD interest
→ US-India Business Council
US-India Pol'ce Action C'ttee has a
wide US o'reach grp + has lobbied Congress
to support it

19) See also → - US - Civilian Nuclear ~
Agree't ~ to place civil nuclear facil't
~ India under IAEA - to enable US to deal~
~ India on nuclear issues